I0911549

Counselling Skills

Third Edition

Third Edition

Counselling Skills

Theory, Research and Practice

Julia McLeod
and John McLeod

Open University Press

Open University Press
McGraw Hill
8th Floor, 338 Euston Road
London
England
NW1 3BH

email: enquiries@openup.co.uk
world wide web: www.openup.co.uk

First edition published 2007
Second edition published 2011

Copyright © Open International Publishing Limited, 2022

All rights reserved. Except for the quotation of short passages for the purposes of criticism
and review, no part of this publication may be reproduced, stored in a retrieval system, or
transmitted, in any form or by any means, electronic, mechanical, photocopying, recording
or otherwise, without the prior written permission of the publisher or a licence from the
Copyright Licensing Agency Limited. Details of such licences (for reprographic reproduction)
may be obtained from the Copyright Licensing Agency Ltd of Saffron House, 6–10 Kirby
Street, London EC1N 8TS.

A catalogue record of this book is available from the British Library

ISBN-13: 9780335250158
ISBN-10: 0335250157
eISBN: 9780335250165

Commissioning Editor: Clara Heathcock
Associate Editor: Beth Summers
Content Product Manager: Ali Davis
Senior Marketing Manager: Bryony Waters

Library of Congress Cataloging-in-Publication Data
CIP data applied for

Typeset by Transforma Pvt. Ltd., Chennai, India

Fictitious names of companies, products, people, characters and/or data that may be used
herein (in case studies or in examples) are not intended to represent any real individual,
company, product or event.

Praise for this book

"This outstanding book achieves something unique in the well-populated world of therapy skills writing: it expertly handles both depth and specificity. Readers will find here a clear and accessible skills anthology, designed to help you acquire and develop your own wide-ranging abilities. This is held within a critical consideration of the notion of 'skill', inspiring readers to see beyond the assumptions inherent to the term. As a therapy trainer I find here a substantial, engaging, and comprehensive skills curriculum. For students of counselling and psychotherapy, this is an invaluable resource that you will keep returning to, during and beyond training."

Nicola Blunden, Director of Studies, Person-Centred Pluralist Counselling, Metanoia Institute, UK

"John and Julia McLeod have a talent for engaging the reader and painting a picture with words. This third version is a comprehensive text on Counselling Skills and has been greatly supplemented and enhanced. An ideal companion for any therapy programme for both the beginner and the most experienced practitioner looking for ways of refining skills they already possess. It is essential reading for those wishing to be skills competent including counsellors, psychotherapists, psychologists, psychiatrists, social workers, teachers, and many other helping professionals. Clearly the authors have considered a plurality of learning styles, with structured, creative, and collaborative approaches included."

Dr. Marcella Finnerty, IICP College President, Dublin, Ireland

"An excellent introduction to the fundamentals of change promoting conversations. Examining the depth and breadth of the core concepts, as well as offering vivid illustrations, the authors provide an invaluable source for developing skills in counselling and psychotherapy. Immensely inspiring as well as effectively useful. Essential reading for any student, trainee, or experienced professional in the field."

Hanne Weie Oddli, PhD, Clinical psychologist and Associate professor at the Department of Psychology, University of Oslo, Norway

"The importance of counselling skills in developing and maintaining a meaningful collaborative and respectful helping relationship cannot be over-stated. Sitting at the core of the work of many professional groups,

Julia and John McLeod have, over several years, made a critical contribution in explaining in accessible language both the importance and application of such skills. This third edition is yet another outstanding contribution to the field, offering clear definitions supported by meaningful exploration of the use of counselling skills in helping relationships. This text really is a must-have for all involved in working with others; to empower and enable through a collaborative process."

Prof Andrew Reeves, Professor in Counselling Professions and Mental Health, University of Chester and BACP Senior Accredited Counsellor/ Psychotherapist, UK

"This excellent book provides a comprehensive guide to the core counselling skills every mental health trainee needs to acquire to competently work in the field. The text is practical and accessible while also being grounded in rigorous empirical research. Notably, the authors are two of the leading psychologists in the field of pluralistic psychotherapy, meaning that they deeply understand the complex relationship between specific therapy models and the "common factors" of counselling practice. This knowledge is threaded throughout the book and will provide trainees with a productive orientation towards professional development that should benefit them throughout their career."

Dr Tony Rousmaniere, University of Washington, USA

"This is an extremely informative and accessible foundational resource for counselling skills training, that is relevant across a range of helping professions. The learning activities are an invitation to explore concepts and theories in greater depth – with particular emphasis on developing self-awareness and understanding. Research evidence is presented in a clear and straightforward way, wonderfully accessible for those who may be unsure of how to link theory and practice. The practical and engaging style of this text will have broad appeal and I particularly appreciate a resource that promotes intentional collaboration at the heart of counselling skills practice!"

Dr Steff Revell, Principle Lecturer, Otago Polytechnic, Aotearoa New Zealand

For Kate, Emma and Hannah

Contents

How to use this book

This book is intended for students and trainees involved in developing counselling skills, as well as more experienced practitioners looking for ways of reflecting on and refining skills that they already possess. Counselling skills such as listening, questioning and challenging are basic tools for facilitating personal learning, growth and recovery. Such skills represent essential competencies for counsellors, psychotherapists, life coaches, career counsellors, psychologists, psychiatrists, social workers, teachers, mental health nurses and members of many other helping professions.

The approach taken in this book is that the development of counselling skills requires an active commitment to learning in the areas of self-awareness, cognitive understanding and practice. Our approach to skills training is strongly influenced by principles of deliberate practice, in which learners use feedback from others to identify areas in which they need to improve, then devise a skills action plan, and finally engage in focused practice with learning partners until a more satisfactory level of performance is achieved. We take the view that counselling skills are grounded in interpersonal helping, communication and caring skills that everyone uses in their everyday lives. Counselling skills represent the adaptation and application of these basic life skills to meet the challenges arising from the responsibility and intensity of acting in the role of counsellor.

Approaches to therapy, such as psychodynamic, cognitive-behavioural therapy (CBT), person-centred, narrative and others, can be regarded as different ways of assembling and utilizing an underlying set of core counselling skills. This book is therefore relevant for trainees and practitioners in all theoretical traditions. A fundamental theoretical assumption that informs the book is that all forms of effective therapy are built on skills for facilitating client–therapist collaboration and shared decision-making.

The terms counselling, psychotherapy and therapy are used interchangeably throughout the book, in recognition of the fact that practitioners in these professional roles draw on a single body of core skills.

We refer to relevant research evidence throughout the book. Counsellors either already work, or are preparing to work, in professional environments in which research evidence informs policy and practice, or are preparing to enter employment in such contexts. If counselling skills and emotional support are to be taken seriously in these settings it is essential to be able to use research evidence as a guide for practice, and to support research initiatives so that more and better studies of the processes and outcomes of the use of counselling skills can be carried out.

It is likely that many readers of this book will be undertaking a module or course in counselling/psychotherapeutic skills as part of a broader programme of study. Each chapter of the book has been written in a way that makes it possible to use it to support teaching sessions on core topics within such programmes. Each chapter includes background theory, a central focus on two or three key topics of skills, and learning activities that can form the basis for seminars, experiential workshops, reflective journal writing, blogs and written assignments. We recommend that each skill should be supported by sessions in which trainees practise skills on and with each other.

Developing and maintaining counselling skills should be viewed as activities that require lifelong learning. The present book represents a starting point: there are many valuable skills that we have not had the space to discuss in detail. Ongoing, career-long attention to counselling skills can involve revisiting, renewing and refreshing skills competence, learning about new research evidence and acquiring new/emergent ways of using skills.

To learn counselling skills, or use them in practice, it is necessary to be able to draw on theories and concepts that facilitate detailed reflection and analysis, and an appreciation of professional issues such as confidentiality, informed consent, boundaries and other aspects of client safeguarding. These topics are not addressed in any depth in this book: readers are directed towards relevant sections of McLeod (2019) where such information can be found.

Our experience over several decades of delivering counselling skills training is that this area of learning is typically experienced by participants as challenging, enjoyable and potentially life-changing. Reflecting on everyday interpersonal skills that are largely taken for granted, and then expanding or relearning these practices from a counselling perspective, often leads to a reappraisal of how one relates to other people in one's life. We strongly believe that it is essential for such processes to take place within a supportive learning community in which tutors appreciate the importance of their duty of care and trust.

Acknowledgements

W e would like to record our appreciation to the many friends and colleagues whose ideas and conversations have deepened our understanding of counselling, including Sophia Balamoutsou, Mick Cooper, Robert Elliott, Marcella Finnerty, Soti Grafanaki, Margrethe Seeger Halvorsen, Hanne Haavind, Triona Kearns, Heidi Levitt, Sally Lumsdaine, Thomas Mackrill, Catherine Marriott, Dave Mearns, Hanne Oddli, David O'Regan, Brian Rodgers, Marit Råbu, Andrew Reeves, David Rennie, Steff Revell, Alison Rouse, Alison Shoemark, Erik Stänicke, Rolf Sundet, Mhairi Thurston, Biljana van Rijn, Tony Rousmaniere, Kate Smith, Fiona Stirling, Marcia Stoll, Lynne Thomas, Dot Weaks, Sue Wheeler, and Mark Widdowson. We are grateful to Beth Summers and her colleagues at the Open University Press, for their generous encouragement and advice, and efficient and timely practical assistance throughout the process of writing and production. We are also grateful for all that we have learned from our students on the counselling training programme at Abertay University. Our greatest debt is to our daughters Kate, Emma and Hannah, their partners Edd and Jack, and our grandchildren Eva, Isaac and Ella. Their lives are a source of joy and wonder to us both.

Why counselling skills are important

Introduction

Counselling provides an opportunity for a person who is concerned about some aspect of their life to enlist the assistance of another person to talk that issue through. Counselling can be of value in response to a wide range of types of problems in living, including difficulties in relationships, lack of meaning in life, behaviour change, and forms of emotional pain such as loneliness, sadness, fear and worry, low mood and depression, and fatigue. The way that counselling works is to create a safe and confidential space in which the person can tell their story and work together with their counsellor to make sense of what has happened in their life, and develop and implement strategies that will enable them to move on. This kind of process, and these skills, are integral elements of helping relationships in many areas of life: not only counselling and psychotherapy, but also in situations such as peer support, doctor–patient interaction, teaching, social work and other arenas.

1

A *counselling skill* can be defined as a concrete, specific, flexible and demarcated sequence of action, usually of brief time duration (typically less than two minutes) that is deployed by a therapist with the intention of facilitating accomplishment of a therapy task. A skill incorporates a mix of cognitive, affective and physical aspects, and is performed with reference to contextual considerations (e.g. how much time there is, how the recipient reacts). It is a micro-event or micro-episode with a beginning and an end. In the therapy literature and professional discourse, practitioners mainly talk, write or otherwise focus on skills in relation to monitoring their work and enhancing its quality: skills are usually taken for granted, and become an object of attention only when something goes wrong.

The aim of this book is to support readers to develop effective counselling skills. In order to make sense of counselling skills, and learn how to use them, it is first of all necessary to unpack and explore the concept of skill. The following sections explore a range of perspectives on counselling skills. We begin by examining the meaning of the concept of a 'skill' and what is implied when we use that term. This is followed by a brief discussion of the history and emergence of the idea of counselling skills in the counselling and psychotherapy professional literature, and the broader social and cultural factors that have shaped these developments. Differences between skills and other widely used therapy terms such as competencies, processes and interventions are discussed. Further sections of the chapter consider the evidence around the relationship between counselling skills and therapy outcomes, and how skills are acquired and developed. Taken together, these perspectives are intended to offer an invitation to think about skills in a critical, self-reflective manner that will enrich the discussion of specific skills that takes place in later chapters.

The concept of skill

At one level, we all know what we mean when we talk about skills, because they permeate all aspects of everyday life. Learning to play tennis involves developing simple physical skills, such as tossing the ball in the air to make a serve, as well as more complex cognitive skills such as managing a rally to get to a point of being able to play a winning shot. Cooking a meal requires being able to stir, pour and measure. A skill is an activity that is teachable. We understand that there exist varying levels of skilfulness – some people are better at these things than others. We are able to pay attention to our level of skilfulness in any particular situation, so we can learn about how to improve at that specific activity.

In order to inform professional training and practice, this kind of common-sense or everyday understanding of skills needs to be expanded and refined. Analysis of the historical linguistic roots of the word 'skill' refers to a broad set of meanings that cluster within two main themes: skills represent practical and personal (as opposed to theoretical) forms of knowledge and understanding; and skilfulness reflects a capacity for discerning differences or parts of some kind of activity or entity. Various writers have interpreted these core meanings as implying the following defining attributes of skilled performance:

- a series of actions carried out for a specific purpose
- capable of repetition (i.e. not due to chance or accident, but under personal control): a deliberate application of human intelligence
- an outcome that is tangible (i.e. measurable or observable) in some way
- a skill may be simple or highly complex
- exercising a skill calls for care, intelligence and reflective monitoring
- performance of a skill makes use of some kind of internal cognitive map, model or image of how to proceed
- an individual exhibiting a skill is unlikely to be consciously aware of, or able to articulate, the entirety of the implicit or tacit knowledge that underpins their performance
- skill use draws on embodied knowing as well as cognitive understanding
- skills refer to activities that are important for future well-being or survival
- effective application of a skill is not automatic, but depends on the situation: skill sequences are modified, adapted or improvised according to context
- skills can be transferred from one setting to another
- skills are learned
- skills are passed on from one person to another, through demonstration, observation and practice
- skilfulness and expertise, in any area of human activity, is a highly prized attribute
- on the whole, we are able to recognize skilled performance when we see it
- novices and experts differ in the way they use the same skill
- there is a sense of intrinsic satisfaction and pleasure associated with effective performance of a skill.

This list of attributes of skill use is drawn from a range of sources, including Claxton (2012), Ericsson and Pool (2016), Flyvbjerg (2001), Hinchliffe (2002), Lindwall and Ekström (2012) and Sudnow and Dreyfus (2001). The list serves as a reminder of the complexity, richness and meaningfulness of skills as an essential element of human life. The capacity to use skill draws on a range of physical, cognitive, social/relational and aesthetic capabilities. The list also operates to alert us to what we need to be thinking about when studying and developing counselling skills. There is an important critical dimension here: the research and practice literature, and widely used training procedures, rarely take account of all the elements outlined above.

A social history of counselling skills

In an evolutionary context, human beings were neither faster or stronger than competitor species, nor possessed a particularly acute sense of smell, hearing or vision. The distinctive attribute that gave the human race an evolutionary advantage was its capacity to communicate intentions and work collaboratively in a flexible manner (Tomasello et al. 2005; Tomasello 2015). Being able to take account of the emotions of other people, share information, and resolve differences and disputes has been a core characteristic of human survival. These essential interpersonal skills were structured into the nervous system over millennia, long before the emergence of agrarian societies within the most recent 6000 years, and have been expressed and reinforced through cultural forms such as language, ritual, dance, music and song.

In the modern era, the existence of this broad range of skills around empathic responsiveness to others, awareness of personal emotions, creative problem solving and conflict resolution has made it possible to negotiate a way through an increasingly intense pace of cultural and technological change. In acknowledgement of the significance of the 'commons' in social life – the shared ownership and stewardship of land, water, shelter and many other material resources – the supportive web of shared experience, compassion, love and caring that allows people to live and work together has been described as a *psycommons* (Postle 2021).

A programme of research into how people offer ordinary, everyday emotional support (i.e. the psycommons) was carried out by the sociologist Julie Brownlie (2014; Brownlie and Anderson 2017; Brownlie and Shaw 2019), using interviews, diaries and social media data. A key theme to emerge from this research was the importance of 'being there' – another person doing something helpful with no expectation of reciprocation. Research informants described such episodes of generosity, caring and kindness as allowing them to feel safer and more connected within the large city where they lived. Elsewhere in this research, informants were asked about their attitude to professional forms of social support, such as counselling. Although most had a positive attitude to counselling, there was also a sense of ambivalence about talking to a stranger about personal matters, a wish to keep certain matters private, and an appreciation of 'being there' and doing things together in ways that were not talk-based (Anderson and Brownlie 2011; Brownlie 2011). Other sources of everyday emotional support and informal counselling have been reported in a range of studies (see, for example, Cowen 1982; McLellan 1991).

This reservoir of awareness, kindness, coping skills, activities and capacity to just 'be there' for each other can be regarded as a folk psychology that provides the cultural origins for all counselling and psychotherapy ideas and interventions. A key feature of modern industrial societies has been a trend towards specialization, professionalization, commercialization and state control of functions of life – such as social and health care – that were previously carried out within families and communities. An example of this line of development has been the way that traditional beliefs, rituals and practices around death and bereavement have increasingly been supplanted by professional counselling. Within this domain of life, a significant segment of everyday caring skills has gradually become demarcated as counselling skills. In similar fashion, other segments of everyday life skills have become designated as interpersonal skills, human relations skills or communication skills.

There are several ways in which it can be valuable to take account of social and historical perspectives when thinking about, learning and using counselling skills. First, it makes it possible to see that all counselling skills have their origins in everyday accomplishments and capabilities. As a consequence, acquiring counselling skills does not start with a blank page, but is more appropriately regarded as a process of adapting everyday interpersonal skills to the requirements of a counselling role. A second implication is that everyday skills and folk wisdom are much wider than counselling skills – there will always be further threads of everyday helping practices that have the potential to be woven into a counselling approach. Finally, because both counsellors, and those who seek support from them, have spent their whole lives offering and receiving emotional support and participating in the psycommons, all of us have an intuitive ability to know whether a helping response is facilitative or otherwise. This factor has important implications for training in counselling skills. Competence in counselling skills can never be adequately assessed by external observers, rating scales, or even by the counsellor themselves – the crucial criterion is the judgement of the recipient or client. As a result, effective learning and training (discussed in Chapter 4) always involves setting up a situation where the trainee counselling skills user can receive honest feedback from the person they are trying to help.

Differences between counselling skills and everyday emotional support

Counselling skills do not represent a new skill set, fundamentally different from the common knowledge of how to offer emotional support that is part of the fabric of everyday relationships. Instead, counselling skills comprise a particular version of everyday interpersonal skills, designed to be relevant to the specific situation of a conversation between a helper who is operating in a formal or professional role, and a person who is in some degree of crisis. In such a situation, the helper needs to possess better skills than they would generally require in the context of supporting a friend, work colleague or family member. Their skills need to be better because they are responding to a stranger, and do not have the advantage of already knowing how to communicate with that person. They also need to be better because the stakes are higher – there is a greater weight of responsibility to get it right. Finally, it is likely that the helper will need to be able to sustain the therapeutic conversation over a longer period of time. Troubles talk between friends or family members tends to oscillate back and forward between each person sharing a story of 'a similar thing that happened to me'. By contrast, a counsellor needs to be able to keep the focus on the client.

History and emergence of the idea of counselling skills

The early histories of both psychology and counselling/psychotherapy did not include the use of the concept of a 'skill'. The idea that psychological processes and interpersonal behaviour can be viewed as skills began to emerge in the 1950s. During World War II, psychologists had been employed by the British armed forces to analyse the kinds of tasks performed by soldiers and aircrew, such as assembling and firing a weapon, with the aim of discovering how these tasks could be performed more effectively and accurately, and the best ways in which training could be provided for people carrying them out. These psychologists came up with the idea of breaking down each task or function into a set of component skills, which could be learned separately and then built up into the final complete task sequence. The model of skill that emerged emphasized the sequence of actions that the operator needed to go through, and the operator's attention to feedback around whether each operation had been effective in achieving its intended goals.

In the immediate post-war years, the concept of skill proved to be valuable as a means of analysing task performance in a variety of areas. In particular, the concept of skill was embraced by social psychologists such as Michael Argyle, who were interested in understanding the way that people interacted with each other. Interesting and important advances were made in applied social psychology, which established the idea that the concept of skill could usefully be applied to the analysis of social interaction and performance. By the 1970s, under the leadership of the British clinical psychologist Peter Trower, the concept of social skill that had been developed by Argyle was being applied in work with people reporting a variety of mental health difficulties (Trower et al. 1978). One of the key ideas in this approach was that, instead of viewing intervention for mental health problems as a form of treatment, it was now regarded as a form of *training*, in which the patient could be guided through a series of learning or skill-acquisition activities. Over the succeeding decades, principles of social skills training have been widely applied in such areas as assertiveness and interviewing, and support for individuals (e.g. those with learning difficulties or severe and enduring mental health problems) who struggle to cope with social interaction (Matson and Burns 2017).

In the USA, a parallel development was taking place in respect of the concept of skills. The late 1940s and early 1950s saw a vast expansion of the psychological therapies in the USA, largely stimulated by the need to respond to mental health problems in armed services personnel returning from war. A great deal of investment at that time was directed into the development of client-centred therapy, an approach to counselling and psychotherapy developed in the 1940s by Carl Rogers. Motivated by the pressure to train counsellors effectively and quickly, some of Rogers' students and colleagues – for example Charles Truax and Robert Carkhuff – came to the conclusion that it would be sensible to treat the core concepts of client-centred therapy, such as non-directiveness, empathy and unconditional positive regard, as skills. These psychologists then developed training programmes in which students were taught, and practised, a set of counselling skills. This approach became known as the Human Resources Development model (Carkhuff 1969a, 1969b; Cash 1984). In the 1960s, a large number of counselling and helping skills programmes were developed by influential figures in the counselling and psychology professions in the USA, such as Allen Ivey (Ivey and Galvin 1984), Thomas Gordon (1984), Norman Kagan (1984), Bernard Guerney (1984) and Gerald Goodman (1984). The high point of these developments was a book edited by Dale Larson (1984), which brought together examples of many of the major skills approaches.

Larson (1984), along with the contributors to his book, believed that the development of brief training in counselling skills represented a fundamental shift in the relationship between therapy/psychology and society. Rather than therapeutic support and interventions being provided solely by professional experts, the counselling skills movement was viewed as having a democratizing function, through making evidence-based helping skills and knowledge available to all, leading to the possibility that therapy could be provided by paraprofessionals, non-psychologists and members of peer support groups (Boukydis 1984; Gendlin 1984).

This radical edge of the counselling skills movement still exists, for example in the form of peer support services using counselling skills that are available in many contexts. However, over time, theory and research on counselling skills gradually became incorporated into mainstream training of professional counsellors, psychotherapists, social workers and other mental health workers. An important aspect of this professional focus has been an accumulation of research into methods of training in counselling skills (Hill and Lent 2006; Hill et al. 2007).

Taken together, the various threads within the historical development of counselling skills have converged on a lack of appreciation of the value of a skills approach in relation to helping people to overcome problems in living. Counselling and psychotherapy have largely consolidated their position in society by defining themselves through theoretical concepts (see McLeod 2019). Practical skills have been relegated to introductory stages in the curriculum, with academic and research interests mainly restricted to consideration of how skills are taught rather than what they are and what they mean.

How and why counselling skills are essential elements of effective therapy

The issue of identifying the factors that contribute to an outcome has comprised a major focus for research in counselling and psychotherapy. Although much of that research effort has been devoted to analysing differences in effectiveness associated with distinct theoretical approaches to therapy (e.g.

cognitive-behavioural therapy (CBT), psychodynamic, person-centred, narrative, etc.), the emerging consensus is that therapy model/approach does not make a significant difference. By contrast, the factors that appear to make a more substantial contribution to therapy effectiveness are the quality of the therapy relationship, the therapist as a person (i.e. some therapists record much better client outcomes than others), and the extent to which therapy is aligned with the preferences and cultural identity of the client (see McLeod 2019 for further discussion of these topics).

Until recently, therapist skills have not been given much attention within therapy outcome literature. This has been mainly due to the prevailing view that differences in therapy effectiveness must be due to therapy models and approaches. Also, for researchers, it has probably seemed reasonable to take for granted that any competent therapist (i.e. a therapist included in an outcome study) would possess adequate skills, in the sense of being able to listen to a client, challenge the client when appropriate, and so on. From a research point of view, it is also technically quite hard to track with any reliability the effect of micro-responses to a client (e.g. a skilful or awkward question) on an outcome that occurs perhaps weeks or months later. As a consequence, there have been few studies that have directly examined the impact of counselling skills on the eventual outcomes of therapy. A notable exception is a study by Ziv-Beiman et al. (2017) that observed a link between therapist use of the skill of immediacy and the level of client symptoms, which demonstrates that this kind of investigation is feasible.

However, despite these methodological difficulties, the importance of counselling skills has been highlighted in an influential line of research into the relationship between counselling skills and outcomes, developed by Timothy Anderson and colleagues at Ohio University (Anderson and Hill 2017; Anderson et al. 2009, 2016a, 2016b, 2019, 2020). Earlier studies by Binder and Strupp (1997) had found that well-trained therapists achieved poor results with clients who were angry, hostile or critical towards them. Anderson and colleagues hypothesized that this might be happening because, even though the interpersonal skills of these therapists were sufficient to deal with most therapy situations, they broke down under interpersonal pressure. To test this idea, they developed a technique for assessing 'facilitative interpersonal skills' (FIS) under conditions of challenge or pressure. Research participants were asked to respond to video clips of eight brief (one-minute) simulated therapy situations, each of which depicted a challenging client response (e.g. confrontational and angry; passive, silent and withdrawn; passively controlling; actively controlling and blaming). A series of studies using this technique was conducted with therapists at various stages of training. Prospective therapists were presented with the video clips and were prompted to respond at predefined moments 'as if' they were the therapist in the situation. Their verbal responses were audio-recorded and rated in terms of the extent to which they exhibited interpersonal skills such as warmth, empathy, emotional sensitivity and collaborativeness. Months later, data were collected on the effectiveness of these trainees in terms of their outcomes with real clients. Trainees with high levels of FIS achieved better outcomes with clients than did colleagues with low FIS ratings but similar levels of qualifications and experience. A particularly notable finding was that FIS ratings obtained in the first week of training predicted outcomes with clients seen during the first clinical placement more than 12 months later: in other words, training did not bring the lower FIS students up to the level of their high FIS classmates. The credibility of the results of this set of studies is heightened by the fact that a very brief (i.e. less than ten-minute) role-play assessment of interpersonal skills could have a consistent measurable effect on client benefit. Furthermore, the students who participated in these studies were enrolled in a high-status university with competitive entry procedures that selected for therapeutic potential.

It is important that the Ohio findings are replicated in other settings and with other therapists. Nevertheless, these studies suggest that, in challenging situations, therapists fall back on core interpersonal skills that are deeply ingrained on the basis of life experience, and not easily shifted by routine training. It seems likely that a capacity to be open to client negativity, and able to respond to it in a respectful and constructive manner, would have implications for therapy helpfulness beyond these specific moments. For example, a therapist who felt unable to handle client negativity could be less willing to engage with difficult areas of client experience, and respond in ways that were more likely to keep the therapy process at a safe level.

The relationship between skills and other therapy concepts

At the present time, there does not exist a unified theory of counselling or psychotherapy within which all relevant concepts are carefully defined and their connection to each other spelled out. In particular, the concept of skill largely exists in a space by itself, somewhat apart from other terms that have similar or overlapping meanings. Some ways of making sense of how skills sit alongside other therapy concepts are outlined below.

Counselling or therapy *competencies* refer to broad areas of therapist capability, that typically encompass theoretical ideas, self-awareness and practical skills. For example, in the model of therapist cultural competence developed by Tummala-Narra (2015), one of the key competencies is described as 'attending to experiences of social oppression'. This area of capability requires the use of multiple counselling skills (listening, linguistic sensitivity and responsiveness, broaching, etc.) alongside a theoretical understanding of oppression and awareness of internalized prejudices. In a programme of work to develop a CBT competency framework to inform the selection and employment of therapists within the Improving Access to Psychological Therapies (IAPT) service, Roth and Pilling (2008) constructed a list that included items such as 'knowledge of basic principles of CBT' and 'ability to explain and demonstrate rationale for CBT to the client'. Again, being able to demonstrate and explain a CBT treatment approach necessarily draws on multiple counselling skills as well as propositional/ theoretical knowledge. In the therapy literature and professional discourse, the term competency is mainly used in the context of professional standards, employability and readiness to practise.

The concept of therapy *process* is used in different ways by different theorists and writers. A broad definition of process is that the term can be used to describe any phenomenon that changes over time: a process is any kind of unfolding cause–effect sequence. This broad perspective can also reflect a value position: process as an essential quality of being human. For example, Rogers (1958) took the position that to be a person meant always being in a state of becoming. An alternative way of making sense of process exists within the research literature. A lot of therapy research is organized around a distinction between 'process' research (investigations of the ingredients of therapy) and 'outcome' research (i.e. the extent to which the client has improved, recovered, etc.). Therapeutic processes are the ingredients that contribute to outcomes. An 'ingredients' definition of process encompasses any factors (e.g. therapist empathy, goal orientation, therapeutic alliance – there is a huge list) that may promote or inhibit therapeutic effects in clients. Within a definition of process as a cause–effect sequence, the act of using a counselling skill can be viewed as reflecting a micro-process that unfolds over a short time. Later chapters of this book reflect this idea, in trying to give a sense of various choice-points within the process of using a skill such as active listening or challenging. However, many therapy processes unfold over considerable periods of time. For example, the process of coming to terms with, or assimilating, a problematic experience may require many sessions of therapy (Honos-Webb and Stiles 1998; Stiles 2001, 2011). To facilitate and deepen such a process, a therapist will use many different skills at different times. Finally, within research studies, skills such as immediacy and self-disclosure have been treated as process ingredients.

Therapy *interventions* (sometimes also described as techniques or methods) are therapist actions that function to produce different types of therapeutic change. The underlying image of an intervention is something that is externally imposed on what is happening, in order to initiate a decisive shift. Different interventions are associated with different approaches to therapy, and different presenting problems. Over the years, a very extensive range of therapy interventions have been devised. In one programme of research, a core set of 30 distinct interventions was identified (McCarthy and Barber 2009; Solomonov et al. 2019). These included such activities as 'the therapist and the client discussed the client's dreams, fantasies, or wishes' and 'the therapist encouraged the client to question his/her beliefs or to discover flaws in his/her reasoning'. While it makes sense to consider such interventions as capable of being implemented skilfully or awkwardly, it seems clear that they are too complex to be considered as specific skills. Instead, a therapist will make use of various skills to deliver an intervention. For instance, a cognitive intervention that aims to enable a client to discover flaws in their reasoning might involve judicious use of counselling skills such as listening, questioning, explaining and challenging.

Although the concept of *task* is used in therapy in a variety of ways, it most often refers to a discrete set of activities undertaken by the therapist and client together, in order to make progress towards a therapy goal. For example, a client who defined their goal for therapy as developing more satisfying and enduring relationships with others might need to complete certain tasks along the way, such as resolving harsh self-criticism ('I am not good/likeable enough for anyone to want to be my friend'), and developing anger control (losing friends by getting angry with them for letting me down). From a counselling skills perspective, such tasks can be viewed as requiring the application of multiple skills in the service of accomplishing a specific task.

This brief discussion demonstrates how the meaning of the concept of skill both is different from, and overlaps with, the meaning of other therapy concepts such as competence, process, intervention and task. As a result, it is not hard to find examples in the literature of a blurring of conceptual boundaries. For instance, the questionnaire developed by Solomonov et al. (2019) includes the skill of listening as a category of intervention. In an excellent paper by Kivlighan Jr (2014) on key clinical processes in interpersonal therapy, immediacy (i.e. bringing the discussion into the here-and-now) is described as a process, whereas elsewhere (including the present book) it is viewed as a skill. These authors are leading figures in the profession. It is important to recognize that what they have written is not confused or mistaken. Instead, this blurring arises from the intrinsic difficulty of doing justice to a complex therapeutic reality that defies precise categorization.

Conclusions

This chapter has explored a range of perspectives on counselling skills, and discussed some of the implications of these perspectives for acquiring skills and applying them in practice. The key take-home messages of this chapter, in terms of being a therapist, are that the development of counselling skills is potentially a highly challenging endeavour because it involves critical personal reflection on deeply ingrained and culturally normative ways of interacting with other people, and because the concept and meaning of a skill is both intrinsically complex and under-researched in the counselling and psychotherapy literature.

Learning activities

The following activities may be explored individually, and/or with a group of learning partners.

1   Take a few minutes to make a list of the skills you are able to use to offer emotional support to other people in your everyday life (i.e. friends, family and work colleagues rather than clients or service users), in order to help them to work through life dilemmas, deal with interpersonal conflict, and other counselling-type tasks. Where and how did you acquire these skills? What are the implications of your reflection on this topic for your development of counselling skills that you will deploy in professional contexts?

2   In relation to counselling skills training in which you are currently engaged (or training that you have done in the past), how is/was the concept of 'skill' conceptualized, in terms of definitions, theories and research evidence? On the basis of these sources, alongside the ideas presented in this chapter, what are the ways of thinking about skills that are most helpful to you in relation to your own skills development?

3   A key contribution to an understanding of counselling skills has been Anderson's analysis of the need for such skills to be able to operate in conditions of pressure. Comparing everyday life helping encounters with what happens in therapy, make a list of (a) which helping skills may be easier to implement in therapy contexts (and why), and (b) which skills may be harder to implement in therapy settings (and why – i.e. the sources of pressure that may be present in therapy interactions). What are the implications of what you have learned from this exercise, for (i) your own learning and use of counselling skills, and (ii) the ways in which counselling skills training is organized?

An A–Z of counselling skills

Introduction

The aim of the present chapter is to anchor the book in a straightforward, plain language description of a set of core counselling skills. Taken together, these skills map out the basic competencies required for anyone involved in offering a counselling relationship. The skills are introduced in alphabetical order, to reflect a position that each of them has equal importance. Although it is possible to separate out these skills for purposes of training and research, in practice they are all interconnected and form part of a general way of being with a person that is characteristic of all approaches to counselling.

The ultimate criterion of whether a counselling skill has been used appropriately is the client's response. For example, it does not matter how elegantly a counsellor empathizes with a client – if the counsellor's statement does not make a difference to the client, then it is of little value. Conversely, some counsellor responses that may appear to observers to be awkward or idiosyncratic may be experienced by the client as very helpful. There are several broad categories of client response that can be observed:

- Counsellor responses that have the effect of helping the client to *tell their story*: what the counsellor says and does has the effect of enabling the person to continue talking, in a deeper and more personally meaningful manner.

- *Developing the relationship*: the counsellor's response has the effect of building connection between counsellor and client, by conveying to the client that the counsellor is interested and caring, and believes in the client's capacity to resolve the issues that are being explored.

- *Enabling reflection and choice*: what the counsellor says or does may open up a space for the client to be more aware of what he or she is experiencing, begin to make sense of what that experience means, or to consider alternative courses of action.
- *Creating a new experience*: sometimes, the deployment of a counselling skill creates an opportunity for a client to engage in an experience that he or she may have rarely undergone before – for example, a withdrawn person may engage in eye contact, or a highly talkative person may sit in silence for a few moments.

When reading through the list of counselling skills in this chapter (see Table 2.1), it can be useful to reflect on how each skill has the potential to contribute to each of these client outcomes.

A–Z of counselling skills

Table 2.1 Core counselling skills

Accessing strengths	Listening
Aligning	Making sense/interpreting
Attending	Metacommunication
Attunement	Naming
Authenticity	Normalizing
Being emotionally touched or moved	Observing
Being open to feedback	Offering feedback
Boundary management	Positioning
Broaching difference	Process monitoring
Caring	Providing and evaluating information
Challenging	Questioning
Checking out/clarifying	Reflecting/restating
Conversational resourcefulness	Reframing
Courage	Remembering
Curiosity	Repair
Eliciting and receiving feedback	Self-disclosure
Embodied presence	Self-monitoring/self-awareness
Empathy	Silence
Future orientation	Structuring
Giving advice/making suggestions	Using props
Immediacy	Witnessing

Accessing strengths

A defining characteristic of counselling is that a person seeking help is troubled in some way, for example through persistent painful feelings and emotions, self-defeating patterns of behaviour, being ground down by adversity, or a sense of something missing in their life. While it is essential to engage with these sources of difficulty, effective counselling also requires a capacity to make use of a client's strengths. This skill is expressed in several different ways. A counsellor operates from a general assumption that the client does possess strengths and capabilities, no matter how defeated by life they might appear to be. Their awareness of the client's strengths is offered back to the client at appropriate moments. The relevance of these strengths is explored in relation to the task of addressing the problems in living that brought the client to counselling. Overall, there is a sense of acknowledging, celebrating and activating the resourcefulness, resilience and knowledge-from-experience of the client. A strengths-oriented counsellor will be open to learning from the client.

Aligning

A fundamental aspect of being human is to have a sense of purpose and direction. Even though someone who consults a counsellor may see themselves as stuck in their life, with no future horizon of what to aim for or hope for, it is always possible to find some indication of what a better life might look like. For example, the act of coming to a counselling appointment may reflect a small step in some kind of positive direction. At the same time, a counsellor also operates from their own sense of purpose and direction, for instance in terms of therapeutic tasks to be fulfilled, or their assumptions around how the process of change might unfold, or even practical matters such as monitoring and deciding how to make best use of the remaining time in a session. A useful way of looking at these characteristics of the experience of both the client and counsellor is that each of them is proceeding along certain lines. From this perspective, it is then clear that it is necessary for each to stay in alignment with the other. It is also possible to see that some degree of misalignment is likely to occur on a regular basis, for instance as each participant moves off in a slightly (or seriously) different direction, or perhaps moves ahead too rapidly or lags behind. In such scenarios it is necessary to realign. On the whole, the responsibility for maintaining alignment is the job of the counsellor. This counselling skill involves making sure that they are routinely checking in on the directionality of the client, communicating their own sense of direction sufficiently clearly to the client, and doing whatever needs to be done to get back to a state of thinking and moving along the same lines.

Attending

In a counselling relationship, the person seeking help should be the primary focus of attention. It can be distracting for the client if they are trying to talk about an issue and they start to think that their counsellor is not really paying attention. There are two sides to the skill of *attending* – internal and external.

At an internal level, in their own mind the counsellor needs to be genuinely focused on the client, rather than thinking about other matters. At an external level, the quality of the counsellor's attention needs to be conveyed to the client. Some of the ways in which attending can be conveyed are through a slight forward lean, facial expression and gestures that are responsive to the client, appropriate eye contact, and 'minimal encouragers' – noises or brief statements such as 'mmm' or 'yes'. As with any skill, trying too hard or doing too much can be counterproductive. For example, too much eye contact can be embarrassing or shaming for some clients. There are important cultural differences in accept- able styles of attending: Northern Europeans mainly prefer a more distanced style, while many other cultural groups expect a more animated response.

It is not possible for anyone to give their complete attention to someone else on a continual basis – some lapses will always occur. Skilful attending therefore also involves being able to acknowledge to the client that this has happened. Although this is not the primary focus of their attention, a client is also attending to the therapist, at least from time to time. However, particular moments of client attention to what is happening in the therapist may be highly significant. For example, when a client describes what they regard as a shameful or embarrass- ing event in their life, they are likely to pay keen attention to how the counsellor responds ('Is my counsellor judging me?'). Some clients, such as people who have grown up with abusive and unpredictable parents, may be particularly highly vigilant around how other people react. As a consequence, the counsellor's attention needs to take account of how the client is attending to them.

Attunement

An effective counsellor seeks to tune into what the client is experiencing, and to the client's way of expressing these experiences. *Attunement* refers to a wide range of ways in which this kind of person-to-person alignment can take place. For example, at an emotional level, an attuned counsellor may feel, within their own body, emotions that are present for the client. Attunement also refers to using the same words as the client (for example, if a client states that he was 'down', it may be discordant for the counsellor to respond by using the term 'depressed'). In addition, it can be helpful for the counsellor to follow the pace and rhythm with which the client speaks, and even to mirror the client's body language. When the process of attunement works well, the client will tend to have a sense that the counsellor is 'with' them. When it is absent, the counselling process may have a stop-start quality, marked by a failure to develop topics, and the client (and counsellor) becoming self-conscious around a sense that things are not going well between them. In the longer term, failure of attunement makes it hard for the counsellor to know what tasks and methods are right for a partic- ular client, and to evaluate whether the counselling is being helpful. The concept of attunement is a musical metaphor that invokes other musical notions such as harmony, resonating, improvising, grace notes and pacing. These (and other) musical and non-verbal images and ideas can provide a useful of way of thinking about those aspects of counselling that are beyond words.

Authenticity

A common theme in client descriptions of therapists who were helpful to them is that the counsellor was genuine, real, honest, open, down to earth and transparent. These qualities can be summed up as comprising elements of a more general notion of authenticity. What this means to clients is probably different from what it means to therapists. The therapy literature – understandably – emphasizes what counsellors can do to be highly authentic. From the point of view of the client, the issue is not so much whether they meet a therapist who offers them a new insight into how real it is possible to be. The question is more that the therapist is not hiding behind a professional role, or pretending to care, or offering suggestions that they obviously do not believe in themselves. Given that a central aspect of being sufficiently troubled to seek help from a therapist is that the person has possibly spent months or years pretending (to themselves and those around them) that everything is all right, then more pretending is not what they want or need. Being a counsellor is not intrinsically a high authenticity role, in the way that being a best friend or family member should be. At the end of the day, being a counsellor is a professional role that requires a willingness and capacity to channel one's genuine reactions in the service of the client. As a skill, therapist authenticity is based on being sufficiently comfortable and accepting of oneself in that role, and sufficiently open to questioning and challenging from the client, to be experienced as being trustworthy.

Being emotionally touched or moved

When another person tells the story of their struggle to overcome adversity, it may trigger an emotional response in the listener of being emotionally touched or moved. Some of the key characteristics of this reaction include moist eyes or tears, a lump in the throat and tight chest. Being moved can be understood as a 'social' emotion, that conveys and reinforces a sense of basic human solidarity. There are many occasions in social life that trigger such reactions, such as marriage and funeral ceremonies; theatre, cinema and poetry reading; political speeches; radio and TV documentaries; children's stories and performances; and private or family rituals. Times when a client can see that their counsellor has been moved by their story can have the effect of allowing the client to see that their therapist genuinely cares, bringing them together, and creating a shared point of reference that can be drawn on at later stages in therapy. Although being moved is an automatic bodily response that does not need to be learned, in the context of counselling it can be viewed as a skill. This is because a lot of the time a counsellor may be unwilling to let themselves go in this manner, and as a consequence will actively suppress or rationalize such reactions. The skill lies in the counsellor allowing themselves to be sufficiently emotionally available and present to be aware of such a reaction, and then to allow the client to see it. A further aspect of this skill is confidence in being able to handle the client's response to your reaction – for example if the client then wants to take care of you because they have upset you.

Being open to feedback

The experience of being a client includes some kind of sense of whether, on a moment-by-moment basis, the interaction with a counsellor is helpful or hindering. Helpfulness is not necessarily the same as feeling good or feeling better – most people appreciate that the process of overcoming a problem in living may at times involve talking about painful experiences, or trying out new ways of being that are initially scary. But even in these rough patches there is usually an appreciation that progress is being made. The client's intuitive understanding of whether therapy is on track (perhaps on track in some respects but not others) is essential information for their counsellor to know about. As a consequence, the capacity to elicit, receive and act on client feedback is an important counselling skill. It is quite rare for clients to offer unsolicited feedback. Instead, counsellors need to be able to take the initiative and ask clients how therapy is going for them, and if they have any suggestions for changes to how they are working together. This kind of feedback process can take the form of a regular checking-in procedure at the start or finish of a session (or at regular intervals over the course of therapy), or can be introduced at a suitable moment in a session. Some counsellors augment direct personal requests for feedback with brief questionnaires that provide the client with a way of structuring their feedback response. While it is always necessary for a counsellor to observe the client's engagement in therapy (see below: observation as a skill), this is kind of feedback is never sufficient, because the client may be concealing dissatisfaction. Also, it requires the counsellor to interpret what they are observing. In explicitly asking for feedback, the counsellor is giving the client every opportunity to have their say. They are also reinforcing the idea that the client is a knowledgeable person whose views are important. Finally, a capacity to work in a feedback-informed way requires a counsellor to examine their own lifetime experience of feedback, and what feedback means to them, in order to minimize their own personal barriers to both criticism and praise.

Boundary management

Counselling can be defined as making a space to talk it through: it is the responsibility of the counsellor to ensure that the boundary of the space is secure enough to contain whatever the 'it' might be that a person needs to explore. A large part of the skill of boundary management is practical: providing and maintaining a private confidential place to meet, no interruptions, an agreed start and finish time, and so on. Another element of boundary management is contractual, for example in respect of issues such as frequency of meetings, or situations in which information would need to be reported to an authority (e.g. disclosure of illegal activity, self-harm, abuse or serious suicidal intent).

A more subtle aspect of boundary management is concerned with the limits of the counsellor–client relationship. For example, either the client or the counsellor may desire to pull the relationship out of a counselling space and into a different kind of interpersonal space, such as the territory of friendship, business or sexual intimacy. A further boundary issue is the extent to which the counsellor is willing to share their own experience with the client. Some counsellors choose to remain in a fairly distanced professional role in relation to patients and clients, with very limited use of self-disclosure. Others take the view that there can be times when self-disclosure on the part of the counsellor can be helpful for the client.

The skill of boundary management involves the development of strategies for how to deal with all of these situations. Component elements of this area of skill encompass the capacity to understand and apply ethical codes, appreciation of the needs and preferences of the client, counsellor and other stakeholders, and an understanding of the meaning of particular boundaries in respect of the client–therapist relationship and the personal issues being explored by the client.

Broaching difference

There are always objective differences between a client and counsellor in respect of social identity markers such as age, gender, sexual orientation, religion, ethnicity, social class, disability and other factors. These differences may be apparent from the first moment of meeting. In general, people are highly effective in instantly scanning and categorizing new acquaintances in respect of such dimensions. Social identity markers always influence the kind of relationship that two people can have. Sometimes there can be an immediate sense of affinity, while in other instances there is a sense that it may be hard to get on the same wavelength. Occasionally, one or both participants has personal or culturally shared memories of being treated badly by the social category represented by the other person. In everyday situations, there are many strategies that are available for dealing with difference in social identity, ranging from actively embracing differences as an opportunity for learning, through to politeness and gracefulness, and then to avoidance and attack. Counselling is an unusual situation in that there is an expectation that two people will be able to work closely together, regardless of their differences. Given that social identity differences are likely to be apparent from the start, it is helpful for a counsellor to take action to prevent such factors becoming the 'elephant in the room'. The skill of broaching difference involves the counsellor sharing the fact that they are aware that there are differences in background and life experience between the client and themselves, and that it will be useful to keep this issue under review to prevent any misunderstandings from occurring. It can be helpful to ask the client whether it is alright for the counsellor to mention it if they think that a misunderstanding has happened or seems likely to happen, and if they would agree to do likewise. This skill comprises not only that kind of opening gambit, but also a capacity to follow through and respond appropriately to whatever comes up later on as a result. In this respect, responsiveness to difference can be seen as a particular form of using feedback.

Caring

From the point of view of the person receiving counselling, one of the most valued aspects of the process is a feeling that the counsellor genuinely cares. Caring can be expressed in a variety of ways. Small acts of caring can involve responding to the person's physical needs, such as for a more comfortable chair or a glass of water. Caring can be conveyed through remembering information that is significant for a client, such as specific incidents from earlier sessions, or the date when a loved one died. For some clients, the active involvement of the counsellor is experienced as caring – for instance, rather than passively reflecting back what the person has said, the counsellor cares enough to make suggestions, or initiate activities or exercises. An essential facet of caring is bound up in anticipating how certain events might have an impact on a person – for example, looking ahead to emotionally difficult holiday periods, such as Christmas. Satisfied clients sometimes refer to this factor when they describe their counsellor as not being bound by a professional role, treating them as someone 'special', or being willing to 'go the extra mile' for them. In this context, small acts of caring have the potential to have a big impact on a client, as indicators of shared humanity. For a counsellor, the skill of caring starts with a genuine interest in a client, which in turn is built around a capacity to resist burnout and emotional distancing through effective professional self-care. Important aspects of the skill of caring include being able to communicate this quality to clients in ways that make sense to them, and the capacity to provide more intensive caring when necessary (e.g. the counsellor as a safe and soothing presence for a client exploring trauma).

Challenging

Someone who is seeking help will usually want their counsellor to be on their side, to offer a supportive, safe relationship. However, clients also want their counsellor to be honest with them, to point out when they seem to be not making sense, contradicting themselves, avoiding things or indulging in self-destructive behaviour. The skill of *confronting* or *challenging* is hard for many counsellors, who tend to be people who avoid conflict and hold a preference for harmonious, close relationships. Counsellors often believe that to challenge a client runs the risk of undermining the therapeutic relationship. There is of course wisdom in adopting caution around the use of challenging – a high proportion of people who seek counselling do so because they have been exposed to critical and demeaning responses from other people in their lives, and are therefore highly sensitive to any hint of judgementalism on the part of their counsellor. However, it can be important for counsellors to keep a hold of the idea that what they are doing when they challenge a client is not only potentially useful in itself, as a means of stimulating new understanding or new behaviour, but also represents an opportunity for the client to learn about *supportive* challenging, that arises from a position of empathic caring.

There are three key principles involved in supportive challenging. First, the counsellor signals that he or she is concerned about some aspect of what the client is doing or saying, and would like to challenge the client. The counsellor asks if this would be a good point at which to share these concerns, or whether doing so would interrupt the flow of whatever else the client wanted to explore at that moment. One way of saying this might be: 'I have some thoughts about this – would you like to hear from me?' Second, the challenge or confrontation is framed in terms of a tentative statement around a possible contradiction between different statements that the client has made. Examples: 'You mentioned that you wanted to use the counselling to deal with the arguments you have with your spouse, but we have met twice and you haven't mentioned this issue again…'; 'You say you feel OK and relaxed, and yet you sound angry…'; 'You want to be more honest with your mother, and yet it seems to me that you have just described a conversation with her where you did everything in your power to hide information about…'. The crucial aspect of this kind of formulation is that it is grounded in evidence, and is specific to a particular issue rather than being generalized. (Totalizing or general statements such as 'You are resistant to looking at your own behaviour' are rarely facilitative, because they merely trigger either an avoidance response or angry and resentful fighting back.) A third principle of challenging a client is to observe what happens next and to be willing to work with whatever process then ensues. Does the client openly engage with the issue, or do they change the topic? If the latter, it can be helpful for the counsellor to point out that this is what the client seems to have done.

Checking out/clarifying

At its core, the role of counsellor hinges on a capacity for *listening* to someone who needs to talk through an issue. However, although listening is fundamental and essential, it is more helpful when combined with a willingness to check with the speaker that what is being heard and understood is accurate. Some of the least helpful counselling responses, in the long run, take the form of reacting to a client by saying 'I know how you feel', 'I understand' (or variants of such statements). How can the client believe that you know how they feel, if you have not attempted to put into words what you believe their feeling state consists of? Further – how sure can a counsellor be that he or she really grasps what the client is feeling, rather than misunderstanding or misinterpreting the emotional signals that are being sent? It is only when the counsellor regularly checks out with the client that their understanding is accurate that both of them can proceed in the confidence that they are on the same wavelength.

Sometimes, checking out requires little more than reflecting or restating what the person has said, or summarizing the various threads of meaning that have been gleaned from what has been said. This kind of minimal checking out has the advantage of reassuring the client that they are being understood, while not interrupting the flow of what they are talking about. However, it can also be facilitative, from time to time, to make longer checking out statements that seek to encompass the connections between experiences or events, or convey the counsellor's understanding of the client's whole story. A basic reflective checking out might take the form, 'My sense is that what you are feeling is a sense of frustration and anger, and maybe also a little sadness that it had to come to this... is that the way it is for you?' A more complex or narrative type of checking out would tend to add a further layer of cause-and-effect sequencing: 'I'd like to just check with you that I'm understanding what you are feeling. It's as though when your brother behaves in this self-destructive way, as he did last week, that you have a sense of frustration and anger, and maybe also a little sadness that it had to come to this, and then when you feel like that you just want to withdraw from him and have nothing to do with him, which then leads to feeling depressed and guilty – is that about right?' An important aspect of checking out can involve seeking to *clarify* the meaning of what the client has said. If a counsellor feels confused when a client is talking, or has a sense that there are things that aren't being said, then it can be helpful to follow this up through a process of checking out. For example: 'I can see in the way you are talking about what happened that you are angry. But I'm not quite sure where the sadness fits with that. Could you say a bit more about that feeling of being sad?'

There are several key component skills that contribute to effective checking out: *timing* (finding the right moment to interrupt the flow of the client's self-expression), *observing* how the person responds to the checking out statement (particularly looking for signs that the statement was not fully accurate), and *phrasing* (conveying the nuanced complexity of what the client has said while remaining succinct). Good checking out also encompasses *non-verbal* aspects of what the client has conveyed (e.g. voice quality, gesture and posture) as well as their actual words.

Conversational resourcefulness

Counselling is to a large extent a particular type of conversation or discussion, which is similar in some respects to troubles talk in everyday life contexts but in other ways is radically different. People often turn to counselling because their everyday conversations around problems in living have not been helpful for them. This may mean that the personal difficulty they are trying to address is something they find hard to talk about. In addition, counselling clients are drawn from a wide range of social backgrounds, each of which is associated with different communication rules and norms. As a result of these factors, it is essential for counsellors to be conversationally resourceful, in terms of being able to adjust their own way of talking as necessary, and to offer alternative conversational templates. For example, some clients talk in very factual and descriptive ways, while others make a lot of use of metaphors and images. Some clients prefer to just talk, whereas others prefer it when the counsellor supplies prompts and questions to help them keep going. Minor aspects of language use, such as word choice, or the difference between 'I' and 'you' statements, as against 'we' formulations, have a significant influence on how the counselling process unfolds.

Courage

Counsellors are similar to first responders (e.g. firefighters, police officers and paramedics) in being willing to move towards and into places of danger that other people are running away from. The places of danger presented by clients are the situations, emotions, memories and self-beliefs that they themselves are avoiding. It can take courage for a counsellor to step towards such areas of experience rather than standing back, because the consequences of going into and through the experience are not entirely predictable or controllable. For example, a client may mention, in passing, that they would be better off dead. At that moment, it is unlikely that the counsellor will know whether this is just a way of talking, or is an indication of something deeper. Neither will the counsellor be able to predict how the client will react if they inquire about the statement that was made. Courage is a skill that is based in a judicious willingness to step out of one's comfort zone.

Curiosity

A counsellor is not just a sounding board, mirror or travel companion. Rather, a counsellor needs to be someone who is actively curious about the client's life and experience, and trying to piece together an understanding of what they are learning about the client. Curiosity is grounded in an attitude of making discoveries and learning new things, rather than an attitude of interrogation and hypothesis-testing. Curiosity is associated with other qualities that are characteristic of effective therapists, such as humility, tentativeness and a 'not-knowing' stance. As a skill, curiosity is manifested in sessions as a conversational style that incorporates openness to whatever the client has to say (listening and following) alongside gentle questioning and invitations to elaborate. It is manifested between sessions as continuing to think about the client, and possibly also accessing further information that is relevant to understanding the client. A key aspect of the skill of being curious is imagination – creating an image or map of what the client's life is like for them.

Embodied presence

Embodied presence refers to a capacity to make use of information from non-verbal cues and the physical presence of both client and counsellor. Most counselling takes place in face-to-face interactions in which the emphasis is on verbal expression. But these words are produced by bodies, and are accompanied by multiple bodily cues. Skilled counsellors are able to observe bodily phenomena in themselves ('I am aware that I am sitting hunched up and with my legs crossed – what could that mean?') and in their clients, integrate these data into the verbal and aural information they are receiving, and use it to inform the process of counselling. An appreciation of this skill is heightened by experience in modes of therapy that involve physical activity, such as adventure therapy, dance therapy or psychodrama, or by watching video recordings of face-to-face therapy sessions with the sound turned off. Even minimal experience of any of these activities will make it clear that a great deal of meaning is expressed through body posture and movement, and that the quality of a relationship is conveyed through an interpersonal 'dance' that takes place between two people. The skill of using embodied presence is exhibited through fluidity and synchrony in the physical movements of counsellor and client. This level of interactive connectedness involves responses within time periods that are too brief to allow for conscious processing. Effective use of this area of skill therefore calls on a capacity to let go, and just be, or be spontaneous, within a framework of shared decision-making and feedback that makes it possible to assess what is appropriate for any particular client at any specific point in time.

Empathy

Empathy is a multifaceted skill that encompasses aspects of listening, attunement, checking out, reflection and remembering. The concept of empathy refers to the capacity to enter the internal reality of the other person, in a way that is sensitive to the multiple threads of the person's experience of the world. Evidence from many research studies confirms that the ability to be empathic consistently produces good client outcomes.

Future orientation

Counselling and psychotherapy are things that you turn to when you have tried to deal with your difficulties in every way that you know, but without success. Clients often describe themselves as stuck, or in a hole, or not able to see their way forward. However, despite that very real sense of impasse, in the background there is always an image or hope of a better future. While counselling may need to take account of how and why problems developed, and what is happening right now, it also needs to be future oriented, both in terms of an immediate nextness and more far-reaching ideas about what a good life would look like. Skills in relation to future orientation can involve identifying goals and completing goal attainment forms, or inviting the client to elaborate on their tentative, barely acknowledged hopes and possibilities. Other aspects of this dimension of therapy may involve defusing catastrophizing fantasies of awful things that might happen, rehearsing alternative ways of responding to certain situations, and making action plans. At a micro level, a collaborative approach to counselling based on shared decisions around questions such as 'what is the priority for today's session?' provides small steps towards a preferred future.

Giving advice/making suggestions

Everyone knows that counsellors do not offer advice. The position that most counsellors take on advice is that they are not there to tell the client what to do, but to facilitate them through some kind of process by which they can arrive at their own solutions and make their own decisions. The wisdom of this position is reinforced by an appreciation of the futility of advice-giving in everyday life. Many (or most) friends or family members respond to the problems of those close to them by offering well-meaning advice ('why don't you…?'), only for the troubled one to say 'yes, but…'. On the other hand, clients can sometimes ask for advice, and may do so on the basis of knowing that the counsellor is in possession of knowledge and experience around the issue for which they seek advice, or may have an inkling that the counsellor does have a position on the issue. In this kind of situation, the client may be puzzled and may feel rejected ('I am not important enough for him to tell me what he really thinks I should do…') if the counsellor does not respond to a request for advice. The skill of offering advice when in a counsellor role therefore hinges on an appreciation of the pros and cons and implications of advice-giving.

It is seldom helpful, in a counselling role, to offer unsolicited advice. Usually, all this does is give the counsellor a false sense that they are doing something useful, while distracting the client from talking about what they need to talk about. When a person explicitly asks their counsellor for advice on a matter, it may be valuable to take an opportunity to acknowledge the person's own resources in relation to the matter in hand ('I'm happy to suggest what I think you might do, but I feel sure that you have thought a lot about this yourself – what are the options that you have been looking at yourself?') and their capacity to enlist the help of other people in their life ('… and I was wondering who else you have talked to about this, and what they have said'). This kind of preamble has the effect of placing the counsellor's advice in the context of other advice, and thus defusing any notion that what the counsellor might suggest has any social authoritative status – it keeps the client in the driving seat. It can then also be useful to hedge the advice that is offered ('You need to be aware that what I'm going to say comes from my perspective – there are definitely other ways of approaching this issue'). Once the advice is offered, it is good to be curious about what the client has made of it ('How does that sound to you… is there something there that you think you can use, or not?'). Throughout the whole process of advice-giving, the counsellor should not imply that they have any investment in whether or not the client follows their advice.

Immediacy

A lot of what is discussed in counselling refers to what is happening or has happened 'out there' in the client's life. Occasionally, it can also be useful to focus on what is happening right here and now, in the counselling room. The skill of being able to make use of here-and-now processes is generally discussed in terms of the concept of *immediacy*. There are two broad types of immediacy. The first involves paying attention to something that the client is doing right now (example: 'You said that you agreed with my analysis of the situation, but when you spoke you clenched your fist and looked away… I'm wondering if there is something else that you are maybe finding hard to say? Could you maybe just stay with that feeling for a moment, and try to find words for it?'). The second type of immediacy occurs when the counsellor describes his or her personal response to the client. This second form of immediacy is sometimes described as counsellor *self-involvement*. An example might be, 'When you say that you agree with me and then look away and act sort of angry then I have a sense of being dismissed, as though I'm a little boy who doesn't get to hear what the grown-ups are talking about', or: 'I don't know if this is relevant, but I just felt scared there, as if I had said the wrong thing and was in trouble.' A key element in all counsellor training is about enabling students to feel confident about using the skill of immediacy. This is because the rules of 'normal' or 'polite' conversation generally proscribe this kind of bluntness or honesty, and also because immediacy is scary – once you open the door to this kind of statement, who knows where the conversation might go? Despite these difficulties, counselling trainers tend to push the value of immediacy, because it can deepen the level of intimacy or connectedness in the client–counsellor relationship, and can also help the client to begin to move beyond a cautious or 'safe' account of their troubles, and begin to talk in a more emotionally honest manner about the things that really matter to them.

Listening

The art of listening lies at the heart of counselling – good counsellors are good listeners. A crucial dimension of listening involves letting the other person know that you are listening. This skill was described earlier in the chapter, in the section on *attending*. It can be disconcerting and disturbing for a person to start to talk about something that is meaningful for them, and to have a sense that their interlocutor is not paying attention to them. Effective attending therefore functions as a means of communicating to the client that their counsellor is still listening. However, the appearance of attending is not much help to the client if real listening is not taking place. Genuine listening involves making an effort to grasp the *whole* of what a person is saying (or expressing through their voice quality and non-verbal cues such as posture). Genuine listening involves suspending or bracketing off any assumptions about the meaning of what a person is saying, and instead being open to what is actually there. Effective listening requires switching off one's internal dialogue in order to tune into the other person's story. It calls for a willingness to be there in the moment.

None of this is easy. In everyday conversations, we listen to each other, but only up to a point – at least some of the time, we are rehearsing what we intend to say when our turn comes round. In many professional situations, we are trained to listen *for* specific types of information. For example, a doctor or nurse learns to listen for symptoms, or for information that will confirm a particular diagnosis. A police officer may be trained to listen for evasions and contradictions in the story told by a suspect or witness. The listening that counsellors do is more open-ended than this. It is more like listening for the person behind the story. Also, as he or she listens to the person, a skilled counsellor also listens to themselves (see below: *self-monitoring*).

There are perhaps at least two observable manifestations of counsellor listening. First, when a counsellor is sufficiently tuned into the client's story, they may get to a point of becoming able to finish the client's sentences, seamlessly making links between what is being said now and what was said in previous conversations, or effortlessly knowing when it is their turn to speak. This comes across to observers as a conversation that is *flowing*, with each speaker in synchrony with the other. A second observable feature of good listening is the occurrence of pauses and silences. Because a counsellor is listening in this kind of holistic manner, they may find it hard to formulate an immediate response when the time comes for them to speak. Typically, if a counsellor has been listening well enough, they may need a few moments to reflect on what has been said before they begin to speak. What this kind of deep listening makes possible, is for the counsellor to gain a sense of the many facets of whatever issue the person is exploring. It can be very powerful for the client if as much as possible of this complexity can then be reflected back to them in the counsellor's response, because it subtly invites the possibility that an issue or problem can be viewed in different ways. As with other counselling skills, developing a capacity to listen effectively is something that can only be acquired through practice and experiment with other people who are willing to provide honest constructive feedback. Also, for any counsellor, reflection on one's ability to listen is likely to lead to the identification of personal issues and vulnerabilities: no matter how good a listener someone is, there are always some topics that cause the shutters to come down.

Making sense/interpreting

One of the most common triggers for seeking help from a counsellor is the experience of not being able to make sense of some aspect of one's life. The person may be frightened, overwhelmed or confused by experiences that they are having. Making sense of these experiences allows the person to gain some control over events, or 'get a handle' on what is happening. Gaining understanding also tends to reduce the emotional pressure on a person, because they are more able to see things in perspective and as a result acquire some distance from their feelings. The skill of being able to work with a client to make sense of a problem therefore represents a crucial area of competence for any counsellor.

There are three broad sense-making strategies that are typically used by counsellors. The first strategy is to invite the person to explain how they personally make sense of the problem or issue that is bothering them, possibly by using an open question such as 'This is clearly a big issue for you, and I'm sure that you must have really thought deeply about why it is happening...'. A variant on this approach is to listen for explanatory accounts that are implicit in the way the person talks about a problem (example: 'As I'm listening to you, it seems to me that you think you can't give up smoking because you are weak-willed – is that the way you make sense of it?'). A further variant is to ask the person how they make sense of similar situations (example: 'you mentioned to me that you have already changed your lifestyle in the area of taking more exercise – how do you understand how you were able to do that?'). Tapping into the sense-making frameworks that the person already espouses is always a good idea. A second sense-making strategy is to create a space for developing understanding by listing, displaying or mapping the events or experiences that are puzzling for the person. Visual diagrams can be very useful in this kind of work. For example, when a person can see, laid out in front of them on a flip chart page, the sequence of events that leads to a crisis, it may be much easier for them to find a meaningful pattern that allows them to make sense of what has been happening. The third strategy is for the counsellor to offer the client an explanatory framework that is based on some kind of pre-existing theory or model. This type of approach has an educative dimension, because the counsellor is trying to teach the client some new ideas. The dangers associated with this strategy are that the client can become confused by the new ideas, or can defer to what they perceive as the greater wisdom of the counsellor (while in truth not regarding the counsellor's explanation as credible or useful). A lot of the time, clients who are baffled by a counsellor's theories will not say so to the therapist, for fear of being impolite or ungrateful. These risks are exacerbated by the fact that offering a client an explanatory framework can feed into a counsellor's self-aggrandizing desire to appear knowledgeable, wise and clever. Having said all that, there are times when a counsellor-supplied theory can make a huge difference to a client: all of us draw on ideas and theories to help us to make sense of various aspects of life, and we learned these ideas from somewhere.

Naming

A really lovely skill, which some counsellors are able to use to powerful effect, is that of finding the right word to describe an experience. This skill applies in situations where there is some aspect of a person's life that is implicit and unsaid. For example, a counsellor working with a woman who was consistently self-critical struggled to find a way of referring to the client's positive qualities, and eventually struck on the word 'feisty'. This concept had a lot of meaning for the client, and the two of them were then able to talk about 'that feisty side of you' or 'the feistier option' – conversational possibilities that were not available up until that point.

Normalizing

Quite often, a therapy client may not only be suffering from a life-limiting way of being in the world (e.g. feeling worried and anxious and having occasional panic attacks) but also suffers from the additional burden of fearing that these responses mean that they are irretrievably mentally ill or on the edge of a complete breakdown. The skill of normalizing comprises two key components. First, the counsellor does not participate in an alarmist interpretation of what has been happening in the person's life, but instead approaches it in a calm and businesslike manner that involves looking at the anxiety and panic episodes in detail. This strategy usually leads to the mutual discovery that there are some processes occurring that would 'normally' make anyone anxious. Examples of anxiety-heightening factors might include drinking too much coffee, poor diet, not enough sleep, health problems, not enough exercise, unresolved sources of stress, panic in situations associated with previous trauma, etc. This kind of normalizing approach does not diminish the seriousness of the client's distress, but breaks at least some of it down into understandable and credible mechanisms, with which the client is almost certainly already familiar, that are associated with practical possibilities for change. Even if none of these mechanisms turn out to be a magic bullet that transforms the client's problem, the chances are that addressing them will begin to alleviate it, and provide the client with enough hope and confidence to keep working at the issue. A potentially helpful phrase in the context of normalizing is 'It makes sense that you feel like that ...'.

Observing

Being observant is a skill that tends not to get sufficient recognition in the counselling literature. Where a person sits, how they move, what they do with their hands, where they look, how they dress, how these and other characteristics change from day to day or moment to moment (and what triggers such changes) – these are all valuable sources of information for a counsellor. The purpose of observation in counselling is not to collect information to lead to a diagnosis, but instead to use every means possible to enter the personal world of the client, and to create opportunities for reflection and learning. It can be useful for clients to share the outcomes of observation: 'I noticed that when you started to talk about your father you bit your lip and hunched up in your chair... I don't know if that means anything, but it somehow struck me as significant...'. A particularly important time to observe the client is in the moment following a statement or intervention made by the counsellor – does the client look as though what you said has deepened their process of exploration and meaning-making, or do they look confused or frustrated? A standard learning exercise around the development of observation skills is to watch a video of a counselling session with the sound turned off. It is usually possible to understand a lot of what is happening, even in the absence of words.

Offering feedback

There is an aspect of counselling that is like being a mirror for the person who is seeking help. It is as though the person is caught up in the complexity and stuckness of their problem, and needs to be able to ask someone external to the situation a question such as 'What does this look like to you?', or even 'What (or who) do *I* look like to you?' Responding to this kind of question involves a process of providing feedback to a person. Giving feedback is therefore potentially very important for some clients, but can be a risky business. There are probably three main risks. There is a danger of making what can be categorized as a *totalizing* statement, or blanket description of a person's actions. Example: the client is talking about a situation that is hard to handle, and asks the counsellor how their behaviour comes across to them, as a therapist. The counsellor says: 'Well, what I see is someone who is avoiding facing up to something.' The client interprets this as: 'She thinks I am being a *complete coward*.' This example also illustrates a second risk, associated with feedback that is generalized rather than anchored in observations of specific behaviour. What might have been better for this counsellor to have said is, 'When you spend the evening with your wife and don't mention this issue, that looks to me as if you are avoiding it, and yet I also know that you are spending a lot of time talking to your best friend, and to me, about how to face up to it.' This statement is explicit about where the avoiding is happening (and implicitly is opening up the possibility of a conversation about how that pattern might be changed), and also balances different items of feedback against each other (thus not falling into the trap of totalizing). A third form of unhelpful feedback is when the statement made by the counsellor is too *bland* (example: 'What I see is someone who is struggling with some really difficult choices in his life' – a statement that could be made at almost any time to almost any client). Bland or empty feedback can make the client wonder whether the counsellor really cares, or has been really paying attention, or perhaps even suspect that the counsellor has chosen to conceal the awfulness of what they have observed ('She thinks I am pathetic but she can't bring herself to say it').

Effective feedback is timely, specific, nuanced, comprehensive and owned ('what I see is X' rather than 'you are X'). In some situations the activity of providing feedback overlaps with the skill of *immediacy*, for instance when the feedback refers to how the counsellor feels when a client says or does some particular thing. On counselling skills training courses, participants usually gain a lot of experience in giving and receiving feedback to and from each other, and thereby gain essential first-hand experience around the types of feedback that can be facilitative or otherwise.

Positioning

In any conversation, the speaker talks in such a way as to position themselves and the listener as occupying specific niches in society, and as participants in a particular type of relationship to them. This is accomplished through use of words like 'I', 'we' and 'you', tone of voice, word choice, and controlling turn-taking. In counselling, if the therapist positions themselves as an expert who is collecting diagnostic information, and the client as a patient to be treated, there is little space for active client involvement or the development of a collaborative relationship. Alternatively, a client may position themselves as deficient, or as a victim of circumstances. In these (and other) scenarios, a counsellor might use positioning skills and awareness to introduce alternative subject positions into the conversation, such as talking in a way that indicated a genuine interest in the client's suggestions, using 'we' formulations to encourage joint action, and restating the client's story as an account of what they did, rather than what was done to them. There are also ways that counsellor-initiated positioning can be unhelpful. For instance, many people regard themselves first as members of a family and community, and only secondarily (if at all) as autonomous individuals. In these cases, any attempt to position the client as having choices that do not involve taking account of the views of others might lead to a breakdown in the client–therapist relationship.

Process monitoring

What happens in a counselling session unfolds and changes from moment to moment. These phenomena can be understood as comprising the *process* of counselling – therapeutic processes that occur on many different levels in the thoughts and feelings of each participant and in the interaction and relationship between them. A skilled counsellor needs to be aware of, or monitor, this process as a means of keeping track of what is happening. Some examples of types of information that may be relevant to an understanding of the counselling process include:

- topic shifts (the client or the counsellor abruptly stops talking about one issue, and changes tack)

- change in interpersonal connectedness (I feel a lot closer to/more distant from the client, compared to a few minutes ago)
- change in depth of emotional processing (the client moves from superficial discussion of a topic, to exploring their deepest feelings around it – or vice versa)
- shifts in client self-concept (a month ago, all they talked about was how useless they were, and now they are starting to acknowledge their own strengths).

Awareness of these (and other) types of process information can help the counsellor to identify what works for each individual client, what kinds of intervention may be counterproductive (e.g. a clumsy interpretation may lead to the client shifting from exploring deep feelings to a more superficial or distanced account of his problems), and how well the client and counsellor are working together. The skill of process monitoring involves paying attention to process factors while retaining a primary focus on the content of what the person is actually talking about. Most of the time, process monitoring feeds into fine-tuning and minor adjustments to the counsellor's approach to the client.

Providing and evaluating information

Someone in the role of counsellor is a potential source of information for the person seeking help. Some of this information may relate to the counsellor themselves – when they are available, the limits to the confidentiality they can offer, their training and experience, etc. Other information may relate to alternative sources of help – specialist counselling and psychotherapy services that may be available, clinics, support groups and so on. There are information sources that in themselves constitute forms of therapeutic assistance, such as self-help books and websites. There are also information sources that address health and social care issues that the client may be experiencing, from how to support a family member with dementia, through to how to claim housing benefits. These information sources may be suggested and supplied by the counsellor, or the client may find information that they might then wish to check out or discuss with their counsellor. All of these types of information can be regarded as resources that have potential to assist the person in working through their difficulties and moving on in their life. We live in a culture in which hard-pressed healthcare systems try to reduce the burden on health professionals by providing patients with leaflets, websites and call centres where they can acquire information about how they can take care of themselves. All this can be useful, but it can also result in people having a sense of being 'fobbed off' with a leaflet rather than being allowed to talk to a person who is an enduring caring presence in their life. It can also result in mountains of unread leaflets. Skilfully providing information in counselling therefore requires that the counsellor finds ways to include the information within the counselling conversation and therapeutic relationship, rather than just suggesting or supplying information and expecting the client to assimilate it on their own.

Questioning

Questions comprise one of the basic elements of language use. Human beings have evolved language as a means of communication, and questions represent a linguistic form that has obvious survival value: asking another person for information or assistance. Question-and-answer sequences comprise a large part of the discourse that occurs between people who are close to each other: 'What did you do at the weekend?', 'Do you like my new haircut?' For many students, one of the hardest parts of counsellor training is associated with the process of learning *not* to ask questions, or learning how to ask particular types of questions for particular purposes.

Being a counsellor involves putting to one side one's 'natural' or taken-for-granted way of asking questions, and acquiring instead a more consciously intentional approach to the art of questioning. Why is this? There are two main problems with the unreflective use of questions in counselling. First, in many counselling situations, the aim is to help the client to tell their story in their own words. Asking questions runs the risk that the ongoing flow of the client's story will be broken – they lose the thread of what they are trying to put into words, by having to break off and answer the counsellor's questions. In other words, there is the possibility that a question will alter the client's process in an unhelpful manner. Second, a question tends to be formulated from the frame of reference of the questioner, and subtly convey the questioner's assumptions about the topic that is being discussed. This aspect of questioning is summed up in the idea that 'behind every question is a statement'. For example, if a client is talking about feeling anxious in social situations, their counsellor might respond by posing a question such as: 'When did this anxiety start… what was the first time you were aware of being affected in this way?' The statement behind this question could be summed up as: 'I believe that it is important for us to look at how this all started, because that is the best way to find out what needs to be done to change it.' However, it may be that the client either does not see the relevance of thinking about how it all started, or is puzzled by why the counsellor might want to know that specific piece of information at that particular point in their story. For some clients, questions may be experienced as a diagnostic rather than a therapeutic process.

Reflecting/restating

As a person seeking help talks about the issues that are bothering them, it can be helpful for their counsellor to simply reflect back to them the main gist of what they have been saying. This allows the person to know that the counsellor is listening, following and understanding, and it enables the counsellor to know that her own understanding of the client's story is broadly in tune with what the client is intending to convey. A reflection or restatement is typically a brief statement, which does not interrupt the flow of the client's narrative. In addition to the main function of confirming a basic level of contact and shared meaning between client and counsellor, the skill of reflection can serve further important therapeutic purposes. It can be useful for a client to hear their inner concerns and feelings being articulated by another person. Quite often, a person who seeks counselling help may have never previously spoken about that issue to anyone else, or may never have voiced particularly embarrassing, shameful or emotionally painful facets of the issue. As a result, their dilemma or problem may have been played in their mind over and over again, as a repetitive inner monologue. In this kind of situation, it can make a huge difference to speak the words out loud, and then to hear these words being said by another person. Even this simple act can allow the person a certain amount of emotional relief and perspective.

Another potentially valuable aspect of simple restatement is that it serves to slow down the flow of the person's talk. If a person is talking about an issue that is emotionally painful or embarrassing, he may well talk quickly as a means of keeping his feelings at a distance, or to avoid having to think more deeply about the issue. Reflection or restatement offers the person brief moments of pause or reflection that allow the beginnings of a process of assimilating and coming to terms with their problematic experience. With some clients, the opposite may occur – the topic is so hard to speak about that they go quiet, or there are long gaps in their discourse. Here, a brief restatement can function as a gentle nudge ('I am interested, and here is what I have picked up so far…') that encourages the person to continue their story. Making reflective statements can also be useful for the counsellor, as way of staying focused. If a client talks for a long time, their counsellor can become overwhelmed with information. Occasional brief restatements or reflections can operate as a strategy for organizing the client's story into more memorable 'chunks'.

For all these reasons, reflection or restatement is a routine counselling skill that has wide applicability. Done well, the act of reflection can carry a great deal of meaning. Mechanical repetition of the last words the client has said is likely to have a negative impact on the client–counsellor relationship. Sensitive reflection, by contrast, is carefully timed and uses words or images that resonate with the client, communicated with a voice quality that subtly conveys a sense of caring and active engagement, and emotional attunement with the client's feeling state.

Reframing

All approaches to counselling make creative use of a distinction between feelings and behaviour on the one side, and on the other side the way that the person interprets or makes sense of these experiences. It is certainly possible to construct massive theoretical debates and research programmes around the nature and implications of this distinction. In terms of counselling skills, however, the action/emotion vs cognition split has a straightforward application, in terms of the use of *reframing*. This skill involves two steps. The first step is to find out how the person makes sense of a problematic experience (behaviour pattern or emotional state), and for the counsellor to let the client know that they understand and appreciate their point of view. The second step is to invite the client to consider an alternative way of making sense of the problematic experience. Some examples:

- Joe is terrified about speaking in public at an important conference; his counsellor asks him whether it might be possible that his *fear* could be viewed in a different light, as *excitement* about being able to influence other people with his ideas.

- Sheila believes that she is a *failure* because she has not been able to achieve some important life goals; her counsellor responds by listing the many ways that Sheila has been successful in her life, and suggests that a different way to look at these problematic life goals might be to regard them as *incomplete* or ongoing.

- Alison fails an exam, and berates herself for not being intelligent enough to pass her degree; her counsellor agrees that a lack of intelligence can be a factor in poor academic performance, but goes on to add that, from what she has heard about Alison's approach to exam revision, a lack of effective study skills and planning might offer a more accurate explanation.

In each of these examples, the counsellor is not dismissing the client's definition of the situation, and is offering a reframed understanding that can be backed up with reference to information that the client has already provided. The underlying manoeuvre that is involved in the skill of reframing is a shift from seeing an event from a standpoint of 'I am worthless and stupid' to a standpoint of 'I am a resourceful person with positive strengths and attributes.' For this intervention to be effective, the counsellor needs to believe in the alternative perspective that she is offering, and be willing and able to explain why she thinks that it represents a valid way of thinking about the situation. Typically, a client will not buy into a reframe straight away, but may need to try it on for size or be reminded about it at regular intervals. What can also happen is that the act of reframing can trigger further conversation and exploration of the more general issue of how, why, where and when the person self-sabotages himself, or is dominated by their 'inner critic'.

Remembering

Another skill that does not receive nearly enough attention and acknowledgement in the counselling world is the ability to *remember* what the client has said and done. A big part of what a counsellor does is to be able to stay with the client in the present moment, for example by reflecting back what has been said, or being willing to sit in silence. However, another vital aspect of counselling involves helping the client to make connections between different chapters of their life story, or different areas of their experience. An underlying difficulty that influences many people to seek counselling is a sense of a lack of coherence in their life, as if they are in possession of different pieces of a jigsaw that do not fit together. In a counselling session, a client may start off by talking about one issue, and then move into another issue, or begin by stating a particular goal and then start exploring something that does not seem relevant to that goal. In these scenarios it is part of the job of the counsellor to hold the first bit of information in the back of their mind and then, at what seems an appropriate point, to reintroduce it into the conversation. Example: 'I'm aware that for the past few minutes you have been talking about your conflict with one of your work colleagues, yet at the start of the session you said that you wanted to really focus on what you are feeling about the results of your medical tests... I'm wondering if there might be a connection between these things, and I was also remembering how you said to me once that when you are scared about something you start a fight...'

The skill of remembering can involve practical strategies such as keeping notes, reading notes before a counselling session, or writing down key phrases during a session. Some of what is being remembered is information (e.g. how many children a person has, and their ages and names), but most of it takes the form of a map of the emotional and relational world of the person. New counsellors may often worry about whether they will be able to remember what the client has said to them, and may try to deal with this fear by taking detailed notes during sessions. This is seldom effective, because it can turn a counselling session into a fact-finding interview in which lots of data are collected but nothing changes in the client's life. In the end, a counsellor needs to trust themself to be capable of remembering whatever needs to be remembered. A training exercise that can be illuminating is to make a recording of a counselling session, and at the end of the session to make notes of the information and themes that have been conveyed by the client. If the session is then transcribed and read carefully, it will be apparent that the post-session notes have missed a great deal of valuable information. This phenomenon occurs not because the counsellor lacks competence, but because clients always say more than we hear – our memories are always partial.

Repair

It is not realistic to expect that the process of counselling will always proceed smoothly. It is inevitable that there will be occasions when a therapist and client misunderstand each other, or even act in ways that are hurtful to the other. It is therefore important as a therapist to possess skills in repairing relationships. Having confidence in one's capacity for repair makes it easier for a therapist to take risks, in the sense of making suggestions or interpretations that may be challenging for the client to hear, or perhaps may be based on intuition rather than the accumulation of observational evidence. Such risks have the potential to contribute to breakthrough moments, and to a general willingness to be honest and immediate in both client and therapist. By contrast, absence of repair skills and strategies may contribute to a somewhat wooden, safe and limited therapy process. The experience of having worked through a rupture together may strengthen the client–therapist relationship and help the client to learn about how to repair relationships in their everyday life.

Self-disclosure

Self-disclosure refers to the act of sharing personal information with another individual. In counselling, it is taken for granted that the client will engage in a great deal of self-disclosure. Usually, in order to allow the client the maximum space in which to talk, and to be clear about who is the one who is helping and who is the recipient of help, a counsellor will engage in little or no self-disclosure. This arrangement is fundamentally different from most social interaction, in which disclosure by one person tends to lead to parallel disclosure by the other. For example, if two friends are talking and one of them tells a story about 'the best restaurant I have ever visited', then it is highly probable that the other person will follow with their own restaurant story. By contrast, in counselling if a client tells a story of 'how I feel overweight and disgusted by how I look', then there is a very low probability that the counsellor will respond by talking about her own body image issues, because she knows that her role is to assist the person to explore the unique challenges in *his* life. However, there are times when this 'rule' may be threatened. For example, a client who is talking about dieting may look at his counsellor (who appears to be 'sorted' in this respect) and ask: 'Do you really understand what I am talking about? Have you ever had to watch your calories?' What should the counsellor say? Alternatively, a counsellor may be listening to a client, and thinking to herself, 'I have been there, I know exactly what that feels like... would it be helpful for me to tell this client what it was like for me?'

In the past, most counselling training strongly emphasized the idea that counsellor self-disclosure was unhelpful, and that a counsellor should resist any temptation to disclose, and deflect back to the client and request for disclosure ('I sense that it might be reassuring for you if you knew that I had experienced similar issues around my weight...'). More recently, practical experience and research evidence suggests that careful counsellor self-disclosure can in fact be highly facilitative for some clients. What does 'careful' mean in this context? A key factor in helpful counsellor self-disclosure is that it is *in the service of the client* – it does not create a situation in which the client feels that they need to take care of the counsellor, or where the session starts to focus on the counsellor's problems at the expense of the client's agenda.

A further factor is that the counsellor includes some kind of statement along the lines that people are different, and that their experience of, say, body image issues may be quite different from the situation being faced by the client. Finally, *how* the disclosure is handled will determine whether it is ultimately helpful for the client. For example, a counsellor might acknowledge something of her own battle with binge eating in a manner that conveys a sense of superiority ('I have dealt with this when I was a teenager – there must be something seriously wrong with you if you haven't been able to deal with it after all this time'), or in a manner that encourages and invites the client to engage in further dialogue and exploration ('Yes, it has been a challenge for me at different points in my life, and has really made me think about the meaning of food in my own life and in our culture as a whole'). For a counsellor, skilful use of self-disclosure arises from having worked through personal issues to a point of being able to use personal life experience in a selective and intentional manner, rather than sharing personal information that is still raw and unresolved. It should be noted that there is an important distinction to be made between self-disclosure (sharing biographical information from life outside the counselling room) and *immediacy* (sharing one's response to what is happening in the here-and-now counselling interaction). Both skills involve the counsellor talking about herself, but in different ways and for different purposes.

Self-monitoring/self-awareness

In a counselling relationship, the person in the role of counsellor is doing his or her best to be with the client and focus on the client's concerns and their story. During this activity, the counsellor does everything possible to lay aside or 'bracket off' the issues in their own life. In this situation, feelings, emotions, action tendencies, images or fantasies that arise in the counsellor may represent vital pieces of information about the client's world and the way that the client relates to other people. A key counsellor skill therefore consists of a capacity to engage in ongoing *self-monitoring* throughout the process of a counselling interaction. A good counsellor listens to her client, and at the same time listens to themselves listening to the client. Examples of the potentially relevant types of counsellor experience that can arise in response to clients include:

- *feelings*: a general sense that something is being left unsaid; a sense of hopelessness or despair
- *specific emotions*: anger, sadness, boredom, fear
- *physical reactions*: tummy rumbling, itchiness, yawning, pain
- *action tendencies:* running away, moving closer, holding
- *images*: the client as a child in school, counsellor as an interrogator
- *fantasies*: we are in a chess match; it's like a scene from Little Red Riding Hood.

There are basically three sources of these phenomena. First, the response can simply arise from something that is happening in the counsellor's life. For instance, the counsellor may already be feeling sad before the counselling session begins, because of the death of a family member. It is important for counsellors to be sufficiently self-aware to be able to differentiate between reactions to clients that arise from their own personal 'stuff', and reactions that represent some kind of capacity to 'resonate' with the reality of the client. A second source of feelings, images and other internal phenomena experienced by a counsellor may be that these experiences reflect aspects of what the client is experiencing. It is as though at that moment the counsellor is sensitively 'tuned in' to the client, and picking up some hidden or unspoken element of what the client is feeling and thinking. For example, a client may be talking about positive hopes for the future – if the counsellor at that point feels sadness it may indicate that for the client there is also some sense of loss involved in making a decision to move on in their life. A third way of making sense of these reactions is that the counsellor may be reacting to the client in a similar fashion to the ways that other people react. For example, a client's life may be full of contradictions and unkept promises, with the result that their friends and family get frustrated and angry with them. When their counsellor also feels frustrated and angry, they can perhaps begin to explore in the present moment how this kind of response is triggered, and what it might mean.

Effective counselling skills training and practice creates opportunities for trainees to experiment with different ways of engaging in self-monitoring and productively bringing these inner experiences into the counselling conversation. It should also provide opportunities for observing how other counsellors make use of self-monitoring, and for being on the receiving end of this kind of intervention. When offering clients the fruits of self-monitoring, it is essential to be tentative and to invite the client to consider the *possibility* that what the counsellor is feeling, or the image that has jumped into her head, may have some meaning for the client. To *assume* or *insist* that these counsellor experiences *must* be relevant for the client, is oppressive.

Silence

The spaces between words are highly significant in any counselling conversation. In these spaces a client may be engaged in a process of experiencing an unfolding of feelings or memories, they may be reflecting on the meaning or implications of something that has just been said or felt, or they may be desperately struggling to find some way to avoid talking about something that is in their awareness but which is too hard to put into words at that precise moment. There are also times when a counsellor may wish to take some moments to reflect on how they have understood what has been said. There are times when a counsellor may decide to wait for the client to speak, rather than initiating conversation, as a way of enacting the idea that the client is in charge of the agenda. These are all constructive uses of silence. There are also less positive uses of silence, for example where the counsellor emotionally withdraws from the client, or conveys a signal that a particular topic is not something that they are willing to talk about. And clients may 'clam up' because they are annoyed or disappointed with their counsellor and don't feel safe enough to mention an issue. The skill of *using silence* therefore involves being sufficiently comfortable with silence to allow it to occur, and being sensitive to the possible meanings associated with different types of silence.

Structuring

In any counselling encounter, part of the role of the counsellor is to be mindful of the time that is available, and to take responsibility for initiating collaborative discussion around how that time might be used. Although clients are free to make suggestions or requests about the use of time – for example by saying that they have had enough for today, or asking for more time – an important implicit dimension of a counselling session usually consists of a tacit agreement that the client has the freedom to 'let go' and 'just talk', while the counsellor takes care of time boundaries. A key aspect of the skill of *structuring* therefore consists of an awareness of the use of time, and a willingness to check out with the client and make suggestions regarding how long a session might last, how often meetings might occur, and the length of time remaining in a session. Typically, counsellors try to avoid situations where the client is in full flow and the session just comes to an abrupt end. It is better, in most situations, to seek to build in a few minutes to review what has been discussed, and look at what might be done next.

The other aspect of structuring consists of organizing the work that needs to be done. For example, if the client identifies several goals, which of these will be tackled first? If the client wants to work on a specific problem, what are the step-by-step tasks that might need to be accomplished in order to resolve that problem, and in what order would it be best to take them? Agreeing time structures and task structures helps both the client and the counsellor to be confident that they are working together in an effective manner. Knowing that there is a clear structure for the work that is being done (even if it is a structure that can be renegotiated if necessary) helps the client to have a sense of safety and security, at a point where some areas of their life may feel as though they are out of control and unmanageable.

Using props

Although therapy primarily operates through conversation and dialogue, most counsellors use props – material objects that provide additional and alternative methods of communication. Therapy props can include forms and worksheets, art materials, cushions, books, musical instruments and much else. Counsellors who incorporate these resources into their practice need to develop skills in how to introduce them to clients and how to facilitate client involvement.

Witnessing

The final skill in this list consists of the act of *witnessing*. It is a mistake in counselling to assume that when a person talks about an issue that is important or painful for them, that they necessarily want the counsellor to help them to 'do something' about that issue. Obviously, many clients want to change aspects of their lives, and want their counsellor to help them to achieve this. But just being able to talk about an issue is in itself a potentially powerful experience. When they talk about an issue in counselling, many clients are telling their story, or certain elements of their story, for the first time. In this kind of situation, just to know that someone is fully present and listening can be a healing experience. There can also be a sense of relief at putting words to emotions and memories that may have been a source of repetitive internal rumination for months or years. By being a witness to someone else's suffering, a counsellor has the possibility of affirming the essential humanity of that person. If a person tells a painful or shameful story, and has an experience of being accepted by their counsellor, they takes a step out of aloneness, and into connectedness and mutual support.

Conclusions

The discussion of counselling skills in this chapter shows how skills have multiple functions, and are interconnected in multiple ways. It is therefore not possible to arrive at an ultimate definitive list of skills – counselling skills books and research studies tend to use slightly different terminology and definitions. It is essential to develop your own way of talking about counselling skills, including adding items to the list, and merging items, where necessary for your learning. From Chapter 5 through to the end of the book, the skills introduced in the present chapter are explored in more detail, with references to relevant theory and research.

Learning activities

The following activities may be explored individually, and/or with a group of learning partners.

1   **Identifying your counselling skills strengths and limitations**. One of the key functions of this chapter is to support you in conducting an audit or review of your confidence and competence in the use of counselling skills. This involves working through the A–Z list and making notes on your ability to implement each skill. It can also be useful to rate your competence with each skill on a 1–5 scale (5=entirely comfortable, competent and confident with using this skill; 4=mainly competent; 3=mixed: able to use this skill in some situations but not others; 2=limited ability to use this skill; 1=do not feel competent at all, and would avoid using this skill).

2   **Consulting other people about your counselling skills abilities**. Ask other people – ideally people who know you in different situations – about how they experience your capacity to use counselling/helping skills. It is valuable to collect their views on both what you are good at, as well as what they regard as areas where you could improve. What does this feedback tell you about: (a) the accuracy of your own skills self-evaluation; and (b) specific skills situations or scenarios that are particularly challenging for you?

3   **Constructing an action plan to develop your skills**. For skills you have rated 1 or 2 in your self-audit, take some time to work out (in consultation with others, if possible) what you might do to become more competent and confident in the use of that skill. A variety of skills learning strategies is discussed in Chapter 4.

4   **Monitoring your skills competence over the course of training**. Carry out further skills self-audits on a regular basis using the same 1–5 scale.

An experience that often occurs in participants on counselling skills training courses is that they feel as though their counselling gets worse before it gets better. This phenomenon occurs for two reasons. First, skills ratings at the start of training may reflect an overpositive self-estimate – practising skills and getting feedback may lead to realizing that you were not as proficient with an area of skill as you thought you were. Second, learning a skill can involve a certain amount of unlearning, as habits that are not optimal are changed or dropped in order to allow more complex sequences of skills and action to be constructed. Another way of looking at this issue is that, by reading books about counselling skills and observing skilled practitioners at work, trainees become more aware of the subtle aspects of particular skills, and as a result may go through a phase of being quite critical about their own performance. The sense of getting worse before you get better should therefore be regarded as a sign of meaningful learning.

5 **Skills that are particularly important in specific contexts**. Your use of counselling skills will inevitably be shaped by the kind of clients that you see. For example, some people who come for counselling as a result of trauma, abuse or betrayal may need and prefer their counsellor to be supportive and caring rather than challenging. Some younger clients can often be very uncomfortable with silence. What are the implications of your work setting and career aims for your counselling skills profile?

6 **Negative and unhelpful aspects of counselling skills**. The discussion of counselling skills in this chapter concentrated on how these ways of interacting with people can have beneficial effects. However, it is also important to be aware that counselling skills can have *negative* effects: anything that is powerful enough to do good can also do harm. In respect of specific skills that are particularly relevant to you, can you imagine situations in which: (i) the use of that skill might be harmful or hindering for a client; (ii) the absence of that skill might undermine the effectiveness of counselling. What are the implications of these issues for your counselling practice?

Theoretical frameworks

Introduction

When using counselling skills, it is helpful to be able to draw on a model or theoretical framework of how different skills fit together. Theoretical concepts function to focus attention and deepen reflection on practice, as well as providing a shared language that facilitates consultation and supervision conversations with colleagues. The aim of this chapter is to introduce the main theories of counselling skills that are currently influential in the professional literature. Particular emphasis is given to a collaborative theoretical and philosophical perspective that underpins the approach adopted in this book. The chapter also discusses the contribution and relevance for counselling skills of broader theories of psychotherapy.

Counselling skills models

The intense interest in counselling skills that emerged in the period between 1950 and the 1980s had the effect of generating both a wide range of training methods and a set of theoretical models that continue to provide a basis for learning and practice. Key figures in this tradition have been Robert Carkhuff, Allen Ivey and Gerard Egan, later joined by Clara Hill. The key theoretical questions that they sought to address were:

- Are there core skills, that form the fundamentals of practice, that may combine into more complex skills?
- What are the functions or outcomes of specific skills?
- How is it possible to decide when to use a particular skill? For example, are different skills more relevant at different stages of the helping process?

The answers to these questions formulated by Carkhuff and others were significantly influenced by the theories of therapy that prevailed at the time: client-centred/person-centred, cognitive-behavioural and psychodynamic (see McLeod 2019 for an explanation of these approaches). However, because they were aiming to develop skills frameworks that would be relevant to trainees from all therapy orientations, as well as lay helpers who would not be expected to be interested in therapy concepts, these theoretical sources were not explicitly highlighted or emphasized.

The microskills approach

The *microskills* model, developed by the American psychologist Allen Ivey and his colleagues (Ivey et al. 2018), has been widely adopted in counselling skills training programmes, and is supported by an extensive programme of research. The microskills model has been around since the 1960s, with new ideas being added on a regular basis, resulting in a complex multidimensional framework for practice. The basic ideas that inform the microskills approach are that:

- there are some core skills that are essential in all helping situations
- there are certain interaction sequences that tend to be useful for clients.

In addition, the microskills approach places a strong emphasis on the idea that effective helpers are *intentional* in the way that they work with clients. In this context, the notion of intentionality refers to a capacity to decide from among a range of alternative actions. For example, a counsellor might select a particular skill (e.g. listening vs questioning) on the basis of which one is most appropriate and responsive to the needs and preferences of the client at that moment. In the microskills approach, the aim of skills training is to enable the counsellor or helper to be aware of what they are doing, and to build up a repertoire of responses they might make to the person, so that they can select the intervention that is most productive in any particular situation.

The concept of intentionality represents an important and distinctive element in the microskills model, because it functions as a reminder that it is not helpful to assume that there is any single, fixed counselling formula that will be appropriate for all clients. One of the hallmarks of Ivey's writing over several decades has been a commitment to acknowledging cultural diversity, and the notion of intentionality is his way of emphasizing that it is essential to be flexible in the face of different needs, and different assumptions about helping and healing, that are associated with people from diverse backgrounds and life experiences.

In the microskills model, the core skills that underpin all forms of helping are *attending* skills. These skills encompass eye contact, a warm and interested tone of voice, 'verbal tracking' (willingness to stick with the client's story rather than changing the subject) and appropriate body language (for example: facing the person, leaning forward, using encouraging gestures). These characteristics are summarized by Ivey et al. (2018) as comprising 'the three Vs + B: visuals, vocals, verbals, and body language'.

A further level of the microskills framework involves integrating basic attending skills into a 'well-formed interview'. Ivey et al. (2018) suggest that, from the perspective of the client, an effective interview or counselling session typically consists of the following sequence:

- *Developing a relationship.* Initiating the session, offering structure and establishing rapport.
- *Story and strengths.* Gathering data about the person's story, concerns and issues, and personal strengths.
- *Goals.* Identifying what the client wants to happen.
- *Restorying.* Exploring alternatives and confronting incongruities in the story.
- *Action.* Acting on new stories and understandings. Ending the session.

If the counsellor and client are able to meet on a number of occasions, this sequence is repeated for different aspects of the client's issue or problem, as it evolves in response to the client's previous attempts to resolve it. A key assumption that informs this aspect of the model is that failure to complete the sequence within a meeting runs the risk of leaving the client frustrated or with a sense of hopelessness, whereas completing the sequence produces a sense that progress is being made.

Although this interview sequence can be accomplished with the application of basic attending skills, in some situations the sequence calls for a capacity to make use of more advanced *influencing skills*. These advanced skills include: identifying contradictions and mixed messages in the client's story; challenging the client in a supportive manner; clarifying issues; looking at the issue from multiple perspectives; reframing or reinterpreting the client's experience; and working with the immediate, here-and-now responses of the client.

Ivey et al. (2018) view these skills as fitting together into a hierarchy, which they visualize as being like a pyramid. At the apex of the pyramid is the integration of different layers of microskills into the counsellor's *personal style*, which reflects their individual strengths and weaknesses, cultural context and values. The microskills model provides a powerful resource for organizing training programmes, because it specifies basic skills that represent a starting point for training, and then offers a framework that explains how and why these core skills can be combined into an interview sequence, augmented (by advanced influencing skills and interventions) and then finally it can be personalized by the trainee into their own distinctive style of being a therapist.

Three-stage models of counselling skills

There are a number of theorists who suggest that the process of helping a person to deal with a problem can be broken down into three stages. The original version of this type of approach emerged in Human Resources theory, developed by Robert Carkhuff (1969a, 1969b), who was a colleague of Carl Rogers. More recently, the most influential three-stage models are associated with the writings of Clara Hill and Gerard Egan.

Helping Skills Model

The *Helping Skills Model* developed by Clara Hill (2019) suggests that the helping or counselling process consists of three stages: *exploration, insight* and *action*. The main counsellor skills and tasks at each stage are:

Exploration
Skills: Using open questions, attending, listening, restatement, reflection of feelings, self-disclosure of insight, and silence as means of:

- establishing rapport and developing a therapeutic relationship
- encouraging the client to tell their story
- encouraging the client to share their thoughts and feelings
- facilitating expression of emotions
- learning about the client's own perspective on their problem.

Insight
Skills: Using challenges, interpretation, self-disclosure of insight, and immediacy in order to:

- work with clients to construct new insight
- encourage clients to determine their role in their thoughts, feelings and actions
- work with clients to address issues in the relationship (e.g. misunderstandings).

Action
Skills: Offering information, feedback and guidance, homework assignments, and techniques such as relaxation and role-play, for the purpose of:

- encouraging clients to explore possible new behaviours

  » assisting clients in deciding on actions
  » facilitating the development of skills for action
  » providing feedback about attempted changes
  » assisting clients in evaluating changes and modifying action plans.

For Hill (2019), the underlying development that takes place through these stages can be summarized as a process that begins by taking clients 'down and into' understanding themselves, before moving into a phase of applying what has been learned 'up and out' into the world. The use of the model to guide training has been supported by extensive research, and it has been used as a practice framework to inform therapeutic work with dreams (Hill 2003) and the search for meaning in life (Hill 2018).

Skilled Helper Model
The *Skilled Helper Model*, devised by Gerard Egan (1984; Egan and Reese 2021), proposes a three-stage approach to facilitating change:

Stage 1: Helping the client to tell their story
  Tuning in – empathic presence
  Listening to verbal and non-verbal communication
  Communicating back to the client what you have understood
  Highlighting core issues in the client's story
  Probing and summarizing
  Identifying problems and opportunities
  Identifying contradictions in the story and challenging the client

Stage 2: Helping the client to determine what they need and want
  Goal setting
  Decision-making
  Identifying possibilities for a better future
  Moving from possibilities to choices
  Making a commitment to change

Stage 3: Implementing action strategies to help the client to get what they need and want
  Identifying and evaluating strategies
  Making an action plan
  Making change happen

The Skilled Helper Model has been applied in a wide range of situations, including organizational change interventions as well as counselling (Wosket 2008).

EMPOWERS model

The EMPOWERS model of helping skills was developed by Links et al. (2020) on the basis of a systematic review of research studies looking at how counselling and helping skills are used in various healthcare practice settings. This model identifies the key characteristics of a helpful conversation or consultation as consisting of a preparatory stage (e.g. practical arrangements about time and place) followed by three stages. The opening phase involves **E**xpressing empathy and emotions, and **M**anaging the agenda. In the middle phase, participants share their **P**erspectives – starting with the client's perspective, and then the helper/counsellor shares their own **O**bservations. They then **W**ork together to establish goals, involving **E**nabling or empowering the client by paying close attention to their preferences, and then **R**eaching an agreement on future action. The closing phase of the meeting or session focuses on **S**ummarizing what has been discussed. There is then a period of time in which the plan is enacted, possibly leading to any further sessions that are necessary to monitor, revise and fine-tune what has been agreed.

The EMPOWERS model is similar to the Egan and Hill models in suggesting a three-stage process of client–counsellor activity. However, it is more explicitly focused on providing a template for single sessions, rather than a way of looking at the whole of a therapy treatment episode. The distinctive features of the model are attention to what happens before and after a session, and an emphasis on counsellor openness about their perceptions. As a recently developed model, the EMPOWERS approach has not generated the kind of rich literature and wealth of examples associated with the Egan and Hill models, nor has it been road-tested by counsellors in everyday practice. However, it is fundamentally evidence-based and in principle offers a potentially valuable second-generation counselling skills model that may turn out to possess great utility.

OSCAR model

The OSCAR model for structuring sessions, and the course of counselling as a whole, is widely used in coaching contexts (Rogers 2016). It comprises the following phases: **O**utcome – the destination, in respect of that particular session and over the longer term; **S**ituation – what is actually happening now and what makes it an issue: **C**hoices and consequences – how have you already tried to address this situation? What are the options as you see them?; **A**ctions – a detailed action plan; **R**eview – how will you/we monitor progress? Distinctive features of this framework are the extent to which it emphasizes the agency, responsibility and resourcefulness of the client, and the inclusion of an explicit review/feedback phase.

The strengths and limitations of microskills and three-stage models

The idea that the counselling process can be organized into three stages (exploration-insight-action, or exploration-goals-action) is meaningful and has practical utility. A three-stage model offers a sense of direction and momentum to counselling and helps trainees to appreciate the aims and purpose of specific skills that they are using. For many helpers who have been socialized into a controlling, advice-giving, 'fix-it' style of interacting with others, three-stage models make it clear that a problem needs to be described and understood before it can be resolved. This offers the counsellor a rationale for being patient and listening. At the same time, the model emphasizes that just talking about an issue is not enough – at some point the person needs to make changes in his or her life in order to move on, and the counsellor needs to be willing to be more active and exert an influence on the client.

There are, however, also some limitations associated with three-stage models. In practice, the process of counselling is far from tidy. The person may get to a stage of taking action, find that these changes are not effective, and loop back into the exploration stage. Some clients just want assistance in making changes that they have worked out for themselves, and are not interested in insight or exploration. Other clients are not ready to change, and may just wish to tell their story and receive support. Possibly the most significant weakness of any three-stage model is that it implies that effective counselling *should* involve progress through these three domains. This expectation can result in counsellors pushing their clients through the stages before they are ready. In deference to the counsellor, the client may then accede to a false resolution of their issues. In addition, skills may occur anywhere in the cycle – for example, listening is just as relevant at the action stage as it is during initial exploration of an issue.

A further limitation of both microskills and three-stage models is that they do not take sufficient account of the quality of the client–therapist relationship – a factor that has been shown to have a significant impact on the success of therapy – or how that relationship can be built and nurtured. Although Carkhuff, Egan, Hill and Ivey are experienced and knowledgeable therapists who are well aware of the importance of both the client–therapist alliance and the therapist's personal response to the client, their theories convey a sequence of events that is primarily driven forward by therapist skills. By contrast, a great deal of research has shown that therapy is unlikely to be productive unless the client feels understood and accepted, trusts their therapist and has a sense of working together.

A collaborative approach to counselling skills

From a collaborative perspective, any person seeking the support of a counsellor or other helper to resolve and move on from a problem in living is assumed to possess considerable previous life experience, personal knowledge, strengths and resources relevant to this endeavour. The job of the counsellor or helper is to work with the individual to combine the skills and ideas of both client and therapist together in ways that allow therapeutic tasks to be accomplished. An emphasis on collaboration, shared decision-making and co-production of outcomes underpins contemporary practice in many areas of counselling, psychotherapy, mental health and social care (Anderson 1996, 2007; Strong 2000; Sundet et al. 2020).

The present book is grounded in a collaborative approach to helping, based on the pluralistic model of therapy (Cooper and McLeod 2011; McLeod 2018). A pluralistic framework for practice is organized around the following key principles:

- A client or service user has preferences around what they believe would be helpful (or unhelpful) for them.
- Different people need different things at different times.
- The process of working together is anchored in a shared understanding of what the client wants (their goals) …
- and a shared understanding of the step-by-step tasks that might need to be accomplished in order to attain these goals.
- To stay on track in relation to tasks and goals, the counsellor needs to be responsive to feedback from the client on whether progress is being made and whether their way of working together needs to be modified.

From a collaborative perspective, counselling skills are actions through which a counsellor or other helper facilitates such processes as agreeing goals, engaging in shared decision-making, eliciting feedback and completion of tasks.

For example, a person may enter counselling or psychotherapy because they feel depressed, routinely undermine themselves through harsh self-criticism and feel tired a lot of the time. Initial discussion with their counsellor focuses on identifying and agreeing tasks that the therapist and client can work on together to make a difference to these concerns. For example, the client might want to develop an understanding of how this pattern developed and how it is triggered, in order to minimize its occurrence in future. They might want to learn how to replace self-criticism with a more compassionate way of assessing their life choices and behaviour. A further task might be to integrate energizing and meaningful activities into their everyday life. The therapist will make use of counselling skills not only to facilitate the shared decision-making process, but also to assist the client to find their way forward in relation to each of these tasks. For example, in relation to the task of understanding how a pattern of vicious self-criticism emerged in the client's life, a therapist might use skills such as listening, checking out that they have heard and understood the person accurately, expressing curiosity, encouraging the person to describe their experience and tell their story, perhaps asking questions and pointing out or challenging apparent contradictions in what the person has said, being aware of their personal emotional response to the client, possibly reframing some aspects of the client's story, possibly offering an interpretation of how aspects of the story might be understood, and checking out whether their reframes or interpretations made sense to the client. At various points in this sequence, the counsellor might invite feedback from the client around whether the overall approach being taken to the task is helpful, how it might need to be adjusted or what suggestions the client might have for doing things differently.

In a collaborative approach to therapy, counselling skills are used to promote an authentic dialogue in which both participants are able to talk openly and honestly. The idea that one of the main functions of interpersonal skills and counselling skills is to sustain and deepen connection and dialogue is the basis for a widely used skills textbook by John Stewart (2011) titled *Bridges not Walls*. A key theme is that whatever else is happening in a helping conversation, there should at the same time be a constant process of building bridges that enable growth in solidarity and pooling of resources. Stewart (2011) characterizes this process as comprising a rhythm that shifts back and forth between an outbreath of allowing oneself to be known to the other, and an inbreath of being open to the other's expression of self. The philosophical ideas that underpin this approach to helping are discussed by Arnett et al. (2008).

Another useful way of imagining the process of collaboration is in terms of interwoven lines – the client or person being helped is on a track or journey towards a more satisfying or fulfilling future, and the job of the counsellor is to do their best to remain in alignment with that journey or directionality (McLeod 2018).

A further metaphor for collaboration is of two people working together to build or *make* something: designing and trying out ways of dealing with difficult situations, making plans and decisions, constructing a way of making sense of a problematic experience, creating a picture or object that symbolizes a memory or a hope, arranging the pattern of everyday life to access a wider range of feelings rather than being locked into depression and sadness, repairing relationships, and so on.

A collaborative stance has important implications for the way that counselling skills are understood and used. While acknowledging the value of the skills frameworks developed by Egan, Ivey, Hill and other writers and trainers, it extends these models in ways that have important implications for practice. Aspects of counselling skills that are highlighted from a collaborative perspective include:

- The counsellor's skills are deployed in the service of the client's goals or purposes. This principle is an extension of Ivey's concept of intentional use of skills (i.e. being able to draw on a repertoire of responses): the most helpful response is the one that has the effect of supporting the client to make progress in relation to an agreed task or goal.
- Checking out with a client whether a particular skill is timely or appropriate. For example, it can be helpful to use silence to give the client the opportunity for inner reflection, or to use challenging to draw attention to apparent contradictions in the client's story or goals. However, for some clients at some points in counselling, silence can be experienced as abandonment, and challenge as an uncaring attack. A collaborative approach may involve asking, 'Would it be helpful to just have a moment of silence to stay with that feeling?' or, after the event, 'I was wondering how that moment of silence was for you – my sense was that it seemed helpful for you, but maybe it was not.'

- Paying close attention to the client's own skills, and finding ways of harnessing or cultivating them. In a collaborative approach to helping, it is not just the counsellor who possesses relevant skills, knowledge and awareness – so does the client. For example, a counsellor should have a repertoire of ways of talking about feelings, for instance a rich vocabulary of feeling words, and a sensitivity to non-verbal expression of feeling. There may be some clients who find it hard to engage with such skills, but have an ability to express feelings in music or colour, or by drawing an image on a piece of paper. In this kind of situation, there may be important ways that the client can learn from the counsellor (e.g. using emotion words) but also important ways in which the counsellor can learn from the client.

- Explaining your working: to make choices and express preferences, a client needs to know what their counsellor is able to offer, or why a counsellor regards a particular way of working together as potentially helpful. An important skill in collaborative counselling is the capacity to communicate counselling concepts in an accessible and transparent manner.

- The counsellor's capacity and skilfulness in using their own personal response to the client, in the form of feelings, memories, images and action tendencies that arise during the counselling process. From a collaborative perspective the counsellor and client function together as an interactive or dynamic system: the counsellor's internal experience therefore represents a potentially valuable source of information about implicit or unspoken aspects of the client's story, or what is happening in the client–counsellor relationship.

- Being there: to be able to function as a partner in a collaborative way of working, a client needs to trust their counsellor and believe that their counsellor respects them, cares about them and affirms them as a person of value. In general, counsellor statements to these ends tend to lack credibility – belief that a counsellor is genuinely there for them is more likely to arise through small things and acts of kindness that transcend a professional role.

Taken together, these collaboration skills represent a subtle but significant pivot in the way that counselling skills are understood. Rather than just regarding skills as ways of having an effect on the client (e.g. helping the client to express feeling, reflect on the meaning of an experience or change their behaviour), the emphasis shifts towards using skills to create a relationship in which 'we' (the two of us together – or more than two if family members are involved) are able to pool our respective knowledge and experience to achieve these outcomes.

Culturally informed practice

When using counselling skills to help and support another person, it is essential to be responsive to differences in the social identities, cultural backgrounds and life experiences of the therapist and client – for example in respect of age, gender, ethnicity, social class, disability and sexual orientation.

Most approaches to counselling and psychotherapy (e.g. psychodynamic, cognitive-behavioural therapy (CBT), person-centred) and models of counselling skills were originally developed in Western societies – mainly Europe and North America – with minimal consideration to cultural differences. Over the years there has emerged an appreciation that such approaches reflect a specific cultural point of view and set of values, and need to be significantly modified if they are to be relevant to people from other cultural backgrounds. For example, most therapy approaches are grounded in an individualist image of the person, whereas many cultural groups adopt a more collectivist philosophy of life. In addition, most therapy is rational and secular, in contrast to the emphasis on faith and spirituality that is characteristic of many indigenous healing practices. Alongside the work on revisiting underlying assumptions, there has also been a greater degree of openness to therapeutic ideas and methods from non-Western cultural traditions – the most striking example being the integration of mindfulness meditation into CBT. Important outcomes of these lines of development have been the construction of competency frameworks for multicultural practice, and a recognition that counsellor self-awareness of their own cultural identity is a crucial aspect of such competence. Further discussion on how the therapy professions have struggled to come to terms with issues around difference, equality and power can be found in McLeod (2019).

Although the question of how to be responsive to cultural difference has received relatively little attention in the counselling skills literature, it is possible to identify a set of principles for culturally-responsive practice. Effective counselling needs to be sensitive to implicit cultural rules and norms about how people should interact, such as how close to sit together, how men and women (or people from different age or social class groups) should be with each other, and how much eye contact or touch is acceptable. There are also different ways of talking about emotions, for instance using emotion words such as 'depressed' or 'sad', as against referring to bodily feelings such as 'pain in my heart'. A counsellor and client need to find sufficient common ground, in relation to these cultural factors, to be able to work together constructively. A study by Joo et al. (2019) interviewed counsellors in Korea about their experiences of learning helping skills and using them with clients in their home country. Research participants reported that counselling skills needed to be used in ways that took account of cultural patterns of indirect rather than direct ways of talking about feelings and problems, and expectations that the counsellor would be an expert who provided information and advice. They also related that they felt awkward using exploratory and insight-oriented skills with Korean clients. Similar experiences around needing to recalibrate counselling skills in response to local cultural norms were found in studies of counselling skills training in Afghanistan (Berdondini et al. 2014, 2019) and Lesotho (Gilbert 2002).

Interviews with Chinese clients found that counsellor effectiveness was evaluated not so much in terms of the therapist's level of empathy, but instead in relation to kindness, 'having a heart to help' and whether they had sufficient knowledge and experience to provide reliable advice and guidance (Ng and James 2013). Shoaib and Peel (2003) interviewed Kashmiri women living in Oldham, England about their views of counselling. A central theme to emerge from this study was the difficulty that many of these women had in translating statements about their emotional life into English. Some Kashmiri emotional terms did not have any meaningful English-language equivalent. The authors noted that many phrases for emotions made use of the head and the heart, such as 'emptying the heart', 'in my head the weight will lighten' and 'my heart's pain'. These findings confirm the results of other studies of emotional expressiveness in members of Asian and other non-Western cultural groups. In these cultures and languages, emotions are not denoted by psychological terms such as 'anger' or 'anxiety', but tend largely to be indicated by reference to parts of the body such as the head, heart and stomach.

A notable aspect of all of these studies is that a Western model of counselling skills was regarded by clients from other cultural backgrounds as providing a valuable addition to local or indigenous ways of offering emotional support, despite obvious cultural challenges. Part of the reason for the success of these initiatives appeared to be the fact that the counsellors were individuals who were comfortable in both cultural arenas, for instance through being fluent English speakers or having lived for a time outside their native country. As a result, they possessed a personal capacity to improvise culturally adapted versions of counselling skills as necessary, and operated as culture brokers, able to bridge different cultural traditions (Miklavcic and LeBlanc 2014; Brar-Josan and Yohani 2019). It is clearly much harder for counsellors who do not possess this breadth of cultural experience to be confident and competent in using counselling skills in situations of cultural difference.

Another way that diversity can influence the use of counselling skills is that relationships between white and non-white individuals take place in a context of a long history of oppression, cruelty, loss and unearned privilege. Similar tensions exist in other cross-cultural encounters, such as between working-class and upper-class people, or between individuals with different sexual orientations or religious affiliations. In relation to counselling skills, what this means is that the challenge of diversity does not consist merely of finding ways to connect with each other in the face of different ways of talking, or different styles of non-verbal interaction. Instead, underlying issues of power, control and oppression may have the effect of inhibiting the process of counselling (e.g. the client and/or therapist are uncomfortable, cautious and guarded), or even producing a process that is hurtful or harmful.

It is relatively rare that overt racism, classism or homophobia are expressed in a counselling situation. Rather, unconscious or unexamined negative attitudes tend to be expressed through microaggressions – subtle responses that may seem harmless or amusing, or may be intended as helpful, but in reality are slights or snubs that exhibit a rejection or invalidation of the cultural identity of the recipient of the remark (Sue 2010; Shelton and Delgado-Romero 2011; Ong et al. 2013). There is evidence that, in counselling where the counsellor is from a more privileged or high-status background, counsellor-initiated microaggression routinely occurs and is experienced by clients as harmful (Owen et al. 2013, 2014). Moreover, counsellors tend to lack awareness that this is happening (Sue et al. 2007; Owen et al. 2018). As a result, there is a higher rate of dropout in therapy where the client and therapist are from different cultural groups. In response to this issue, there exist many culturally specific counselling and psychotherapy services where clients can be guaranteed to see a therapist from the same, or a similar, cultural background.

In counselling and psychotherapy training, as in other fields such as education, healthcare, social work and criminal justice, issues of exclusion and discrimination have been addressed though a broad range of strategies at a policy level – for instance around recruitment of trainees and tutors from diverse backgrounds, equality guidelines, ethical principles, and curriculum requirements, as well as through more directly practice-facing strategies such as collection of research evidence, design of training and supervision activities and development of culturally informed theory. All of these approaches are relevant to the culturally sensitive use of counselling skills. In addition, there are two specific skills domains that are crucially important: broaching and language use.

The skill of broaching refers to the counsellor actively inviting and facilitating a conversation about any potentially relevant ways in which they and their client are different. Traditionally, counsellors have not used this skill to any great extent, but instead have assumed that if some aspect of difference is important, it will emerge at some point as a topic in the counselling process, and that the best interests of the client are served by just responding to whatever issues and topics they choose to mention. This traditional approach has turned out to be misguided, because it leads to situations in which the client is aware of difference but feels anxious about saying anything about it because it does not seem to be an area in which the counsellor has shown any interest. The longer this kind of 'elephant in the room' scenario continues, the harder it becomes to do anything about it. What can then happen is that the client quits, or the counselling drifts into vague discussions of superficial issues. By contrast, if the counsellor takes the initiative early on, by acknowledging difference and highlighting it as something to be explored and reviewed at any point, then the client is given permission and encouragement to bring this aspect of their experience into the conversation whenever it seems relevant.

Broaching is an important skill in any counselling situation, because no counsellor–client dyad is culturally identical – there will always be differences in beliefs, values and experience that have the potential to influence the therapy process. There is a growing evidence base around how to use broaching effectively (Jones and Welfare 2017; Day-Vines et al. 2018, 2020, 2021; King and Borders 2019; King 2021; Sahu et al. 2021). In practice, it sits alongside other skills that promote a client–therapist collaborative stance, such as metacommunication (pausing the ongoing flow of counselling to check out or clarify if what is happening is helpful) and use of feedback.

Linguistic flexibility represents a further key area of skill in respect of using counselling skills in a culturally responsive manner. The single most significant way in which cultural identity is expressed, and cultural difference is negotiated, is through the way that a person talks (Lee 2017). In general, a professional helper, such as a counsellor, social worker or teacher, will be a fluent speaker of the official language of the country in which they are working. This means that they will have a wide repertoire of words and phrases at their disposal, they may talk quite rapidly, and they will use a relatively formal way of talking that does not include colloquial terms and uses a decontextualized or abstract form of discourse. By contrast, a client or service user may have a more restricted vocabulary, may struggle to keep up with what is being said, and may be more used to a way of talking based in stories about concrete events that have happened. In some cultures, in a first meeting between people the conversation would usually involve a phase of establishing mutual points of connection in respect of family, place and shared acquaintances. Linguistic flexibility may involve encouraging a client to use words and phrases from their culture of origin (language switching), or the use of translators (Costa and Dewaele 2018; Costa 2020). Other aspects of linguistic flexibility are discussed in Chapter 10.

Responsiveness to client–therapist differences in social identity needs to take account of the existence of intersectionality. The way that someone sees the world is not just a matter of being black or white, male or female, etc. Each person's identity consists of intersecting identity statuses. For example, the life experience of a working-class Asian-British person is different from that of someone else who is Asian British, has had a public-school education and comes from a wealthy family. Intersectionality underscores the value of a collaborative approach to counselling in which the beliefs and preferences of each client feed into a process of shared decision-making about how therapy will proceed.

Conclusions

This chapter has explored ways of understanding how counselling skills contribute towards the ultimate outcomes of counselling, such as being able to accomplish goals and live a more satisfying life. A key theme throughout the chapter has been the importance of using skills in a collaborative, flexible manner that is responsive to the preferences and cultural identity of the client.

In addition to specific skills-oriented models, there are also more comprehensive theories of therapy that are relevant to the process of learning counselling skills. For example, the person-centred theoretical approach developed by Carl Rogers and his colleagues introduced detailed conceptual and research-based analyses of therapist empathy that are invaluable resources for anyone wanting to acquire a deeper understanding of counselling skills such as reflecting and checking out. Similarly, psychoanalytic and psychodynamic theory around the concept of countertransference has the potential to hugely expand the understanding of counselling skills such as immediacy and self-monitoring. Because the aim of this book is to focus on the practical use of skills, this kind of supporting research and theoretical literature is not examined in detail. Where relevant, key concepts from theories of therapy are briefly outlined, with an indication of where to find further information in the companion textbook (McLeod 2019).

Learning activities

The following activities may be explored individually, and/or with a group of learning partners.

1   Take a few moments to reflect on your experience as a client, either in formal counselling/psychotherapy or in a situation where you were being helped by a teacher, social worker, doctor or other practitioner. To what extent did the process of counselling correspond to the kinds of stages described in this chapter?

2   Identify an episode in your life where you were able to collaborate effectively and in a satisfying way with other people (in any sphere of your life) to accomplish a task. What were the factors that contributed to successful collaboration? Were there any specific skills and strategies that seemed to make a crucial contribution to the success of this venture? In what ways can these skills and strategies be imported into your work as a counsellor?

3   Reflect on counselling/psychotherapy (or similar experiences) that you have had in your life. How collaborative were the individuals from whom you were seeking help? What skills did they use, that facilitated

working together? What skills would you have wanted them to use? Reflect on the relevance of these experiences for your own practice as a counsellor.

4   In what ways have significant life experiences (in your family, at school, with peers, with spouse/life partner, work relationships, etc.) shaped your capacity to collaborate with others? In what ways can the positive gifts and capabilities around collaboration, arising from your life experience, be channelled into your work as a counsellor? What lessons have you learned from negative experiences of collaboration that might inform your work as a counsellor?

5   How might your cultural identity influence your use of counselling skills? A useful way to appreciate the complex nature of cultural identity is to reflect on the cultural influences in your own life. Take a large sheet of paper and some coloured pens, and spend some time drawing or mapping the different elements of your own cultural identity. Use a broad understanding of culture, encompassing age, gender, ethnicity, social class, disability and sexual orientation. Some prompts that may help you to engage with this task:

   • Write as many answers as possible to the question, 'who am I?'

   • What does 'home' mean to me? Where and when have I felt most at home?

   • What are (or were) the cultural identities or cultural worlds of my parents and grandparents? Which aspects of their cultural norms and beliefs have I incorporated into my own life?

   • How has cultural curiosity manifested itself in my life? What cultures have I been interested in, and become familiar with?

6   Once you have constructed and reflected on your cultural identity map, allow yourself some more time to consider the implications of this exercise for your role as a counsellor. How might some clients view you (or pigeonhole you) in cultural terms, and what might be the implications of this kind of labelling – could it inhibit some clients from talking about certain issues? In which areas might your counselling skills and concepts reflect cultural assumptions that might not match those of clients from different cultural backgrounds? How might you deal with such areas of mismatch?

CHAPTER 4

Learning and training

Introduction

The development of counselling skills represents a key element of training to become a counsellor, psychotherapist, clinical or counselling psychologist, life coach or careers adviser, as well as being included in preparation to enter other occupations. In each of these fields, training programmes are available in a wide range of colleges, independent institutes and universities, supported by an extensive literature around models of training, and research. There also exist codes of practice, published by professional associations, that recommend standards for training programmes. The general consensus within this domain of education and training is that there are four broad areas that should be addressed in the curriculum. First, any person offering a counselling (or similar) relationship to others should possess an ability to make sense of what they are doing, in the form of a model or theoretical framework, supported by relevant research evidence. Second, training should involve an extensive period of practical learning, in which the person develops competencies and critical awareness around skills, methods and intervention strategies. This area of training characteristically involves observing expert practitioners (live or on video), practising methods with and on other members of a training group, and – crucially – recording and analysing counselling sessions with people actually seeking help (i.e. clients). Third, training in counselling and similar professions requires development of self-awareness. Effective counselling depends on the quality of the relationship between person and counsellor. It is therefore essential that the counsellor understands what they bring to that relationship, in terms of their own relationship needs and patterns, and their capacity to respond constructively to the type of relationship that is preferred by the person seeking their help. On training courses, the development of self-awareness is typically facilitated through a range of activities such as participation in experiential groups and workshops, the experience of being a user or client of counselling, and keeping a personal learning journal. Finally, training courses need to cover professional and ethical issues, such as maintaining confidentiality and using supervision or consultative support. Taken together, these areas of learning provide a context within which the development of counselling skills takes place.

The present chapter focuses on the kinds of activities that have been found to be helpful in relation to the specific goal of becoming more competent and resourceful in the use of counselling skills in helping relationships. It begins by offering an overview of core principles and processes associated with the development of counselling skills, then explores the contribution of specific learning activities and models.

Developing competence in the use of counselling skills: general principles

There are some general aspects of skill acquisition and usage that have significant implications for the way that counselling skills are learned and applied. Any complex skill always consists of a combination of pre-existing simpler skills. For people who are learning to be counsellors, or to enhance their counselling competence in another professional role, the counselling skills that they are taught are always in some sense already there. From an early age, babies learn how to observe others, how to smile, how to detect emotional signals and how to take turns in conversation or other kinds of interaction. Later in life, we learn how to empathize with others, and how to be supportive and helpful when another person is in distress. These are some of the core interpersonal skills that are required to be able to carry out counselling skills such as paraphrasing the meaning of a statement that the client has made, or using an open-ended question to encourage a client to explore their feelings around an issue. Counselling skills are therefore grounded in life experience. Someone who is being trained in counselling skills should not be learning anything they did not know already – what they should be learning is how to apply what they already know in a more purposeful and aware manner, to achieve a particular result. Effective counselling skills training involves self-reflection on the part of trainees, as a means of allowing the learner to be more in touch with their own personal experiences of helping and being helped, which in turn heightens their awareness of the basic skills to which they were exposed, or which they were able to use, in these situations.

Another crucial aspect of counselling skills is that they almost always have a physical, *embodied* dimension to them. It is possible to envisage skills that are purely cognitive (for example, doing a complex multiplication calculation in your head). However, most practical skills involve actual physical activity. This is certainly true for counselling, which is more like learning to dance than like learning to do sums in one's head. So, a book such as this one, that offers a verbal explanation of counselling skills, can never function as a sufficient basis for learning these skills. It is always essential to be able to see how someone else does a skill (modelling), and to get feedback on one's own performance of a skill.

A further element of the application of any skill is that it involves paying attention to the effect of each micro-action within a skill, and using that information to make adjustments to the next action that forms part of the skill sequence. For example, making a serve in tennis begins by throwing the ball in the air. The server needs to watch the ball. At a very basic level, they need to detect whether they have thrown it high enough and straight enough to hit it, or whether the throw has been too unbalanced to make the ball hittable (in which case, the intended serve is not followed through). The requirement, in effective skill use, to make use of moment-by-moment monitoring introduces another embodied dimension to the process: a skilful person is someone who has learned what to look at, listen to and viscerally sense, and who knows what to do with this information. As a result, careful and accurate *observation* is intrinsic to skill use – an accomplished skill user is able to observe the impact of their use of a skill (has it achieved the result that was expected?) and is a keen observer of how other people use skills (and how they themselves use them).

An additional critical aspect of any skill is that it involves a *sequence* of activity. As a person becomes more skilful, they make sense of what they are doing in terms of longer sequences. For example, a novice chess player may only be capable of thinking one or two moves ahead: 'If I move this rook, that will avoid it being captured by my opponent's Queen.' By contrast, expert chess players call on conceptual strategies that involve an appreciation of complex possibilities that may occur over a lengthy sequence of moves. This phenomenon underlies one of the paradoxes of counselling skills training – experienced counsellors do not tend to think in terms of specific skills. When *learning* about counselling, it tends to be useful to pay attention to specific, discrete skills such as 'listening', 'attending' and 'reflecting back'. Eventually, though, the aim is to be able to take these specific skills for granted, and to be able to think instead about the work with a client in terms of whether a sufficient degree of empathic engagement is being maintained: 'empathic engagement' is a more abstract concept that can be understood as a process that encompasses complex sequences of basic skills such as listening, reflecting and so on.

A crucial facet of the experience of skill acquisition is the phenomenon of *awkwardness*. Most people have a baseline of practical and interpersonal skills with which they feel comfortable – they know how to use them, and feel confident when they are using them. Invariably, moving on and becoming more skilled involves some degree of awkwardness, because it requires the person to try something that they don't yet know how to do properly. Sometimes, learning a skill may involve *unlearning* other skills. For example, it is possible to produce a perfectly acceptable tennis serve from a square-on stance, but if a player wants to learn how to make a top-spin serve they need to change their stance so that they are at right angles to the baseline – this can feel very awkward!

Taken together, these aspects of skill use underscore the fact that skill acquisition involves active *practice* – receiving instruction, watching how someone else does it, trying it out yourself, getting feedback, trying again, and so on. This process inevitably incorporates lots of mistakes, as the learner tries out different skills in different sequences. Counselling training therefore usually includes many opportunities for practice, in an environment in which it is acceptable to make mistakes. Usually, at least at the start, counselling trainees practise their skills on each other, before moving on to 'real' clients.

Beyond the elements of skill learning discussed above, there are two important contextual factors that influence the process of developing competence in the use of counselling skills. For most learners, the experience of skills training includes moments of anxiety. For example, learners may feel threatened by the possibility of receiving negative feedback, self-conscious about being observed and self-critical around exposing personal limitations and lack of awareness. To address and minimize these issues, most training programmes endeavour to create a supportive group environment that involves sharing experience through regular check-ins. A further strategy involves channelling stress and anxiety into energy and excitement through the use of creative activities such as warm-up exercises and use of techniques from the expressive arts.

An additional contextual dimension in counselling skills training is the effect it has on the trainee as a person, their relationships with others, and possibly even their world view and values. The process of practising counselling skills opens up many opportunities for self-reflection: Do I really listen to others? Am I aware of feelings and emotions? Am I capable of engaging in authentic collaboration? The answers to such questions that emerge over the course of training can have significant implications for pre-existing relationships and the trainee's sense of self.

Approaches to counselling skills training

There are several contrasting models of counselling skills training that have evolved over the years. Although each of them reflects basic principles of breaking down complex skills and competencies into component elements that are then mastered and consolidated through repetitive practice, they implement these basic ideas in different ways.

The microskills approach

The microskills perspective, originating in the work of Ivey et al. (2018) and Truax and Carkhuff, has generated a technology of counselling training that has been widely adopted by universities, colleges and training institutions around the world. Typically, students or trainees listen to an explanation of a specific skill, and observe a demonstration, live or on video. These steps allow the learner to identify separate skills and begin to differentiate between helpful and unhelpful examples of the use of that skill. They then practise the skill in small groups, on each other, and receive feedback from a tutor and from fellow students. Once a sufficiently wide set of skills has been acquired, the trainee begins to work with actual clients. Contemporary examples of how this approach is implemented, and how effective it can be, include studies by Chui et al. (2014) and Hill et al. (2014, 2020). A consistent theme in studies of microskills training is that learners rate the opportunity to engage in practice as particularly important.

Reviews of research into the effectiveness of the microskills training model can be found in Baker et al. (1990) and Ridley et al. (2011). The latter review highlights the limitations of the approach in respect of developing complex skills, attention to the counsellor's emotional response to the client, and the development of multicultural competencies. While these criticisms are undoubtedly valid, they do not sufficiently take account of the fact that such higher-level skills and competencies would usually be addressed in other parts of the training curriculum.

There have been some valuable and important areas of innovation within the broad microskills paradigm. McCarthy and French (2017) introduced guided viewing of online video material as a means of learning to differentiate between skills. Swank and McCarthy (2013, 2015) focused on the capacity of trainees to provide accurate and constructive feedback to each other, and developed a specific feedback training module. Rantanen and Soini (2013, 2018) have created a structured approach to facilitate trainee work in small groups.

The persistence of the microskills approach over several decades, alongside examples of ongoing innovation, represents a strong testimony to the value of this framework. The success of this model of skills training can be attributed to a number of factors. Breaking down the activity of counselling into a set of component skills makes it possible to develop a structured curriculum, with clear learning objectives, thus allowing counselling skills training to be readily incorporated into standard university or college modular structures. Also, the cycle of demonstration-practice-feedback provides an excellent vehicle for systematic reflection on practice.

Interpersonal process recall (IPR)

Like the microskills model, interpersonal process recall (IPR) is a training approach that emerged in the 1960s. Developed by Norman Kagan (Kagan et al. 1969; Kagan 1980, 1984; Kagan and Kagan 1990), IPR has been widely used in skills training, therapy supervision and therapy research. The trainee or supervisee makes an audio or video recording, then listens/watches it, pausing the recording at points where they wish to reflect on or discuss what was happening during the session. The underlying assumption is that if the recording is reviewed in this way within about 24 hours of the original events, the participant will retain a detailed recollection of what they were thinking or feeling at that time. Reflection and analysis of the recording can focus on specific episodes or processes within the session, and may be facilitated by probe questions from a trainer or supervisor, or a group of fellow trainees or colleagues. In some situations, observations may also be available from the client. In research studies, a recording is made of a therapy session and then reviewed by the client or therapist. In any of these scenarios the aim is to enable stimulated recall of experiences and processes that would otherwise not be readily available for scrutiny. In training situations, the discussion that is triggered by examining a specific episode in a counselling session may include suggestions and rehearsal by the trainee, and/or modelling by the trainer of possible alternative responses that might have been made. In recent years, Murphy et al. (2019, 2020) have developed mPath, an online system that enables trainees to engage in detailed reflection on video recordings of counselling skills practice sessions, and receive feedback from colleagues and trainers. Similar technology has been used by Swift et al. (2017) in a study of client perceptions of helpful and unhelpful events in therapy. IPR can also be used to focus on specific areas of skill, such as multicultural competencies (Ivers et al. 2017).

In both research and training contexts, IPR is generally described by participants as creating a powerful learning experience that involves the shock of close self-examination alongside an opportunity to become more aware of the intricate interpersonal dance that occurs between two people (Crews et al. 2005; Macaskie et al. 2015). Although, unlike microskills training, the IPR model does not highlight repetitive practice, it nevertheless generates many ideas about next steps in practice. Being based on recordings, IPR feedback refers to observable sequences that can be replayed over and over again.

Being in the client's chair

Over 90 per cent of counsellors and psychotherapists have had the experience of being a client, either prior to entering training, during training, over the course of their working career, or all three. Although the majority of these therapy episodes are primarily initiated in response to personal issues (Bike et al. 2009), there is also consistent evidence that being on the receiving end of counselling skills and techniques is a massive influence for many practitioners in terms of their use of counselling skills (Kumari 2011; Probst 2015). Many therapy training programmes require students to work with a therapist from the same therapy approach as the training, in order to consolidate their skills in that model of practice. In the microskills model of training (see above) students routinely play the role of client for each other, with subsequent frequent opportunities to observe skills from a client perspective.

Creative methods

Many counselling skills trainers and training programmes have adapted arts-based and creative activities to support the development of counselling skills. Such processes have the potential to enable learners to try out different ways of being and relating in a playful, non-serious and energizing manner. For example, the tradition of theatre improvisation ('impro') encompasses many exercises and routines that require participants to observe behaviour and interaction, experiment with different ways of responding, and authentically co-create the 'reality of the moment' (Bayne and Jangha 2016; Kelly et al. 2019; Romanelli and Tishby 2019). From within the tradition of psychodrama, Dogan (2018) has exploited the relevance for counselling skills development of 'doubling': standing behind the protagonist/client, imitating their posture and walk, voicing their feelings. Such a procedure is similar to advanced empathy skills – seeking to express attitudes and feelings that are either outside the conscious awareness of the protagonist/client or are too threatening or painful to put into words. A similar technique was developed in the 1980s by one of the leading figures in multicultural counselling, Paul Pederson. In his 'triad' activity, the client was joined by a 'pro-counsellor' behind one shoulder and an 'anti-counsellor' behind the other. The task of the 'pro-counsellor' was to articulate the cultural attitudes of the client that might lead them to value the counsellor's responses, while the job of the 'anti-counsellor' was to whisper in the client's ear about culturally based doubts and scepticism about therapy. The task of the actual counsellor was to find a way of acknowledging both polarities while still working with the client's main presenting issue (Pedersen 1994). This multicultural skill learning activity represents just one among a wide range of creative simulation exercises developed by Pedersen and his colleagues in this field of practice (Yoshida 2020). Other counselling trainers have used visual arts, music and poetry to facilitate aspects of counselling skills. For example, Warren and Nash (2019) describe a technique that uses drawing to help trainees to be more sensitive to emotional content.

Other skills learning approaches

There are many strategies for supporting the development of counselling skills that are used in particular training programmes but have received relatively little attention in the literature. One of these areas consists of the task of taking stock of skills: being aware of the skills that one already possesses and those that require further attention. Some programmes ask participants to keep personal journals in which they reflect on their experience of learning skills, and develop personal learning plans. In some instances, a tutor may even audit and comment on journal entries on a weekly basis. Another strategy for taking stock is to complete a self-reported counselling skills questionnaire or rating scale on a regular basis. Many such measures have been developed. A particularly clear and comprehensive skills measure is the Counselor Activity Self-Efficacy (COSE) scale (Lent et al. 2003). Details of the scale items are provided in the published article as well as being available on the internet. It is important, when using such a measure, to be aware of what has been described as the 'response shift' phenomenon – a change in ratings may not only reflect an increase (or decrease) in skills competence, but may also be influenced by a shift in the meaning of the questions. For example, some trainees using such scales report that they became aware that the answers they gave at the start of their training were too positive – it was only when they started to practise certain skills that they realized how much they had to learn. Either type of learning (i.e. discovering a change in skilfulness and/or a change in awareness) can be valuable.

Another approach to skills learning that has been used in some training programmes is the use of reflection teams (Meekums et al. 2016). A reflection team is a group of people who silently observe a counselling session (or part of one) and then at the end share their experience of what they have witnessed. The aim is not to provide a technical or theoretical analysis, but instead to offer a genuine human reaction to what happened in terms of how they were touched, or what they remembered from their own life in response to what they heard and saw. This technique is used, in a variety of ways, in family therapy and narrative therapy, with the aim of opening up a range of perspectives that might assist the client and therapist to see the issues that are being explored, and the quality of their contact with each other, in new ways. Descriptions of how this procedure has been used in counselling skills training can be found in Hawley (2006) and Paré (1999). One of the advantages of reflecting teams, compared to the type of feedback and discussion that occurs in microskillls training and IPR, is that skills are explored in the context of a broader appreciation of the meaning of what is happening in a counselling session, rather than the focus being more narrowly on the performance of a specific skill.

Deliberate practice and self-practice

In recent years, a new approach to the development of counselling skills has emerged, based on sustained, focused activity to master specific skills that are problematic for the learner. There are two versions of this approach: deliberate practice and self-practice.

The concept of deliberate practice refers to purposeful, repetitive skills practice outside of the actual immediate work or performance setting. This perspective has its roots in the work of the Swedish psychologist K. Anders Ericsson into the characteristics of expert performers in many areas of life, such as musicians, chess players, athletes and surgeons (Ericsson and Pool 2016). The research carried out by Ericsson and his colleagues has shown that while the competence of most members of such occupational groups steadily improves over the course of training, it then hits a plateau and ceases to improve. These are individuals who are engaged in 'practice' (i.e. they do their jobs) with little or no additional commitment to enhancing their abilities. By contrast, there is a smaller group of performers who continue to improve over the course of their career. When Ericsson examined what made these people different, what he found was that they paid close attention to negative feedback (i.e. when things went wrong), identified the underlying deficit in their skills and knowledge, formulated a strategy for remedying this deficit, engaged in practising these new skills in a safe environment outside of the front-line work situation, and monitored whether all of this had then produced a tangible improvement in their effectiveness in real-life work settings.

The idea of 'deliberate' practice reflects the principle that the best way to hone a skill is to deliberately focus on that particular skill. For example, on the practice court, a leading tennis player such as Andy Murray will work for hours on a specific shot, rather than just playing bounce matches with his pals. Another aspect of 'deliberateness' is choosing which skills to work on. The key principle here is to use deliberate practice to remedy skill deficits – i.e. paying attention to and learning from failure and negative feedback. In the field of counselling and psychotherapy, there is a growing body of evidence showing the significance of deliberate practice in relationship to therapist effectiveness (see, for example, Chow et al. 2015; Rousmaniere 2016, 2018; Rousmaniere et al. 2017).

Deliberate practice can be understood as representing, on the part of a counsellor, a sustained commitment over a period of time to a cyclical process of learning and continual improvement that involves:

- identifying areas for further learning, by monitoring performance in counselling (and other similar) situations
- reflecting on what the actual learning needs consist of (i.e. what is missing from the learner's current knowledge and skills)
- devising and implementing a systematic plan for improvement, including repeated practice of specific skills until they become routine
- developing a mental representation or image of the skill, to guide its application in different situations
- monitoring/reviewing one's performance in situations that had previously been problematic, to confirm that the skill was now able to be utilized effectively.

This process can be carried out alone, through consultation with tutors/trainers and supervisors, and with the assistance of colleagues on a training programme (or other people who may be able to help you in your learning). An important aspect of deliberate practice learning activities is the level of emotional arousal of the learner. If the activity makes the learner too anxious, it becomes impossible to learn anything. On the other hand, if the activity is too easy, it is probably not sufficiently challenging. The aim is to carry out as much of a learning episode as possible somewhere between these extremes.

The concept of self-practice refers to learning activities in which practitioners develop therapeutic skills by applying them to issues in their own life (Bennett-Levy and Finlay-Jones 2018; Bennett-Levy 2019). This approach is widely used in training for cognitive-behavioural therapists: the cognitive-behavioural therapy (CBT) training manual produced by Bennett-Levy et al. (2015) teaches students how to use CBT interventions for anxiety and depression by leading them through a step-by-step application in relation to their own personal episodes of low mood or worry. This approach can also be used to support the development of specific counselling skills. For example, awareness of the process of giving and receiving feedback in counselling can be deepened by identifying moments in one's own life when feedback was avoided, or handled awkwardly. Or awareness of the dynamics of conversational silence can similarly be enhanced by paying attention to thoughts and feelings associated with silence (or its avoidance) in everyday interactions. A consistent finding in studies of self-practice is that both skills development and trainee satisfaction are enhanced by routinely writing about the process of learning in a journal or blog, and being a member of a supportive group of like-minded trainees (Bennett-Levy 2019). Each of these elements has the effect of consolidating learning and understanding through reflection on practice, and maintaining motivation.

Deliberate practice and self-practice have a number of advantages compared to widely used counselling skills training approaches such as microskills and IPR. First, they concentrate on skills that need to be improved rather than spending time on skills in which the learner may be quite fluent. Second, the emphasis on repetitive practice means that learners need to continue working on the skill until they achieve an acceptable level of competence. By contrast, with microskills and IPR training programmes, skills practice is restricted to a fixed block of time with a scheduled class. Third, deliberate practice and self-practice enable the learner to engage in practice and reflection in a wide range of contexts and scenarios.

A research-based initiative to incorporate self-practice and deliberate practice into a year-long counselling skills training programme was carried out by McLeod (2021). In this project, students were introduced to the principles of deliberate practice and self-practice at the start of the course, and then supported and encouraged in pursuing this mode of learning over the following months. Most participants devoted at least two hours each week to this activity, over and above classroom attendance. Some of this time was spent in self-practice, for example cognitive rehearsal of skills, or analysing recordings of their use of skills. However, most of the time was used in self-organized meetings with two or three learning partners (fellow trainees, professional colleagues, and in some instances even family members). A typical example of the kind of learning process that occurred was the case of a student who received feedback in the context of an in-class skills training session that her physical presence and use of non-verbal skills was somewhat stiff and frozen, and inhibiting to others. This student watched videos to learn about how experienced counsellors conveyed warmth, and rehearsed alternative facial expressions and ways of sitting and moving on her own, in front of a mirror. She then met with other trainees to try out these new ways of responding in practice sessions, receiving detailed feedback from them. As she began to be more capable around this set of skills, she began to notice that, compared to learning partners, she had a limited capacity for awareness of internal emotional reactions to clients, or noticing or reflecting back the feelings and emotions that were either explicitly or implicitly conveyed by clients. This set in motion a further sequence of self-practice and deliberate practice.

This example illustrates the potential of a deliberate practice approach. In contrast to other methods for the development of counselling skills, it operates not only as a structure for initial training, but also as a mechanism for lifelong learning. Through paying close attention to skills deficits and failure episodes, it encourages counsellor receptiveness to client feedback. Unlike other skills training procedures, it is much more driven by the learner, and more attuned to a collaborative approach to practice. However, engaging in deliberate practice is not a straightforward matter. A central theme in the McLeod (2021) study was the necessity for trainees to understand and internalize a deliberate practice model of learning. They achieved this using a variety of strategies. Some adopted a trial and error approach in which they tried out different deliberate practice activities, and went back to Ericsson and Pool (2016) or Rousmaniere (2016), or talked to a tutor, for further guidance if things did not work out. Another strategy was to make connections with earlier learning experiences over the course of their life, to retrieve memories of occasions when they had successfully implemented aspects of deliberate practice in the past.

A useful source of further information and learning resources on deliberate practice is the *DP Institute* website (https://www.dpfortherapists.com), set up by two leading figures in the deliberate practice movement, Tony Rousmaniere and Alex Vaz. This website includes open access skills practice exercises as well as online lectures and interviews. Further resources being produced by members of the Institute are books on deliberate practice activities for learning emotion-focused therapy (EFT) (Goldman et al. 2021) and CBT (Boswell and Constantino 2021), with other titles forthcoming. Although these books focus on skills for specific therapy approaches, they also provide exercises that are relevant for the development of general counselling skills. For example, the EFT book includes several exercises on empathy skills, and the CBT book covers skills for structuring an agenda for a session.

Process analysis

A significant assessment task in many counselling skills training modules and programmes is the presentation of a process analysis. This task involves selecting and transcribing a segment of a counselling session conducted with a learning partner or actual client, and analysing the process of counselling that took place. In broad terms this learning activity is similar to the type of reflection on practice that can take place in a microskills workshop or IPR session, but carried out with greater thoroughness and attention to detail. Typically, the centrepiece of a process analysis comprises a transcript of the therapy episode being analysed, with one or more additional columns that provide supplementary information on:

- the internal reactions of the counsellor at key moments, for instance what they were thinking and feeling, images and memories that came to mind, and action tendencies
- the non-verbal behaviour of the counsellor and client
- the skills used by the counsellor
- the change process that was unfolding.

This material is often preceded by an explanation of the context in which the session took place, and an account of what happened in the period leading up to the target event. The transcript is followed by a reflective and theoretically informed commentary and analysis of key processes and turning points in the therapy episode, including indications of alternative responses that might have been more helpful at different points. Often the report will conclude by identifying personal learning arising from the exercise, and outlining implications for further development such as deliberate practice activities. In many instances the report may also include feedback from others, such as the client in the session, and observers.

A useful general strategy in carrying out a process analysis is to look closely at 'triples': a series of speaking turns (usually three) comprising a client statement followed by a counsellor response, followed by the client's next statement (Sachse and Elliott 2002). This approach provides a means of assessing whether the therapist's use of a skill such as empathic reflection or silence is effective and appropriate by looking at (a) the extent to which it represented a satisfactory response to the client's preceding statement, and, crucially, (b) whether it had the result of encouraging and deepening the client's ongoing exploration and expression, or otherwise. Effective use of skills produces a series of speaking turns that build towards the accomplishment of a therapy goal or task. By contrast, unskilled responses can slow the client down, confuse them, or lead them in a direction that lacks relevance.

At the initial stages of counsellor training, a process analysis would tend to be restricted to reflection on skills and basic processes occurring with the therapy episode being examined. At later stages of training a process analysis might be embedded in, or refer to, a broader exploration of a case as a whole. In some programmes, the process analysis serves as a starting point for a viva that may expand to consider wider aspects of the candidate's competence and awareness.

Alternatively, a transcript or process analysis can form the basis of a group discussion or seminar.

Although different programmes may emphasize different aspects of the process analysis learning task, there is a shared understanding that this kind of task allows a trainee to use critical reflection to deepen, and then demonstrate, their appreciation of what Ivey described as counsellor intentionality – the capacity to be aware of different possible ways of responding to a client. Because the work involved in transcribing a counselling episode and then completing a process analysis takes a great deal of time, the trainee is forced to confront their own practice. For these reasons, doing a process analysis is experienced by many students and trainees as a key point in their development as a competent user of counselling skills. It can also function as a template for what is possible in clinical supervision.

There are some important underlying assumptions that inform the use of process analysis. One significant aspect of this learning activity is that it highlights the complexity and interconnectedness of what happens in a counselling session, and the extent to which many elements of the process unfold out of conscious awareness (but may become evident once a recording is scrutinized in detail). Another aspect is the degree to which general processes, such as the capacity to connect with a client, or sensitivity to language, are exhibited in micro-moments of interaction.

A more in-depth version of a process analysis, known as comprehensive process analysis (CPA), has been used in therapy research as a means of developing an understanding of different types of change event (see, for example, Balmforth and Elliott 2012; Rees et al. 2001). For anyone undertaking a process analysis as part of their training, it can be useful to read such articles as a way of appreciating the underlying logic of a process approach, and also getting a sense of what is possible when a team of researchers works on a transcript (and other supporting data) over an extended period. However, it is also essential to keep in mind that the aim of a CPA study is the development of theory and evidence, whereas the aim of a process report is the personal and professional development of the author.

Developing counselling skills as a collaborative interpersonal process

A consistent theme in all approaches to facilitating the development of counselling skills is that this is an area of learning that requires commitment to working with other people. The main drivers of skills learning are being able to observe others, feedback and practice. While it can be valuable to observe video demonstrations of skills, it is even more useful to be able to participate in live, interactive demonstrations that allow for questions and discussion around how and why certain skills were deployed, and the client's views as to how helpful they were. Feedback is an essential part of the learning process. It is necessary to be able to ask for, provide and receive feedback in constructive ways. Tutor or trainer modelling of feedback, and willingness to intervene to minimize potentially destructive feedback, contributes to the creation of an appropriate culture of feedback. For many learners, participation in feedback can be highly stressful, because it can evoke memories of childhood humiliation, criticism and exclusion in family, school and peer group situations (Alexander and Hulse-Killacky 2005; Hulse-Killacky et al. 2006; Stroud et al. 2016). Openness to corrective feedback is a capacity that is important not just during training, but also over the course of a career as a therapist or helper (Brattland et al. 2018), and touches on highly significant areas of personal development around relationships with others and one's sense of being loveable and worthy. Counselling skills training can trigger deep reflection on the participant's sense of self and relationships with others (Nerdrum and Rønnestad 2002, 2004). In response to these factors, Johnson et al. (2014) have argued that all counsellor and psychotherapist training needs to take place in a learning environment that is experienced as a supportive community.

Conclusions

The main message of this chapter is that developing an effective and responsive counselling skills repertoire is not an easy matter. Learning counselling skills is challenging because of the difficulty in altering deeply ingrained ways of interacting with others that have been acquired over a lifetime. Counselling skills trainers and tutors have devised a wide range of frameworks and activities to facilitate this kind of work. These approaches all draw on some combination of a set of key elements: cognitive understanding, observing others model good and poor performance, personal practice of skills, receiving feedback from others (clients and observers), and reflection on practice. In addition, all of them employ strategies for accommodating the emotional demands of this kind of learning, primarily through membership of a supportive learning group. The deliberate practice approach represents a particularly valuable overarching framework for learning counselling skills, because it incorporates all of the key elements listed above and because it is backed up by strong evidence in many occupational contexts. The learning activities provided at the end of each chapter reflect a deliberate practice/self-practice philosophy of learning, in the sense of identifying possibilities for practice that can then be pursued in whatever training contexts are available to the reader.

Learning activities

If possible, it can be helpful to meet with others to share and discuss the insights triggered by these learning exercises.

1   **Reflecting on your personal experience of learning a practical skill**. Think about a practical skill that you have recently acquired or developed. This could be work-related, or arising from your involvement in sport, or concerned with some aspect of domestic life. Examples could be: learning to use a new application on your phone or PC; a sporting accomplishment such as being able to make a top-spin serve in tennis; being able to prune fruit trees properly. Once you have decided on a specific skill that has been meaningful for you, take some time to reflect on the following questions:

   • What were the pre-existing skills that you already had, that you had to develop further or bring together in order to master this new skill?

   • What was the *process* of acquiring this new skill? What stages did you go through?

   • What types of assistance and tuition from other people were helpful or unhelpful?

Finally, taking your responses to these questions as a whole, what are the implications of what you discovered about the experience of learning a practical skill, for your learning and development in relation to counselling skills?

2   **Learning needs, preferences and choices**. This chapter has described several different approaches to developing counselling skills. Which approaches are most relevant and potentially valuable for you at this point in your training? Which approaches seem to be less useful? What is it about different approaches, or specific activities within them, that makes them attractive and meaningful to you (or otherwise)? What kinds of learning approaches and activities are available to you? What are the implications of these questions for how you make best use of the time you are able to devote to developing counselling skills?

3   **Your capacity to use feedback**. Being open to feedback from clients, learning partners, observers and tutors is a vital element in skills training. Use the prompts outlined below to explore your experience of receiving feedback in a skills training context:

   a. Background of the event (situation, who was present, etc).

   b. What was the feedback, and how was it communicated?

   c. What did you think during the feedback process? How did you feel? How did you react?

   d. What did you learn? How did you act on the feedback? In what ways has the experience influenced your use of counselling skills, or approach to learning skills?

It can be valuable to use this format for reflection on practice on a regular basis, for example as part of a learning journal. It can also be supportive and informative to share feedback experiences with learning partners, and to compare your own experiences with the findings of feedback research studies by Alexander and Hulse-Killacky (2005), Brattland et al. (2018), Hulse-Killacky et al. (2006) and Stroud et al. (2016).

4   **Using deliberate practice**. Read the study by McLeod (2021) of how counselling students used deliberate practice to support their development of counselling skills. This is an open access article that is free to download. In what ways does this study (i) help you to appreciate the nature of deliberate practice and how it fits alongside other learning activities, and (ii) inspire you to imagine deliberate practice exercises that might assist your own learning?

Making a counselling space

5

Introduction

At the heart of any form of counselling is *making a space to talk it through*. The idea of a counselling *space* arises from an understanding of people as living their lives in a personal niche that they have made for themselves within their society and culture. This personal world can at times be hard to live in – things go wrong. When this happens, counselling provides a space outside of the person's everyday life, where they can stand back from their routine and reflect on what they might wish to do to change things to make them better. A counselling space is like a bubble, haven, refuge, sanctuary, vantage point or place of emotional safety that the person can occupy for a period of time, and to which they can return when necessary. This chapter explores the skills and strategies that contribute to the construction and maintenance of a counselling space, and its eventual closure.

Before the first meeting

There are many important aspects of a counselling space that need to be planned, or will already be in existence, before the first meeting between a client and their therapist. These include:

- some kind of administrative structure, with its own organizational culture and style of engaging with clients (Brown et al. 2011; Kehoe et al. 2016; Sandage et al. 2017)
- a booking system, that allows clients possibilities and limits regarding timing, frequency and number of sessions (Carey et al. 2013; Churchman et al. 2020)
- website, leaflet, posters, etc. that inform clients about the existence of the therapy clinic or service, and what it offers
- rooms (or online environment) that provide the location where therapy will take place (Jackson 2018; Jones 2018, 2020; Punzi and Singer 2018)
- an intake procedure – for example an assessment interview or telephone call prior to seeing a therapist
- a system for collecting client information, including data about name, next of kin, contact numbers etc., but perhaps also including questionnaires completed by the client regarding symptoms, quality of therapy relationship and satisfaction with the service.

Each of these elements makes a difference to the client experience, in the sense of priming them to view therapy in a particular way. They also provide the framework in which the therapist needs to operate. This framework can be supportive, in the sense that certain practical matters are already decided. But it can also place limits on what a therapist can do, for instance in relation to the number of sessions. In addition, there is a subtler emotional dimension associated with these organizational factors, which Kehoe et al. (2016) have described as *administrative attachment* – the extent to which clients feel welcomed, are treated respectfully as an individual and have a feeling of being taken care of. This dimension is particularly significant for clients (or potential clients) from disadvantaged and socially excluded groups (Brown et al. 2011).

These contextual elements of therapy that operate prior to the first therapy session are clearly highly significant in terms of both setting the scene for therapy and screening out clients who are not able to negotiate their way through what is required from them. However, there no established, widely agreed or evidence-based models, guidelines or skills associated with these aspects of the task of building a space for counselling. At the present time, counsellors need to develop their competency in these areas by learning from published studies, speaking to colleagues, reflecting on their own experience as clients/service users and therapists, and taking account of how such matters are handled in other types of human service agencies.

The first meeting: what do you say after you say hello?

The first actual meeting between a client and therapist is a highly significant moment in therapy. What happens at that meeting will almost certainly establish a pattern of interaction and direction of travel that will be hard to renegotiate if it turns out to be unhelpful. There is a potentially very long list of practical matters that may need to be handled. The client is also likely to be feeling apprehensive. In addition to these challenges, also in play is the underlying human capacity to make instant appraisals of other people (Gladwell 2006). It is not surprising, therefore, that as many as 30 per cent of clients do not return after the first session.

The extent to which practical issues may need to be addressed in a first session will depend on the kind of intake procedure that a client has already undergone. For example, explaining confidentiality and risk management procedures, in a manner that allows the client to ask questions, can take several minutes. Given that the client may be anxious and uncertain about what will happen and what is expected of them, it is extremely valuable for a counsellor to formulate, practise and become familiar with a potential script for a first session, including a repertoire of possible statements that can be included. Being prepared in this way makes it easier to actually listen to the client and keep track of time. We strongly advocate starting a first meeting – after saying hello, introducing yourself, making sure that the client is comfortable, etc. – with a brief overview of what you would like to cover in the first session (and why), and an invitation to the client to feel free to ask questions at any point. This helps the client to feel in control and gives them a few moments to orient themselves in the room or become accustomed to the online portal. It is also useful, early on, to inquire about the client's experience of their contact with the service up to that point and the information they have received or have provided.

In a first session, a balance is usually needed between addressing practical issues around information-giving, arrangements and assessment, and a process of beginning to explore and make sense of the client's concerns. Lavik et al. (2018) reviewed studies into client experiences of early sessions of therapy and found that clients came into therapy hoping to meet a therapist who was competent and warm, who would try to understand them as a whole person rather than as a psychiatric category or bundle of symptoms. They wanted the first or second session to alleviate their fears about entering therapy, and give them a sense of being accepted and validated, with new strength and hope for the future.

There are several useful sources that discuss therapist skills and strategies for achieving such outcomes in the first session. Chow (2018) includes a wide range of ideas about how to enable clients to leave the first session with a sense of having learned something new about themselves and a sense of direction. Other sources that similarly discuss skills for handling the start of therapy are King and Boswell (2019), Sommers-Flanagan and Bequette (2013), Spencer et al. (2019) and Tsai et al. (2019). Key general themes emerging in these papers include: exploring the client's sense of their preferred future; identifying client goals and tentatively mapping how they might be tackled; helping the client to recognize their own strengths and resources; shared decision-making around how therapy will work; conveying a sense of therapist humility, hopefulness and openness to encourage the client to actively engage in the therapy process.

A particularly crucial point in a first session is the moment when the therapist invites the client to talk about their problem. There are many ways of phrasing such a statement, for example:

- What brings you for counselling?
- What brings you here?
- What is the problem that is troubling you?
- How can I be of help?
- Just tell me what is on your mind.
- Where do you want to start?

Such statements are open-ended and allow the client to proceed at their own pace. A tentative and general statement such as 'What is around for you right now?', perhaps accompanied by a pause or brief silence, can be a good way to initiate a therapy process that draws on unconscious material, or engages with here-and-now experiencing. But it is always important to keep in mind that any counsellor statement will have the effect of subtly directing the client's process. For example, 'What is around for you right now?' invites the client to pay attention to some aspects of their experience (i.e. what is happening now) rather than others (e.g. their hopes, intentions or goals).

In a first session context, in which a client is possibly quite apprehensive and perhaps unsure of what an appropriate answer might look like, it can be helpful to offer more structure, by using a statement along the lines of:

> What would be useful for me would be if you could tell me what has brought you to counselling, for example what concerns you, and also what you would like to get from counselling. Is that OK for you?

This more extended statement also includes a reference to the client's goals ('what you would like to get from counselling') and functions as a prompt in respect of the client's sense of a preferred future (Bohart 1993; Cooper 2021; Oddli et al. 2021).

Shared understanding of goals (what we are trying to achieve together) is an essential element of collaboration. If you are working together to cook a meal, or decorate a room, or develop a Covid vaccine, you need to agree on what the end point is likely to be. If you do not have an agreed goal, you are not collaborating – either one person is leading and the other is following, or you are essentially working on different projects. It is therefore valuable in a first session not only to listen to what the client has to say about the concern, issue or problem that brought them to therapy, but also to begin to get a handle on what they hope to gain from therapy in terms of an end point or destination.

Active curiosity is a crucial skill in relation to exploring client concerns and goals in a first session, for example through follow-up questions. If you started with a statement that did not convey an interest in the client's goal, or if the client responded to your opening statement by just talking about concerns and problems rather than goals, it may be useful at the first or second speaking turn to sum up and check out your understanding of their concern/problem, and then ask about what they would want to achieve. For example:

> Can I just check that I am hearing you correctly? What you are saying is that feeling anxious and terrified in social situations is a major thing for you in your life at the moment... Is that about right?
>
> [Client replies...]
>
> I was wondering how you see counselling helping with that issue – for example, do you have a sense of what you would want to get from our time today, or maybe even where you would like to be by the end of counselling as a whole?

At a later point, it can also be helpful to offer tentative/candidate goal formulations that try to sum up what the client has said about their aims for therapy:

> In terms of that issue – feeling anxious and terrified in social situations – that you have said is the most important thing for you just now, it would be useful for me if you could let me know where you would like to get to today, what you would like to achieve by the end of the session. I'm not clear whether at this point you maybe want to just talk, to get things off your chest and use our time together to just start to get a better appreciation of the whole situation. That would be fine. But I was also wondering whether you might want to make sense of what has happened in that area of life, so you could kind of get a handle on it – for example understanding how it developed, or what triggers it in particular situations. Or maybe what you would want is to begin to look at skills or ways of coping, such as techniques that would allow you to deal with the situation in a different way... I'm OK with any of these directions, or all of them. Or there may be something else that you want to get from counselling...

It is important to keep in mind that it is unlikely to be easy for a client to come up with a clear and concise statement of what they want from therapy. Also, there is no one point in therapy where goals are addressed: being goal-oriented or future-oriented is a process. What you say about goals at the start should come across as an indication of your interest in learning more, and a topic that you will invite the client to come back to. A useful source for ideas, strategies and skills around what is involved in a goal-informed approach to therapy is Cooper and Law (2018). Mackrill et al. (2018) emphasize the importance of being open to the broader meaning of therapy goals in relation to the client's life as a whole.

Some possibilities to be considered in developing your way of working with client goals are:

- Writing down agreed goals on a form, and rating the degree to which these goals have been accomplished, may provide a useful anchor point, and a concrete means of reviewing, and if necessary redefining, goals. But it is not enough in itself. It needs to be backed up by what happens during sessions.
- Developing a flexible and responsive language for talking about goals. For example, the word 'goal' may have negative connotations for many clients (see Chapter 10 for alternative ways of talking about goals).
- Achieving greater goal clarity and specificity is often a sign of progress in therapy.
- Some clients use therapy to review and reflect on their wider life goals – for them, a key goal of therapy is to develop more satisfying and meaningful life goals.
- We live in a consumerist society based on persuading us to pursue false goals – there may be situations in which stated goals are in conflict with a client's underlying values.
- No purpose, no future, no hope, no goals... – these are characteristics of being ground down by adversity.

The more personal reflection, reading and discussion you do around the concept of goals, the more sensitive you will be to nuances in the client's account of what they want, and the more you will be able to engage in productive dialogue around this topic.

As well as beginning to establish what the client wants from therapy, at some point in a first session it is also useful to open up a conversation about the client's strengths, for instance by acknowledging that the client has thought about the issue a lot, has worked out ways of dealing with it and has their own understanding of what has been happening for them. Although it is unlikely that a client will talk much about these factors in a first session, it is useful to put down a marker for later conversations around preferences, ways of understanding, strengths and the everyday cultural resources that are available to them. It is also useful to talk in a way that implies collaboration, for example through phrases such as 'it would be helpful for me if...', 'it will help us to work together if...'.

In a first session, the value of beginning to explore the client's goals and ways of making sense of their difficulties – in addition to hearing about their problems and handling practical aspects of therapy – becomes clear when considering how to end the session. A key point made by Chow (2018) is that clients are more likely to come back for a second session if they have left the first session with something useful that they can take away with them. If a first session predominantly focuses on the client's problems and distress, there is a chance that they may leave in a worse state than when they arrived, because they have had an experience of being exposed and vulnerable – opening up their worries and anxieties without any indication of how things might get better. By contrast, if some degree of tentative agreement around goals has been achieved, and there has been a conversation about how to make sense of the problem, the therapist becomes able, in the closing minutes of the session, to highlight how these lines of direction can be taken forward in subsequent meetings. This take-home message can be reinforced by cautiously suggesting possible activities the client might undertake before the next session ('I was wondering if maybe this work-sheet might be helpful for you, as a way of collecting your own information on what happens when you feel anxious…?'). Some therapists may even write down take-home messages on a card they give to the client at the end of the session, or in an email letter sent (if the client agrees to such contact) after the session.

Later sessions

The general principles of how to handle a first session are also relevant to the question of how to start later sessions. Additional skills and strategies can also be used, that build on what was discussed in the first session:

- asking the client if they have further thoughts about what was explored in the first (or a previous) session
- exploring the client's experience with between-session tasks
- sharing your own thoughts that have emerged since the previous session
- discussing the client's experience of completing an outcome monitoring form (if this is part of therapy) at the start of the session, and looking at implications of how items have been answered, the overall score on the measure, etc.
- recap of goals and tasks agreed previously – are they still valid, do they need to be reworded or refocused?
- agreeing an agenda for the session.

It is important to be responsive to what the client needs or wants at the start of a session, rather than initiating the topics listed above in a mechanistic way. For example, a client may come into a session feeling upset about something that has happened in their life, and may not be ready or able to think about anything else until they have had a chance to talk about these emotions. Similarly, there may be a success or positive breakthrough that the client is bursting to report.

A key counselling skill is that of being able to *punctuate* sessions in a sensitive and helpful way. For example, if more than one goal or task is being pursued in a session, it can be useful to agree at the start roughly how much time is to be allocated to each one, and for the counsellor to check out at the appropriate time whether the client would like to move to the next topic. It may be that the client is so intensively involved in the initial topic that they choose not to shift emphasis at that moment. Acting as the timekeeper and navigator can allow the client to give themselves up to whatever they want to work on. It also functions as a way of embedding practical collaboration and shared decision-making into the therapy process.

Using time between sessions

Thinking about counselling as a space within the broader landscape of the client's life makes it easier to construct points of contact between what happens in therapy and what happens in other contexts. Many approaches to therapy make use of between-session activities such as homework tasks, projects, journaling, reading, collecting dream specimens, practising skills such as mindfulness meditation, making art, engaging in life-enhancing activities such as outdoor pursuits, accessing other therapies, and using bridging forms and worksheets to reflect on the previous session and identify areas to be explored in the following session. Stewart and Schröder (2015) use the phrase 'emotional homework' to describe this aspect of the experience of being a client. Facilitating the planning and monitoring of these activities, and their effective integration into therapy, requires specific skills and strategies. A useful discussion of how therapists can engage with this dimension of practice, specifically focused on client self-help, is available in Norcross (2006) and in Edwards-Stewart and Norcross (2019).

For their part, therapists use time between sessions to engage in supervision and consultation, and to participate in reading, study, seminars and training courses that are relevant to their work with a client. They also reflect on how their work with a client has touched them at a personal level (Arnd-Caddigan 2012, 2013; Bimont and Werbart 2018; Knox et al. 2018; Schröder et al. 2009; Smith 2019). These therapist between-session activities deepen their level of engagement with a particular client. While therapists rarely say much about their between-session process in their conversations with clients, it can be helpful to do so. For example, even briefly mentioning that you have been thinking about a client, or outlining what these thoughts have been about, can be a powerful signal to a client that you care, and are committed to their well-being. Such interventions can have the effect of strengthening trust and the therapeutic alliance.

Ending therapy: what do you say when you say goodbye?

The ending of therapy – closing down the therapeutic space – is a key phase in therapy. Typically, a client may benefit from the routine of knowing that they will have someone to talk to each week about their personal issues. In terms of making changes in one's life, it is also helpful to have someone who will function as a dependable source of support and encouragement. The end of therapy represents a shift into a situation where the person needs to rely on their own personal capabilities, and the support of people other than their therapist. Endings may reflect a sense of achievement on being ready to move on in life. Alternatively, they may reflect a sense of disappointment at missed opportunities, or even of having been harmed or damaged by the experience of therapy. In situations where therapy operates within predetermined limits regarding the number of sessions, the therapist is suddenly not available (e.g. they have become ill), or the client decides to quit, there may not be time to go through an ending phase. From the point of view of the client, leaving their therapist may evoke earlier painful episodes of loss in their life.

The development of skills and strategies around facilitating a good therapy ending is problematic because it is not a situation that can be easily replicated in practice sessions with learning partners. As a result, becoming skilful in handling endings is generally based on a combination of using supervision to guide one through the ending process of early cases during training, and drawing on the collective wisdom and experience of colleagues. In terms of the latter sources, papers by Goode et al. (2017) and Norcross et al. (2017) provide very helpful accounts of the ways that experienced therapists collaborate with their clients to create the best possible endings. Additional insights on therapy endings can be found in Bamford and Akhurst (2014), Råbu and Haavind (2018), Shafran et al. (2020), Tsai et al. (2017) and Webb et al. (2019). For example, Shafran et al. (2020) have shown that client active participation in dialogue around the meaning of ending tends to be an indicator that therapy has been helpful, while closing sessions in which the therapist dominates the conversation are more likely to occur when the client has not been satisfied with what they have gained from therapy.

In relation to handling endings, it is important to develop an approach to ending that is consistent with your own approach to therapy, the types of clients that you see, and the requirements of the organizational setting in which you work. There are many different types of ending ritual or procedure that can be implemented, including reviewing the therapy journey, reinforcing the client's accomplishments, looking at ways that gains can be maintained and relapse prevented, writing a letter to the client, exchanging gifts, and arranging follow-up sessions. A collaborative approach to therapy emphasizes routinely reflecting on the therapy process and relationship – this can lay the groundwork for shared decision-making around when therapy should end and what the ending might look like. For example, if the therapy has involved identifying goals, then the attainment of these goals can readily become one of the topics for an ending session. Similarly, if the client has offered feedback to the therapist, in ways that have made a difference to the progress of therapy, then these events provide evidence of client resourcefulness that can be acknowledged.

Conclusions

On the whole, skills for building, maintaining and closing a therapeutic space have not comprised a significant topic for therapy research and training. Research and training are carried out by therapists, and from a therapist's point of view there is an assumption that powerful therapy interventions, along with a strong working alliance, are what makes a difference. However, from the point of view of the client, what makes a difference is the experience of being able to access a place, block of time and person that are set up to be responsive to your needs, are reliable, consistent and trustworthy, and provide a context for facing up to personal challenges and dilemmas. This is particularly important at the start of therapy – many clients walk away because they do not understand what is happening in sessions and how or how it could be useful for them.

Learning activities

The following activities may be explored individually, and/or with a group of learning partners.

1   Meet up with learning partners, and take turns in being counsellor, client and observer for brief ten-minute sessions. The participant who is the counsellor should try out different opening statements (e.g. 'Where would you like to start...?'), either taken from the list in this chapter, found in other published sources or invented by the counsellor. Participants in the client and observer roles should concentrate on giving honest feedback on what they perceive to be the helpful and unhelpful aspects of each opening statement. Reflecting on the experience of being a client is important, as a way of getting a sense of what it is like to be a recipient of alternative opening statements. It can then be useful to design other opening statements that might be more facilitative, and road test them in a further learning session.

2   Create a plan for a first meeting with a client – either in the context of a counselling agency in which you work, or in an ideal independent practice setting. What topics would you include? How would you explore each topic? How long might you allocate to each section, and to the meeting as a whole? A useful example of a first session template (in a coaching context, but still relevant for counselling) can be found in Rogers (2016: Appendix 1).

3   If you have received therapy yourself, as a client, how did your therapist (or different therapists you may have consulted) handle the types of situations described in this chapter, such as the beginning and ending of

therapy, the start and finish of sessions, and identifying goals? What did they do in relation to these aspects of therapy that you thought was helpful or unhelpful for you? Which elements of their approach might you integrate into your own practice, and which would you want to avoid? Although this learning activity may be explored on an individual basis, it can be particularly useful to share experiences in a learning group as a means of developing a broader perspective.

4   Assemble a file of public, client-facing information (e.g. leaflets, web pages, posters) produced by counselling/psychotherapy services and private practice therapists in the area where you live. What do these sources of information convey to clients about how to understand their problems, and what they can personally do to enhance their recovery? What information is missing from these sources, that you believe should be provided? Although this learning activity may be carried out on an individual basis, it can be particularly useful to work in a group where each member prepares a report on two or three clinics/practices.

5   Imagine that it is ten years in the future. You have completed your training as a therapist, and have been successful in your career. You now have an opportunity to design your own therapy room or space (this can be in whatever setting you would see yourself as working in – e.g. private practice, a therapy clinic, an outdoor centre, etc.). What would your room look like, and why? Although this learning activity may be explored on an individual basis, it can be interesting and informative to share your ideas with learning partners as a means of developing a broader perspective.

6   Having completed Learning activity 4, read the study by Punzi and Singer (2018), in which experienced therapists were interviewed about the therapy rooms they used. This is an open access paper, available free of charge on the internet. In what ways do the findings reported by Punzi and Singer (2018) help you to develop a more complete understanding of this issue?

Listening

6

Introduction

Listening is a basic aspect of human relationships. You do not need to learn how to listen – we all do this in many situations every day. Imagine the following scenarios:

- cooking the evening meal while listening to your child's story of what happened at school today
- listening to music and being moved
- listening to a new neighbour who is a Syrian refugee tell you about how they lost a member of their family crossing the Mediterranean
- listening to a talk given by a widely respected teacher
- receiving instructions on how to find a particular street in an unfamiliar city
- listening to your doctor delivering a diagnosis
- listening to a colleague sharing office gossip.

Each of these situations evokes a different style of listening. How you handle these situations, as a listener, can have profound personal implications for both yourself and the speaker.

The theoretical and research literature on listening encompasses analyses of listening in many contexts, such as employee–manager interactions, teacher–pupil communication, political discourse, within families, language learning and in medical consultations (Jones 2011; Worthington and Bodie 2020). The question of what it means to listen to, and understand, the experience of another person is an issue that has been extensively explored by key figures in philosophy (Haroutunian-Gordon and Laverty 2011; Notess 2019). The pervasiveness of listening, including the experience of not being able to listen and not being heard, means that the use of listening in counselling and psychotherapy draws on a massive amount of both everyday understanding and academic discussion of this topic.

The counselling literature on listening focuses on the experience of a specific type of listening: conversations that are intended to be emotionally and psychologically supportive and facilitative, where the speaker talks about personal concerns, troubles or problems and the listener is in some kind of professional counselling or helping role. Compared to listening in other situations, listening in counselling is more oriented towards learning about the *meaning* of the events and experiences that are being recounted, particularly their emotional significance, rather than acquiring factual information. Listening is carried out in the service of an overall aim of contributing to the awareness and resourcefulness of the speaker. The listener is in a position of offering an acknowledgement, or being a witness to, the suffering of the speaker. There is only a limited degree of mutuality – the person seeking help is not expected to listen to the counsellor to any great extent.

A capacity to listen lies at the heart of counselling – good counsellors are good listeners. Although helpful counselling undoubtedly involves many other activities and processes in addition to listening, it is unlikely that these will be helpful if the counsellor is unable to truly grasp the meaning and implications of what their client is trying to express, or the client lacks confidence in their counsellor's capacity to 'get' them. All counselling skills – for example challenging, questioning, silence – are built around the process of listening.

From a counselling perspective, listening can be defined as: *an active process of developing a comprehensive and accurate awareness and understanding of the client's world, with a particular emphasis on the concerns that the client is seeking to address in therapy*. The key idea here is that therapeutic listening is an *active* process – something that the counsellor works hard to achieve, in ways that are apparent to the client. We may listen to a fitness instructor who is giving us information about how much time to spend on each exercise, or on the safety features of a cross-training machine. While this kind of listening for factual information does occur in therapy (our clients will want us to remember whether they are married, and how many children they have), therapeutic listening inevitably goes beyond data collection, to encompass the implicit and underlying meaning and significance of what is being said.

The present chapter analyses listening skills in relation to how to make sense of this way of relating to clients, the challenges involved in listening and how to listen effectively.

Research evidence on the importance of listening in therapy

Because listening is such a taken-for-granted aspect of counselling, there are relatively few studies that specifically focus on it as a primary topic. However, there are many studies based on interviews with clients and therapists, in which listening is described as a key helpful factor in therapy. Examples include adolescent clients' experience of therapy to address the effect of being bullied at school (Versammy and Cooper 2021), clients' views about what makes for a supportive therapy relationship (Dollarhide et al. 2012) and an analysis of the kind of deep listening that is essential for effective therapy for clients who are suicidal (Østlie et al. 2018). A particularly important theme in this area of research has been exploration of the impact of not being heard and listened to, for example in female victims of violence (Brazelton 2019) and women who become depressed (Jack and Ali 2010). A major international research programme exists on the effectiveness of listening visits conducted by community nurses with women at risk of experiencing postnatal depression (Shakespeare et al. 2006; Segre et al. 2010; Brock et al. 2017). These studies – and many others – provide valuable insights into how listening skills combine with other skills and interventions, in a range of therapy settings, to produce beneficial client outcomes.

The function or purpose of listening

There are many different aspects of what can happen in the listening process, for the listener and speaker:

- the listener to learn what the speaker is trying to say
- the speaker to express themselves – in a counselling situation, to talk about what is bothering them
- talking to an engaged and sensitive listener has the effect of opening up a conversation or dialogue:
  - this kind of talking can function as a means of enabling the speaker to reflect on what they have said
  - … and perhaps being able to see patterns or meanings they had not been aware of before

  - talking to someone who is a good listener may create a bond or sense of connection between both people
  - careful and respectful listening positions the speaker as someone of value, whose story is worth being heard
  - genuine dialogue (as opposed to debate or argument) requires each person to listen and appreciate the point of view of the other
  - the establishment of an effective pattern of talking and listening may make it possible for a therapist and client to revert to that mode when communication between them hits a rocky patch
  - for both speaker and listener, a listening episode may be a memorable resource that can be mentally revisited at times of trouble
  - failure to listen can be highly destructive.

All in all, there can be a lot happening when one person is listening to another. A counsellor needs to be aware of the potential relevance of each of these functions of listening.

The internal experience and intentions of the listener

Most people who become counsellors take listening seriously and are interested in becoming better listeners. A key aspect of listening centres on how to make constructive and helpful use of the internal experience of being in that role. The intention of the listener (i.e. their sense of what they are trying to achieve) represents what is probably the most fundamental dimension of this process. In their classic book on skills learning and the development of exercise, Ericsson and Pool (2016) argue that effective performance of any kind of complex skill depends on building a flexible and detailed *mental representation* of how to carry it out. A mental representation is a kind of cognitive structure that can be expressed in different ways, depending on the situation: a mental image or video, a map that shows how to get from one place to another, a set of concepts, a theoretical model.

Carl Rogers was one of the most gifted exponents of therapeutic listening – his books, articles and therapy videos are still widely influential. In a detailed historical account of the development of how Rogers understood the intention of the listener/counsellor in a therapy session, Arnold (2014) identifies four different mental representations that Rogers adopted in respect of his listening stance at different points in his 50-year career.

In his initial training, Rogers was introduced to the notion that the therapist's job was to listen *for content* that was deemed relevant in terms of their theory of therapy. For example, a psychoanalyst would listen for transference, or a behaviour therapist would listen for examples of how behaviour was reinforced. He quickly rejected this kind of interpretative or selective style of listening as a mental representation that he came to regard as judgemental, intrusive and potentially threatening to the client, and undermining of an authentic relationship. He replaced this strategy or mental representation with an intention of being a *mirror* to the client's internal frame of reference. By being accepting and non-directive, the aim was to allow the client the freedom to express whatever was important to them, and follow their own path towards being the person they wanted to be. Nevertheless, after a while, Rogers and his colleagues realized that seeing oneself as operating like a mirror could all too often come across as insincere and false.

This led to the formulation of yet another intentional stance or mental representation, in which the therapist's listening response took account of their own inner congruent or authentic reaction to the client: *listening from the inside*. In this approach, the act of listening was subsumed under a broader concept of empathy. However, over time he came to see this approach to listening, grounded in therapist empathy and congruence (i.e. the Rogerian 'core conditions'), as not giving sufficient weight to the client's contribution to a process of building a shared understanding. His final position on listening, therefore, was a mental representation in which the therapist actively checked out their understanding with the client; empathic listening was a *joint activity,* carried out between client and therapist working together.

Although the four intentional stances identified by Arnold (2014) – ranging from theoretically distanced to actively relational – are apparent in the evolving therapy approach of Carl Rogers, they still comprise mental representations that most, or even all, therapists adopt at various points in their work with each client they see. The conclusion reached by Arnold (2014), which we share, is that the kind of collaborative, relational style of listening that Rogers articulated towards the end of his career is on balance the best option, because it is less likely to go astray (the therapist is actively checking out whether their understanding is accurate), more likely to create spaces where the client can fill in the gaps in terms of what has not been said, and more effective in building a platform for working together.

This is not to say that the other forms of listening intention highlighted by Arnold (2014) – interpretative, mirroring and guided by personal authenticity – are necessarily bad things to do. In fact, at times each of them may be highly appropriate. For example, there may be times in therapy when it is helpful to selectively listen (i.e. interpret the client's experience) for specific themes, such as client strengths and solutions, harsh self-criticism or risk of self-harm. With fragile clients, or those who find it hard to trust their therapist, a good way to build some kind of connection may be to simply reflect back. An absence of willingness to be authentic (to listen from inside) is likely to inhibit creativity and use of intuition, as well as leading to client uncertainty about the emotional honesty and trustworthiness of their therapist.

Difficulties in listening

Throughout his career, Rogers advocated a form of listening that attempted to be responsive to the totality of what a person was trying to convey. One of the most valuable aspects of his work was his effort to describe and analyse helpful, effective and optimal forms of active listening. By contrast, other commentators have focused on what is happening when there are lapses or failures in listening (Nemec et al. 2017).

Patterns of listening difficulty include:

Distraction. The listener is not paying attention to the speaker because they are thinking about something else – for example, how long until the end of the session, what they are planning to do that evening, etc.

Rehearsing. The listener pays too much attention to formulating their response to the speaker, for example in terms of what they are going to say and when they are going to say it. As a consequence, they may fail to hear important segments of the speaker's account of their experience, or switch off from tuning into the underlying feeling or emotional tone of what is being talked about. This pattern can often occur with novice helpers, or in situations where there is time pressure or the listener is concerned about making a mistake (e.g. the speaker/client is in a vulnerable state). In everyday conversations, we listen to each other, but only up to a point – at least some of the time, we are rehearsing what we intend to say when our turn comes around.

Being self-consciousness and anxious. It is generally useful for a listener, helper or counsellor to be tentative rather than overconfident. However, when a listener lacks basic confidence in their own ability to be helpful, they may engage in a spiral of anxious rumination (e.g. negative thoughts such as 'I am lost', 'This is all too overwhelming and confusing', 'I will never be able to say the right thing') and bodily tension. As with rehearsing, this kind of internal activity has the effect of distracting the listener from hearing what the speaker is saying. The non-verbal anxiety cues emitted by the listener, such as physical tension, looking worried, lack of responsiveness, nervousness when they say something, etc., may also make the speaker wonder what is happening.

Filtering. Sometimes a listener may be operating in terms of some kind of implicit or explicit model or theory, with the consequence that they are only listening for what they expect to hear. For example, a listener may assume that they need to know about factual matters, such as what the person has been doing, or when the problem started, and as a consequence not be sensitive to feelings and emotions that are being expressed. Alternatively, a listener may be so focused on collecting information to make a diagnosis that they do not register examples of positive strengths and achievements being described by the speaker. In many professional situations, we are trained to listen *for* specific types of information. For example, a doctor or nurse learns to listen for symptoms, or for information that will confirm a particular diagnosis. A police officer may be trained to listen for evasions and contradictions in the story told by a suspect or witness.

Advising and 'rescuing'. Helpers may assume that their job is to fix or solve the speaker's problem. Their response to the speaker may therefore consist of well-intentioned advice. Even when the advice is sensible or wise, this kind of listener response can have the effect of leaving the listener wondering whether they have been truly 'heard' – for instance if the listener has paid attention to their existing efforts to resolve the problem, or to their wish to just 'get things off their chest' rather than achieve an instant solution. A 'rescuing' response may also convey a sense that the listener does not want to hear any more of the speaker's troubles or difficulties, and just wants to talk about positive or 'feel good' topics.

Unbalanced turn-taking: the listener says too much or too little. In ordinary everyday conversation, when one person describes a problem, the standard response is for the other person to share an example of when they had a similar problem and were able to solve it. This kind of interaction maintains equality between speakers, and is generally experienced as supportive. However, it is not usually the best strategy in a helping situation. When someone is seeking help, they need the other person to be quiet and listen. There is usually a balance of speaking time that greatly favours the person seeking help: the listener takes up much less of the stage. The therapist speaking too much may come across as a kind of helping by lecturing/teaching, or as the therapist moving into the role of client. At the same time, saying too little is not an effective way of actively listening, for two reasons. First, the speaker or help-seeker is left wondering whether the listener is actually present and engaged. Second, the listener may be so overwhelmed by the amount of information they are receiving, that they get confused or are only able to acknowledge a fraction of what has been said (when they eventually speak). Effective listening involves an appropriate balance of turn-taking – not too much and not too little.

Being a skilled listener involves being aware of these traps, noticing when they occur in a therapy session, and being able to switch back into listening mode. Some of these difficulties, for example self-criticism and rescuing, may highlight issues that need to be addressed in the trainee's personal development work.

Strategies for effective listening

Experienced therapists use a range of strategies to enhance their listening effectiveness. The most straightforward strategy is preparation, for example through taking a few minutes immediately before a client arrives to reduce the likelihood of internal mental distraction by relaxing, clearing your mind and becoming centred. Another useful form of preparation is to maintain energy levels through exercise and appropriate diet. It can be helpful to think about the client before they arrive for a session – in effect to begin listening to them before they are there. A further standard means of increasing the likelihood of accurate listening is to routinely use reflective statements or summaries to check with the client that what you have heard or gleaned is accurate. This is not always an entirely satisfactory technique, because clients may be reluctant to be critical of their therapist. On the other hand, clients can sometimes be quite forthright in feeding back that a therapist's reflection or summary is inadequate. The likelihood of useful feedback is increased if a collaborative way of working together has already been established.

A widely used set of strategies for effective listening is based on adopting a mindset of openness. In psychoanalysis, this has been described as an attitude of free-floating or evenly hovering attention. The key idea here is that the therapist does not try to make sense of what the client is saying, for instance by identifying themes or applying theoretical concepts, but instead adopts a kind of meditative stance of merging with, or being immersed in, the client's world or reality on a moment-by-moment basis. More recently, some psychoanalysts have described this as a state of *reverie.* Although it discusses reverie primarily in relation to research interviews, a paper by Holmes (2017) includes an explanation of reverie that is highly relevant to therapy. Other therapists, mainly in psychodynamic and family therapy, have used the term 'not-knowing' stance or attitude to refer to this way of being (Rober 2002). In existential therapy, the concept of phenomenological 'bracketing' serves a similar function (Cooper 2012). It is clear that free-floating attention, reverie, a not-knowing stance or bracketing can never be all-encompassing – a therapist always has a purpose and a model of therapy in the back of their mind (Spence 1984). Also, giving oneself over to this kind of unstructured way of listening may be more difficult to accomplish in short-term therapy where there is considerable time pressure (Nissen 2018). Nevertheless, the extensive literature on these perspectives on listening represents an invaluable resource for anyone seeking to develop skills in this area.

Another technique that can be valuable in the context of therapeutic listening is to pay attention to what is *not* said, or what seems to be on the edge or horizon of the client's awareness. This may include:

- gaps in the person's story
- the speaker's voice quality and tempo, and the feelings evoked by these features
- metaphors/images used by the speaker
- aspects of what the speaker is saying that seem to be in conflict with each other (e.g. wish to change vs not ready to change; a harsh/critical voice vs a vulnerable voice)
- whether the speaker seems to be keeping you at a distance vs inviting you into their world.

The advantage of this approach is that it helps the listener to pick up more than the basic content of what the client is talking about, but without adopting the more radical or all-encompassing commitment to openness required by psychoanalytic free-floating attention. A valuable perspective on the principle of listening for what is not being said can be found in the Listening Guide developed by Gilligan (2015; Gilligan and Eddy 2017), which provides training materials for sensitivity to such aspects of a client narrative as 'who is speaking?' and 'to whom are they speaking?'

In some situations, the incorporation of props into the counselling process (e.g. art materials, cups of tea, forms to be filled in and handed over, photographs to be looked at, etc.) may enable more effective listening. Shirota (2021) has analysed the phenomenon of *nagara* listening in Japan – the widespread tendency in that culture to conduct meaningful conversations while doing something else at the same time. What seemed to be happening in *nagara* episodes was that multitasking made it possible for participants to minimize the occurrence of potentially disruptive distractions, by relating such intrusions to routinized and automatic behaviours. Such actions also functioned as ways of managing differences in status between interlocutors. In some respects, this type of conversational multitasking seems the exact opposite of the kind of intensely focused person-to-person attending that is associated with counselling and psychotherapy. On the other hand, props are widely used in therapy (see Chapter 11). Further research needs to be carried out if *nagara* listening is to become as facilitative in therapy as it is in everyday life settings in Japan.

Observable aspects of effective listening

There are some observable characteristics of episodes in which a therapist is listening effectively, and the client feels heard:

Flow. When a counsellor is sufficiently tuned into the client's story, they may begin to finish the client's sentences, or seamlessly make links between what is being said now and what was said in previous conversations. This comes across to observers as a conversation that is *flowing*, with the speaker staying 'on track', and a sense of each person being in synchrony with the other.

Pauses and silences. A second observable feature of good listening is the occurrence of pauses and silences. Typically, if a counsellor has been listening well enough, they may need a few moments to reflect on what has been said before they begin to speak.

Rich detail. Deep listening makes it possible for the counsellor to gain a sense of the many facets of whatever issue the person is exploring. As a result, the counsellor's response to the client, in a reflection or summary statement, will convey a richly detailed and nuanced sense of the client's reality. By contrast, less sensitive listening leads to therapist reflection that merely contains one or two broad-brush generalizations.

Embodied attending. A crucial dimension of listening involves letting the other person know that you are listening. This aspect of the skill of listening can be described as *attending*, and consists of body movements, posture and minimal encouragers. It can be disconcerting and disturbing for a person to start to talk about something that is meaningful for them, and to have a sense that their interlocutor is not paying attention to them. Effective attending therefore functions as a means of communicating to the client that their counsellor is still listening. However, the appearance of attending is not much help to the client if real listening is not taking place.

Affirmation and validation. There is a sense of openness, welcoming and acceptance in the physical presence and utterances of the listener: they are responding from a position of affirmation and belief in the value of the other (rather than a position of suspicion or interrogation – see Josselson 2004).

These are all features of listening that can lead to the establishment of a dialogue between client and therapist. By contrast, partial or distracted listening tends to be associated with a disjointed conversational flow, awkward silences and possibly a sense of therapist distancing and disapproval.

Learning to listen

Reflecting on the experience of acquiring skills in therapeutic listening – moving from an everyday life approach to listening to a more intensive mode – represents a valuable means of understanding important aspects of the role of listening in counselling. Lee and Prior (2013, 2016) interviewed participants who had completed an early stage of counsellor training that incorporated many hours of listening skills practice in small groups. Three key themes emerged from this material. First, trainees learned a lot about themselves, in terms of how they defended against being fully open to the experience of the other person. Second, the process of listening built a relationship between the client and themselves, including a heightened sense of the 'otherness' of the other person. Third, by the end of the training they had become aware that they had acquired a capacity for a broader understanding of the other person. An important implication of this programme of research is that it takes time, and repetitive practice, to develop listening skills, and that it is a process that involves both emotional and cognitive learning.

Conclusions

Genuine listening involves making an effort to grasp the *whole* of what a person is saying – not only in their words but also through their voice quality and non-verbal cues such as posture. Genuine listening involves suspending or bracketing off any assumptions about the meaning of what a person is saying, and instead being open to what is actually there. Effective listening requires switching off one's internal dialogue in order to tune into the other person's story. It calls for a willingness to be there in the moment. None of this is easy. The listening that counsellors do is more open-ended than listening that occurs in other situations: it requires not only listening to the story being told, but also to the person and the social world behind the story.

The reason that listening is so powerful is that it creates an experience, for the person seeking help, of being-with another person in relation to their problem in living. For the person seeking help, there are always significant parts of their experience, or their story, that they have had to carry alone. The more that the helper listens, the more the problem emerges as something that they both know. It is almost as though the problem, and the pain, fear, shame and confusion that accompanies it, begins to be brought into being in the room between them. Once this happens, they can begin to 'walk around' the problem together, examining it from different angles and deciding what to do with it. To some extent, listening is about information-gathering, learning about the facts of what happened in the person's life, who was involved, how the problem grew. But more than that, it is about being willing to enter the life of the other, by being a companion and a witness. Listening, in the fullest sense, is always personal. It always involves an emotional and a moral commitment from one person to another. The person seeking counselling is making a commitment to being known, and the counsellor is investing themselves in a willingness to know.

Learning activities

The following activities may be explored individually, and/or with a group of learning partners.

1   If you are undergoing counselling or psychotherapy training, you will almost certainly have many opportunities to use your therapeutic listening skills, and receive feedback on these skills from others. Use the ideas and perspectives introduced in this chapter to inform your further reflection on your capacity for listening.

2   What was the listening culture that you were exposed to in your childhood? To what extent, in what ways and in what situations did members

of your family listen to each other? What are the implications of this personal listening history for your work as a counsellor?

3   What occupational listening cultures have you been socialized into in your work career as an adult? What are the implications of your occupational listening history for your work as a counsellor?

4   Reflect on times when you have been trying to really listen deeply to another person. This could be in a formal counselling/helping situation, or in another context. What did you do that seemed to be helpful? What did you do that was unhelpful?

5   Reflect on times when you have had the experience of being really 'heard' and listened to by another person. What was this like for you, and what effect did it have on you? What did the other person do that seemed to be effective? How did you let the other person know (either explicitly, or through unconscious cues) that they were being helpful?

6   What might you do to be able to listen more effectively? How can you practise these strategies and get feedback on whether they are working?

7   Research by Bodie et al. (2013) has identified four distinct listening styles:

• *Relational listening*: listening that is primarily guided by a wish to understand the feelings of the speaker, in order to build a relationship

• *Analytical listening*: a listening approach that is mainly based on collecting facts and information, and all sides of the issue being discussed, in order to arrive at a valid judgement

• *Task-oriented listening*: a listening style that encourages the speaker to get to the point; impatience with people who ramble on during a conversation

• *Critical listening*: paying particular attention to contradictions and errors in what the speaker is saying.

When you listen to a recording of yourself in a counselling practice session, which of these modes of listening do you use most often, and least often? How do your client and observers (if available) rate your use of these listening styles? What are the implications of your listening style profile for your work as a counsellor?

Shared understanding

Introduction

The intention to establish a shared understanding, drawing on the implicit and explicit theories and assumptions of both the client and the therapist, represents a fundamental aspect of a collaborative approach to counselling. Many approaches to therapy use the counsellor's ideas and theoretical model as the sole guiding principles that determine the course of therapy. But from a collaborative perspective, this kind of expert-driven stance has three limitations: it fails to take advantage of the client's knowledge and experience as an active therapeutic resource; it contributes to situations in which the client may reject the therapist's ideas because they clash with their own personal beliefs and perspectives; and it positions the client as an object of analysis rather than as a partner or co-participant. Skills and strategies for developing shared understanding are therefore crucial aspects of an ability to work collaboratively.

The main focus of this chapter is on the use of empathic engagement as a skill for building shared understanding. Empathy is a process through which one person is open to the experience of the other. It involves entering, appreciating, sensing and building a picture, map or understanding of how the world is experienced by that other person. Empathic engagement takes this a step further, by seeking to check out with the person that what has been understood fits for them. Gradually, these small acts of checking establish enough points of connection to allow participants to feel that they possess a sufficiently secure and reliable shared understanding to support their collaboration on tasks that may be hard for each of them.

Skills for building shared understanding

Shared understanding refers to ideas and information generated within the counselling relationship that build into a body of knowledge that is available to both counsellor and client as they work together to enable the client to move on in their life. Shared understanding draws on a range of sources:

- explicit, formal theory (e.g. ideas and concepts from psychodynamic, cognitive-behavioural therapy (CBT), etc.) with which the therapist and/or client are familiar
- implicit theories (e.g. a client may believe that individual willpower is a vital aspect of change, without ever having thought much about this idea or read about it; the therapist may have an implicit bias towards therapeutic activities that helped them in their own life)
- wider cultural knowledge and values (e.g. a client or therapist may believe in the healing power of nature, or a religious faith)
- the facts of the client's life, such as concrete information about sources of influence, key turning points, decisions, life events and strengths
- facts of the therapist's life
- the client's ideas about how therapy can be most helpful for them
- the therapist's ideas about how therapy can help this particular client
- the shared history of the client and therapist working together – memories and learnings associated with what was helpful or unhelpful, mis-steps that were sorted, moments of closeness and distance, etc.

The shared understanding that is co-created by a client and therapist is unique and distinctive to their relationship.

The following anonymized episode from therapy that one of us provided for a young man who was depressed provides a brief example of what shared understanding means in practice. In the early sessions of therapy we shared our ideas about how each of us thought that therapy might be helpful. The client talked in detail about key episodes in his life that he saw as contributing to his current difficulties. On the basis of these conversations, we used a timeline to agree on a plan of action that included participation in a range of everyday activities that provided positive and energizing experiences, alongside exploration of the continuing influence of specific childhood events that had resulted in the client still feeling emotionally vulnerable when in similar situations as an adult. Although this plan was significantly influenced by the therapist's theories of effective therapy for depression, it was consistent with the client's life experience and beliefs. After a few sessions, the client decided that it was too upsetting for him to continue exploring painful childhood experiences. On the basis of the shared understanding that had built up between them, the therapist could readily appreciate that the client's response did not reflect avoidance of something that he needed to face up to, but was an entirely appropriate decision for him to make given the circumstances in his life at that time. The defusing childhood memories therapy task was then wrapped up, and therapy proceeded on the basis of the other elements of the agreed plan. While many aspects of this therapy were challenging for both the client and therapist, the existence of mutual understanding made it possible to jointly navigate a way forward and reach a satisfactory conclusion.

The client's pre-existing understanding

By signing up for therapy and describing a problem or concern that they want to deal with, a client is providing two important starting points for developing a shared understanding. It is then necessary for the counsellor to invite the client to expand on these pieces of information by describing how the problem fits into their life as a whole, and how they think therapy might be helpful. Examples of prompts that convey the therapist's wish to develop a more complete appreciation of the client's pre-existing understanding include:

- 'It would be helpful for me to really understand how this issue fits into your life as a whole – would it be OK if I asked you a few questions about that? You don't need to answer these questions, if for any reason they are intrusive – and you don't need to explain why you're not answering them – you're in charge. Also, it's fine to ask me why I'm interested in particular things.'
- 'It might be useful for us to look at what you would ideally like your life to look like, beyond therapy. You have said that you want therapy to help you to get a handle on worrying so much and being so self-critical, and to become more confident in social situations. It's good to be so clear about that. But what comes next? Is there a bigger picture that you have, about what you want to do with your life?'
- 'I was wondering if you made any connections between these concerns and issues you have now, and anything that happened to you at earlier points in your life?'
- 'I can see, from what you have already told me, that you have done everything possible to make sense of these issues and concerns, and to cope with

them. It would be useful for our work together if you could tell me about how you make sense of these experiences, and what has been helpful or unhelpful in terms of coping – what I'm thinking is that it would be good if we could work together to build on what has worked for you in the past, and avoid ideas or techniques that you already know are not relevant or useful for you.'

- 'Have you had any therapy before, or taken medication, or used other ways of dealing with the difficulties you have told me about, such as yoga or exercise?'

These prompts are ways of initiating discussion of the client's ways of making sense of their problems and how these problems can be addressed. Other opportunities to explore the client's understanding occur in the context of listening to the client's story, or when asking them to identify their goals for therapy. It may also be appropriate to invite the client to complete questionnaires that have been designed to evaluate therapy preferences, and then discuss the implications of their answers (see, for example, Cooper and Norcross 2016; Norcross and Cooper 2021).

The therapist's pre-existing understanding

Shared understanding requires pooling of knowledge from both sides. The client needs to be able to empathically enter the world of their therapist. The therapist needs to be sufficiently open to being known to allow this to happen. A collaborative therapist needs to be able to articulate their ideas about therapy, and how therapy might be helpful in relation to a particular problem, in a way that a client can follow, and that does not take up too much time. Some clients are interested in reading about the type of therapy their counsellor is offering – it can be useful to be able to recommend specific books, articles or websites. It is important to encourage the client to ask questions about theories and techniques – and to be willing to answer them. It can be helpful for a therapist to offer examples of their personal life experience that might be relevant for a client – the topic of therapist self-disclosure is discussed in Chapter 9.

Empathy

Empathy is a core building block of any meaningful counselling conversation. The concept of empathy has been central to the practice of counselling and psychotherapy ever since the pioneering research of the American psychologist Carl Rogers in the 1950s. There is substantial evidence that the ability of a counsellor to empathize sensitively and accurately with the experience of their client is a major component in therapeutic effectiveness (Elliott et al. 2018). Empathy refers to the capacity of one person to 'tune in' to the reality of another person, to 'walk in their shoes', to see the world from that other person's perspective or frame of reference. In counselling, this is expressed through the therapist's active empathic *engagement* with the person. It is not enough merely to empathize silently – a good counsellor *communicates* their empathic understanding in a form that the person can receive, usually a brief empathic reflection that summarizes the main threads of what the client has said, in a brief counsellor statement. This type of counsellor response is usually delivered tentatively, or accompanied by a specific checking-out probe (e.g. '… does that seem about right?'). Over time, these empathic reflections, and the client's corrections to them or verifications that they are accurate – along with the initial client statements to which they refer – accumulate to form the core of a body of shared understanding available to both participants.

Empathy is not a matter of analysing the other person or dissecting their personality. It is about moving forward together.

A considerable literature exists around the use of empathy in therapy. Key sources for learning about how empathic engagement functions in therapy are Rogers (1961, 1975) and Mearns and Thorne (2013). An accessible and informative account of how post-Rogerian theory, training and practice around empathy has developed is available in Neukrug et al. (2013). The toxic effect of absence of therapist empathy is discussed by Moyers and Miller (2013).

As with other counselling skills, the use of empathy in therapy requires adapting and refocusing an everyday understanding of this quality. Specifically, it is crucial to recognize that therapeutic empathy is different from sympathy or compassion. While these are valuable human qualities in their own right, they imply a rather narrower response, which expresses fellow feeling or solidarity for the suffering that a person is experiencing. Empathy, by contrast, embraces a rather wider attempt to take in all, or as much as possible, of the experiential world of the other person, rather than just responding to a particular negative experience. Empathy can also be confused with identification with the speaker, another central aspect of everyday helping. For example, a counsellor might respond to a client with an everyday conversational rejoinder such as 'I feel, or have felt, that too', 'I know how you feel', or 'that happened to me, therefore I know what you are talking about'. While therapeutic empathy always encompasses some degree of capacity to imagine or recall aspects of one's own life that are similar to that of the client, it seeks to go beyond those aspects of the other's experience that are familiar, and connect with aspects that are unfamiliar or different. Similarity to the other (e.g. 'we have both had the experience of being unemployed') may undermine or limit the capacity to respond empathically, by assuming that the experience of the other maps onto one's own. True empathic engagement calls for a holistic response to the other, including cognitive, feeling and moral dimensions of the way the person experiences the world, and also an appreciation of the direction in which the person is moving.

How empathy is helpful
To be able to use empathic engagement as a skill in therapy, it is necessary to appreciate not only that it is helpful, but *how* it helps. The question of how empathy works can be understood from two perspectives: individual and relational.

At an individual level, each empathic reflection has the potential to enhance the process of client learning and change in significant ways. For example, Vanaerschot (1993) analysed how accurate, sensitive empathic engagement can 'release' a variety of significant 'micro-processes' in the person:

- feeling valued and accepted as a person
- learning to accept feelings, by hearing another person put one's own personal feelings into words without shame or embarrassment
- alienation is dissolved: 'I am not abnormal, different and strange – there is someone else who can understand me'
- learning to trust one's own experience, through the affirmation of that experience by the counsellor
- focusing the person's attention on the core aspects of their issue or problem
- facilitating recall of information – previously 'forgotten' or 'repressed' aspects of the issue may surface
- organizing information – the empathic statement may put things in order when the client has been talking in a fragmented or disjointed manner.

A further useful way of understanding how empathic engagement operates at an individual level is through the idea of the client's 'track', as defined by Rennie (1998). When a client starts talking about an issue, it is as though they are on a track – their account has direction and momentum. Non-empathic responses by a counsellor can throw the person off their track, because they indicate to the person that the counsellor has not understood them. At such a moment, the person finds themself wondering whether they need to stop and explain things to the counsellor, or perhaps even thinking that there may be little point in talking to someone who does not latch onto what they are trying to say. By contrast, an accurate empathic response enables the client to keep going. Using an analogy from driving, consistent empathic engagement is about keeping the car on the road – a basic requirement for any kind of journey to take place.

All of these individual processes enable the client to explore their experience more fully, become more aware of aspects of experience that had previously been out of awareness or on the edge of awareness, accept aspects that had previously been suppressed or denied, and move forward in their life. These are all very significant therapeutic effects.

In addition to the processes outlined above, a relational or collaborative perspective on therapist empathic engagement also considers the cumulative effect of multiple moments of empathic connection over a period of time. Therapist empathic engagement helps the client to tell their story in a more detailed and nuanced way. This allows the therapist to get a much closer view into the client's life, and the client hears themselves saying things that they had possibly never said before (or had not been able to say in the same way). The therapist is also checking out whether their grasp of the client's reality is along the right lines. Through these repeated interactions, a shared understanding is gradually built up.

Collaboration requires mutual empathy. Clients are empathic too, and trying to figure out where their therapist is coming from. The client is aware of how their words affect the therapist. The experience of receiving empathic responses involves paying attention to how the therapist does this, which can be transported to how they themselves can be more empathic in non-therapy relationships. The process of mutual empathy as part of the shared history of the client–therapist relationship is beautifully described by Jordan (2000).

A further cumulative effect of empathy includes the fact that later empathic reflections are never only responses to the client's prior statement, but draw on the entire thread of shared understanding that has been established. Over time, empathy may become a dependable baseline mode of interacting that can be called upon when therapy becomes hard work, or there is a rupture in the relationship. This allows both client and counsellor to be more confident around being more open with each other, and being more immediate and honest, as time goes on.

Empathy skills: a cyclical model

Carl Rogers (1975) described empathy as a way of being. However, some of his colleagues sought to identify the practical skills and strategies that made it possible to maintain an empathic way of being. Godfrey (Goff) Barrett-Lennard is an Australian psychologist who worked with Carl Rogers in the 1960s on some of the landmark research into the role of empathy in counselling (Barrett-Lennard 1998). During that time, Barrett-Lennard had the opportunity to study in depth what happened when a counsellor was able to engage empathically with a person seeking help. He came to the view that the best way to understand what was happening was to regard empathy as a cyclical process, comprising a series of moment-by-moment interactions between person and helper. His model (Barrett-Lennard 1981, 1993) can be described in terms of a series of five steps (see Table 7.1).

This simple model has a great deal of practical significance, in relation to what a counsellor actually does during the process of empathic engagement. The model suggests that there are key skills that an empathic counsellor is able to utilize:

- A readiness to hear the person – this requires being able to set aside any other distracting thoughts.
- An ability to 'resonate' – to allow the emotional meaning of what the person is saying to be felt at a gut level.
- A capacity to use language to summarize accurately, sensitively, tentatively and succinctly their sense of what the person is trying to communicate.
- Observational skill and openness to feedback information – watching and listening to how the client receives what has been offered. If the counsellor's

Table 7.1 The Barrett-Lennard empathy cycle model

	The person seeking help	The counsellor
Step 1	Is aware of an issue that he or she wishes to explore	Open and attentive – signalling a readiness to hear what the person has to say
Step 2	Talks about the issue or concern	Actively listens, and allows the emotional meaning of what the person is talking about to physically 'resonate' in them
Step 3	Pauses to hear what the counsellor has to say	Expresses their understanding of what the client has said, usually in the form of a summary
Step 4	Receives what the counsellor has said and conveys their sense of the extent to which the counsellor's summary was accurate and helpful	Observes the person's response to their attempt to summarize and convey understanding
Step 5	Resumes talking... the cycle continues	Resumes attentive listening... the cycle continues

response has been accurate, then there is often a visible sign of relief on the part of the client, as if he or she is saying 'yes, that's it'. If, on the other hand, the counsellor's response is not quite right, the client may look away, reply with a 'yes, but' statement, or look confused.

- Holding and keeping in mind the unfolding shared understanding that is being created – each empathic response builds on previous ones.
- Responsiveness to evidence (Step 4) around whether their empathic statement was helpful or otherwise – being able to make corrections or try again.

This cycle of empathic engagement typically occurs many times within a counselling session. On each occasion, if the counsellor is successful in capturing enough of the essence of what the person is trying to say, then the person will gradually move into a deeper and more personal exploration of the topic. If, on the other hand, the counsellor continues to get it wrong, or not quite right, the client may lose the thread of what they are talking about, may stop trying to communicate, by moving on to more superficial topics, or may resort to more vivid and forceful language (e.g. metaphors) to try to get their point across. In such a situation, a good counsellor will try to find some way to repair the situation and get the conversation back 'on track'.

The empathy cycle model not only provides a valuable set of guidelines for skills that counsellors can reflect on in supervision and practise in training, but also makes it clear why the concept of empathy is complex and hard to understand. The model suggests that there are three quite different vantage points in relation to estimating the level of empathic engagement in a counselling conversation. First, there is the counsellor's sense of how open and empathic they are being (Steps 1 and 2). Second, there is the quality of empathy exhibited in what the counsellor says to the person (Step 3) – this is what an external observer would mainly pick up on. Finally, there is the person or client's sense of whether they themselves felt that what the counsellor has said did indeed 'hit the mark' for them (Step 4).

A more detailed account of the Barrett-Lennard empathy cycle model, emphasizing collaborative aspects of this process, can be found in McLeod (1999). The following sections explore further issues that are relevant to the development of empathy skills: the nature of advanced empathy; the difference between empathy and interpretation; the co-creation of meaning; and the use of language.

Advanced empathy

Anyone who has watched videos of counselling sessions is able to differentiate between empathic responses that are luminous, and those that are mundane or muddled. From the earliest studies of empathy, by Truax and Carkhuff, there have been attempts to define the characteristics of advanced or additive empathy responses, and how they differ from 'subtractive' empathic statements (Neukrug et al. 2013). Copies of rating scales designed to measure different levels of empathic quality can readily be found on the internet. However, even though clients and observers are clearly able to differentiate between high and low levels of empathy, it has been difficult to arrive at an agreed list of attributes of advanced empathy responses. This is probably because highly effective empathic statements are very much idiosyncratic products of the moment, in almost poetically capturing a sense of what is being expressed at that instant (Bozarth 1984). Some of the qualities that tend to be associated with particularly helpful therapist empathic reflections:

- delivered in a tentative manner
- coherent – makes sense
- crystallizes or captures the heart or core of the client's experience
- identifies multiple threads of meaning
- identifies tensions and contradictions ('part of you wants… while another part wishes that…)
- mentions feeling aspects of the client's experience
- acknowledges what it means to talk about the issue ('and it's so hard to even say that word…', 'it's such a relief to be able to…', 'talking about that here, with me, is…')
- offers some kind of indication of how different aspects of the client's experience fit together ('you feel… because…', 'when… you…')
- conveys a sense of the future horizon/possibilities of the topic being explored ('… and you want to…'; 'if that was to happen, then you…')
- brings together themes from earlier points in the session, or earlier stages of therapy (Omer 1997).

By contrast, less satisfactory empathic responses are more likely to: be descriptive of facts and actions; focus on what other people did rather than on the client's experience, be muddled, hard to follow and vague; and introduce concepts or interpretations that were not part of what the client was talking about.

The difference between empathy and interpretation

In the field of psychotherapy, the concept of interpretation is used to refer to therapist statements that make sense of the client's experience from a particular theoretical perspective. In principle, this is clearly not the same as empathy, which is a concept used for therapist statements that seek to reflect the client's reality in its own terms. In practice, however, it can be hard to tell the difference between an advanced empathic statement and a well-crafted interpretation. Both are grounded in the client's experience, while offering a new way of seeing that experience. Analyses of transcripts of therapy sessions of Carl Rogers have frequently categorized his responses as interpretations. However, less gifted empathic responses and interpretations are much easier to tell apart. The former are descriptive restatements of what the client said, and the latter are obviously anchored in a theoretical stance.

Co-creation of meaning

The training literature on empathy tends to assume that empathic engagement essentially comprises an act of reflection. Typical training exercises involve practising reflecting feelings, or reflecting meaning. Critical feedback to trainees may highlight their reflection of content rather than meaning, or reflection of only some aspects of what the client said rather than the whole of it. From a collaborative perspective, meanings, feelings and experience are never merely expressed or exhibited by a person, but instead are always shaped by the context in which they occur, particularly the relationship between speaker and listener. Research carried out using micro-analysis of conversational patterns shows that meanings are always co-constructed in a subtle interplay between speaker and listener. Although the Barrett-Lennard model was not based in that research tradition, it can nevertheless offer a way of making sense of empathy as a co-creative process. Understanding that empathic engagement is a co-created process, that depends on the joint action of client and therapist, is a liberating and helpful perspective to espouse. Rather than thinking that your empathic response is either on target (i.e. nailing the client's reality) or off target, it suggests that both therapist and client are in it together. For example, the client needs to offer empathic windows of opportunity, in the form of ways of talking (e.g. vivid stories) that allow the therapist to get close to their experience. This implies that it may be necessary for the therapist to find ways of supporting the client to make such opportunities. Another implication of a co-construction perspective is that it usually takes more than a single empathic response to engage successfully with the client's experience – what is important is to be able to sustain an empathic connection over several speaking turns.

Linguistic aspects of counsellor empathy

Following a client statement about some aspect of their life experience, a counsellor will usually make an empathic response that conveys what they have heard and understood. There are various linguistic options open to a counsellor when making this kind of response:

Repeating back what the client has said using the client's own words, or using slightly different words. Using the actual words of the client may help the client to, in effect, hear themselves, which may have the effect of enabling them to stay with that word and consider what it means, or to gain more of a sense of how they come across to others. Using actual client words also minimizes the risk of counsellor misunderstanding. To be able to use the client's actual words, a counsellor may need or want to write them down as the client is speaking, which in some cases may have the effect of creating a distance between counsellor and client (e.g. by reducing eye contact or therapist awareness of client non-verbal cues). Using slightly different words provides an opportunity to explore implicit or emerging aspects of the client's experience. For example, a client may talk about being 'sad', and the counsellor may respond with a phrase such as 'profound sadness' or 'constant sadness' to convey a particular quality of the client's experience that they believe is implied in the client's general way of talking about their sadness.

Repeating back what the client has said using a direct personal response, or through proxy voicing. For example, a client may say: 'When my mother comes to stay at Christmas, it is as though I revert to being a rebellious teenager.' A direct counsellor response to such a statement might take the form of 'you revert to being a rebellious teenager when...' or 'what I am hearing is that you revert to...'. By contrast, in a proxy voice formulation the therapist would speak as if they were the client (Seedall and Butler 2006; Zemel 2016), for instance by saying 'Almost as though "I am a teenager again... you come back into my life and all I can do is to rebel against you..."'. A direct counsellor response is a kind of default way of talking that maintains the to-and-fro of the conversation. By contrast, proxy voicing has the possibility of dramatizing and highlighting the significance of a particular statement, particularly if the voicing is accompanied by an evocative tone of voice. Carl Rogers was masterful in the judicious use of proxy voicing to accomplish these types of outcomes.

Using tentativeness. Close examination of empathic reflections made by experienced therapists shows that they rarely just repeat back what the client has said, even in situations in which the content of their response is built around the exact words of the client. Typically, a therapist empathic response will include various forms of tentativeness and hedging (Gordon and Toukmanian 2002; Oddli and Rønnestad 2012; Tay 2014). For example, a client may state that 'Every time I get into a close relationship, something goes wrong – usually I back off because I can't seem to tolerate the threat of losing my own space and freedom.' A tentative response to such a statement might take the form: 'It's almost as though, maybe, getting really close to someone, really loving them maybe, is what you want but then becomes something that... is a loss, or is intolerable, and possibly also a threat...' In such a response, brief gaps and silences, and hedging phrases such as 'maybe' and 'possibly' function as opportunities for the client to disagree, or add further clarification detail. In this way, tentativeness allows and encourages new meaning to emerge, and if necessary allows the client to remain at a slight distance from a description that they may not be ready to embrace fully.

Limiting the use of distancing words. Many counsellors use empathic responses that begin with 'so' or 'it': 'So you are feeling...', 'It seems as though you are feeling...'. While these ways of talking generally make sense to a client, they may have the effect of distancing the therapist from the client, or distancing the client from their own experience. For instance, the term 'it' refers to a vague, undefined entity. Positioning the therapist as 'it' deflects from the therapist actually owning their statement as representing their personal perception. A detailed analysis of the meaning of the word 'so' in therapist empathic responses has been carried out by Hollingworth (2017). Linguistically, the word 'so' introduces or claims a logical implication between the preceding utterance (i.e. the client's statement) and what follows (the therapist's empathic response). By invoking the implicit authority of a 'so' formulation, the therapist is constraining the client's possibilities in their next speaking turn – essentially they can only either agree or disagree. Hollingworth (2017) concludes that 'so' statements are not consistent with a collaborative stance, and notes that the narrative therapy community (which strongly espouses a collaborative approach) has for several years been training therapists to eschew such formulations. It is of interest, in this context, that a study by Thompson et al. (2016) found that 'so...' responses were generally rated as more facilitative than other types of response made by psychiatrists to their patients. This seemed to be because, compared to the other – even more directive – types of question used by psychiatrists, 'so...' statements at least allowed the patient to determine whether or not their problems had been understood. In conclusion, it is likely that although occasional use of 'so' and 'it' formulations is not harmful, it is better if the majority of empathic responses are formulated in a more collaborative style, for example by hedging, making a direct statement or prefacing a response with terms such as 'I...', 'you...' or 'we...'.

Shared language: metaphor and imagery

A tangible source of evidence for the emergence of shared understanding is the development of a shared language. Over time, a therapist and client will build up a set of words and phrases that they routinely use, because they know that each of them has a similar understanding of what these words mean, and how they apply to the situations that the client is talking about. Most of the time, shared language is reflected in word choice. For example, a client who finds it hard to cope with social interaction may not be comfortable with a term such as 'anxiety' because it is too medical, and may feel that 'worry' does not capture the extent to which they have a strong bodily reaction to such events. Together with the therapist, they settle on 'agitated' as a word that they agree to use to indicate the experience of being in difficult social situations. In addition to that kind of prosaic word choice, another aspect of shared language centres on metaphors and images. A metaphor or image represents the use of vivid, sensory, evocative language that compresses multiple threads of meaning into a brief word or phrase. This kind of language can be highly significant in therapy, because a client may use a metaphor or image to communicate an emerging or implicit sense, or understanding, that they are not yet able to explain in more explicit terms. As a result, a metaphor or image provides the client and therapist with a potentially valuable point of entry into a new or expanded way of making sense of an issue. For example, the socially anxious client mentioned earlier might say that in social situations 'it's like I have crashed, like a computer – screen goes blank, cursor is stuck, frozen'. The image or metaphor of a crashed computer encapsulates multiple meanings (seeing oneself as like a machine, something is happening that is beyond personal control, helplessness, watching from the outside, etc.). It can also lead to useful conversations around such questions as how it might be possible to prevent a computer from crashing, how to get it going again when it has crashed, and so on.

There is further discussion of skills associated with the use of language and metaphor in Chapter 10.

Questions for clarification

Therapist questions are an important part of the process of working collaboratively to develop a shared understanding. A therapist may need to use closed questions to clarify points of detail ('Were you taking any medication?') and open questions to invite the client to expand or elaborate on an important aspect of their story ('I am wondering: would you be able to tell me how you decided whether or not to take medication at that stage in your life? This would help me to understand your ideas about how you make sense of your depression and what you think is helpful or unhelpful in respect of dealing with it.') Examples of this approach to using questions to augment empathy and facilitate shared understanding can be found in McCarthy et al. (2020) and Renger (2021).

Therapist use of questions can be perceived by a client as valuable. For example, questions can convey the genuine curiosity of the counsellor. Sometimes, people want to talk, but find it hard to get started, and appreciate questions that help them to open up. However, too much questioning, or the wrong type of questioning, can have the effect of closing the conversation down. The reason why questioning can be problematic in counselling is that any question constructs a relationship of control: the questioner is in control, because they are directing the attention and awareness of the other person towards coming up with an answer. Being asked a question momentarily overrides the agency and 'track' of the person answering, and forces them to think about what the questioner has asked. Even rejecting the question ('Sorry, I don't want to think about that right now') diverts the person from the ongoing flow of their thinking and feeling for the time it takes to ponder on the question and formulate the response of saying that you do not want to respond. Questioning therefore does not fit well within a way of talking that seeks to demonstrate empathic engagement. The essence of being empathic lies in actively checking out with the person that you understand what they are trying to express, in a way that encourages a deepening of the conversation.

A question such as 'Were you taking any medication?' may be heard by the client as a gentle invitation to keep talking. On the other hand, it may be heard in a more confrontational or even authoritarian manner, as: 'I am interviewing you… give me the facts…'. One of the difficulties with questioning is that there is a (usually hidden) statement behind every question. So, a question such as 'Were you taking medication?' will almost always arise from the counsellor's assumption or hypothesis that this information is significant in some way (e.g. 'I have been wondering whether some of the experiences you had around that time could be attributed to medication side effects'). Rather than using a simple question (which hides the hypothesis), it is usually better to use a more elaborate form of words that allows the counsellor's meaning and intention to be more transparent. Turning a question into a statement, or prefacing it with a clarifying statement, has the effect of: (i) emphasizing that the person seeking help is the expert on their own life, and is in control; (ii) building a collaborative relationship, by sharing aims and assumptions whenever possible; and (iii) giving the client more options for replying.

The discussion of questions in this section focuses on the specific use of questions to supplement empathy and other strategies for building a shared understanding. Questions can also be used for more actively interventionist purposes, to stimulate client reflectiveness and meaning-making. This further aspect of questioning as a counselling skill is explored in Chapter 12.

Creative methods

Most of the time in therapy, empathic engagement and shared understanding are articulated through the use of language. However, there are many situations in which it can be valuable to use creative and expressive methods to facilitate expression of experience and to represent how that experience is understood. For example, a client might realize that it was hard for them to communicate a key aspect of their experience in the course of a conversation with the therapist, and decide to bring in a poem, photograph or object from their home that conveys what they wanted to say. This might lead to a conversation around the meaning of the expressive object. Alternatively, the client and therapist might draw images or lines on a single piece of paper as they talk, and then look at the pattern that emerged. These, and many other expressive and creative techniques, are reviewed in McLeod (2019), along with suggestions for further reading on this topic. A case example of how one therapist facilitated empathic engagement with a client by inviting them to select pieces of music that were meaningful for them is reported in Duffey and Haberstroh (2013). Many counsellors develop skills in integrating arts-based activities into their practice.

Stories

Storytelling is a basic human accomplishment, acquired early in childhood. We use stories to communicate to each other the important or memorable things that happen to us. In our heads, and in our own lives, each of us lives out a story or stories, and constructs our identity and sense of self through creating a story of our life, our autobiography. Culturally, the beliefs, values and world view of a set of people are carried through narrative, in the form of myth, scripture, literature and 'news'. A story conveys information about an event that unfolds over time, involves intention and purpose, reveals the relationship between the protagonist or central figure of the story and other people, and communicates feeling and emotion.

One of the most basic ways that counselling is helpful, is that it gives the person an opportunity to tell their story. When a person experiences a stressful or difficult situation in their life, there seems to be a natural tendency to want to tell the story of these events to at least one other person. Telling the story has a number of positive effects. Organizing a set of memories, images and feelings into a story enables the person to sort out a mass of information that might have previously been whirling around in their mind. The structure of a story allows the person to put these events into a cause and effect sequence ('he said this, and then I did that') which links together action (what happened), intention (goals and plans) and emotion (what was felt). A story also usually includes an evaluative or moral dimension, which weaves in how the person stands in relation to the events that are being recounted – whether they were pleasurable, disgusting, shameful, prideful and so on. Quite often, a person will seek a counselling relationship within which to tell their story because they do not have anywhere else to tell it. The story that the person wishes to tell may be threatening or embarrassing to other people in their life, or it may be that they are isolated and do not have access to other people who are willing to listen to what they have to say. The need to tell the story can also arise in situations where the person has only been allowed to tell a 'thin' or selective version of their story, and has not had the chance to give voice to a 'thick' version that expresses more fully what they thought, felt and did. An important outcome of telling the story of what has happened is that it allows the person to make sense of something that has happened, by organizing and ordering feelings and events into some kind of sequence.

The client's stories function as the essential bedrock of client–therapist shared understanding. In a counselling situation, when a person tells a rich and vivid story of something that has happened in their life, it has the effect of allowing the counsellor to know them much better. Such a story is like a scene from a movie that takes the counsellor right inside the world of the client. The sharing of a story therefore provides the counsellor with invaluable information about the person, which allows any subsequent response to be better grounded in the reality of the person's experience. Stories told by the client gradually build up a shared point of reference for the counsellor and client.

There are several counselling skills and strategies that contribute to the process of using client storytelling to build shared understanding:

Appreciation of the value of different types of story. Shared understanding comprises the story of the client's life as a whole, stories of significant events, and how they imagine their story to develop in the future. In relation to the story of the client's life as a whole, valuable strategies include the use of a timeline (McLeod and McLeod 2020) or the idea of dividing a life into chapters (McAdams 1993). The future horizon of a client's life story can be explored by inviting them to imagine what they would like their life to look like 10 or 20 years in the future, or by using ideas and questions from the literature on the psychology of possible selves (Markus and Nurius 1986; Oyserman et al. 2002). The therapy approach developed by Lynne Angus (Angus and Greenberg 2011; Angus 2012) identifies different types of client story that provide crucial insights into the way that the person makes sense of their life:

  - *the same old story*: repetitive accounts of similar patterns of negative experience
  - *absent stories*: strong emotions not linked to a story
  - *broken stories*: narratives that are incoherent and hard to follow
  - *untold stories*: important events that are described for the first time in therapy
  - *unexpected outcome stories*: being surprised by having been able temporarily to be free from a persistent problem
  - *healing stories*: the experience of successfully overcoming a problem.

  Further categories of client story that may be emotionally significant in terms of developing a shared understanding of what life means to a client are *autobiographical narratives* (stories of specific events that the client uses to anchor their overall story of who they are and what life means to them (Singer et al. 2013)) and *early memories* (the client's earliest memory usually encapsulates feelings and relationship patterns that persist across their life as a whole (Fowler et al. 2000)).

Asking the client to give a specific example. A client may report that an issue is concerning them, but then talk about that issue in general terms, without giving the listener much of a sense of what actually happened. It may be useful in such situations to offer an invitation along the lines of: 'When you mention that you feel anxious a lot of the time, I'm wondering if it might be helpful if you could tell about a particular occasion when this happened, so that I can get a better understanding of what this issue is like for you?'

Allow the client to get to the end of the story. The end point of a story will usually take the form of a 'coda', which brings the conversation back to the present moment, such as '… and that's why I told you that I kept feeling so anxious last week'. There may often be a pause in the conversation at the end of the story – as though the teller can stop for breath, or look around, having finished something that needed to be done. This moment is highly significant, in terms of what the counsellor does next. During the telling of the story, the teller has 'held the stage', and in all likelihood the counsellor has said little. At the completion of the story, it is the counsellor's turn to say something. It is crucial to acknowledge and affirm the story before attempting any kind of discussion of what it might mean. The medical anthropologist Arthur Kleinman (1988, 2012) has written very sensitively about a process that he describes as *empathic witnessing* – one human being responding to the troubles, pain and suffering of another human being. This kind of fundamental affirmation of the experience of the teller, and of his or her courage in telling the story, can be tremendously meaningful for a person. Following the telling of a story, there is often much for the person and counsellor to reflect on: a story will often encompass many significant threads of insight into a person's life, and how he or she copes with events. A story can be viewed as an opening, or invitation into the person's subjective world.

The therapeutic significance of stories reflects the idea that core emotional and interpersonal issues with which a client struggles over the course of their life are encapsulated in a small number of vivid 'scenes'. A person's life story as a whole can be viewed as a drama – a play or movie that consists of a series of scenes in which core issues are enacted. Each of the different types of story outlined above provides insight into the different characters in the client's life, and how the patterns of interaction between them lead to endings that can be happy or sad. Empathic engagement, as discussed in earlier sections of this chapter, has predominantly been regarded in therapy theory and practice as involving reflections on specific, relatively brief, client statements. Stories function as more substantial blocks of communication that convey more complex meanings, and function as anchor points for the client's sense of who they are. A narrative perspective (McLeod 1997) suggests that it can be helpful to empathically engage with stories.

Conclusions

Listening, the capacity to use self, and empathic engagement are key skills that permeate all aspects of the counselling process. Lack of ability to use these skills – either temporarily in a particular situation, or more generally – tends to lead to poor therapy outcomes. Being an effective counsellor requires understanding what empathy is, how and why it is a necessary aspect of therapy and how to provide it. A reputation for being empathic, in everyday life situations with friends, family and work colleagues, does not necessarily translate into a capacity for empathic engagement in a counselling context. Counselling clients are a more heterogeneous group than one's social circle, they are talking about things that are more sensitive, and empathic connection needs to be established much more quickly. This chapter has focused on skills for facilitating empathic engagement in order to build a shared understanding with the client that will support a collaborative approach to addressing the client's concerns and helping them to accomplish their goals for therapy.

Learning activities

The following activities may be explored individually, and/or with a group of learning partners.

1   **Using questions**. What kinds of questioning strategies do you employ in your everyday life? Over the course of a day, make a note of the types of questions you ask. Pay particular attention to the proportion of open and closed questions, and the situations in which they are used. What are your aims or purposes in asking these questions? Can you identify statements behind these questions? To what extent are these questioning strategies suitable for a counselling role?

2   **The stories you tell about yourself**. Make a note of stories that you tell about yourself, over the course of a few days. What patterns can you identify in the way you describe yourself and other people, the way you interact with other people, and how the story ends? In what way are these patterns consistent with issues in your life that you might want to explore (or are currently exploring) with a therapist?

3   **Feeling really understood**. At the heart of therapy is the hope that someone else can accept and understand us for who we are, without judgement or analysis. The aim of this exercise is to encourage you to explore the significance, in your own life, of this type of moment. Sit quietly for a few seconds... and think about the *last time you felt really accepted and understood by another person*.

Once you have identified such an occasion, write notes about:

- what the circumstances were
- how you felt
- the consequences or effects on you of this experience of being accepted and understood.

4   What are the implications of what you have learned from this exercise, for your work as a therapist?

Further reading

A research study which has analysed the experience of being understood is: A. Bachelor, (1988) How clients perceive therapist empathy: a content analysis of 'received' empathy, *Psychotherapy*, 25(2): 227–40. You may find it interesting to look at how your own experience compares with what was reported by participants in this investigation.

5   **Empathy skills exercise**. Below are three client statements. Each statement is followed by a number of possible counsellor empathic responses. In the light of what you have read in this chapter, make notes on the helpful and unhelpful aspects of each response. You can also summarize your overall sense of the level of empathy you think is demonstrated by each response using a 5-point scale:

1=Absent/Subtractive, 2=Slight, 3=Moderate empathy, 4=High level of empathy, 5=Very High/Additive/Advanced

Statement 1:   *It's all getting too much for me. I'm not getting on well with my studies. I can't concentrate on what I'm doing and am feeling really fed up with the course. I'm thinking of dropping out, but I don't know what else to do with my life.*

Rating   Response

A [ ] I'd like to hear more about the problem if you would like to talk about it.

B [ ] So it's really a major choice point for you...?

C [ ] You sound rather gloomy and depressed at the moment about your studies, and perhaps concerned and anxious about whether you are going about your work in the right way and where you go from here.

D [ ] You know what's best for you is to...

E [ ] There are a few things here, that are bit different but connected – how you are feeling, your actual work on the course, the decision of whether to leave the course, and then also the much bigger question of what you do with your life. Does that seem to capture

what it looks like for you? There's a lot we could look at – I'm
wondering if you have a sense of what the priority might be?

F [ ] It would be a pity if you dropped out of the course as I know you
have put a great deal of time and effort into it. I'm sure everything
will turn out OK if you stick at it.

G [ ] The course is not difficult. You should try to pull yourself together.

Statement 2:   *I'm worried about my relationship with my partner. We've been*
together for two years. We never have sex together any more.
It was good at the start but now they are just not interested.
I've tried talking about it with them, but they avoid the topic.

Rating Response

A [ ] It sounds like a good sex life is important to you.

B [ ] You know, I've never understood why people make such a song
and dance about sex. It's always seemed overrated to me.

C [ ] Have you ever tried spending a bit more time in each other's company?

D [ ] I'd like to hear more about the problem if you would like to talk
about it.

E [ ] It's like you have reached an impasse?

F [ ] I can hear you expressing concern and anxiety about how you are
getting on with your partner and that it seems you're not as close
as you used to be.

G [ ] I can refer you to a sex therapist if you would find this helpful.

Statement 3:   *I'm just not getting on with my colleagues at work. I find it*
hard to live up to their expectations of me and I feel that
they've now begun to exclude me from things.

Rating Response

A [ ] From what you have told me before, your team has a reputation for
being difficult. I wouldn't worry.

B [ ] I know just what it's like. I was in exactly the same situation as you
last year. Work teams are all the same.

C [ ] That's a really difficult situation to be in – being left out. It would
be helpful for me if you could maybe just say a bit more, to let me
get more of a sense of what is happening – would that be OK?

D [ ] What I'm hearing is that there are several bits to this. One is how
you are feeling about being excluded – maybe hurt, or angry even?
Another is how you make sense of why this has happened –
something around meeting expectations? I'd like to know more
about how you understand that and how it might have happened.
Then, also it's as though you are asking yourself, or me: 'is there
anything I can do to change this pattern?'

E [ ] You are still new and I'm sure that things will improve in time.
F [ ] It seems like you are concerned about how you are relating to your
         colleagues and that is causing you a lot of anxiety at present.
G [ ] I wonder why you are having this problem.

It can be helpful to work though this exercise on your own, then share and
discuss your analysis and ratings with learning partners. It can be interesting to formulate other potential responses to these client statements, that
might be even more empathic, and see what the group makes of them.
A further activity that is worth trying is to read aloud each client statement
and counsellor response, or to have different people take each role. Reading aloud makes it possible to convey more of the emotional meaning of
each statement. Also, different readers are likely to perform statements in
slightly different ways. A final possibility is to use these statements as
starting points for more extended client–therapist imagined interaction –
what might the client say or do next, and how might the counsellor respond
to that, etc.?

Building a collaborative relationship

Introduction

Problems in living that lead people to seek counselling can usually be resolved in other ways. For example, if a person is experiencing work stress and over-load, they can sit down with a piece of paper and make a plan of action, take up yoga and meditation as a means of relaxation or read a self-help manual. Each of these methods of stress management can be effective. The distinctive feature of counselling, in comparison with these other coping or change strategies, is that counselling primarily operates through the formation of a *relationship*. But what does this mean? What kind of relationship can exist between a person and their counsellor? And how and why does this relationship necessarily have a positive impact? After all, if we look at our lives, we can all identify relationships that are at times destructive or limiting, and may even have difficulty in identifying relationships that have unequivocally been good for us. What is it about a counselling relationship that is distinctive?

At one level, the relationship in counselling is straightforward – it is someone to talk to. If you need to talk something through, then it is essential to have someone who will listen. Beyond this, the relationship in counselling is a relationship with a person who stands outside of the problem, who is independent of one's family, friendship network or work group, and who can respond to the problem in a fresh and unbiased fashion. There is also a deeper meaning to the idea of a relationship. A relationship implies an encounter with an *other*, a person who is separate from oneself. At some level, the challenge of making contact with this *other* evokes a long list of questions that a person may have about how they connect with other people in general. For example: Can another person be trustworthy? Can I be understood (do I make sense or am I crazy?) and accepted? Can I be really honest with another person? Can I allow someone else to care for me? A great deal of what happens in counselling always comes back to questions around 'Who am I and how do I relate to other people?' In talking about these questions, a person expresses their subjectivity (this is who I am) in relation to the 'you' or 'other' represented by the counsellor. In turn, the counsellor is trying to find a way to work together ('How can *we* tackle this…?'). This core issue, of aloneness and separateness in life, runs through all counselling conversations, sometimes in the background, at other times up front.

This chapter looks at how to build a facilitative therapy relationship by exploring two key competencies: making sense of the complex nature of the therapy relationship, and developing skills around working collaboratively with clients.

Making sense of the therapy relationship

It is not possible to directly observe a therapy relationship. In terms of offering counselling to a client, one's moment-by-moment attention is taken up with listening, formulating a response, taking account of how much time is left and other practical matters. The relationship represents a more abstract, higher-order pattern that comprises all of these observable actions. In order to be able to think relationally about therapy, it is necessary to piece together one's own mental representation or map of relational processes and concepts. It is also important to develop a repertoire of strategies for actively building, maintaining, deepening and repairing the therapy relationship (Råbu et al. 2011; Vandenberghe et al. 2018).

Understanding how and why the quality of the client–therapist relationship is important

Many research studies, on a wide range of client groups, therapy approaches and presenting issues, have found that the quality of the therapist–client relationship that has been established by around the third session is the largest single factor that predicts the eventual outcome of therapy (i.e. whether the client reports that their problems and symptoms have significantly reduced). Different therapy approaches (e.g. psychodynamic, cognitive-behavioural therapy (CBT), person-centred) have generated alternative theoretical models of the therapy relationship. Further information about this body of theory and research, along with suggestions for further reading, can be found in McLeod (2019). Taken as a whole, the therapy literature identifies many ways in which the client–therapist relationship operates to facilitate client learning and growth, and the accomplishment of their goals for therapy:

- Trust and belief in the therapist makes it possible for the client to face up to aspects of their life that they have been avoiding – for example, someone who has never talked about awful experiences from their childhood may do so for the first time because they believe that their counsellor is a safe and reliable person for them.

- Therapy skills, interventions and activities do not function in the same way for every client, and need to be adapted and modified in response to the client's preferences and life experience – the therapist needs to know the client well enough and have a sufficient degree of rapport and connection, to do this successfully.

- The therapist is a model of how to function in a relationship in a caring and effective manner – for example, a client might watch the intensity of how their therapist listens, or how they maintain certain boundaries, and begin to apply this learning in their own life.

- The therapist functions as a representative of the wider society – when the therapist accepts and affirms the value of the client as a person, or refuses to judge them for something they have done, it can strengthen the client's capacity for active citizenship and creative participation in society as a whole. The therapist functions as an empathic witness to the client's suffering.

- Many clients are afraid that their problems in living are an indication that there is something fundamentally wrong and different about them – being understood by someone who is knowledgeable, and in whom you can trust, can represent a vital step in the direction of self-acceptance and healing.

- There will inevitably be parallels between the life of the client and that of the therapist – the latter may be able to draw on personal examples in ways that make certain learning points particularly meaningful for the client.

- Destructive and self-defeating relationship patterns from a person's life are played out within the client–therapist relationship, but with a different result – the therapist is able to help the client to reflect on what they are doing, and then to begin to create new and different ways of relating. For example, a client who has grown up to expect others to ignore their wants and needs may move in therapy from a position of being very guarded in what they say to their therapist, to learning to be more open, and then to implementing this new relationship style in their life outside the therapy room (see, for example, Sandberg et al. 2017).

A therapist needs to be able to be aware of, and able to work with, each of these relationship dimensions, because they are all present to a greater or lesser extent in every case. However, these aspects of a therapy relationship vary in salience in different situations. For example, short-term counselling with a client who presents with a clear-cut goals agenda may only need a relationship in which the client's therapist is responsive enough to adapt techniques to the client's preferences. By contrast, in long-term therapy with a client who has a lifetime history of troubled relationships the client–therapist relationship is likely to feature much more as a central vehicle for learning.

Therapist relational qualities

There are some counsellor attributes, qualities and values that clients generally regard as necessary for the establishment of their relationship with a therapist. A counsellor needs to be someone who is unequivocally on the side of the person, whose aim and purpose is to be helpful. By contrast, a counsellor is not someone who has any intention of using, abusing, harming or exploiting the person who comes for help. The counsellor has no axe to grind, no stake in whether the person decides to do one thing, or the opposite. The counsellor is a person who can be *trusted*.

An important facet of trust is concerned with how a counsellor responds to a person on a moment-by-moment basis. If there are too many discrepancies between what the counsellor says and how they appear, the person on the receiving end will quickly begin to wonder what is going on. For example, if someone who is gay, lesbian or bisexual is told by a counsellor that their sexual orientation is something to be valued and celebrated, but the counsellor looks uncomfortable when they say it, then the person may feel that the counsellor may not be allowing themselves to be totally honest and transparent. In such a situation, the person seeking counselling would be likely to become very cautious about talking about their sexuality or lifestyle to this particular counsellor. Carl Rogers (1961) used the term *congruence* to describe this aspect of the counselling relationship, as a means of drawing attention to the importance for a counsellor of maintaining consistency between what they subjectively thought or felt, and what they said to their clients. Research carried out by Rogers and his colleagues showed that counsellor *incongruence*, falseness or inauthenticity undermined the counselling process. People do not want to talk about their personal issues to someone who is pretending to listen, or pretending to accept their experience, or who seems to be just playing a professional role.

For a counsellor, entering a relationship of trust can represent a challenge on two fronts. It is hard for a person to be trusted if they do not feel worthy of trust.

From the counsellor's side, being willing to be available to another person in a counselling role implies believing in one's own capacity to deserve trust. Acceptance of this can be difficult for some counsellors, for example if they struggle to overcome their own tendency to harsh self-criticism. At the same time, it is important for a counsellor to recognize that, most of the time, the people who come to them for help will not trust them unconditionally, and will continue to test them out as a means of guarding against betrayal or disappointment. The issues that people bring to counselling are often topics or events that are hard for them to talk about, because of guilt, shame or embarrassment: it may require a high level of trust before the person feels safe enough to talk openly about what really matters.

A further key counsellor quality that is a vital part of the therapy relationship is *caring*. In deciding to enter a counselling relationship, a person is looking for someone who will care about them. The concept of care has been largely ignored or devalued in the counselling literature, probably because it might be taken to imply a lack of professional expertise and detachment. This is a pity, because, as the philosopher Heidegger has pointed out, caring represents a fundamental aspect of involvement in the world: the experience of caring discloses what is important and has meaning for us. In a counselling relationship, caring can be expressed by small acts of kindness, remembering information about the person's life, thinking about the person when they are not there, proceeding gently and slowly, and with patience – checking things out, and celebrating the person's achievements.

Skills for developing a collaborative relationship

The preceding sections in this chapter have outlined the multifaceted nature of the client–therapist relationship, and the extent to which it is grounded in the personal qualities of the therapist and how these are received by the client. The relationship pervades all aspects of the experience and process of counselling. Everything that the client or therapist says or does can be understood from a relational perspective. An important consequence of this complexity is that a counsellor can be overwhelmed and paralysed by the immensity of the potential relationship agenda and landscape with which they are confronted. As a means of coping with this issue, it is valuable for a counsellor to be able to access some kind of relatively simple framework (i.e. theory or model) for guiding their thinking about relational aspects of practice.

The early development of therapy was associated with two alternative models of the therapy relationship. One model, arising from the work of Freud and other psychoanalytic and psychodynamic theorists, was based on the idea that the client unconsciously projects their dysfunctional relationship patterns and feelings, that have originated in their childhood, onto their therapist. This is described as transference. In turn, this triggers feelings and relationship patterns in the therapist (countertransference). The aim of therapy is to enable the client to gain insight into these processes so that they can develop more satisfying relationships in their everyday lives.

A second highly influential model of the therapy relationship was developed by Carl Rogers. This perspective suggested that if the therapist was able to respond to the client in ways that were accepting, empathic and genuine, the client would gradually become more able to accept aspects of their own self, and experience, that they had previously suppressed.

Both of these relationship perspectives have been refined over the years, and remain cornerstones of practice for many therapists. However, neither of them gives any significant weight to the active participation of the client in the relationship. The *working alliance* model developed by the American psychotherapist Ed Bordin represents a perspective on the therapy relationship that fills that gap. Bordin (1979) suggested that there are three main elements of a therapy relationship: client–therapist agreement over the *goals* of therapy, client–therapist agreement over the *tasks* to be undertaken to fulfil these goals, and a client–therapist emotional *bond*. For the last 40 years, this model has functioned as a shared point of contact between therapists of all backgrounds and theoretical orientations. In addition, a massive amount of research has shown that higher levels of these elements (particularly as perceived by the client) make a major contribution to therapy outcomes.

In emphasizing agreement between client and therapist, backed up by trust and belief in each other, the alliance model is essentially a theory of collaboration. A major theme in contemporary research and training in psychotherapy has centred on the question of developing an understanding of what therapists can do to build a collaborative relationship, and what such a relationship looks like from the point of view of the client. Studies that provide useful entry points into how this topic has been investigated include Bedi et al. (2005), Bedi and Duff (2014), Lavik et al. (2018) and Owen et al. (2013). This research has shown that a collaborative relationship requires rapport-building responses such as warmth, posture, respectful listening, etc. but – crucially – it also depends on the experience of successfully working together (e.g. actively agreeing goals and tasks, developing a shared understanding, giving and receiving feedback). This is similar to any area of life – if you meet someone new, you create a friendship through doing enjoyable and meaningful things together.

A valuable way of thinking about what can happen as a result of collaboration is the list of five good things that characterize satisfying relationships, developed in relational-cultural therapy (Miller 1992; Jordan 2017): zest, clarity, sense of worth, productivity and a desire for more connection.

The following sections focus on counselling skills for building a collaborative relationship. The process of collaboration involves working together as partners and allies, drawing on what each participant brings to the relationship. Effective collaboration is a matter of *putting difference to work*. Effective counsellors need to develop skills in building, and then tending and maintaining, collaborative relationships with individuals and families with different personalities, values and ideas about what will be helpful for them, and from different cultural backgrounds. A collaborative mode of working needs to be established in the first session. Essential skills for working collaboratively include: shared decision-making, metacommunication, immediacy, feedback and restoring alignment.

Shared decision-making

In any situation that involves people collaborating together, it is necessary to make shared decisions about the aims of the project, how tasks will be allocated, deadlines and so on. Similarly, client–therapist collaboration in therapy requires shared decision-making. In practice, what this involves is inviting the client to consider options around central aspects of the process of therapy, such as:

- what the client wants to achieve through therapy (goals)
- what kinds of therapeutic activity (tasks and methods) might contribute to achieving these goals
- how to make sense of the client's problems (shared understanding)
- arrangements for therapy (e.g. number, length and timing of sessions, location, whether family members will participate, follow-up sessions, etc.)
- when therapy will end, and how that ending might be conducted.

In addition, there are likely to be many recurring micro-decisions that need to be made, around such questions as the focus for a particular session and allocation of time within a session. In any situation, shared decision-making needs to be based on a body of relevant knowledge and information. In therapy, this body of knowledge comprises the shared understanding that has been built up by client and counsellor (see Chapter 7). Decision-making conversations both draw on, and contribute to, client–therapist shared understanding.

At the present time, there is almost no literature at all, or training, in shared decision-making in counselling and psychotherapy. However, there has been substantial attention to this topic in the field of healthcare (Gulbrandsen et al. 2016; Keij et al. 2021; Stiggelbout et al. 2015). In that context, there can often be several alternative treatments that are broadly equivalent in effectiveness (e.g. certain types of back pain may be helped by exercise, physiotherapy, yoga, medication, physiotherapy, surgery, etc). Shared decision-making therefore comprises a consultation with a doctor or nurse in advance of starting actual treatment, to allow the patient to express their preferences and ask questions. The evidence from healthcare is that patients are more likely to adhere to a treatment plan if it has been based on a shared decision-making process. Models of shared decision-making, training programmes for health professionals and decision aids for patients have been developed.

There are important areas of similarity between shared decision-making in medicine and in psychotherapy, for example around the importance of equalization of power and control, providing relevant information to service users in a form that makes sense to them, and allowing enough time for a genuine dialogue to take place. However, there are also significant differences. For example, most medical interventions do not involve the kind of ongoing process of decision-making that occurs in psychotherapy. Medical treatment options are usually easier to explain than psychotherapy options. Also, the client's ability or willingness to make decisions may be an actual focus for psychotherapeutic work, in a way that is unlikely to occur in other healthcare settings.

One study of shared decision-making in psychotherapy, by Gibson et al. (2020), found that although clients varied in the degree to which they actively engaged with shared decision-making, and how daunting they found it, most of them valued the invitation to take part in this kind of process, and generally found it helpful. Clients reported that it was essential for their therapist to provide a structure for decision-making conversations, and to give enough time to it.

Developing skills in facilitating shared decision-making requires various types of preparatory work. It is necessary to be clear in one's own mind about the degree of flexibility that can be offered. For example, if the administrative system in a clinic can only handle one-hour sessions, there is little point in discussing client preferences around session length. It is also necessary to assemble decision aids, such as information sheets, preference rating forms and agreement contracts. Finally, it is important to be able to rehearse how shared decision-making conversations might be initiated and facilitated, and to have opportunities to learn from more experienced colleagues about how they handle this aspect of therapy.

Metacommunication

Shared decision-making primarily refers to blocks of time during sessions (or during the intake procedure before the start of therapy) that address pivotal choice-points in therapy. Such episodes can be seen almost as rituals in which an underlying principle of 'we are working together' is enacted. A further way of enacting a commitment to collaboration is to initiate micro-choice points during the flow of a session, to check whether what the client and therapist are doing at that moment is consistent with what has previously been agreed. This skill – *metacommunication* – involves reflecting on the process of therapy and the state of the therapy relationship. A capacity to engage in metacommunication is a crucial aspect of collaborative working.

The nature of metacommunication can be illustrated by considering the usual shape and content of a conversation between a person and their counsellor. Most of the time in a counselling situation, both the person seeking help and the counsellor talk about the person's problem. For example, a woman talking about her relationship with her teenage daughter might say: 'We just argue all the time. There doesn't seem to be anything we can do together that doesn't end up in a battle.' The counsellor might reply by saying: 'That sounds really frustrating… it's as though there is a real barrier between you...' And the person seeking help might then go on to say more about other aspects of this issue. In this example, the focus of the conversation is on the problem that has been identified by the person. This kind of conversation happens frequently in counselling encounters – the counsellor acts as a kind of sounding board, and reflects back to the person the main threads of what he or she has been exploring, in a way that helps him or her to expand on the issue and gain some perspective on it.

In addition to this kind of reflective response, it can be useful for a counsellor to build into their conversational repertoire the careful and consistent use of a further way of responding to the person – using metacommunication to check out what is happening at that moment. Checking out basically involves pausing in the flow of the conversation to test out assumptions about what is happening, or to inquire about the assumptions or the experience at that moment of the person who is seeking help. Rennie (1998) described this activity as *talking about the process of talking*. There are many different ways in which checking out or metacommunication can be helpful in a counselling session. Some of the most widely used forms of checking out are listed below, along with examples of how they might be used to enhance the interaction around 'my teenage daughter and I argue all the time' that was introduced above.

Example: A woman talking about her relationship with her teenage daughter states that 'We just argue all the time. There doesn't seem to be anything we can do together that doesn't end up in a battle.' Her counsellor, a worker in a family support centre, responds using these words: 'That sounds really frustrating... it's as though there is a real barrier between you...' The counsellor's response is a fairly standard empathic reflection, that picks up on the main feeling that she senses (the client's frustration) and seeks to find an image to capture the key relationship difficulty that is causing the problem (described by the counsellor as a 'barrier'). However, there are a number of ways in which the counsellor might choose to employ metacommunication to use her response to the client as an opportunity to reinforce the collaborative nature of their relationship. There are at least four metacommunicative strategies that the counsellor could use at this moment:

1 *Checking out the person's reaction to what the counsellor has just said.* The counsellor might wonder whether she had accurately understood the meaning for the person of the situation that was being described, and could check this out by saying: 'That sounds really frustrating... it's as though there is a real barrier between you... Although, as I hear myself saying that, I'm not sure whether I've got it quite right. I'm aware that there's a lot about your situation that I don't know about... Is frustration the right term, or would you use another word... and maybe "barrier" is too strong...?'

2 *The counsellor being open about her strategies and intentions at that point.* The counsellor may be mindful of the fact that, although the person has mentioned a number of issues that are bothering her, she has a gut feeling

that the situation with her daughter is probably the most important, or urgent, of these. This could be expressed by saying: 'I realize that in the last couple of minutes you've told me about lots of things that are hard for you at the moment. But it's what you said about your daughter that really struck home for me, because it seemed very painful for you, and I have a sense that it might be the link between all these other things you mentioned. What's happening with your daughter sounds really frustrating... it's as though there is a real barrier between you... My sense is that it might be useful to stay with this for a bit. What do you think? Does that feel right for you?'

3 *Inviting the client to focus on her own plans, strategies and assumptions.* The counsellor may not be sure about the agenda or goals of the person at this point in the conversation, so might say: 'The situation with your daughter sounds really frustrating... it's as though there is a real barrier between you... But I'm not sure whether that's the thing you want to look at more closely now. Is it? Or is there something else that's more pressing?'

4 *Checking out her assumptions about what the person might be thinking or intending.* Sometimes, a counsellor may come up with a theory, or a guess, about what might lie behind the thoughts or feelings that the person may be experiencing, but without having any real evidence to indicate whether these ideas are valid or not. Often, this kind of counsellor intuition can be sensitive and accurate, and provide a good guide for moving forward. On some occasions, however, the counsellor may have misunderstood the person. It is therefore important to check out any such hunches or theories. In this case, the counsellor may have a sense that the person blames herself in relation to her problem with her daughter. One way of acknowledging this might be to say: 'That sounds really frustrating... it's as though there is a real barrier between you... As you were speaking about your daughter, I just had a strong feeling that you were blaming yourself for what was happening. Have I got that right, or is it something else?' The person might reply that 'I wouldn't call it blaming myself, it's more that I just don't feel adequate – I don't know what to do.' In this instance, the process of checking out has allowed the counsellor to see that her assumption was only partially correct: the person was being self-critical, but not to the extent of actually *blaming* herself.

Each of these metacommunicative strategies has the effect of standing aside from the immediate content of what is being said, to allow a few moments of sharing, discussion and reflection around aspects of the relationship between the counsellor and the person seeking help. In effect, these metacommunicative moves are offering openings to a question that could be summarized as: Are we on the same wavelength – do we each understand and agree with what the other is trying to achieve right now? These moves are also consistently emphasizing the affirming and empowering stance of the counsellor in relation to the person. In effect, they are conveying ideas such as 'you are in charge', 'I believe that you are the person who knows what is helpful for you', 'I can only help you if you let me know if what I am doing is working for you'.

Metacommunication can be particularly important at points in counselling where the topic being talked about shifts in some way. Examples include:

1 A student is talking to their counsellor around their dilemmas about course options, but then suddenly shifts to talking about a recent argument with their flatmate. The counsellor might say: 'I noticed that you started off talking about your module choices, and then switched to telling me about that situation with Frankie at the weekend. I was wondering whether the Frankie thing was more of a priority right at the moment, and you wanted to come back to the course assignment stuff later. Or are the two situations connected in some way…?'

2 A student is talking to their counsellor around their dilemmas about course options, but then conveys in some way that there is an emotional or personal dimension to the issue that they might wish to explore. It can be useful to check out with the person whether he or she would at that moment like to explore their feelings in more depth (i.e. shift the topic): '… you seemed to me to have a lot of feelings around as you were talking… there seemed to be tears in your eyes… I was wondering if you wanted to take a few minutes with me to look at how these feelings might be a factor in the choices you need to make…?'

Metacommunication is also an essential strategy in situations where the relationship between a person and a counsellor may have broken down, or reached a point of impasse – skills and strategies for addressing this kind of scenario are explored in a later section of the present chapter.

Metacommunication conveys to the client that they have choices, and that these choices are important to the counsellor and worthy of being taken seriously. It implies that the counsellor is doing his or her best to be sensitive and responsive to what the person needs at that moment, and might therefore be a person who can be trusted in the future. It suggests that the counsellor is someone who is genuinely curious and interested in the person, and in the totality of what the person might be thinking and feeling – the counsellor is not pursuing a fixed pathway or agenda. Metacommunication also introduces slight pauses in the conversation, moments in which the person might engage in a bit of reflection around what the problem means to them ('Is this about blaming myself?'), or what they can do to change ('Am I willing to look closely at this issue right now?'). It also opens up an awareness that it may be OK to be wrong about some things (e.g. if it emerges that the counsellor has misunderstood the client), and that there are ways of surviving being wrong – a particularly helpful insight for people whose lives may be dominated by perfectionism.

At a deeper philosophical level, metacommunication is a good way of expressing some of the core values of counselling. Rather than viewing the counsellor and client as separate entities, the process of checking out suggests a sense of two people being in a relationship with each other, and requiring to take account of each other's position in order to work effectively together. The idea of being a 'relational self' rather than an isolated, completely separate 'autonomous self' can be helpful to people who have difficulty in getting and giving support, and this simple conversational strategy can represent a useful and unthreatening way of introducing the possibility of relatedness into someone's awareness. The use of metacommunication emphasizes the worth of the person – his or her intentions, preferences and experience are being taken seriously. Useful sources for understanding the concept of metacommunication include McGrath (2013), Papayianni and Cooper (2018) and Rennie (1998).

Immediacy

Metacommunication is part of a cluster of skills that function in a broadly similar manner. Metacommunication refers to an invitation to reflect on the meaning of what is happening at a particular moment in therapy, for example in terms of the intentions and purposes of the client or therapist. It has a particular focus on supporting collaboration, monitoring the alignment of client and therapist and opening up opportunities for realignment and negotiation, as well as functioning to invite the client to engage in reflection, and as an act of affirmation of the client as someone whose perceptions and intentions are valuable. Immediacy and impact disclosure are important skills that overlap with metacommunication:

- *Immediacy* (Hill et al. 2018) – any comment (usually by the therapist, but occasionally also by a client) on what is happening at that moment in therapy. Example: 'You seem to have become more energized when you started to talk about that issue.'
- *Impact disclosure* (Kivlighan Jr. 2014) – the therapist specifically reporting on how they reacted to something the client has said or done. Example: in a discussion of the impending ending of therapy, a client mentions that they will be glad when it is finished, and the therapist replies by saying 'I felt a little hurt to hear you say that – as if it did not matter to you how long we have been working together.'

Immediacy and impact disclosure represent ways of bringing here-and-now experience into the therapy conversation by drawing attention to them. These skills function to highlight moments of connection between client and therapist, which then makes it possible to look at the meaning of these relational events.

A useful aspect of the concept of immediacy, in relation to developing counselling skills, is that there exists a substantial amount of research into this process, both in psychotherapy (Hill et al. 2018) and other healthcare contexts (Ellis et al. 2016). This research has been used to inform training in immediacy skills (Spangler et al. 2014). A further skill that also overlaps with metacommunication – transference interpretation – is discussed in Chapter 9.

Feedback

People who work collaboratively – in any context – need to be open to feedback from each other, to be able to know whether what they are doing is in accordance with what their collaboration partner(s) think they should be doing. Feedback is also necessary as a way of maintaining energy and motivation, by acknowledging and celebrating when good work has been done.

Until recently, the question of how client–therapist feedback processes operate in counselling and psychotherapy had not been the focus of much theory or research. This absence reflects the degree to which mainstream theory and practice in psychotherapy has not been grounded in a collaborative stance. Useful sources for developing an appreciation of contemporary research-based evidence on feedback in therapy include Börjesson and Boström (2020), Brattland et al. (2018), Daniel and McLeod (2006), Kolmes and Taube (2019), Lambert et al. (2018), Mackrill and Sørensen (2020), Moltu et al. (2018), Prescott et al. (2017) and Solstad et al. (2019, 2020, 2021).

It is useful to think about two contrasting and complementary types of client feedback to therapists. First, there are situations where feedback occurs in the ordinary conversational flow of therapy:

- the therapist observes the client's behaving
- the therapist observes their own reactions to the client
- the therapist initiates a progress review discussion
- the client says something to the therapist, on their own initiative.

Second, an increasing proportion of therapists also make use of formal feedback procedures, typically involving the client completing a questionnaire. Many different types of questionnaire have been applied for this purpose.

There are some general processes that occur in all of these forms of feedback. The therapist needs to be open to whatever it is the client has to offer, provide sufficient time to explore their suggestions, and then agree on any changes in their relationship or way of working together that need to be made. All this can be quite difficult and threatening for the therapist, who will generally see themselves as well-intentioned and want to be liked. In addition, at least some of the time, client feedback can be quite personally challenging. From the perspective of the client, it can be hard to be honest, because of a fear that the therapist may take offence or may even punish them in some way (e.g. labelling them as having some kind of disorder). Establishing metacommunication as a routine aspect of the way that a client and therapist work together may make it easier for a constructive feedback process to take place, because multiple micro-opportunities for feedback are being opened up and a culture of feedback is gradually built up.

It is important for any counsellor who seeks to work collaboratively with their clients to work out their position and strategy around eliciting and responding to client feedback, and then rehearse and practise relevant skills. At the present time, there are no published training procedures in this area that we are aware of. However, the general principles of feedback in training contexts, discussed in Chapter 4, are relevant. Finally, from a collaborative perspective, one might imagine that the provision of therapist feedback to the client might also be valuable. This is something that is rarely explicitly discussed in the therapy literature.

Acknowledging difference

It is inevitable that a counsellor and client will be different from each other in respect of one or more dimensions of social identity and life experience. Skills for constructively acknowledging and harnessing difference play an important part in developing a collaborative therapeutic relationship. Effective collaboration is based on putting difference to work, by creating a space in which the contrasting knowledge and experience of client and therapist can be brought together. By contrast, unacknowledged or avoided difference can undermine the client's trust in the therapist. Key skills in this area involve mentioning, or broaching, the issue of difference early in therapy, then routinely monitoring and checking out whether misunderstandings have occurred due to differences in world view and life experience. It is also important to highlight moments in therapy when client–therapist difference may have been helpful.

An example of the kind of opening statement that might be used is: 'Something that I'd like us to keep in mind is that – obviously – we are different people, who have had different life experiences and will see things in slightly different ways. I think that this can be really useful in therapy, because it allows you to share ideas and suggestions that might never occur to me, and vice versa. But it can also lead to misunderstandings. For example, we are both white, and grew up in similar circumstances, as far as I can tell, in respect of our social class and education. So there are a lot of important similarities between us. But you are a woman and I am a man. And we have worked in quite different professions. For example, as a manager you understand what it is like to have other people depend on you for direction – something that I have never really had to do in any job I have had. These experiences may make us see some things in quite different ways. There are probably other differences as well, that are not clear yet. If it's OK with you, I would like it if we could agree to mention it, straight away, if either of us is aware of how our differences might either be useful in terms of alternative ways of thinking about an issue, or might be behind some kind of misunderstanding. How does that sound?'

This statement should be taken as just one possible approach to broaching difference – it is important to work out a way of doing this that fits your approach as a counsellor, and that will make sense to your client. The statement includes a fairly lengthy explanation of what the counsellor is wanting to achieve, and incorporates an example of a possible area where a difference in perspective might arise. It is useful to offer one or two candidate examples, as a way of helping the client to understand what is being suggested. In the absence of concrete examples, the topic of being open about difference can seem mystifying.

The skill of broaching difference was initially developed in the field of multicultural counselling, as a means of addressing issues around cultural difference and racism. The studies that have been carried out on broaching in situations where the client and therapist come from different cultural or ethnic backgrounds have generally found that counsellors feel uncomfortable and anxious around using this skill (Day-Vines et al. 2018, 2020, 2021; Jones and Welfare 2017; King and Borders 2019; King 2021). For example, they worry that broaching may cut across the flow of whatever it is the client needs and wants to talk about at that moment. It may also be scary for a therapist to create a situation in which the client might tell them that they come across as prejudiced or ignorant. However, these studies were not carried out with therapists who were already using a collaborative approach. From the perspective of a collaborative model of therapy, broaching complements and sits alongside other skills that promote a client–therapist collaborative stance, such as metacommunication (pausing the ongoing flow of counselling to check out or clarify whether what is happening is helpful) and use of feedback (Sahu et al. 2021).

Although the skill of acknowledging difference builds on the use of broaching in multicultural counselling, it represents a more general relationship-building strategy that is used with all clients. From the perspective of the counsellor, when this skill is routinely deployed with all clients, it quickly becomes a comfortable and positive aspect of the therapy process.

Restoring alignment

It is not realistic to expect the counselling relationship to proceed smoothly at all times – there will inevitably be points at which a person feels that they are not getting what they need from the counsellor, or the counsellor misunderstands them. At these moments of misalignment, it is valuable for the counsellor to be able to 'hit the pause button', and engage in metacommunication that invites reflection from both participants around what has been happening. It is particularly important for the counsellor to be willing and able to acknowledge his or her role in the difficulties that have arisen – a counsellor who insists on attributing the sole cause of any problems to inadequacies on the part of the person or client is not really demonstrating a collaborative style of working, and may come across as blaming and persecutory.

A useful way of thinking about client–therapist misalignment is to see it as a rupture in the working alliance. Over the past 30 years, a substantial international programme of research around the rupture-repair cycle, led by Jeremy Safran, Christopher Muran and Catherine Eubanks, has yielded important practical insights into how this type of situation can be handled effectively (Safran 1993; Safran and Muran 2000; Muran and Eubanks 2020; Eubanks et al. 2021; Muran et al. 2021). If the bond between client and therapist is threatened or broken, the client may be reluctant to engage with the process of change, or may even quit therapy. On the other hand, successfully repairing a rupture can strengthen the bond, as well as leading to valuable learning for the client about how to deal with difficult relationships in everyday life.

An alliance rupture has its origins in the client's belief that their therapist has misunderstood them, has not listened well enough, has made unhelpful suggestions or has behaved in a manner that is insensitive, aggressive or hurtful. This leads to the client either withdrawing from the therapist, or becoming angry with them. The rupture-repair model suggests that an optimal therapist response consists of the following sequence of therapist actions:

- Therapist is aware that the ongoing flow or process of therapy has become stuck. This will usually involve acknowledgement of, and reflection on, feelings that are arising in the session, their own feelings such as anxiety, sadness or boredom.

- Therapist invites the client to look together at what is happening, using the skill of metacommunication in the form of statements such as 'Let's look at what's happening between us right now' or 'I'm aware that something is not quite right in our work together... I wonder if you're feeling something similar...?'

- Each participant talks about what they have been feeling, and their contribution to the impasse between them. It is crucial that the therapist owns their own part in what has happened.

- Agreement around changes to how they work together.

- Linking: exploring implications for the client in respect of other relationships in their life.

This kind of repair process is typically quite hard for therapists to implement (Kline et al. 2019). To begin with, many ruptures are subtle, or are hidden by clients who are themselves reluctant to stand up for their own rights. This means that, quite often, it is difficult for a therapist to know whether a rupture may have occurred at all. A further difficulty arises from the fact that, on the whole, therapists are individuals who see themselves as empathic, supportive and helpful, and are uncomfortable with conflict or others becoming angry with them. As a result, there may be a tendency for the therapist to avoid acknowledging that a rupture has occurred, or avoid talking about it in detail. In addition, the theoretical model espoused by the therapist may lead them to attribute relationship difficulties to the client's resistance, dysfunctional patterns or lack of motivation. Finally, the therapist may want to protect or defend themselves against perceived attack, or possibly even push back in the form of challenging or disparaging the client.

The successful resolution of a rupture can be regarded as an example of collaboration under pressure, which then reinforces the capacity for effective collaboration in the future. Failure to address relationship ruptures can lead to a state of impasse and deadlock between client and therapist, which can result in the client dropping out (Werbert et al. 2020).

Chang et al. (2021) have suggested that therapy relationships reflect patterns of power and privilege that exist in the broader cultural context in which therapy takes place, and that many ruptures can be understood as coming from microaggression and discounting arising from underlying racist, classist, sexist, ableist (and other) biases of the therapist. This means that the meaning of a rupture may encompass not only psychological and interpersonal processes (e.g. how willing each person is to be honest about what they are feeling, how adequately they have discussed how to pursue a particular therapeutic task, etc.) but also the exploration of their positions in society, and their social identities. Chang et al. (2021) argue that exploring such issues in the therapy room has the potential to be extremely valuable for clients, but is only possible if the therapist has sufficiently developed their own understanding of oppression. What makes this additional cultural-relational level of processing of rupture events helpful, is the opportunity to develop compassion and mutual acceptance around aspects of life, and enduring hurts, that are seldom talked about.

Beyond collaboration

The emphasis in this chapter has been on skills for building a collaborative relationship that functions as a scaffolding that helps the client move in the direction of accomplishing their therapeutic goals and constructing a more satisfying life. These skills can be seen as ways of expressing and channelling therapist qualities such as trustworthiness and genuineness. These skills and qualities are always important in therapy. However, there exists another level of relatedness that can emerge in therapy, in which the relationship with the therapist has a transformational effect. This quality of relationship is reflected in situations where the client develops an internal representation of their therapist that they access as a means of support in times of trouble (Knox, S. et al. 1999; Myers and White 2010), intense relational depth with their therapist (Knox, R. et al. 2013) or moments of shared humanity (Skatvedt 2017; Topor et al. 2018). These forms of relational experience in therapy are not necessary for therapy to be beneficial. Instead, they can be seen as a kind of unexpected bonus. There is no evidence that such episodes can be facilitated by specific skills or techniques – their occurrence seems to arise from some combination of an underlying affinity or chemistry between client and therapist, along with a willingness and courage to take advantage of potential openings for authentic contact when such moments arise (Stiver et al. 2008).

Conclusions

This chapter has explored some of the skills, activities and qualities through which a counselling relationship may be built, and some of the ways in which it might be understood. It cannot be emphasized often enough that a good relationship is ultimately what counselling is about. No matter how skilled a practitioner might be at exploring painful emotional issues, and facilitating change, if the person does not trust them, and does not feel a bond and connection, then they will not open up enough to allow the knowledge, experience and competencies of the counsellor to have much of an impact on them. The next chapter explores a crucial aspect of the capacity to build a therapeutic relationship – the therapist's ability to use their own internal response to the client, and their life experience, as a relational resource.

Learning activities

The following activities may be explored individually, and/or with a group of learning partners.

1   **Facilitative relationships in your own life.** Take a few moments to think about the people in your life with whom you have had relationships that allowed you to express yourself most fully. Describe the qualities of these people. In what ways can your internal image of these relationships be valuable for your role as a counsellor?

2   **The impact of being genuine.** In terms of the people to whom you offer a service, how often are you able to be congruent, authentic or fully 'present' with them? What is the effect on your relationship with your clients when you are able to be genuine with them? What are the organizational factors that facilitate or inhibit the expression of genuineness?

3   **Repairing fractured relationships.** Reflect on your own experience of relationship ruptures. How were they resolved? What have you learned from these episodes in your life, in terms of cognitive understanding, practical skills and self-awareness, that can inform your capacity to facilitate the repair of alliance ruptures in counselling?

4   **Dealing with endings and loss.** Most of us find it hard to cope with endings and losses. What have you learned, from your experience of loss and endings in your personal life, that might be relevant to your capacity to handle the process of collaboratively negotiating the end of therapy with a client?

5 **Your relationship learning agenda**. Reflecting on this chapter as a whole, what would you identify as being your relationship strengths, and what are the areas of relational competence that require further learning, study and practice? In respect of these relationship issues, formulate an action plan based on specific, achievable self-practice, deliberate practice and other training and learning activities that would allow you to develop stronger theory relationship skills.

Using counsellor self-awareness

Introduction

Anyone observing a counselling session would be able to witness that the client talked most of the time, about who they were as a person and what troubled them. They would also see that the therapist spoke much less often, and rarely referred to who they were as a person. Turn this around, so that the point of observation is what the counsellor is aware of. From that perspective it is impossible to ignore the steady stream of personal memories, feelings and internal self-talk that accompanies the counsellor's effort to listen and attend to the client. For anyone reading a therapy textbook or research study, the therapist is portrayed as a person of a particular age and gender, who has been trained in a particular therapy approach. However, for the client sitting opposite that therapist, what they see is a live person with a unique physical presence that conveys innumerable identity cues relating to values, social class, life history, fitness level, marital status and much else. The client may wonder – who do they remind me of…? These observations reflect the fact that the person of the therapist is an unavoidable element in the process of therapy. The aim of this chapter is to explore how a counsellor can make skilful use of who they are – their awareness and sense of self – in constructive ways within therapy.

Behind the scenes

The main focus of this chapter is on the development of practical skills that counsellors can use in sessions to draw on aspects of their personal experience in the service of the client. It is important to recognize that this can only be done in a helpful or facilitative manner if it builds on considerable work behind the scenes, in the form of counsellor commitment to personal development and self-awareness. For the majority of therapists, the decision to enter this occupation is preceded by an extensive, sometimes lifelong, passionate interest in how people deal with problems in living. This interest may have been triggered by experiences of personal adversity, or by being forced to take the role of carer for a family member. Whatever personal pathway is followed, an individual who gravitates towards a career choice as a therapist has almost certainly already – before entering training – personally tried out on themselves several models or theoretical perspectives, and several therapeutic techniques and activities. Most training programmes require students to engage in personal development during the course, in the form of personal therapy, participation in experiential groups, journaling, mindfulness training, immersion in unfamiliar cultures, etc. However, these activities do not represent a new departure for the trainee, but instead are extending a trajectory that is already established into a phase of preparation for using such personal knowledge in a formal professional role. Fascination with the process of learning from life experience is a characteristic of effective therapists over the course of their entire careers (Jennings and Skovholt 1999, 2016). Domains of self-awareness that tend to be most relevant for therapists are discussed by Knapp et al. (2017) and McLeod and McLeod (2013). A useful framework for thinking about how life experience can be channelled into therapeutic skill is the Person of the Therapist Training Model (Aponte and Kissil 2014, 2016).

The skills that are introduced in the following sections of this chapter require an underlying capacity for the therapist to be aware of their own reactions to others, and an understanding of what these reactions might mean. They also depend on the therapist possessing a sufficient familiarity with fateful and critical moments in their own life history, and emotional wounds associated with them, to the extent that these wounds are not triggered to an unmanageable extent if and when a client brings up similar episodes. The assumption is not that someone who is, or is training to become, a therapist has reached a stage of total self-acceptance and self-understanding. Such an aspiration is not realistic and not possible – personal learning and development is never complete. The assumption is, instead, that a therapist has sufficient experience and confidence around reflecting on their own personal troubles to be readily able to bring these capabilities into the therapy room when required.

Skills for therapist use of self

The domain of counsellor skills addressed in this chapter is sometimes described as therapist use of self. Valuable sources for accessing the extensive literature that exists around this topic include Baldwin (2013), Gelso and Perez-Rojas (2017), Hansen (2009) and Kahn (2001). In this context 'self' does not refer to any particular theoretical concept of self, but rather should be taken as a way of talking about any aspect of life experience that may be relevant for practice. Use of self permeates all aspects of the therapy process and relationship. However, it is possible to identify a set of key learnable skills through which it can be implemented productively: *being centred; double listening; bracketing off; not disconnecting; using personal knowledge; expressing self through the design and layout of the therapy room; authenticity, congruence and presence; being moved; troubling here-and-now personal reactions to the client; self-disclosure.* Because authenticity, troubling reactions and self-disclosure can be particularly problematic for therapists, they are discussed in most detail.

Being centred

Making effective use of personal experience in the service of the client requires being open to one's own moment-by-moment reactions and responses to the client during a session. A lot of the time these reactions may be subtle and elusive, or there may be a lack of clarity over whether they are in fact responses to the client rather than the residue of other interactions (e.g. still thinking about the previous client). Many therapists try to maximize their receptiveness by using grounding and centring techniques before and during a session. For example, before a session it can be helpful to meditate, pray, engage in a body awareness activity such as breathing or walking, or mentally rehearse your sense of the client's strengths. During a session it can be useful to monitor one's breathing, make sure that one's feet are grounded on the floor or carry out a brief scan of internal awareness. More broadly, everyday self-care activities around diet, exercise, enjoyable time with other people, etc. have the effect of increasing the chances of being able to be centred when in the therapy room.

Double listening

All of the skills discussed in this chapter draw on a basic skill of being able to listen to oneself. At the same time as listening to a client, a therapist will have a background awareness of what is happening within themselves, in terms of feelings, thoughts, memories, images, metaphors and action tendencies. At the end of a skills practice session, or when compiling a process analysis (see Chapter 4), it should be possible to recall and reconstruct one's internal process throughout the session.

Bracketing off

The concept of bracketing refers to a cognitive process of being able to put one's assumptions or interpretation around what is happening to one side, in order to consider the question 'What else is there?' Bracketing is a central aspect of phenomenological philosophy and existential therapy (Cooper 2012). It represents a crucial skill in respect of use of self in therapy because it is likely that one's response to a client comprises multiple strands of feeling and meaning. To use the response in the most effective way, it is necessary to be able to tease apart these threads so that one can either feed back to the client those meanings that seem most relevant at that moment, or offer one's sense of the whole of what is happening within oneself at that moment. The opposite of this – consistently offering a response to the client based on just a single idea – is unhelpful because it reduces the range of possibilities open to the client and may be received as a defining label that cannot be questioned. Being able to offer a differentiated response, achieved as a result of a process of internal bracketing and generating many 'what else's' supports collaboration by allowing the client to move forward with whatever bit of the therapist's statement is meaningful for them.

Not disconnecting

The importance of maintaining a satisfying and supportive connection with others is an aspect of life that most people can identify with, and it informs most approaches to therapy to a greater or lesser extent. Relational-cultural therapy is an approach that places a particularly strong emphasis on connection as a cornerstone of practice (Jordan 2000; Jordan et al. 2004). In that theory, the concept of *strategies of disconnection* offers a distinctive perspective on therapist self-awareness and use of self that has broad implications. Strategies of disconnection are the ways that therapists avoid engaging with clients, both routinely as well as during particularly challenging and stressful moments in a session. Studies have shown that therapists are readily aware of what they do to disconnect from clients, and when they do it (Cooper and Knox 2018; Gross and Elliott 2017). Disconnecting during a therapy session occurs when distancing mechanisms to ensure emotional safety, acquired and practised in everyday life situations, are triggered by the client's story or way of being. A valuable skill, in respect of using self in therapy, is to be aware of when and how one is disconnecting, and to develop strategies for reconnecting.

Using personal knowledge

An important theme in this book is that anyone training to be a counsellor is able to draw on a massive amount of relevant pre-existing knowledge and experience arising from their journey through life up to that point. Even if this knowledge is not explicitly shared with a client, it can still enrich the therapist's response to the client in many ways. For example, a therapist who has a background in music or art knows about putting things together to create something new, struggling to get something quite right, deciding when it is good enough to be shared, taking the risk of performing/exhibiting and being open to praise or criticism, and so on. A therapist who has been a parent or carer has an enormous understanding of how to support others, cope with the demands of others, appreciate small gains, etc. It is clearly not helpful to assume that one's own experience of a creative process, or dealing with a child's tantrum will directly map onto the experience of a client who is struggling to express their potential, or feels helpless to influence the behaviour of another person. Nevertheless, at these moments during a session, relevant personal knowledge and experience can sensitize the therapist and help them to stay close to the client's reality. A therapist who has had a previous career as a nurse offering end-of-life care is likely to be more comfortable and grounded with a client who wants to explore the experience of being with their father when he died, than a therapist who has never been in the presence of death. A useful learning activity can be to meet with therapist colleagues to share and reflect on specific personal examples and stories of how personal knowledge from life experience has shaped their practice.

Expressing self through the design and layout of the therapy room

The social identity of a therapist is conveyed through the way they dress, and possibly also by the way their therapy room is laid out (e.g. private practice therapists who design their own rooms). Important aspects of a room may correspond to the therapist's values, beliefs and model of practice. For example, a therapist who believes that feelings are conveyed through bodily movement may create a counselling room that includes objects that can be touched and handled. A therapist who believes that therapy is a journey into an inner self may have mandala-type pictures on the wall that depict this theme. The choice of books on a shelf says a lot. A wholly neutral room and dress choice may indicate a therapist who does not want to be known.

Authenticity and congruence

The concept of authenticity refers to a crucial aspect of the way that a therapist is experienced by the client in sessions. If the therapist is viewed as having an authentic presence, the client is more likely to trust them (what you see is what you get) and treat them as a credible and reliable source of support. On the other hand, a therapist who is regarded as inauthentic is treated with suspicion, as someone who is playing a professional role, not honest, and not believing in what they are doing. Authenticity is a concept from existentialist theory, and is hard to define in precise terms. Over the years, it has been discussed and investigated using a range of labels, including congruence, genuineness, transparency, realness, openness and honesty. The following paragraphs largely draw on the person-centred therapy literature, originating in the work of Carl Rogers, on the meaning and use of *congruence* – the perspective on authenticity that has had most influence on counselling skills training.

Congruence/incongruence refers to the capacity of a person (therapist or client) to be aware of, and appropriately communicate, what they are experiencing at a particular moment. In this model, there are two main aspects of congruence: (a) awareness of moment-by-moment experiencing, and (b) when appropriate, communicating that awareness, usually through verbal means but also possibly by physical movement or some form of creative expression. From a person-centred perspective, incongruence is a common factor in clients at the start of therapy. It is important to note that the term 'congruence' is also sometimes used in the therapy literature to refer to something completely different: similarity between therapist and client (e.g. congruence in social class, age or personality).

To understand the person-centred concept of congruence, it is helpful to know how it developed. Early client-centred/person-centred therapy, which emerged in the mid-1940s, emphasized therapist qualities of empathy, acceptance and non-directiveness. In the 1960s, Rogers and his colleagues were involved in a major study into client-centred therapy for hospitalized 'schizophrenic' patients. What they found was that empathy was limited in value for clients who were uncommunicative and suspicious of them. They discovered that the therapist's capacity to use their own inner response to the client was a key factor in successful therapy with these clients. This led to the role of congruence being given much more prominence in subsequent person-centred theory and practice. It is important to note that the significance of congruence became apparent in a clinical situation with clients whose life experience had led them to be reluctant to trust professional helpers. An accessible and inspiring account of this episode can be found in Rogers and Stevens (1968).

To develop a congruent way of responding to clients, it is important to have a clear idea about what it is. Mearns and Thorne (2013) define it in terms of the match or correspondence between the therapist's outward response to a client and their inner feelings and sensations. Rogers (1961) regards this quality as based in a capacity to accept or embrace one's inner response rather than being afraid of it, and adds that no one is ever able to fully achieve an attitude. Another way of defining congruence is to look at how it is measured. The Barrett-Lennard Relationship Inventory (BLRI) (Barrett-Lennard 2014; available on the internet) includes subscales for congruence and the similar construct of 'willingness to be known', that provide a detailed picture of how clients perceive the authenticity of their therapist (or its absence). Items from the client versions of these scales are: 'I do not think that my therapist hides anything from themselves that they feel with me' (congruence); 'My therapist has unspoken feelings or concerns that are getting in the way of our relationship' (incongruence); 'My therapist is willing to tell me their own thoughts and feelings when they are sure that I really want to know them' (willingness to be known); 'My therapist adopts a professional role that makes it hard for me to know what they are like as a person' (lack of willingness to be known). Therapist congruence is not the same as self-disclosure (e.g. sharing information such as 'I am married' or 'I have been depressed in my own life') – therapist self-disclosure of biographical information is discussed in a later section.

Congruence is often regarded as comprising a way of being (i.e. how a person is, rather than what they do) rather than a counselling skill that is turned on or off. Nevertheless, it is possible to identify observable, skill-like manifestations of this quality:

- often involves using the word 'I' (or equivalents such as 'for me', 'in me', etc.)
- brief but regular moments of therapist self-attention in which they attend to their internal bodily feelings
- use of the word 'and' – congruence is likely to be communicated in terms of several strands rather than one feeling: 'I am aware that I am feeling kind of pleased *and* also wondering what happens next...'
- may be accompanied by movement or gesture indicating where in the body feelings are located
- sometimes follows a moment of incongruence (i.e. realization of falseness of a response triggers the therapist to correct themselves and search for a more authentic reaction)
- sometimes associated with mutual congruence (client and therapist both being congruent at same time; high level of verbal and non-verbal synchrony).

Most of the time, congruence operates in the background, as a source of information that the therapist can draw on, alongside other sources such as listening to what the client is saying. The decision to make an explicitly congruent statement or response to the client depends on several factors. Some person-centred therapists advise against being openly congruent (i.e. saying something) until the relationship is strong enough and the therapist is confident about what they want to say (e.g. have felt something consistently over a period of time). On the other hand, it may be better to make self-referential congruent statements more regularly, because otherwise a therapist 'I' statement can then come as a surprise/ shock to clients, and delay could risk a loss of immediacy and spontaneity – you may end up with a rather wooden response that has little emotional resonance (Goldstein and Suzuki 2015). Useful accounts of how therapists deal with these dilemmas can be found in Burks and Robbins (2011).

Examples of what a congruent statement might look like are:

- 'As you have been talking, I have felt… and… and… I was wondering – are these feelings that you have too? Am I picking up these feelings, or some of them, from you? Maybe these feelings have nothing to do with you – let me know…?'
- 'I just feel so happy to hear you say that. I just feel so pleased.'
- 'I have a sense of being pushed away, as if you don't want me to know any more about this issue.'
- 'As you were talking just now, I had an image of being on a roller coaster, going up and down and faster and faster – does that make any sense to you?'
- 'I'm aware that there are tears in my eyes as I listen to you.'
- 'Could I just say something for a minute? Every time you have talked about XXX, I have had a similar feeling. It's there right now, it's like an angry feeling… I'm wondering what that might be about. Are you angry with XXX?'

It is important to realize that incongruence is not necessarily harmful: correcting yourself and admitting you got it wrong can strengthen the client's trust in you. Also, disconnection from inner feelings is sometimes necessary to allow a therapist to reflect on what the client is saying or doing. Many therapists prepare themselves for being congruent by using mindfulness, meditation, yoga and other grounding activities (Goldberg and Sachter 2018). Therapy training typically involves participation in experiential groups or personal development groups that are based on being empathic and congruent in relationships, rather than engaging in intellectual discussion (Austin and Austin 2018). Evidence of the relationship between therapist congruence and client outcomes is reviewed by Kolden et al. (2018). Studies that have explored the meaning of therapist congruence from the point of view of the client include Dollarhide et al. (2012) and Schnellbacher and Leijssen (2009).

Presence

Congruence refers to a process that primarily takes place within the therapist, and then has an impact on the client. The concept of presence represents a valuable way of making sense of what congruence looks like from the perspective of the client (Greenberg and Geller 2001). A congruent or authentic therapist is someone who is experienced as being there, and present, in the moment (Colosimo and Pos 2015). Research by Geller suggests that there are three key criteria that clients use to assess the level of presence of their therapist: the extent to which the therapist was 'fully there in the moment with me', responded in a way that was 'really in tune with what I was experiencing in the moment' and did not seem distracted. Geller (2017) has developed a set of guidelines for therapists around how to be intentionally and intensely present with their clients. Hayes and Vinca (2017) argue that the most effective therapists are those who exhibit the highest levels of presence.

Being moved

In recent years, there has been a growing amount of research on the social emotion of being touched or moved by something that another person has said or done. It is described as a social emotion because it is essentially an experience of connection or human solidarity. Because it is a phenomenon that is understood differently in different cultures, researchers have decided to refer to it using the Sanskrit term 'kama muta' – literally translated as 'moved by love'. Frequently reported aspects of the kama muta response include: a heavy feeling in the centre of the chest, moist eyes, goosebumps, shivers, lump in throat and deep breaths (Fiske 2019; Fiske et al. 2019). In a therapy situation, if a client can see that their therapist has been moved by what they have said, it provides them with strong evidence that their therapist genuinely cares, as opposed to merely responding in a professional role. A not uncommon example of kama muta in therapy interaction is therapist tears (Morgan and Nutt Williams 2021). Studies have shown that even brief episodes of the therapist being moved can be highly affirming and memorable for clients (Skatvedt 2017; Topor et al. 2021). Kama muta has been described as the 'connecting emotion': from the perspective of the therapist it functions as the opposite or antidote to strategies of connection (see earlier section 'Not disconnecting'). A therapist's capacity to allow themselves to be moved is an important skill that supports authenticity and presence.

Troubling here-and-now personal reactions to the client

Concepts or processes such as authenticity, congruence, connection and presence mainly refer to an ongoing flow of internal response to a client, and a sense of being closer to the client or more distanced from them. The concept of being moved refers to a type of specific event or response that is primarily positive, in bringing client and therapist together in a moment of shared humanity. In addition to these processes, there exists a more troubling kind of therapist personal reaction to the client, in which the therapist either thinks or feels something that disturbs them because it seems inappropriate (e.g. sexual attraction to the client, anger) or it throws or 'rubber-bands' the therapist into memories and powerful emotions around an aspect of their personal life that is emotionally raw (Stewart and Joines 2012). Unlike routine authenticity, which is on the whole benign and has the potential to add depth to the conversation, these troubling reactions may lead the therapist to doubt their own competence and suitability for the work, and this can undermine their capacity to continue to facilitate the therapy process until they have been able to re-establish composure.

There are many ways in which these troubling moments can be understood. For example, Berthoud and Noyer (2021) explore how to make sense of therapist anger from a congruence perspective. However, the perspective that represents the most widely studied and applied approach to making sense of these processes is the psychodynamic theory of *transference* and *countertransference*. It is extremely important to appreciate that the theory of transference/countertransference refers to all aspects of the therapist–client relationship, not just to troubling events. Many excellent sources are available for developing an understanding of these ideas, and associated skills and strategies (Maroda 2009; McCluskey and O'Toole 2019; Shedler 2006, 2010). The following discussion focuses specifically on the application of notions of transference and countertransference to instances of troubling and destabilizing therapist here-and-now responses to a client.

Essentially, transference refers to the way that pre-existing patterns of relating to others are enacted by the client in their relationship with their therapist. Countertransference refers to the therapist's conscious and unconscious responses (thoughts, feelings, memories, action tendencies) to the client. In classical Freudian theory and practice, the therapist sought to function as a neutral blank screen on which the client's dysfunctional feelings and style of relating could be projected, thus enabling the therapist to analyse these processes, help the client to make sense of them, and to make decisions about how to respond in different, less self-limiting ways. In this early version of psychoanalysis, the therapist's countertransference was regarded as an unwanted and unhelpful complication that reflected unresolved personal issues in their life, and was to be avoided if at all possible. It is essential to appreciate that psychoanalytic and psychodynamic theory and practice has *moved on* from this view. Specifically, it has become clear that the therapist's countertransference provides crucial information about the client, in two ways:

- The therapist's emotional response to the client may mirror the client's own internal emotional life – the therapist is so closely attuned to the client that they are resonating to feelings and emotions of which the client is not necessarily consciously aware.

- The therapist's emotional response to the client may be similar to the way that other people in the client's life react to them.

Contemporary psychoanalytic/psychodynamic practice therefore requires therapists to be skilful in attending not just to client transference, but also to their own countertransference responses.

This revised way of looking at the client–therapist relationship has important implications for how a therapist can deal with situations where they are troubled by their response to a client. In such a situation, both the content of the therapist's response, and its intensity/quality, need to be taken into account. The intensity of the response is a reflection of a combination of the importance of the topic for the client, and the degree to which they have consciously processed it. If a client has been able to reflect on a topic or issue in the past, and talk about it, it is likely they will introduce it into a therapy session in a calm and rational manner that gradually draws the therapist into the topic, and prepares them to be able to deal with it. If, on the other hand, the topic is highly meaningful for the client but not easy for them to put into words, it is more likely to be introduced suddenly, with its significance being conveyed not in words but through non-verbal cues and actions, and possibly also through words that the client intuitively knows will provoke the therapist. The key idea here is that the client is operating on the basis that 'I cannot tell you how I feel, so I will make you feel it for yourself.' The fact that the therapist is troubled and disturbed is an indication that (a) the client trusts them enough, and feels sufficiently safe, to begin to open the lid on some of the things that are really bothering them, and (b) the therapist is sufficiently open to their own experience to receive the message at a feeling level.

Even equipped with such a rationale, such episodes are hard to deal with, even for experienced therapists who specialize in this way of working (Maroda 2019). Pérez-Rojas et al. (2017) suggest that the following skills and strategies are necessary:

- Self-insight: the therapist has done enough work on self, and has enough self-awareness, to possess a basic confidence that they can handle their own reactions.
- Conceptualizing ability: the therapist has some kind of theoretical understanding that allows them to see what is happening, rather than just being overwhelmed by it.
- Empathy: the therapist is able, even under extreme emotional pressure, to see the process from the client's point of view.
- Anxiety management skills: the therapist has robust techniques for calming themselves down, such as breathing, keeping their feet on the ground, positive self-talk, etc.

In a study by Gait and Halewood (2019), experienced therapists were interviewed about their process of developing confidence and competence in being able to use intense countertransference responses to clients in a constructive manner. The key themes to emerge from this study were that this was a challenging and difficult process, and one that took place across a number of years. The main helpful source mentioned by these therapists was the opportunity to talk honestly about their responses to clients in a supportive environment where there was no fear of criticism. One leading therapist (Cornell 2018) described how he had reached the point of being a qualified and experienced therapist, several years into his career, before a particularly difficult episode with a client (and his unhelpfully defensive response) stimulated him to take countertransference seriously.

The literature on therapist troubling emotional responses to clients almost entirely focuses on situations that reflect personal relationship issues around themes such as anger, influence of parents and early experience, and sexual feelings. Very little attention has been given to looking at how client ways of relating to their therapist, and therapist ways of responding to their client, can be shaped by cultural and social class differences, colonialism, racism, white privilege, etc. For example, it is clear that countertransference arising from therapist–client difference in colour is rarely addressed in therapy training (Goedert 2020), yet this can have a significant negative influence on the course of therapy (Dos Santos and Dallos 2012). The skill of broaching, discussed in Chapters 3 and 8, offers an important strategy for dealing with this issue.

A capacity to handle troubling personal responses to clients is an example of the way that being a therapist calls for an ability to use interpersonal skills in situations of pressure (discussed in Chapter 1). A vivid example of this particular source of pressure, and what can happen if it is not dealt with constructively, can be found in Dalenberg (2004).

Self-disclosure

Therapist self-disclosure refers to the therapist sharing information about themselves with the client. In the literature, two distinct forms of therapist self-disclosure statements have been identified: self-involving or immediacy responses in which the therapist refers to what they are thinking or feeling at that moment, and biographical disclosure statements in which the therapist refers to events from their own life, or aspects of their social identity – for example 'I am married' or 'like you, I have been through a period of depression'. The discussion in this section focuses solely on the latter category – biographical self-disclosure. The skill of therapist immediacy is explored in Chapter 8.

Traditionally, therapist biographical self-disclosure has been viewed in the profession as something to be avoided because the focus should be clearly on the experience of the client. However, more recently, evidence from research studies has suggested both that appropriate and well-timed therapist self-disclosure can have a positive effect, and that on other occasions self-disclosure even from highly skilled practitioners can be unhelpful. The mixed results from research are encapsulated in a study by Audet and Everall (2010), who interviewed nine clients. Some participants reported that they had welcomed therapist self-disclosure at an early stage of therapy, because it created more of a sense of equality. However, others felt confused when this happened, and were concerned about potential role confusion. Some research participants were very positive about self-disclosure later in therapy, because it brought them closer to the therapist, while others felt overwhelmed, or felt misunderstood because they experienced the therapist's personal information as having been irrelevant to them.

On the basis of research findings, various sets of guidelines have been developed to provide a framework for effective therapist biographical self-disclosure (for example: Farber 2006; Henretty and Levitt 2010; Hill et al. 2018). Key suggestions include:

- Too much therapist biographical disclosure is unhelpful – for example, it can lead to a situation where the client feels they need to care for their therapist.
- Self-disclosure should be carried out in the interest of the client.
- If possible, check out with the client in advance whether they think it might be helpful for the therapist to share their experience.
- Observe the client's reaction to the disclosure.
- Afterwards, check if it was useful.
- Do not talk about your unresolved personal problems (this kind of self-disclosure may come across as you wanting/needing the client to take care of you).
- Focus on similarities between therapist and client, not differences.
- Turn the attention back to the client after delivering the disclosure.

It is also important to keep in mind that disclosure of therapist information is not entirely under the control of the therapist. Many clients are curious about the therapist's biographical information and pick up a lot of cues without ever asking questions – they may look for a wedding ring, probe for attitudes to different topics, be curious about objects in the room such as pictures or reasons for taking time off for sickness, or conduct an internet search on the therapist. In addition, clients may explicitly ask their therapist for biographical information that they feel is relevant (Hanson 2005). Skilfulness around self-disclosure includes deciding on strategies for dealing with such requests. For example, at the start of therapy, it may be useful to invite the client to ask any questions they have about you – this approach acknowledges and anticipates their interest in you, and defuses it rather than turning it into an 'elephant in the room'.

Taken as a whole, the research does not indicate any way of guaranteeing that therapist biographical self-disclosure will be helpful or unhelpful, even when guidelines are being followed. The decision about whether or not to self-disclose, and what to say, is often made in the moment, in a situation where it is not possible to take account of guidelines in a comprehensive manner. The most useful way to approach this skill is to read studies and guidelines on therapist biographical self-disclosure and decide what will work for you, in terms of your style as a therapist, your personality, model of practice and client population. This process may involve reflecting on, and perhaps making new decisions around, personal disclosure 'rules' that you have acquired in your family of origin or work career.

A valuable exercise is to work out for yourself what areas of your life you would not want to share – and what you would say if the client asked you about them – and also those parts of your life experience that could be potentially useful for clients. There are many areas of therapy practice – for example around addictions, eating disorders, sexual violence, loss of a child – where a significant proportion of therapists have had personal experience of that issue (e.g. Wasil et al. 2019). There are also some therapy agencies that explicitly advertise themselves as being run by survivors. In these situations, therapists rehearse and practise what they are willing to tell clients about themselves, and what they are not. A study that looked at this question was carried out by Mjelve et al. (2020), who interviewed counsellors working with young people in educational settings about how they handled biographical self-disclosure. Some interviewees described themselves as rarely using this skill, while others used it a lot. All of them had given a lot of thought to what they would share, and the circumstances under which they would share it.

In terms of developing your own style of using biographical self-disclosure, it can be valuable to reflect on the ways that experienced therapists have worked their way through this dilemma (Berg et al. 2016; Newberger 2015; Pinto-Coelho et al. 2018). It is also of interest to think about specific issues associated with attitudes and expectations around self-disclosure in different client groups that you might work with, such as young people (Johnsen and Ding 2021) or people with non-Western cultural backgrounds (Sunderani and Moodley 2020). Finally, the function of therapist disclosure may be quite different in specific therapy approaches such as cognitive-behavioural therapy (CBT) (Miller and McNaught 2018) or collaborative therapy (Berg et al. 2020). For example, in functional analytic psychotherapy, a third-wave CBT approach, the use of therapist biographical self-disclosure is a primary intervention skill, and its application is clearly defined, well understood and a core part of training (Tsai et al. 2010).

Conclusions

Self-awareness, self-understanding and capacity for self-monitoring are important general qualities that therapists need to have. Most therapists have been interested in developing such capabilities throughout their whole lives, prior to entering training, because their personal circumstances and the adversities they have faced have required them to do so. The message of this chapter is that, to make a difference in work with clients, such qualities and capabilities need to be channelled into specific skills and strategies. Appropriate and facilitative use of self in therapy does not just happen – it requires preparation, planning, thinking through, deliberate practice and openness to feedback.

Learning activities

The following activities may be explored individually, and/or with a group of learning partners.

1   What are your own strategies for disconnection, both in real-life relationships and work with clients? In what ways, and to what extent, do these actions undermine your capacity to offer a facilitative therapy relationship? Once you have reflected on your own personal experience and ideas around this issue, use the following sources to deepen and expand your understanding of the topic: Cooper and Knox (2018), Gross and Elliott (2017) and Stiver et al. (2008).

2   What stories from your own life have the potential to function as learning points for clients? Reflect on this question, and write out at least one example of a piece of biographical self-disclosure that you might make to a client. Think about the kind of situation that might stimulate you to offer such a response to a client, including the types of client for whom it might be particularly appropriate, or contraindicated. Also think about how you might introduce the statement to a client. Be mindful of the issues discussed in the self-disclosure section of this chapter, and in your further reading on this topic. If possible, it is valuable to meet with learning partners in a group in which each participant reads out their biographical self-disclosure statement and colleagues offer feedback on their reactions to it.

3   How authentic, congruent and present do other people perceive you to be, both in therapy situations and in everyday relationships? Invite people who know you, and learning partners who have acted as practice clients, to give you feedback around this question. Do not use actual therapy clients. It is possible that it will be hard for those with whom you

consult to answer this question, either because they see it as too vague and general, or because they are being polite. Instead, use items (or the whole scales) from either the presence questionnaire developed by Shari Geller (available at https://www.sharigeller.ca/publications.php) or the congruence and willingness to be known sub-scales of the Barrett-Lennard Relationship Inventory (available online or in Barrett-Lennard 2014). Once you have collected this information, reflect on any implications for your practice as a therapist, and on what you might do to convey your authenticity more effectively to others.

4   If you have been practising counselling skills with learning partners, or working with actual clients, it is highly likely that you would have experienced troubling here-and-now personal reactions to clients. Choose one such episode for further reflection using the ideas presented in the relevant section of this chapter around the meaning of countertransference, and skills/strategies for handling such situations.

Conversational resourcefulness

Introduction

There are many different ways of dealing with mental health difficulties – for example through medication, physical activity, meditation, art-making or engaging in good work that benefits society. The distinctive feature of counselling, both as a healing process in itself and one that can take place in conjunction with these other activities, is the extent to which it is based on conversation and language. All of the counselling skills in this book either directly involve talking, or – in the case of listening skills and non-verbal awareness – involve focused attention that feeds into talking. This chapter focuses on skills for using language more effectively in therapy, particularly around the development of ways of talking that support collaboration.

In addition to the material in the present chapter, linguistic aspects of counselling skills are also discussed in many other places in the book, for example in the context of empathy and shared understanding (Chapter 7), and the challenges associated with working with cultural difference and diversity (Chapter 3).

Skills for using language in counselling

There are three basic assumptions that underpin an understanding of the importance of language in counselling. The first is that language makes a difference. Different words evoke different ways of seeing the world, and different ways of relating to each other. For example, talking about one's difficulties in terms of a psychiatric category such as 'depression' is not the same as talking about the same experiences in terms of a unique personal phrase such as 'the silent darkness'. Similarly, a counsellor referring to themselves as 'I' and the client as 'you' is less collaborative than using the term 'we'. In counselling, the capacity of the counsellor to help the client to develop new ways of seeing things, and new ways of acting, will often depend on finding the right words.

A second basic assumption regarding the use of language in therapy is that it is important for the counsellor and client to develop a shared language. The absence of a sufficient degree of shared language means that the counsellor and client are not understanding each other, and as a consequence are hampered in their ability to work together effectively. In counselling, the intention to establish a shared language implies a process of convergence that requires each interlocutor to accommodate to the other – in this sense, moving towards a shared language is part of building a relationship.

One of the important ways that people learn (about anything) is through being offered new words, phrases and ways of talking from other people with whom they interact. Over the course of therapy, therefore, a client may find themselves adopting words and ways of talking that they have picked up from their therapist, or that have emerged in the course of therapeutic dialogue.

The study of language is a highly complex topic. The following sections do not claim to provide a comprehensive review of the role of language in therapy. Instead, the aim has been to concentrate on how linguistic flexibility and resourcefulness can inform practice.

Word choice

Choice of words is a crucial aspect of therapy. The significance of 'so' as the opening word in a therapist empathic reflection was explored in Chapter 7. Granello and Gibbs (2016), along with many other researchers, have shown how personalized (e.g. 'person with mental health problem') ways of describing people with mental health issues are much less stigmatizing and distancing than phrases such as 'psychiatric patient'. Similar issues exist around ways of describing people with a wide range of disabilities (Dunn and Andrews 2015; Bury et al. 2020; Mousavi et al. 2020; Puhl 2020). In a medical context, Heritage et al. (2007) found that patients' unmet concerns (i.e. issues that they wanted to talk about in a meeting with a doctor, but were unable to do so) were greatly reduced when the doctor used the word 'some' ('Is there something else you want to address in the visit today?') rather than 'any' ('Is there anything else

Table 10.1 Words that refer to goal-like experiences

Goals	Turning
Projects	Achievement
Aims	Attainment
Objectives	Accomplishment
Wishes	Imagined self/future
Pathways	Fulfilment
Trajectories	Becoming
Intentions	Actualization
Purposes	Constructing
Agency	Building
Journey	Making
Destination	Possibility
Wants	Preference
Plans	Advance
Moving forward	Progress
Arriving	Future
Script	Direction

you want to address in the visit today?') – primarily because 'any' tends to be heard as implying 'none'.

In other situations, there may be many alternative words and phrases that might be used. For example, the concept of 'goal' refers to a core aspect of being human, and as a result many different ways of talking about this topic have been generated. The list in Table 10.1 includes a wide range of 'goals' words that all reflect a common core meaning in referring to doing something that leads to a future state of affairs or sense of agency (capacity to make things happen). Although the word goal is widely used in the therapy literature, there are many clients who do not like this term, either because it is too concrete and specific, or because it reminds them of areas of experience that they do not identify with, such as management jargon or sport. A linguistically resourceful counsellor who was seeking to build a collaborative relationship with a client would be sensitive to the client's word preferences around discussions of future-oriented aspects of therapy, and would be able to offer alternative word choices as necessary.

Clarifying the meaning of words

An important aspect of counselling is curiosity – the counsellor's keenness to know more about the experience of the client and what is helpful for them, and the client's openness to learning about themselves and sometimes also their curiosity about their therapist. A useful place where curiosity can be focused is around the meaning of specific words. Often, the words used by a client are meaningful to them in ways that may not be immediately apparent to the therapist. Conversely, the therapist may show curiosity around the client's use of a word: 'I was wondering… you use that word "stress" a lot… I know that can mean different things to different people… it would be helpful for me, in terms of really appreciating what is happening for you in your life, if you could say a bit more about what "stress" means for you…'.

There are three main ways that people elucidate the meaning of a word. They may refer to other words – for instance, the client may explain that they associate stress with pressure, fatigue and hopelessness, and explain why they view it as different from depression. Alternatively, the meaning of a word or phrase can be further elaborated by telling a story or giving an example. So, the stressed client may share a story of the 'most stressed I have ever been in my life' or the therapist may ask them to provide an example of a recent time when they felt particularly stressed. Finally, the person may anchor the meaning of a word or phrase in a bodily state. The stressed client may touch or hold their chest or their head as they talk about being stressed, or may describe physical signs such as 'a knot in my gut' or 'awful tension around my shoulders'. Often, a client will use all three of these sources when asked to explain what a word means to them. Each of these sources could help the therapist to gain a more complete picture of what stress means (and does not mean) for a client. In addition, establishing a web of meaning in this way allows the therapist more points of entry into the world of the client, and more possibilities for facilitating change. For example, stories of being stressed would almost always include other people, and lead to the possibility of exploring relational aspects of stress (i.e. how relationships trigger a stress response, and how they might alleviate it).

A further dimension of clarifying the meaning of words is associated with the client's curiosity around words used by their therapist. Even if a therapist does not use technical terms with clients, they will usually have favourite words such as 'choice', 'inside' or 'depth', that reflect their theoretical stance or underlying assumptions about human personality and identity.

From a collaborative perspective, exploring the meaning of a word or phrase is best done together. Useful examples of how the meaning of a word or phrase can be collaboratively unpacked can be found in a study by Jager et al. (2016) that analysed how therapists responded when an adolescent client replied 'I don't know' when asked to elaborate on their experience or state a preference for some aspect of treatment. The therapists in this study exhibited a range of strategies, including restating the question, offering a candidate answer and checking out whether the client agreed with it, or shifting the focus of the session so that the meaning of not knowing was explored.

Discursive positioning

The concept of discursive positioning has emerged from a constructionist approach to social psychology based on the notion that we co-create the realities we live in, through language and talk. We construct identities by telling stories about ourselves and the groups to which we belong. These identities and realities are constantly being maintained and renegotiated through conversation and other ways of using language, for instance in different types of written text. In this perspective, a *discourse* refers to a way of thinking and talking about a particular issue. To have, or perform an identity as an individual, and to explain or account for one's actions, it is necessary to *position* oneself in relation to prevailing discourses. For example, in Western society there is a strong thread of Christian discourse, which contains within it a fundamentalist wing that asserts that abortion is morally wrong. However, also in Western culture there are discourses of liberalism and feminism, which assert (in slightly different ways) that it is a woman's right to choose. We are all familiar with this debate, and with the forms of language (arguments, imagery, justifications, etc) that are brought to bear by each side. Each of us will, from time to time, find ourselves being called upon to position ourselves in relation to these discourses. An individual can position themselves either by simply adopting a mainstream discourse (such as that promoted by the Catholic Church) or can make an effort to assemble different discourses into a personally coherent account (for example, this would be necessary for anyone who views themselves as both Catholic and liberal).

Examples of how positioning theory can contribute to understanding the process of counselling can be found in McLeod (2004), Sinclair and Monk (2004), Wahlström (2018) and Winslade (2005). Essentially, an awareness of how the client and therapist position themselves, and each other, in relation to topics being addressed in therapy enables the therapist to help a person to find new and different ways to talk about an issue – to reposition themselves.

There are two main strategies that a counsellor can use. First, the counsellor can invite the person to more fully articulate and explore the position that they have adopted. This can be helpful because the person may have never, or seldom, in the past explicitly considered the way he or she has positioned themselves in relation to a topic. The person may discover, as a result, that the position they have adopted is, perhaps, not consistent with positions they have espoused in other areas of their life. Second, in a conversation, a counsellor can offer other positions, which allow the person the opportunity to try out new vantage points on areas of their life. Examples of these strategies are given below.

Inviting reflection on positioning

This skill has been described by Winslade (2005) as '*discursive empathy*'. Rather than empathically reflecting back to the person the meaning or emotional content of what they have said, in this kind of empathic response the counsellor reflects back the discursive position that the person has adopted. For example: Duncan is a manager in a successful IT business. He has had a heart attack, and is undergoing rehabilitation that involves a combination of exercise, physiotherapy and counselling for lifestyle change. The counsellor meets Duncan to discuss how he is feeling about the rehab programme. They have the following conversation:

Counsellor: Would it be OK if we looked at your activity diary now, so we can see what you have been able to do over the last few days?

Duncan: Here it is. You will see that I had a couple of meetings with the section heads in my office. Just to see how they were getting along. I was worried about how they were coping.

Counsellor: That wasn't part of the rehab plan, was it? I thought you had decided to wait a bit longer before making contact with people at work?

Duncan: You're right. But I just felt that I should do it. I guess I felt responsible – like I was just leaving them in the lurch.

Counsellor: I'm thinking that this sense of responsibility is a big thing for you. I've heard you mention it before. You often say that you 'should' be doing this or that. What's that about for you?

Duncan: I suppose I do say that a lot, now that you mention it. I've always felt that I should be responsible.

Counsellor: Could you tell me what that means for you? Feeling responsible?

Duncan: It's like I should look after people. I should do the right thing by other people.

Counsellor: Do you have any idea where that comes from in your life?

Duncan: Well, yes, now that I think about it, that sense of responsibility comes from the church. Growing up in a family that had that sense of service to the community. One of my uncles, and a grandfather, were ministers. You had to sacrifice yourself to others. It was never acceptable to put yourself first. I remember my grandmother saying, over and over again, 'who do you think you are?' whenever anyone put themselves first. All of us in the family are locked into this, I think.

Counsellor: So this way of thinking about things, this "'service to the community'… I'm wondering how relevant it is to the situation you are in now. I'm thinking, well, this is a situation where you might be needing to put yourself first, at least for a while.

In this dialogue, the counsellor invited their client to reflect on the way he positioned himself morally in relation to his work colleagues. Quite quickly, their discussion opened up a space in which Duncan was able to identify the discourse in his own life that he was drawing on in order to account for his actions in this situation. Once he had identified the discourse and noted some of the ways that it structured his actions, the counsellor, in turn, was able to ask him to begin to consider whether there might be alternative ways of positioning himself that might be more consistent with his goal of recovery.

Offering a different position

Another way of working with positioning is to rephrase what a person has said, so that it embodies a different position. This strategy does not invite the person to reflect on the discursive context of their way of talking, but much more directly gives them an opportunity to try out an alternative conversational stance. The most straightforward example of this kind of counselling method can be found in relation to discourses of agency/passivity. For example:

Client (student):	The course is too much for me. There is too much work to do. The other day the lecturer said that we needed to hand in our lab report by the end of term, and it's just impossible. I'm just hopeless at it. There's no way I'm going to get through.
Counsellor:	Right, I'm hearing you saying that you are feeling a lot of pressure of work right now, and you are wondering whether you can handle it. Is that the main thing?
Client:	Yes, it's just too much. There isn't enough time. The books are never in the library when you need them. It's just impossible.
Counsellor:	OK, these are extra pressures – not enough time and books not being in the library. So you're saying to yourself something like 'I just won't be able to get it done.' Is that right?
Client:	Yes.
Counsellor:	I was wondering if we could maybe just break this down step by step. That would help me to understand the challenge that you are facing. Would that be all right? If we looked at it step by step?
Student:	OK.
Counsellor:	Right, well, if we look at it from the point of view of getting the lab report in. What does the lab report involve, for this module?
Client:	I've been working with a small group, to complete a microbiology experiment on cell growth. Each of us needs to write our own separate analysis of the data.
Counsellor:	Could you break that down for me a bit more? What has your bit of it involved? What have you been doing?
Client:	My job is to use the microscope to make readings, and then I write them in a lab book...
Counsellor:	... and that has been OK?
Client:	Yes, there hasn't been any problem with that. In fact, the lab assistant said I had done that well.

In this passage of conversation, the client begins by positioning themselves as a passive victim of external forces (the course, the lecturer, the library, their own inadequacy). It would have been possible for the counsellor to engage empathically with this discursive position, for example by inviting the client to consider the meaning of pressure, or blame, in their life, or the word 'hopeless'. However, the counsellor is aware that client's goal or priority (agreed earlier) is to do well on the course, and anticipates that a potentially valuable way to achieve this might be through adopting a position of agency in relation to the topic. The counsellor therefore offers the client a different way of talking about the issue, a discourse of agency. This is carried out by describing the client's report of problems as something they are saying now, by using the linguistic construction 'so what you are saying is that you are feeling…'. Here, the counsellor is translating a statement originally framed by the client within a discourse of passivity ('it's just impossible') into a discourse of agency, in which the capacity to be responsible for one's actions is foregrounded: 'what *you are saying* is that you are feeling a lot of pressure of work right now, and *you are wondering* whether you can handle it'. The counsellor's restatement of the issue introduces the idea of personal agency in the use of the words 'saying' and 'wondering'. Later, the counsellor invokes another discursive move, which is to shift the conversation away from a total, or totalizing description of a whole situation, described in general terms, and in the direction of descriptions of specific actions taken by the student at different stages ('looking at it step by step'). Acquiescing in this move requires, or at the very least encourages, the client to talk about their problem in terms of what they did in response to specific subtasks. From the counsellor's perspective, this new way of talking about the issues opens up a space where they can observe, and affirm, both positive action that the client has taken, and examples of skills and resources that the client can bring to bear on any subtasks that are proving harder to complete. Once the way of talking about the problem has shifted in this way, possibilities for change, and solutions, tend to emerge naturally in the conversation.

A further aspect of discursive positioning comprises the way that the counsellor and person seeking help position themselves *in relation to each other*. For example, in the case of the counsellor working with Duncan on rehab planning, it would have been easy for them to position themselves in a health adviser role, and merely reinforce the importance of keeping to the agreed rehab schedule. Similarly, the counsellor meeting with the distressed student might well have spoken from the position of the 'voice of the university', by telling/lecturing the client on how it was important to work hard, make sure that you are at the library when it opens, and so on. In both of these cases, the counsellor positioned themselves, instead, within a discourse of collaboration and curiosity, and invited the people they were helping to talk on these terms.

The skills involved in discursive repositioning are widely used by counsellors, most of whom are not aware that discourse theory and research provides a useful way of making sense of what they are doing. An intentional focus on positions adopted in conversations is a particularly valuable perspective and skill set in relation to working collaboratively, because it creates moments at which the counsellor and client can look together at the implications of their ways of talking. The discussion and practical examples available in Wahlström (2018) are a key resource in terms of learning more about this skill.

Opening the door: using vivid language, imagery and metaphor

One of the most powerful dimensions of communication is the occurrence of vivid imagery and metaphor. Metaphors are memorable. By combining many threads of meaning within a single word or phrase, a metaphor creates a new meaning that extends beyond its constituent elements. In therapy, it is always worthwhile to pay attention to the images and metaphors a person uses – the therapist as well as the client. If a word or phrase almost seems to stand out from what the person is saying, as if it had neon lights around it, then it is almost certain that it conveys a lot of meaning for the person – it is as though it operates as shorthand for a longer story that the person could tell. The following sections explore the skill of using metaphor in therapy from two contrasting perspectives: metaphors generated by the client, and those generated by the therapist.

Skills for working with client metaphors

Many aspects of a client's way of talking can be informative about therapeutically relevant issues such as their emotional state, inner world, intentions and relationships: tone of voice, pace and volume of their talk, repetition and emphasis, coherence, etc. One of the most psychologically significant linguistic elements is use of metaphor, imagery or figurative language. Many statements made by a client will convey a single, literal meaning. For example: 'I am sad' or 'I am depressed'. Such statements do not convey much information about what 'sad' or 'depressed' mean to that person. By contrast, a depressed client might use metaphoric statements such as: 'I seem to have *gone downhill* since we started rather than uphill'; '… things would kind of go along the way that I didn't want to and would get me down and then I'd get kind of agitated, and then start *spiralling down*'; 'I feel as if I'm plunging into the *darkness*'. In metaphor, one thing is being compared to something else – for example 'sadness' is compared to a sense of 'spiralling down'. It is clear, from the context of the conversation, that the person is not *literally* 'spiralling down'. The metaphor sets up a tension: the listener has to work out which aspects of 'spiralling down' are relevant and meaningful. A metaphor highlights some aspects of a phenomenon and downplays others. For example, 'spiralling down' highlights meanings such as having started off in a higher place, going round and round, being out of control and heading for a crash. An aspect of depression that this particular metaphor downplays or leaves out is any sense of what triggered the downward movement.

In the ongoing flow of conversation in a therapy session, a metaphor such as 'spiralling down' has the potential to function as:

- a means of bringing the therapist closer to the client's actual lived experience, in all its complexity
- an implicit invitation to the therapist to join in a process of exploring/ unpacking the meaning of the metaphor

⋄ a contribution to developing a unique shared language, that can serve as a point of reference/shorthand.

Metaphors always refer back to basic dimensions of bodily experience (up/down, forward/back, physical actions and sensations, etc.) (Lakoff and Johnson 1980, 1999). As a result, metaphors have the potential to give access to what is fundamentally important for the person (i.e. beyond words). In addition, the sensory qualities of the image are only hinted at in the actual metaphor itself, but are potentially available for further exploration. An image or metaphor operates as the title or headline for a longer story that the person could tell:

⋄ I am spiralling down.
⋄ I am a time bomb waiting to explode.
⋄ I am a prisoner of the past and occasionally on parole.
⋄ Our relationship is like a war.

It is possible to make a distinction between novel metaphors that are vivid and new, and 'dead' or conventional metaphors that permeate all aspects of conversation and are taken for granted, such as 'feeling up', 'feeling down', 'lost the plot', 'feel stuck'. Both types of metaphor seem to be important in therapy. For example, when a client uses the phrase 'lost the plot', it probably carries a lot of meaning, for instance around the existence of a plot, what the plot line was in the past, etc. However, dead/conventional metaphors occur so frequently in the client's talk that is hard to keep track of them.

In terms of working therapeutically with a client's metaphor, there are some key skills, strategies and guiding principles that are relevant:

1 Pay particular attention to metaphors or images that 'hit' you: that jump out or seem intriguing or 'in neon lights'. This kind of impact is a good indicator that – in the context of your relationship with the client and the therapy process at that moment – something important has been said.

2 Check out with the client whether it would be OK with them to take a few moments to look at what that word or phrase might mean. It can be useful to be open and acknowledge that it struck you (the therapist) as potentially important.

3 Stay with the metaphor for at least a few speaking turns – research by Angus, Rennie and Rasmussen suggests that good outcome cases are characterized by a capacity not just to acknowledge or draw attention to a client's metaphor, but to use it as a way of exploring meaning. Their studies also indicated that some clients found it hard to do this, because they had a predominantly concrete style of talking that prevented them from imagining and 'playing' (Angus and Rennie 1988, 1989; Rasmussen and Angus 1996; Rasmussen 2000).

4 Invite the client to describe the sensory qualities of the metaphor (an example of how to do this is given below).

Remember the metaphor, and refer back to it (where relevant) at later points in therapy – the image or metaphor functions as a consistent thread through the therapy process, which gains in meaning every time it is explored (Finlay 2015; McMullen 1989, 1999).

It is also valuable to be sensitive to metaphor themes (clusters of images/ metaphors that all refer to a single underlying way of seeing the world). For example: a general metaphor theme of 'relationship is war' might appear in statements about 'defending myself', 'going into hiding', 'attack', 'armoury', 'scars', etc. Examples of common metaphor themes in therapy include: being at war (Heide 2010); being on a journey (Aronov and Brodsky 2009; Lawson 2005); building bridges (Minulescu 2015); dance (Pistole 2003). New metaphors that arise, or changes in the way a client uses a metaphor or metaphor theme, can be regarded as indicators of change – for instance when a client with marital difficulties stops talking about marriage as war and starts to use images of building bridges. There can also be meaningful shifts within an overall metaphor theme, such as from 'stuck' (negative journey) to 'turned the corner' (positive journey). Therapist curiosity about new/altered metaphors can help the client to consolidate change (Levitt et al. 2000; Sarpavaara and Koski-Jännes 2013).

Vivid and out of the ordinary metaphors are highly memorable. A person is more likely to remember a vivid metaphor, following a counselling session, than they are to remember other topics and ideas that have been discussed. Metaphor can therefore help to link together counselling and everyday life. The use of metaphor allows the possibility to make use of important human resources and strengths such as imagination, creativity and the capacity for play. 'Metaphor talk' in counselling can often be energizing and connecting, and can lead to new discoveries.

In terms of developing practical skills for working therapeutically with client metaphors, it can be useful to start by implementing a set of procedures developed by Kopp and Craw (1998) and Kopp and Eckstein (2004). As with any therapy method, it is important to personalize these guidelines and find a way of using them that works for you and your clients. However, as a learning exercise it may be helpful to just follow the instructions, and practise them two or three times with learning partners, before adapting them.

Step 1. Notice metaphors. During a practice session, have a paper and pen handy and write down the client's metaphor verbatim.

Step 2. Ask the client if they would like to explore the metaphoric image. If they do, ask them: 'When you think of [the metaphor] what image comes to mind?', or 'What does the metaphor look like?'

Step 3. Invite the client to explore the metaphor as a sensory image. Avoid adding content. Use open-ended questions such as: 'What else do you see?', 'Describe the scene', 'What are other people saying or doing?', 'What are the sensory qualities of…?', 'What led up to this?', 'What else is going on?', 'What happens next?', 'How does it turn out?'

Step 4. Invite the client to describe his or her feelings associated with the meta-phoric image.

Step 5. Invite the client to change the image: 'If you could change the image in any way, how would you change it?'

Step 6. Explore the parallels between the metaphoric image and the original sit-uation/issue/goal that they were exploring. Invite the client to think about whether the way that he/she changed the image has any implications for their current situation. 'How might the way you changed the image apply to your present situation?'

Throughout: avoid interrupting the client's process with interpretations, empathic reflections, comments, conclusions or suggestions.

Case example: the stressed teacher

Background: a teacher who is experiencing a high degree of work stress, and has a variety of physical ailments including chronic back pain, has visited his GP three times in the past month for prescriptions for painkillers, none of which have made much difference. On this occasion, the GP suggests that it might be helpful for the patient to try counselling. What follows is an excerpt from the first counselling session.

Client: I had a really bad time a few years ago, and my back was playing up then too. It was really difficult to get through that, and it's always in the back of my mind. Sometimes I just feel as though I'm skating on thin ice – it would not take much and I would fall back into all that awful stuff I was feeling then. I wouldn't call it depres-sion, but…

Counsellor: Would it be OK if we just looked a bit more at what you just said there? My attention was really drawn to that phrase you used – 'skating on thin ice'. It just seems such a vivid image, it really hit me, because it seems to really catch what that situation means to you. I remember you used it before, this morning, to describe your situation. Would it be OK with you to stay with that image for a few moments? I'd be interested to learn more about what that means to you – 'skating on thin ice' …

[Counsellor notices the metaphor, then asks the client if they would like to explore the metaphoric image]

Client: That's OK. When you mention it, I realize that it's something I say a lot.

Counsellor: Right, well maybe you could begin by telling me where you are skating – on a rink, a river…?

[The counsellor encourages the person to 'dwell in' the metaphor, to explore its sensory qualities, to begin to let the story unfold: what went before… what is happening now – who, where, how, why… how will it end…]

Client:	That's funny, it's definitely a frozen lake, with mountains on either side.
Counsellor:	Are you going fast, slow…?
Client:	I'm skating very deliberately. Not fast or slow. I mustn't stop.
Counsellor:	You mustn't stop? What would happen if you stopped?
Client:	If I stopped I would be more likely to fall through the ice. I must keep going.
Counsellor:	So, if you stopped there would be the risk of… what?
Client:	It would just give way.
Counsellor:	And then?
Client:	I would freeze. I would be pulled down. I just wouldn't last for ten minutes. It would be the end.
Counsellor:	So you must keep going. Are you OK if you keep going? How do you keep going?
Client:	If I can get to the other side I'll be fine. I'm not sure how I keep going. I grit my teeth and tense my muscles. If I relaxed for even a moment I'd be gone.
Counsellor:	So you keep going, trying to get to the other side. And is that far away – the other side…? What's it like over there?
Client:	Quite far, but I can see the people there. *[client changes the image]*
Counsellor:	The people…?
Client:	Yes, there are people there who are trying to help me to get to the other side. Giving me advice. I know I'll be all right if I can make it over to where they are, so they can take care of me.
Counsellor:	So these people are really rooting for you?
Client:	Yes, definitely.
Counsellor:	And what are you feeling about all this, as you are telling me about it?
Client:	Kind of shifted from kind of 'weary and scary' when I was talking about skating back and forth, back and forth, to almost excitement, yea and relief too, when I saw these people over there.
Counsellor:	Thanks for that. I know it may seem silly to be talking about skating and so on, but it did seem to me that what you were saying there was somehow important. What came over to me was that you have to keep moving, very carefully and deliberately, or you will disappear into a depression like you had before, right through the ice. But there are also some people who can help, if you can get to them. Is that right?
Client:	Yeah, that's it in a nutshell.
Counsellor:	It's making me think that maybe the pills you are taking may be only part of the answer. Could we look at what would be involved in actually getting this support that's on offer from these people?

[Exploring parallels between the metaphor/image and the client's presenting issue. Then moves on to look at implications – who are these people, what can they offer, how to accept their help, etc.]

The stressed teacher excerpt illustrates some basic features of the use of metaphor and imagery in counselling conversations. The metaphor that was generated by this person – skating on thin ice – could easily have been ignored as a fairly commonplace image. However, for this person, in the context of what he had said before (mainly describing lists of symptoms), this image was vivid and conveyed new meaning. The metaphor functioned as akin to a door into the client's personal world. The key skill, in the work done by this counsellor, relied on remaining open and curious about the meaning of the metaphor for the person: 'Tell me more', 'What's it like?', 'What happens next?' At no point did the counsellor make any assumptions or offer any interpretations about the meaning of the metaphor for the client. The counsellor is curiously trying to fill out the picture, as if they were there with the client in that skating-on-ice scene. The majority of powerful, evocative metaphors refer to physical, bodily qualities. As the client followed the counsellor's invitation to put these tangible and embodied aspects of the metaphor into words ('describe where you are skating… how far away is the other side…'), they became more aware of their own bodily sensations, emotions and feelings that were bound up in the imagery – which in turn allowed deeper/implicit layers of meaning to be expressed. Essentially, what the Kopp and Craw (1988) procedure does is allow the client to stay with the metaphor, in terms of what it means for them, until its wider meaning begins to be revealed. The aim is, as much as possible, to recreate the feelings and sensory experience here and now in the counselling room – *not* to think about, interpret or analyse the meaning of the image/metaphor. In the stressed teacher example, there was an important shift initiated by the client himself. If this does not happen, the counsellor invites the client to change the image, by asking: 'If you could change the image in any way, how would you change it?' (or an equivalent statement).

Skills for working with therapist-generated metaphors

There are two types of therapist metaphor that are relevant in practice. One category consists of spontaneous metaphors/images that capture the meaning of what the client is talking about, or what is happening at that moment in therapy. Examples: 'the way you describe it, it's a long hard road you have been on…'; 'when you said that a moment ago, it was like a light going on in my head…'. It is important that such images and metaphors are offered tentatively and collaboratively, and essential to be open to the possibility that they may not be meaningful to the client, or that the client may want to adapt them: the therapist needs to hold their own spontaneous metaphors lightly.

A second category of therapist metaphor consists of planned and purposefully deployed metaphors, images and teaching stories that are intended to be consistent with, and reinforce, the theoretical approach of the therapist. Examples of this kind of metaphor include:

- psychodynamic: metaphors around mothering, being a child or baby such as 'it's as though you have lost that comfort blanket…'

- humanistic/person-centred: growth metaphors such as 'beneath the surface, there's just that part of you wanting to show itself'
- cognitive-behavioural therapy (CBT): information-processing metaphors, for example – 'there's just too much to take in', 'depression is like wearing dark glasses so nothing ever looks bright'.

Because it emphasizes the importance of the client learning the theory and actively applying it in their life outside therapy, the CBT professional community has developed many metaphors and images to facilitate client understanding. An extremely helpful and informative introduction to this resource is a paper by Killick et al. (2016), in which well-known CBT therapists briefly describe how they introduce clients to therapeutic metaphors. Other useful CBT sources are available (Blenkiron 2010; Friedberg and Wilt 2010; Stoddard and Afari 2014; Stott et al. 2010).

Therapist-generated metaphors are also widely used in narrative therapy, notably the idea of the 'Tree of Life' (Denborough 2008, 2018; Ncube 2006). Clients in a therapy or community development group draw their own personal 'tree of life', including their 'roots' (where they come from), their skills and knowledges, their hopes and dreams, as well as the special people in their lives. Participants then join their trees into a 'forest of life' and, in groups, discuss some of the 'storms' that affect their lives and ways that they respond to these storms, protect themselves and each other. The aim of the Tree of Life is to enable people to speak about their lives in ways that strengthen their relationships with their own history, their culture and significant people in their lives. The success of this technique with people from many different cultural settings and life difficulties reflects the meaningfulness, in all cultures, of the tree as a metaphor and growth as a central principle of life.

Therapists have also developed images and metaphors to facilitate therapy for different client groups. For instance, the literature around counselling with clients from non-Western cultural backgrounds and counselling for people struggling to move on from bereavement illustrate this approach. Genuchi et al. (2017) have described how they use therapist-generated metaphors in therapy with men, particularly around facilitating exploration of emotions. Their key metaphor was 'emotion as information', which could be expanded into related images and metaphors around activities that were particularly meaningful for a specific client, such as sport, engineering or computing.

In terms of developing skills for using planned therapist-generated metaphor, it is vital to find images and metaphors that are meaningful for you and that you are comfortable using. If a metaphor has not assisted your own personal learning and growth, you are unlikely to deploy it in a way that clients perceive as authentic and credible. It is also important to do deliberate practice on how you would offer your chosen metaphors to clients, and how you might follow through on the metaphor to use it to facilitate actual client change. These skills are best seen as representing career-long therapist professional development tasks, rather than competencies that can be acquired in the space of a few months.

Conclusions

This chapter has explored skills and strategies around productive and creative ways of using language to facilitate the process of therapy. The general topic of the role of language in therapy is potentially vast, and has not been sufficiently integrated into therapy theory and training. It is therefore not realistic to expect to be able to gain a comprehensive knowledge of these issues. However, there are many specific points in therapy where awareness and skills around language options can be facilitative. Learning these skills can be awkward, because it inevitably involves paying attention to your own way of talking. This is an area in which it can be particularly helpful to record counselling skills practice sessions, listen for examples of ways of using words that you might want to revise, then stop the recording and say alternative statements out loud. A crucial question to keep in mind is whether a particular way of talking supports collaboration, shared decision-making and dialogue, or closes it down by reinforcing a more controlling and hierarchical form of word use. A particularly useful resource, in terms of developing conversational flexibility, is a book by McHenry and McHenry (2020) that offers a unique collection of examples of ways that therapists talk.

Useful additional resources, in terms of developing conversational flexibility beyond the topics covered in the present chapter, include the book by McHenry and McHenry (2020) that offers examples of ways that therapists talk, research by Banham and Schweitzer (2017) highlighting the effectiveness of therapist use of concrete observational language, and the literature on the therapeutic use of humour (Gladding and Drake Wallace 2016; Irving 2019).

Learning activities

The following activities may be explored individually, and/or with a group of learning partners.

1 This task is intended to get you thinking about metaphor, taking a few moments to reflect on the images and metaphors that come to mind when you think about different aspects of the counselling process. Write whatever comes into your mind when you read the following questions:

- What kind of animal is a counsellor? Or a client?
- What kind of imagery comes to mind when you think about the process of counselling? The interaction between a counsellor and client is similar to...?
- Completing a series of counselling sessions is like...?

This exercise is based on a study by the psychotherapy researcher Lisa Najavits (1993), who asked counsellors and therapists to write down their images for the therapy process. Are there any metaphors from her article that introduced a perspective on therapy that you were not previously aware of? Or that stimulate you to think about therapy in new and possibly helpful ways?

2   An important skill in relation to using language to support collaboration in therapy is to be able to draw on a repertoire of words and images in relation to key ideas. This chapter includes a table of words for talking about goals. Identify other concepts that you might find yourself discussing with a client, for example anxiety, depression, therapy alliance, therapy homework activities, emotions, rupture, strengths or termination. Start with a concept that is particularly meaningful for you in respect of your own style of counselling, and generate a list or word map of possible ways of referring to it. This exercise can be carried out alone, but has added value in a group situation where ideas can be shared. Once you have created a list, take some time to reflect on the ways that different words and phrases have slightly different meanings, and the implications of this for how they might be used in therapy.

3   As you read, attend workshops/training events, watch therapy videos, receive your own therapy or participate in counselling skills practice sessions, keep a note of (a) the ways that therapists respond to and work with client metaphors; (b) the possible consequences of not responding to a client metaphor (i.e. what might the therapist have done to handle this better?); and (c) ways that therapists introduce their own metaphors into therapy. Reflect on what you have learned, in terms of ways of using metaphor that are helpful or unhelpful in relation to your own preferred style or approach as a therapist.

Non-verbal and embodied presence

Introduction

Although Freud characterized therapy as the 'talking cure', it is clear to anyone who is a counsellor or a client that there is a lot happening in a therapy session beyond words. In particular, non-verbal bodily processes and interactions and channels of communication can have a powerful influence on the experience of therapy, the quality of the therapeutic relationship and the depth of connection between therapist and client. This chapter examines skills associated with the capacity to facilitate non-verbal and embodied processes in therapy in helpful ways. Until quite recently, discussion of non-verbal aspects of counselling skills largely centred on readily observable factors such as posture, eye gaze and touch. These topics remain crucially important, and are covered in the present chapter. However, in recent years there has been a massive expansion of research in neuroscience and embodied cognition that has started to transform our understanding of therapy skills. Essentially, findings from these studies have made it possible to identify multiple ways in which cognitive, emotional and relationship processes operate at an embodied level that is outside of conscious awareness. Further information on theories and research studies that have contributed to an understanding of embodied knowing can be found in Claxton (2015), Hauke and Kritikos (2018) and McLeod (2019: Chapter 19).

When reflecting on non-verbal and embodied counselling skills and awareness, it is important to keep in mind that such processes are a two-way street. Some clients are highly sensitive observers of their therapist's non-verbal cues, and highly disciplined in their own transmission of such information, on account of vigilance acquired through growing up with unpredictable or abusive caretakers.

The development of non-verbal skills needs to be based in reflection on practice – actually checking out whether what you are doing is helpful in a particular situation. This is because the meaning of any embodied process is heavily contextualized. For example, the appropriateness of a non-verbal response such as eye contact, touch or voice quality depends on the personal and cultural preferences of those involved, and the particular moment at which it is used. There are very few general rules. Effective non-verbal skills require a capacity to be responsive, including collaboratively checking with the client whether a specific way of responding is helpful. In recognition of this issue, this chapter has been written as an invitation to reflect on some key non-verbal and embodied skills. Each section includes information on what to look for and possibilities around what a counsellor might do.

Further discussion of the use of non-verbal and embodied skills in relation to working with emotions can be found in Chapter 13.

Elements of embodied non-verbal communication

There are several different non-verbal and embodied channels of communication that are relevant in counselling. The followings sections introduce skills and awareness associated with each of these dimensions.

Posture

Posture is a broad concept that refers to the positioning of the counsellor's body during a counselling session. It is generally understood that a crossed-arm posture or a backward lean runs the risk of conveying detachment and possibly also an attitude of judgement. Perhaps the single most widely known idea about non-verbal communication in counselling is the SOLER model developed by Gerard Egan in the 1970s, which describes the optimal posture as: S (Squarely) – the counsellor sits directly opposite the client or at a slight angle; O (Open posture) – arms and legs are not crossed; L (Lean towards the other) – conveys interest, attention and being client-focused; E (Eye contact) – consistent direct eye contact with occasional breaks; R (Relaxed) – not moving around too much or conveying nervousness. More recently, Stickley (2011) has created an alternative model (SURETY), consisting of: S (sitting at an angle); U (uncrossed legs and arms); R (relaxed); E (eye contact); T (touch); and Y (your intuition). The key differences in the Stickley (2011) model are that it is intended to take account of the way that sitting directly opposite someone may be experienced as threatening and inquisitorial, and also to function as a reminder that appropriate touch may be helpful and that it is essential for the counsellor to use their intuition (i.e. sense of what is appropriate in the moment) to inform their response.

The research studies that have investigated the connection between postural factors and client ratings of rapport have broadly supported the validity of the SOLER and SURETY models (Sharpley and Sagris 1995a, 1995b; Sharpley et al. 2001). These findings also suggest that the degree to which the counsellor's posture matches or mirrors that of the client, and the counsellor's capacity to be flexible and intuitive (i.e. not remain in a fixed posture, but respond in different ways at different moments in a session) are important.

Facial expression

In the field of social psychology, several decades of research by the American social psychologist Paul Ekman and his colleagues have generated valuable insights about micro-facial expressions that occur out of awareness. These micro-movements have evolved as culturally universal signalling systems, adapted for survival human groups, that are grounded in autonomic nervous system activity (Ekman and Friesen 2003). Facial micro-movements are highly significant in therapy because they act as a channel of communication for emotions such as disgust and anger, that a person might be consciously trying to suppress. Very subtle facial movements, such as a fleeting smile or moment of anger, may contradict the verbal messages or story offered by the client. There is evidence from both physiological and video monitoring that the recipient (e.g. therapist) reacts to these cues at a neurobiological level, even if they are not able to verbalize their response. In addition, accuracy in understanding subtle facial movements is associated with an ability to manage social interaction. Therapy researchers have identified complex patterns of client–therapist facial interaction patterns associated with productive and unproductive therapy processes and episodes (Benecke et al. 2005; De Roten et al. 2002; Rasting and Beutel 2005). For example, most of the time, if a client smiles and the therapist responds with a smile, the effect is to reinforce their relationship in a productive way. However, if the client smiles in a self-deprecating or self-mocking manner, a reciprocal therapist smile is not helpful (because it is colluding with the dysfunctional behaviour of the client), whereas a neutral facial response is more likely to lead to facilitative processing of the interaction.

A useful approach to developing non-verbal counselling skills is to practise sensitivity to facial expression cues (e.g. watching a slowed-down video of a client's face with colleagues and comparing perceptions of which emotions are being expressed). It can also be valuable to broaden one's awareness, and personal repertoire, in respect of one's own facial expressions. Self-awareness and repertoire can be expanded by watching one's own face on slowed-down video, then practising alternative facial responses in a mirror. Paul Ekman's website includes a great deal of useful material on all aspects of facial expression.

Eye contact

Direct eye contact is associated with interpersonal closeness and connection. By contrast, avoidance of eye contact may convey a lack of trustworthiness or caring. As with most counselling skills, eye contact is a Goldilocks phenomenon – too much (i.e. fixed staring) is as unhelpful as too little. The optimal level of 'just right' eye contact will depend on a wide range of conditions, including cultural norms, personal preferences and the topic being explored at that moment. From a broader perspective, eye contact represents one aspect of the wider phenomenon of gaze, and in particular mutual gaze. In addition to looking at each other, there can be important moments in therapy when counsellor and client look at the same thing together – for example at a diagram the counsellor has drawn on a flip chart page, a painting that the client has made, or through the therapy room window at the snow that has started to fall. The concept of gaze also introduces the quality of the way that one person looks at another. For instance, clients who are overweight may dread the counsellor's fat-shaming gaze. Many clients will treasure the moments when their therapist's loving or compassionate gaze rests on them.

Voice quality

Therapist voice quality – the tone, pace and volume of their voice – has an influence on the client experience (Rice and Wagstaff 1967; Tomicic et al. 2015). For example, when a therapist speaks in a soft, quiet voice it tunes into the client's feelings and evokes a sense of closeness. A natural, relaxed way of speaking can indicate interest, attentiveness and genuineness. By contrast, a more controlling, clipped voice creates more distance, and a sense that the therapist is in control. Research studies have shown that therapist voice quality can produce direct shifts in physiological functioning in the client (Kykyri et al. 2017). In addition, different voices have significant cultural associations (e.g. the therapist speaking like a teacher, or like a mother trying to soothe her baby). An import-ant aspect of therapist voice quality is that it can influence the client in the direction of adopting a similar way of talking. For instance, a client who is anxious may talk at a rapid pace, to avoid accessing underlying painful feelings. When the therapist responds in a more slow-paced and soft/soothing voice, it can help the client to slow down and allow themselves to be more aware of what they are feeling in the moment.

Therapist awareness of client voice quality may provide them with useful clues around how clients are processing their emotions. Rice and Wagstaff (1967) observed four distinctive patterns of client voice quality: emotional, focused (tracking inner experience), externalizing (directing or controlling the listener) and limited (holding back). These different voice qualities also convey informa-tion about how the client is maintaining closeness or distance in their relation-ship with their interlocutor (the therapist). Honos-Webb and Stiles (1998) found that different parts of the self were 'voiced' in different ways. While clients and therapists have an awareness that different vocal qualities are meaningful (Tomicic et al. 2015), it is probable that most of the time they are not consciously paying attention to such information. It therefore functions outside of awareness, as a channel of embodied communication between client and therapist. In terms of becoming more skilful and resourceful in relation to this area of practice, it can be helpful for counsellors to listen to their own voice in session recordings, get feedback from others about how their voice comes across, and pay attention to the voice quality of well-known therapists whose work is available on video. There are also many voice-oriented training exercises used in drama and singing workshops that can provide valuable learning opportunities for counsellors. Aspects of voice quality that relate to cultural and social class background are discussed in Chapter 3.

Gestures and encouragers

Allen Ivey introduced the idea of 'minimal encouragers': brief vocalizations such as 'mm-hmm' and 'uh-huh' that convey the message that the listener is paying attention, and encourage the speaker to keep talking. Other writers have described such actions as 'response tokens'. Judicious use of these modes of communication encourages speakers to keep talking and to add detail to what they are speaking about. A similar function is fulfilled by nodding, smiling and leaning forward. All of these responses provide feedback and encouragement to speakers, without interrupting their flow. Some research has found that these types of response occur a lot in sessions, and function best when they are combined – encouraging noises without accompanying micro-movement seem to be off-putting (Battles and Berman 2012).

Another type of micro-movement that occurs frequently in therapy sessions is gesture. A study by Gerwing and Li (2019) found that client and therapist verbal statements were more meaningful when accompanied by gestures. As with other non-verbal and embodied skills, the use of minimal encouragers, affirmatory micro-movements and gestures seems to be most helpful when the client and therapist converge on a frequency and style of using these responses with which they both feel comfortable (Salazar Kämpf et al. 2020).

Proxemics

The concept of proxemics was developed by the American cultural anthropologist Edward T. Hall in the 1960s, to refer to the use of personal space in different social contexts and cultures. For example, people in Western societies accept a level of being crushed together in a lift or underground train that they would abhor in a shop or on a beach. An appreciation of theory and research in the field of proxemics is highly relevant to the development of counselling skills. Traditionally, most counsellors sit opposite their clients, at a distance between chairs of more than a metre. As pointed out by theorists such as Stickley (2011), such an arrangement impedes potentially valuable forms of therapeutic interaction such as touching, sitting side by side to work collaboratively on a task such as creating a diagram together, or sitting side by side as a means of offering emotional support. Lohr et al. (2018) suggest that therapy clients differ a great deal in their preferences for the amount of distance between their therapist and themselves. A crucial aspect of the layout and furnishing of a therapy room is the scope allowed for adjustment to personal space. This consideration also applies to the design of therapy clinics. For some clients it is very important to have a private space where they can be alone immediately before or after a session. Close scrutiny of videos of face-to-face counselling sessions can reveal many moments at which therapist or client try to get physically closer or more distant, to the extent made possible by the physical space in which they are meeting. A useful exercise that is conducted in many therapy training programmes is to experiment with distance during counselling skills practice sessions – how is the process and experience of a session changed by being closer to each other, or further apart?

Expression of emotions

Feelings and emotions are important in everyday life and in therapy because they function as indicators of the underlying, fundamental significance of a situation or relationship. Counsellors need to be skilful in helping clients to be aware of their feelings, and to be able to use them as a guide for action (Chapter 14). A lot of the time, a client will either name their feelings and emotions, or provide enough of a label ('that yucky feeling') to enable the nature of the feeling to be clarified. However, emotions are complex – they comprise multiple threads of feeling that are bound up in the client's story. Some of these threads may be easier to talk about than others. For example, some people are able to talk about their fears and worries, but not their anger – others are the opposite. For all of these reasons, it is necessary for a counsellor to be able to access as many channels of emotional communication as possible, including non-verbal and embodied sources as well linguistic ones.

A recurring theme in this book is that being able to observe and be aware of relevant phenomena and processes is a crucial aspect of counselling skills. Some of the ways in which a client's emotions may be expressed non-verbally include physical signs such as a flushed face, tense facial expression, agitated movement, bodily tension, fast shallow breathing, yawning, sighing, appearing to almost stop breathing, tummy rumbling, voice quality and fast pace of speech, fatigue, and self-soothing or scratching. Emotions are generally associated with a particular part of their body, for instance disgust with throat and digestive areas, and anger with arms (De Jager et al. 2016; Nummenmaa et al. 2014). A client who is experiencing such emotions, or trying to convey them, may touch or stroke (i.e. soothe) the relevant part of the body.

Other useful information may be available through the therapist's own bodily response. Any of the client emotion cues listed above may be mirrored by the therapist. For example, a therapist may note that they are moving around in their chair, are locked into a particular facial expression, or that their tummy is rumbling. In addition, the therapist may be aware of their own personal inner feeling states that either resonate with those of the client (i.e. are similar to what the client is feeling at that moment) or represent a reaction to the client's feelings (i.e. similar to the way that other people, such as family members, feel when they interact with the client). The therapist may also be aware of internal memories, images or fantasies that symbolize action tendencies associated with specific emotions, such as a fantasy of running away from a wild animal (fear) or searching for something (loss).

There are several approaches to therapy that pay special attention to bodily expression, such as Gestalt therapy, body psychotherapy, and various methods of working with trauma. As a result, there exist a range of counselling skills and strategies that have been developed to facilitate constructive therapeutic use of such phenomena. The most basic skill is to just draw the client's attention to what seems to be a potentially relevant non-verbal process ('I was just aware there that you seemed to tense up your whole body and clench your fists when you talked about that situation'), and invite the client to keep attending to it for a few seconds ('Would it be OK to just stay with that for a moment or two, or maybe even exaggerate it…?') and report on what they are experiencing ('Are there any thoughts or memories, or words that come to mind when you tense your body like that…?'). The therapist might also offer a tentative hypothesis ('When you tensed up like that, I wondered, wow, you are so angry, you are ready for a fight… but maybe I picked that up wrong – how do you make sense of it yourself?').

Breathing

The breathing patterns of both client and therapist are an indicator of emotional states and energy levels. Shallow breathing is often associated with anxiety and panic, while breath-holding is often a sign of an attempt to control painful or terrifying emotions. On the other hand, deep breathing into the abdomen can produce energy and a sense of positivity and well-being. Deep breaths and sighing may be signs of becoming aware of highly meaningful memories or insights. Counsellor non-verbal skills include awareness of client breath patterns, and one's own. In addition, it can be helpful to draw a client's attention to their shallow breathing or breath-holding, and gently invite them to breathe more fully into their abdomen. Sometimes it can be useful to demonstrate or model this action, and take a few moments to breathe together. The relaxation instructions and self-help tapes used in cognitive-behavioural therapy (CBT) for anxiety typically include instructions for breathing well. A routine aspect of outdoor therapies is involvement in physical activity (e.g. walking, canoeing) that inevitably induces deeper breathing. Some approaches to therapy, such as body therapy, Gestalt therapy and yoga-informed therapy, incorporate more specialist skills and interventions based on different breath exercises.

Tears

Client and therapist tears and weeping represent a powerful form of non-verbal communication and interpersonal contact (Morgan and Nutt Williams 2021). From a client perspective, their own tears convey their depth of feeling around an issue in their life, function as a marker that they feel sufficient safety and trust in the therapist to express their feelings directly, and may provide a sense of catharsis or release. Tears may also be significant because they reflect a healing process that is consistent with the client's cultural tradition, in a way that talking to a therapist may not be. Their therapist's tears may allow them to see that the therapist is open to their experience and has been touched by their story. The experience of weeping together may function as a memorable moment of mutuality and togetherness that either of them can refer to at a later point in their work. From the perspective of the therapist, in addition to all of the ways of understanding tears already mentioned, there may also be a sense that the client's tears, or their own tears in response, may not be entirely authentic, and could instead be understood as a familiar form of emotional expression that perhaps serves to mask a level of feeling that is too scary to allow into awareness (e.g. crying rather than getting angry).

Although tears can have different meanings at different times, it is clear that they comprise a highly significant non-verbal and embodied event in therapy. Typically a therapist will punctuate or follow such an episode by using gentle probes or reflections to explore the meaning of tears (for example, 'If your tears had words, what would they be saying?' or 'I just felt, in myself, how completely awful your loss has been… am I picking that up right?'). Although this kind of active meaning-making is helpful, it is also important to acknowledge that there can often be aspects of tears that go beyond words, and just need to be accepted as part of being human.

Sexual feelings

Physical attraction, sexual feelings, and their manifestation in positive anticipation about meeting, excitement and pleasure in spending time together, and flirting are areas of embodied and non-verbal behaviour that are present in some counselling relationships for the client and/or the therapist (Sonne and Jochai 2014). Acting on these feelings, by developing a sexual relationship, has the effect of ending therapy as it is irreversibly turned into something else. It can also be highly damaging for the client, leading to confusion and a sense of being exploited and betrayed by someone they trusted. Professional ethical codes unambiguously forbid sexual relationships of any kind between a therapist and a client. At a level of everyday practice, it is generally accepted that it is unhelpful for a therapist to tell a client that they find them sexually attractive, because it may be heard as a demand or as a condition of ongoing care. These injunctions mean that therapists sometimes do not allow themselves to even be aware that such feelings are occurring.

Gelso et al. (2014) suggest that such a response is not ideal, because it excludes emotions and ways of relating that may be highly significant for the client, and precludes the possibility of using therapy to facilitate learning and development in these areas. Gelso et al. (2014) argue that therapists should be willing to talk about love and attraction in the therapy room, no matter how awkward such conversations might be. They identify two key skills that are required in respect of this process. First, the therapist needs to reflect on their own feelings and fantasies about the client, including discussing the topic with their supervisor or personal therapist. This is necessary as a means of enabling the therapist to understand and separate off their own needs and wishes, so that they can focus on the client. The second skill or strategy is to treat the client's sexual attraction as a feeling just like any other, and a potential source of strength and resource for living, and not create a sense of shame in the client by conveying a sense that what they are feeling is wrong. The dominant tradition in therapy has been to either avoid talking about sexuality, or to treat it as a problem (e.g. as something that might require referral to a sex therapist). An alternative approach is reflected in the model of sex-positivity developed by Mosher (2017), which advocates affirming the client's sexuality as a source of pleasure, energy, intimacy and connection. From such a perspective, the client's sexual feelings towards their therapist become a starting point from which they can build such experiences in their real world, and – if necessary – grieve and make sense of the absence of such opportunities in the past.

Touch

There are many forms of touch that occur in counselling: handshakes, sitting side by side on a sofa, a light touch on the arm to draw attention to something, a hand on the back when entering or leaving a room, hugging, holding, cradling and stroking, a high five to celebrate an achievement. Touch can have many meanings:

an act of connection, caring, soothing or grounding; a boundary being crossed or renegotiated; something to be feared, something that is forbidden, restimulation of earlier experience of physical abuse and violation. There are also examples of proxy touching, in the use of dogs and horses in various types of therapy. Members of therapy groups often touch each other. In general, however, there is a lot of fear and uncertainty associated with the use of touch in one-to-one counselling (Burkholder et al. 2010). While touch is a routine aspect of therapy in many cultural settings (see, for example, Campbell and Wilson 2017), in many Western cultural settings it is often avoided because of concerns that it might lead to unethical sexual contact, recognition that some clients would have been traumatized by previous intrusive touch experiences, and because the counselling encounter is usually a private one-to-one meeting in which exploitative or insensitive touching and complaints about touch are hard to verify. While analyses of the experience of touch in general healthcare settings are generally positive (Kelly et al. 2018, 2020; Wearn et al. 2019), reviews of the literature on touch in psychotherapy yield a much more ambiguous picture (Phelan 2009; Zur and Nordmarken 2011). There are no generally accepted guidelines for the use of touch in psychotherapy. Some therapists never touch their clients. Others restrict themselves to a handshake. Yet others are more open to whatever seems helpful for the client and acceptable to them. Some clients appreciate touch while others do not. When developing skills in using touch it is important to be mindful of any expectations and guidelines that might exist in one's place of employment, and to work out how to check out with a client in advance whether, under what conditions, and what type of touch they might regard as helpful. And then afterwards to check out again whether it has been. It is also important to work out what you might say if a client asks to be touched or held.

Props

It is not sufficient to think about non-verbal and embodied skills as merely a matter of how the counsellor and client interact with each other. A lot of the time, non-verbal meaning is conveyed through the use of props – physical objects that make it possible for different types of bodily interaction to take place. For example, different types of non-verbal information are available if client and counsellor are sitting in upright chairs that limit their capacity to move, as against sitting on sofas or couches that allow more scope for movement and a wider range of postures. Similarly, a room with a choice of seating arrangements – more than two chairs, sofas as well as chairs, seats that can be moved closer to each other or further away – creates a moment of choice and shared decision-making at the start of the session. A collection of photographs of counselling rooms would reveal a wide range of physical objects or props:

Chairs, sofas, couches, tables, plants, coat-stands, slippers, cupboards, bookshelves, books, cushions, blankets, quilts, rugs, yoga mat, tissues, waste bin, heaters, fans, air conditioning

Paper, worksheets and forms, pencils, pens, crayons, paints, rubbers, plasticine

Found or collected objects: driftwood, buttons, stones, flowers, objects of remembrance, gifts

Paintings, drawings, photographs, sculptures

Recording equipment

Musical instruments

A mirror, a magnifying glass

Jugs, glasses, cups, kettles, plates, sugar bowls, food, baby bottles

Cuddly toys, figurines (people, animals), vehicles, games, jigsaws, dolls house, sand tray

A view from a window – sight of birds, trees, hills, weather. Curtains, blinds

A dog.

Each of these objects can function as a source of meaning, and as a go-between in the counsellor–client relationship.

When counselling takes place out of doors, many more material objects and forces come into play. A significant difference in outdoor sessions is that nature is an active participant in the therapy process – client and therapist need to respond to changes in weather, seasons and light levels. In addition to the appearance of birds, animals, insects and plants over which the therapist has no control, working out of doors also introduces the potential for including horses as well as dogs as therapy companions.

Some approaches to therapy, such as arts therapies, horticultural therapies and equine-assisted therapy, make explicit use of props, and train practitioners in how to work with them. However, most of the time, therapists just accumulate objects that seem helpful, and evolve their own routines and rituals around them. Sometimes, clients take the prop home with them so that it becomes a 'transition object' that reminds them of the therapist and the safe space of the therapy room (Arthern and Madill 1999, 2002). This may happen on a regular basis in arts therapies, where the client may accumulate a series of pictures or sculptures that represent their journey through therapy. However, clients in conventionally talk-based therapy may also collect objects from the therapy room – in one study a stone, earring, cuddly bear and cardigan (Arthern and Madill 2002).

Online counselling

Compared to traditional face-to-face working, the practice of counselling at a distance, through phone, online video (i.e. Zoom, Skype, etc.) and text represents a distinctive set of challenges in relation to reduction in the amount of non-verbal information that is available. Both phone and online video counselling have the effect of highlighting voice quality. The latter also enables greater attention to facial cues. Bailenson (2021) has suggested that Zoom counselling can be stressful and tiring for participants because of the intensity of eye contact, and the tendency to work harder at facial expressiveness as a means of compensating for the absence of other non-verbal cues. In addition, he described the effect of seeing one's own image on screen as the equivalent of an 'all-day mirror' that leads to self-consciousness.

Geller (2020) provides a list of ways that therapists can enhance and maintain effective levels of presence online. There are also significant differences in the range and type of props that are available to support embodied presence and interaction. Some clients feel more emotionally secure on account of being in their own personal space during a counselling session. By contrast, others may feel insecure and guarded because of the fear of being overhead by others in their home. In the context of online therapy to adolescent clients, Hart (2020) described examples of creative ways that clients used the space at their end of the call, and even aspects of the Zoom interface, to regulate the embodied non-verbal process between client and therapist. Because online video counselling is a relatively recent development, and particularly because it has expanded to a huge extent during the Covid-19 pandemic, a lot of attention has been paid to the therapeutic implication of a (relatively) disembodied way of working. However, what seems to be emerging is an appreciation, just as in the longer-established practice of telephone counselling, that clients and therapists adapt to the conditions that are available to them. Some clients and therapists find that online video contact (or telephone and text contact) works well for them, while others refuse to have anything to do with it. This pattern almost certainly reflects the way that individual preferences play out in particular settings, rather than being a distinctive aspect of therapy at a distance: there are many people who are far from comfortable with the prospect of sitting in a room for an hour with a therapist looking at them.

Reflecting on non-verbal skills: critical perspectives for practice

On the whole, existing knowledge about non-verbal and embodied counselling skills mainly comprises suggestions about what to think about in situations where things aren't going well, rather than prescriptions around what to do to get things right. As a result, the development of such skills depends to a large extent on creating opportunities to observe oneself (e.g. through video recordings) and benefiting from feedback from clients and observers. It can also be helpful to watch how other therapists manage their embodied presence and that of their clients. In relation to the development of non-verbal skills, when observing one's own performance as a counsellor or inviting comment from clients and colleagues, there are four main perspectives to consider:

* *The client's response*: for each non-verbal or embodied response that you made, how did the client react? Although the client's verbal feedback on how they recalled feeling at the time is also important, it is possible that they may not have a complete recollection of each moment of a session – micro-analysis of their immediate reaction on the video is a valuable tool for reflection on practice.

* *Discrepancies*: were there any differences between what was being said (by the counsellor or client) and their non-verbal/embodied behaviour? Some theorists of non-verbal behaviour, such as Ekman, suggest that the person's authentic truth may leak out through non-verbal 'tells'. It is also possible that a person may tell a powerful story about their experience, but remain physically frozen and still. From a counselling point of view, either of these possibilities are of interest. An important area of skill development is learning to be sensitive to discrepancies, and formulating constructive ways to feed this awareness into the therapy process.

* *Synchrony*: one of the general findings to emerge from studies of non-verbal and embodied process in therapy is that better outcomes are associated with sessions that exhibit a high level of interpersonal synchrony (e.g. therapist and client bodily movement patterns and rates are similar and appear to be as if they are participating in a dance), and that therapist and client converge from their distinct starting points to end up functioning as if a single system. At the same time, moments of lack of synchrony can also be significant in terms of indicating either a general lack of embodied connection, or alternatively a temporary phase that reflects the (unconscious) unwillingness of one participant to buy into the emotional tone being set by the other (Tschacher and Meier 2020).

* *Authenticity*: almost all of the non-verbal skills discussed in this chapter can be faked. For example, a counsellor can lean forward, and emit regular minimal encouragers without actually listening or understanding the client at all. It is not easy to evaluate level of authenticity. Sometimes the client will have an intuitive sense that something is not quite right. Careful micro-analysis of a session video may show that in what appear to be authentic interactions the gap between client embodied action and embodied counsellor response is too long. Data from research analyses of simultaneous monitoring of client and therapist physiological reactions, or their facial movements, tends to indicate that synchrony is almost immediate, and well below the threshold for conscious decision-making (Paulick et al. 2018; Tschacher 2018).

The technique of interpersonal process recall (IPR), described in Chapter 4, provides a basis for reflection and learning of embodied non-verbal counselling skills. The areas of focus outlined above represent suggestions for making the most of IPR sessions. However, the basic experience of IPR – just watching a session and being able to re-enter what it felt like at the time – is itself a powerful learning opportunity.

Conclusions

The non-verbal and embodied dimension of the therapy process – and the skills associated with it – has been a somewhat neglected topic in the therapy training and practice literature. It is hard to do research that demonstrates the impact of non-verbal skills on client outcomes, because these skills are bound up with many other co-occurring processes, and are highly flexible and improvised rather than being fixed units of behaviour. In addition, it is also hard to undertake research that does justice to the enormous complexity of patterns of non-verbal communication, personal space, etc. associated with different cultural traditions. However, the challenges involved in establishing an evidence base for embodied aspects of therapy do not diminish its practical significance.

Learning activities

1   Meet up with one or more learning partners. Pair off as counsellor and client (with observers if possible) and conduct a face-to-face counselling session without words. If there is time, conduct other wordless sessions that involve the use of props that are not language-based, such as lego bricks, plasticine or lines on paper. Reflect on what is gained and what is missing in these scenarios, compared with a talking counselling session.

2   Watch a video recording of yourself as counsellor, with the sound switched off. The first viewing should be just watching what is there and being aware of your immediate response as a viewer. Later viewing may involve: (i) experimenting with what significant parts of the session look like when speeded up, slowed down or paused, and (ii) systematic application of the crucial perspectives introduced towards the end of the chapter.

3   Make a video recording of yourself as a counsellor, then use interpersonal process recall (IPR) (Chapter 4), inviting your client (a colleague or learning partner rather than a real client) to watch the video and pause it when there is an aspect of your non-verbal/embodied responses, and their own, that they regard as significant.

4   Make an audio or video recording of yourself as counsellor. Adjust the sound controls until you can sense the voice quality but not detect the meaning of the words. Make notes on the client's voice quality, and your own, and the interplay between them. It is instructive to conduct a similar learning activity with recordings of well-known therapists – for example the Carl Rogers session with Gloria (available on the internet).

5   If you were able to design your own counselling room, what props would you include in it? For each prop, make notes on how you might use it to support your non-verbal/embodied presence. (A further learning activity could include practising the use of a prop with a learning partner as client.)

Making meaning

Introduction

The baseline or default setting for any counselling encounter is that of allowing the person to talk in a way that enables them to find meaning and possibility in the area of their life space that is troubling them. The aim of this chapter is to consider some of the skills and strategies that a counsellor can use to facilitate a therapeutic conversation so that the client can reflect on their actions and experience. The chapter builds on the discussion of skills for developing client–therapist shared understanding in Chapter 7, in particular the use of empathic engagement, in looking specifically at strategies for generating new perspectives and new ways of understanding that can make a difference to the way that a person lives their life.

Making sense of meaning-making

Facilitating client reflection on the meaning of their experience comprises one of the fundamental core change processes that occur in therapy. It is possible to identify four main processes through which reflection and meaning-making takes place:

1 The client gradually acquires a more effective capacity to think about what they are thinking and doing in their everyday life, rather than just acting in an automatic manner. This capacity is described in various ways in the therapy literature: reflective functioning, mentalizing, metacognitive processing. For example, a client who describes themselves as just losing control and getting angry for no apparent reason becomes able to pause, reflect and make sense of what is triggering their emotional response, and consider the alternative options and responses that are available to them.

2 Making cognitive connections, or constructing meaning bridges, between two areas of experience. For example, a client with a problem in controlling anger may realize that the internal harsh critic that leads to bouts of depression is the same inner voice that tells them that they are a coward if they allow someone else to push in front of them in a queue.

3 Constructing a personal explanatory model or theory. A step beyond a capacity to reflect and make connections is the ability to develop a 'big picture' understanding of where a particular issue fits into one's life as a whole. For example, the angry client may begin to appreciate how the depression, aggression and internal harsh critic are all part of the family environment in which they grew up, and the marital environment that they subsequently created with their partner.

4 Acquiring and applying a new concept or theory offered by the therapist or discovered through reading. For example, the angry client's therapist may feed in ideas that contribute to the making of connections and construction of a model, in the form of interpretations, or more formally present a theoretical account of the client's behaviour through a case formulation.

At one level these processes can be seen to operate on a continuum, with self-generated reflection and meaning-making at one end, and externally provided concepts and ideas at the other. However, in practice, self-generated and externally sourced reflection tend to operate hand in hand. For example, even the most private, personal and internal process of reflection uses words and concepts (that have originated somewhere else) as tools for reflection. Conversely, even direct teaching of concepts (such as in psycho-educational interventions) requires the learner to engage in personal reflection in order to assimilate the ideas that are being offered.

The capacity for reflexivity is a basic human accomplishment: research in developmental psychology has shown that it is transmitted at an early age through interaction and rhythmic playful talk between caretakers and babies. As a result, reflective and meaning-making abilities are bound up in core relationship patterns. Some individuals grow up with a secure sense that other people are trustworthy and reliable partners in meaning-making. Others may emerge from childhood with a core belief that the only person they can rely on is themselves. These differences can shape the way that clients respond to the kinds of skills discussed in this chapter.

Most people are not able to reflect on experience to make meaning and develop understanding to an equal extent in all areas of their life. It is therefore possible that a client who comes to counselling because they are struggling to make sense of intimate relationships, may possess a highly differentiated and sensitive capacity for productive reflection in professional or leisure contexts. One of the general strategies for facilitating client meaning-making around problematic issues is to encourage the client to import or apply reflexive skills that they already use elsewhere in their lives.

It is important to keep in mind that too much reflexivity and meaning-making may not be a good thing. Ideally, reflection on experience is part of a learning cycle in which reflection leads to a plan of action, that is carried out in the form of actual behaviour in the world, producing concrete experiences that are then reflected upon ... and so on. Too much reflection without action can be unhelpful for a client. For example, if someone is depressed, has panic attacks or is too anxious to function in social situations, then acquiring a comprehensive and highly differentiated intellectual understanding of these issues is not beneficial if it still leaves them feeling miserable. While some people may choose to spend long periods of their life engaged in reflection – for example members of contemplative religious orders – most people who come for counselling do not see reflection and insight as an end in itself, but as a necessary step in the direction of living a more satisfying life.

It is necessary to pay attention to the position or stance from which reflection and meaning-making takes place. In particular, it is crucial, in respect of both self-generated and externally provided sources of meaning, for the process of reflection to be grounded in acceptance and self-compassion. There is a toxic and undermining form of meaning-making that is driven by such forces as perfectionism and the demands of a harsh internal self-critic. These are traps.

The writings of Art Bohart are a valuable resource for thinking about the client's active involvement in meaning-making, the ways that therapists can facilitate that process, and how clients adapt therapist interventions to fit their own sense of what is helpful (Bohart and Tallmann 1996, 1999; Bohart 2000, 2021). A further valuable perspective can be found in the writings of Peter Fonagy, Anthony Bateman and their colleagues on the psychoanalytic concepts of mentalizing and reflective functioning – the capacity to make sense of self in relationships with others in terms of possessing an internalized model of how people think, feel and interact (Bateman and Fonagy 2019).

Skills for facilitating client reflection, understanding and meaning-making

The following sections begin with the skill of using silence, which predominantly aims to facilitate client personal reflection and meaning-making in the moment, and ends with case formulation, which makes greater use of externally sourced ideas provided by the therapist. It is important to use these skills in a collaborative manner, for example by establishing an understanding of the client's preferences, checking out whether a particular approach would be welcome at that specific moment, and getting feedback after the event about whether it had been helpful or how it might have been more helpful.

Silence

A potentially useful skill in relation to facilitating client reflection and meaning-making is to allow pauses or periods of silence in which the client is able to stay with their thoughts and feelings in a way that allows some kind of greater understanding to emerge. This can be particularly valuable when a client is speaking rapidly or continuously, in a manner that suggests a degree of avoidance of painful or upsetting memories: rapid-fire talk makes it difficult or impossible for the speaker to process the information that they are communicating.

Moments of silence in a counselling session can mean many different things and serve many different purposes. These include positive and helpful processes such as:

- allowing the client space to reflect or remember
- an opportunity to stay with feelings
- a still moment of peace, tranquillity, safety and belonging
- space for an internal process of discovery to unfold
- a chance for the client to work out an issue in their head or to work on a task such as making a drawing or picture.

Negative and unhelpful processes include:

- the therapist buying time to think what to say next
- client feels frightened and abandoned – triggers memories of being left alone
- client feels confused – What is going on here? What should I do?

- client has been traumatized by something that happened earlier in the session, and is emotionally frozen, unable to speak
- client has learned to be suspicious of anyone in authority so is withdrawing from the therapist or punishing them
- client is stuck – does not have the words to express what they are feeling
- avoidance/shame/embarrassment – either client or therapist (or both) are reluctant to talk about a particular issue
- not speaking is the client's normal mode of interaction, perhaps as a result of an avoidant attachment style
- lack of purpose: it just happens to be what the therapist has been trained to do (e.g. in psychoanalytic training)
- awkwardness – confusion/misunderstanding over whose turn it is to speak
- client is withdrawn, or annoyed with counsellor
- client has entered a dissociative state
- client is physically unwell.

This mixed picture of the potential meanings of silence during a therapy session means that most therapists have needed to develop strategies for working effectively with silence. Surveys and interviews where therapists share their ways of using silence can be a valuable source of learning (Hill et al. 2003; Ladany et al. 2004).

Skills for effectively using silence to support productive client reflection and meaning-making include:

- explaining to the client how and why silence can be useful
- exploring client preferences around silence at an early stage in therapy
- as the silence starts to unfold, quietly checking with client: 'Is this OK, or...?'
- during the silence, watching/observing the client (without staring at them) for clues about what might be going on
- being still and quiet during the silence
- if the silence is due to the therapist's need or wish to think about what to do or say next, it is helpful to briefly explain this to the client ('If it's OK, I just need a few moments to take all that in...'); in many situations the better option may be to think out loud, as a form of metacommunication
- at the end of the period of silence, checking out whether it had been helpful: 'I was aware that there was quite a long period where neither of us spoke – it seemed to me that you were deep in thought, so I didn't say anything...was that OK for you?... What would you want me to do if that situation arose again?'
- afterwards, exploring and processing what had been happening for the client during the silences
- the therapist sharing what they had been experiencing during the silence.

It is also important to be mindful of what you know about the client – e.g. if they had been exposed to punishing silence as a child, or have a history of regularly using techniques for silent reflection such as meditation, prayer, etc. It is also useful to consider the client's cultural background – for example, in some indigenous cultures what is unsaid, or the experience of sitting together in silence, are highly valued (Blue et al. 2015; Lee 1997). In Japanese culture, for example, the concept of *ma* refers to a general expectation and preference that communication will include gaps and spaces (Matsumoto 2020). A further significant aspect of the capacity to use silence skilfully is to have worked through the implications for practice of one's own personal position. For example, a therapist who has grown up in a large family, where everyone competed for air time and silence was a rare commodity, may be uncomfortable and uncertain about pauses and silences during therapy conversations, and as a consequence handle them awkwardly. The discussion of therapist authenticity in Chapter 9 highlighted the importance of pausing in the ongoing flow of the therapy interaction to monitor internal feelings and reactions. The use of pauses and brief silences can be viewed as contributing to building an authentic relationship (see, for example, Hernández and Grafanaki 2014).

Valuable practical insights are available from recent research studies that have explored the complexity of moments of silence. For example, a detailed analysis of silences in therapy sessions concluded that silence episodes that led into more productive and collaborative post-silence dialogue tended to be those where the therapist could sense that the client was engaged in an active internal process of reflection, and the client could sense that the therapist was supportively attentive and present throughout (Cuttler et al. 2019). The process of finding meaning through a process of staying with internal experience during silence is illustrated in case analyses of the importance of silence in long-term therapy, such as Hill et al. (2019a) and MacIntosh (2017).

Silence during in-session activities, such as art-making, has its own meaning and implications, and represents a separate topic (Regev et al. 2016a, 2016b).

In conclusion, it seems most useful to view silences and pauses as most likely to contribute to meaning-making when they spontaneously emerge from the ongoing dialogue between therapist and client. The key skills, in such a scenario, involve checking out that what is happening is helpful, supporting and paying attention to the process, and at the end of the episode of silence respectfully inviting the client to talk about what their experience had been. This works best when it builds on prior shared understanding of preferences around silence and the gradual establishment of a conversational rhythm that incorporates pauses, tentativeness and spaces. Silences that are triggered as a therapist technique, or arise from a breakdown of turn-taking and interpersonal alignment, are less likely to be helpful, and may even in some cases lead to the client deciding to quit therapy. However, uncomfortable silence episodes can provide valuable learning opportunities if the therapist is able to initiate an effective repair process.

Challenging

The use of challenge refers to counsellor activities that involve pointing out contradictions or discrepancies – for example between what the client says their goals are, and how they are behaving, or between inconsistent information they have provided at different times. Some clients explicitly want their counsellor to challenge them – they realize that sometimes they pretend, avoid things or 'fool themselves', and want their counsellor to be an honest observer who tells it as they see it. However, other clients may have been exposed to a lifetime of harsh criticism and are looking for support. Many clients want both challenge and support.

In the history of therapy, there have been approaches that made a lot of use of active confrontation (for example, some addictions models) – these are now regarded as risky and unhelpful. In the field of addictions, Moyers and Miller (2013) have argued that the evidence shows that empathy is generally much more effective than confrontation.

Many therapists are ambivalent about the skill of challenging. On the one hand, there are concerns that being too confrontative runs the risk of damaging the therapy alliance. On the other hand, in some situations a counsellor might be faced with a dilemma – to challenge, or risk colluding with the client's self-destructive behaviour or lack of honesty (Blanchard and Farber 2016; Farber et al. 2019). This ambivalence, along with the history of abusive use of confrontation in some therapy situations, has meant that there has been a limited amount of research into the process of challenge and its impact on therapy outcomes.

There are many different scenarios in which a counsellor might challenge their client, including:

- discrepancies between different things a client says and does:
  - between words and behaviours
  - between thoughts (head) and feelings (heart)
  - between self-acceptance ('I believe that I am basically a good person') and maladaptive thoughts/inner critic ('you are useless')
- client motivation/commitment to change:
  - not turning up for therapy/doing homework
  - withdrawing from the therapy process (tuning out, becoming distracted) during a session
  - persistent addictive behaviour (eating, alcohol, social media, etc.)
- actions that conflict with the values of the client and/or counsellor:
  - partner violence
  - actions that are not consistent with religious or social laws.

The common thread across these situations is a discrepancy between different positions or standpoints espoused by the client – for example between attending therapy and saying that they want to change, and then not seriously participating in therapy tasks. The use of challenge in therapy is therefore primarily concerned with facilitating a process of facing up to, then resolving, such discrepancies.

Skills and strategies for effective challenging are based on a principle of inviting the client to engage in a collaborative process of exploring discrepancies:

- establishing – early in therapy – the client's preference for, and their attitude to, challenge
- ensuring that the relationship is sufficiently solid
- the timing of a challenge is important:
  - challenge as soon as a discrepancy or apparent contradiction has become evident
  - alternatively, 'strike while the iron is cold' (i.e. wait until the client is open, reflective, not in survival mode, etc (Yalom 2002))
  - check out that the client is open to challenge at that particular moment ('Would it be OK if I challenged you a bit in what you just said…? If that's not relevant or helpful right now, just say…')
- pointing out *specific* discrepancies between different things the client says/does/believes, etc. – do not generalize – check out that you have observed/understood these things correctly
- conveying a sense of curiosity and openness, rather than being accusatory
- conveying a collaborative approach: 'We can make sense of this together' or 'Can you help me to understand this?'
- if appropriate, explaining why you are doing this – to achieve awareness and insight/understanding
- making links with goals for therapy.

Pressurizing the client to change (confrontation that comes across as being like a critical parent or teacher figure) is generally not helpful. The extent to which a therapist is able to be effective in their use of challenge is also influenced by their own attitude to confrontation, argument and conflict. In a study of training in skills for challenging, most participants reported that their confidence and competence with this skill was based in what they had learned in their family of origin. Some participants described how they had been exposed to open, supportive, honest and constructive models of challenge in their childhood. In contrast, others acknowledged that destructive patterns of confrontation in their families had made them highly anxious and avoidant around using this skill with clients (Chui et al. 2014).

Questions

The use of both open-ended and closed questions, as a means of supporting empathic engagement in the process of creating shared understanding, was discussed in Chapter 7. The following paragraphs explore skills in using questions in the context of working with a client around meaning-making and the development of new ways of understanding. In such situations, questions can operate as catalysts that allow new insights to emerge (Heron 1976; McCormack 2011). An invaluable source of ideas about strategies for creative use of questions in therapy can be found in McCarthy et al. (2020). Examples of this way of using questions include the following.

Hypothetical (what if?) questions: 'What would it be like for you to tell your boss how you feel?', 'What would happen if you just quit?', 'If you could imagine that you had woken up one morning and all these problems had vanished... what would your life be like?', 'If we were having this conversation in five years' time, what would your life be like?' This category of question can stimulate the client's imagination, and encourage them to think about new possibilities (Newman 2000).

Guided discovery questions (in CBT also described as 'Socratic questioning' or 'Socratic dialogue') invite the client to reflect on their own assumptions (this was the basis of the 'Socratic' method in Greek philosophy):

Client: 'If I don't check that the lights are off, my Dad will get ill and die'
Counsellor: 'What is the connection between switching off the lights and your Dad's health?' … 'What happened the last time you left the lights on?'… 'How true do you think that is [or: how would other people rate that statement] on a scale of 1–100?'

This kind of questioning is usually not intended to function as a stand-alone intervention in itself, but as part of a broader process of gradually enabling the client to change self-limiting and irrational ways of thinking (Kazantzis and Stuckey 2018; Overholser 2018).

Catalytic questions can convey a sense of curiosity or interest as well as helping the client to take a different perspective ('that question really made me think').

'I'-position narration

Sometimes a client will report that they are aware of a pattern of behaviour in which their actions and responses to others remain puzzling for them, despite a sustained personal effort to make sense of what happened. For example, a client might be troubled by situations in which they cannot tolerate being with others, and feel a pressing need to be on their own. A particularly effective means of working on this type of client issue was initially developed by Greenberg et al. (1993) and has become part of emotion-focused therapy (Elliott and Greenberg 2021; Timulak and Keogh 2021). This technique invites the client to retell the story of their puzzling or problematic reaction in a way that highlights the feelings and emotions associated with that event. The method essentially consists of the following stages:

- The client identifies a specific recent episode of the troubling pattern of behaviour – in this instance an incident in which they attended a party with friends, and then decided to just walk out and go home.
- The client is invited to recount, in the first person, the story of a specific event in detail, from an 'I' position ('I did this, and felt that…'). This enables them to vividly re-experience what happened, on a moment-by-moment basis. This way of talking yields a rich description of how the client thought and felt at each point, and particularly highlights their intentions, making it possible to identify the competing intentions that were in play ('I wanted to run away, but at the same time I was telling myself that I needed to face up to the challenge of staying'). It is helpful to use counselling skills in a sensitive manner to facilitate the telling of the story, for example through summarizing and non-verbal signs of attending. Once the client has completed their description of the problematic event, it is valuable to offer an overall narrative summary that encompasses what led up to the event, the unfolding of the event itself, and the later consequences. The counsellor's summary needs to capture and feed back the feelings and emotional themes in the client's experiencing of the event.
- The next stage involves making sense of the event in terms of the conflict between these competing intentions, or parts of the self, and finding a way of making a *bridge* between them, so that these different and contrasting personal impulses or beliefs can work together and be in dialogue rather than in conflict. In emotion-focused therapy, two-chair work (see Chapter 13) is generally used to facilitate this process – each side of the dilemma is enacted from a different chair to allow a dialogue to develop between them. However, it is possible to use more conventional conversational means to achieve this segment of the task, or to invite the client to make a drawing of the conflicting parts of self that were activated by the situation that they were in. In this instance, the bridge was the idea of 'being true to myself and being willing to say no: all of these incidents were times when I was exhausted and depleted by overwork… on that particular occasion I could not say turn down the invitation to attend the party, or even give my apologies and leave… my body took over… this is what always happens'.
- The closing stage of this process involves examining the implications of what the client has learned in the previous stages for how they handle such situations in the future.

The use of 'I'-position narration is an example of a skill that is relatively simple to implement: merely inviting a client to tell their story in a novel way, and then encouraging and supporting them to remain on task until they reach the end. However, it represents a potentially highly effective way to facilitate meaning-making because it takes a dialogical process in the client that has got stuck (i.e. their own efforts to make sense) and allows new meaning to emerge by slowing the story down, making sure that important details are not glossed over, and thereby allowing an implicit underlying conflict to be brought into the open and resolved.

Visual mapping

Creative and expressive techniques (drawing, painting, sculpting, writing, dance, music and drama) can make a valuable contribution to enabling clients to develop new ways of thinking about themselves and their problems in living. By activating and harnessing imagination and playfulness, such methods help clients to see the world in fresh ways. An overview of arts-based approaches to therapy, along with suggestions for further reading, can be found in the companion text (McLeod 2019). In this area of practice, a skill or technique that has provided a valuable entry point has been the use of visual mapping – essentially, having paper and pens available in the counselling room so that the client and therapist can draw diagrams and maps that represent and reflect what they are talking about. Examples of this kind of approach can be found in Oster and Crone (2004), Potter (2020), School of Life (2021) and Withers (2006). In relation to collaborative meaning-making, some particularly useful aspects of visual mapping that stand out are:

- being able to see a representation of the whole of the client's life or problem
- being able to draw connecting lines between life events, to create a personalized causal model
- the client and therapist being able to sit side by side to work on a diagram together.

Completed maps/diagrams also function as props and material objects that can be consulted on future occasions in counselling, and even retained by the client after the end of counselling. Although training workshops are sometimes available, most therapists who use visual mapping tend to evolve their own style of using this technique, because it makes use of simple drawing skills that the majority of people already possess.

Reframing

The skill of reframing involves a therapist statement that provides a different frame of reference or way of looking at a problem. Usually, the alternative frame of reference will be based in a theoretical model or approach with which the therapist is familiar but the client is not – the reframe therefore functions as an implicit invitation to try on the new perspective for size. An example is the *relational reframe* developed by Diamond (2014) in attachment-based family therapy for depressed adolescents. The families that comprise this client group generally come to therapy with an individualist or intrapersonal understanding of the troubled adolescent – for example that they suffer from low self-esteem. By contrast, the assumption that underpins attachment-based family therapy is that it is more helpful to view the problem in relational terms. In the example of a relational reframe provided by Diamond (2014), the therapist does not engage with the feelings of individual family members, but instead asks them from the start about how they offer each other support. The depression is thereby reframed not as an individual issue but as a relational problem.

Reframing can be used with most therapy approaches. For example, from a strengths perspective on therapy (Chapter 14), the fact that a client has made it to therapy at all, even when anxious or depressed, can be reframed as evidence of their resourcefulness, courage and commitment to change. When using this skill, it is essential to appreciate that it is not merely a matter of offering a different way of looking at a problem, but instead is an intentional gateway into an alternative perspective that includes therapeutic activities and a model of change.

Interpretation

An interpretation is similar to an empathic reflection, in that it conveys that the therapist has heard and understood what the client has been trying to convey, and is checking out that their grasp of what the client said is correct. However, an interpretation makes sense of the client's experience not in terms of the client's own understanding (as in empathy) but in terms of a pre-existing theoretical framework. In relation to the task of facilitating the client's capacity to understand their own actions and make meaning, interpretation is in effect a means for the therapist to offer the client a way of making sense of their experience. Although interpretation is used by all therapists to a greater or lesser extent, it is particularly associated with a psychodynamic way of working. A key aim of psychodynamic counselling and psychotherapy is to help the client to see that their current ways of relating to other people are a repetition of ways of relating that they acquired in the past (e.g. with their parents). One of the main ways that this new understanding (or what psychodynamic therapists would describe as 'insight') is accomplished is by interpreting parallels between the client's here-and-now relationship with the therapist and their ways of relating with other people in their present life (e.g. their spouse) and important figures in their early life (e.g. their father). By contrast, a cognitive-behavioural interpretation would tend to interpret the client's experience in terms of dysfunctional ways of thinking. The following example illustrates how this skill might be used:

Client: I don't think that anyone really cares about how bad I feel.
Counsellor 1:   What I'm hearing is you are feeling lost, or maybe alone right now – and what makes it worse is that no one else you know

cares enough to get close *[empathic reflection that seeks to capture what this experience means to the client]*

Counsellor 2:   You feel abandoned and left to fend for yourself – by me, by your partner… and maybe this is similar to what you have described to me about how you felt when your mother and father argued with each other? *[psychodynamic interpretation that highlights roots of this feeling in parental abandonment]*

Counsellor 3:   There is *no one at all* who cares? Or *really* cares? *[cognitive-behavioural interpretation that emphasizes exaggerated thinking as a mechanism that heightens the intensity of negative feelings]*

As a skill, interpretation can have a powerful impact on the client (Leibovich et al. 2020). However, it can also be unhelpful, for example if it is mistimed (e.g. cuts across the client's ongoing flow of talk, or is offered before the client is ready to take it on board), is perceived by the client as lacking in credibility, or is offered in a mechanistic way that does not take sufficient account of the client's experience. An example of how the helpfulness of interpretation depends on the establishment of a collaborative relationship is provided in a case study by Hill et al. (2019b).

Case formulation

Although reframes and interpretations are ultimately grounded in a broader theoretical perspective being used by a therapist, they do not attempt to explain that perspective as a whole. Instead, they function as ways of gradually introducing the client to the theory or perspective, in a piecemeal fashion. An approach to meaning-making that offers the client a more comprehensive understanding is case conceptualization or formulation. A case formulation comprises an episode in therapy in which the therapist shares their understanding of the origins of the client's problems, how they are maintained, and how they might be changed. Some approaches to case formulation adopt a collaborative approach, in which the client and therapist share their respective ways of making sense of these questions, and arrive at a shared model and action plan. A useful way to facilitate this kind of collaborative process is through co-constructing a visual diagram, in the form of a timeline or flow chart. Further information about collaborative-oriented case formulation skills and methods can be found in Johnstone and Dallos (2014), Kuyken et al. (2008) and McLeod and McLeod (2016, 2020). Studies that have interviewed clients about their experience of participating in a case formulation have consistently found that they describe it as having made a major contribution towards developing new ways of understanding their issues (Gibbs et al. 2020; Kahlon et al. 2014; Redhead et al. 2015).

Conclusions

This chapter has explored some of the more widely used therapy skills for helping clients to develop new ways of understanding and making sense of what may often be scary and confusing life experiences and deeply entrenched patterns of behaviour. The key themes in this chapter are that clients are always already actively engaged in efforts to make sense of what is happening in their lives, and that there exist a range of strategies through which therapists can support this process. It is helpful for a therapist to be able to draw on more than one of these skills and strategies, in some shape or form, to be able to be flexibly responsive to client needs and preferences.

Learning activities

The following activities may be explored individually, and/or with a group of learning partners.

1   The capacity to use silence and challenging in effective ways to facilitate client reflection and meaning-making is based on personal experience of these processes in both early life and later work roles. In what ways have your experience of these skills in everyday situations provided you with constructive or negative attitudes and memories that are triggered when you try to use either silence or challenging in counselling or helping situations? What are the implications for your counselling practice?

2   At the heart of the use of silence in counselling is being able to be in connection with another person for a few moments without words, during the process of talking together about an issue. Invite people that you know – friends, family members and learning partners – to experiment with you around introducing this kind of pause into conversations that you would be having anyway. What difference does it make? What have you learned from these experiments about how to nurture these moments effectively?

3   Reflecting on your own life, what recollections do you have of questions that you have been asked that have had the effect of making you think about yourself in a new and helpful way? What can you learn about the timing of these questions, the way they were asked, and your relationship with the questioner, that might be relevant for your work as a counsellor?

4   Find yourself a piece of paper and some coloured pens or pencils and create a timeline of your life. Start with a line towards the lower edge of the page, with marks at birth, now and future. Insert words, phrases or images at relevant places to indicate important events, people, turning points and life decisions. Use coloured lines to draw links between items that seem to be connected, or where one thing has caused or led to another. Include positive strengths, assets and experiences as well as more troubling ones. Give yourself 20 minutes to focus on this task. Just keep going, writing whatever comes into your mind. There are no right or wrong ways of doing it – be guided by your own sense of what is meaningful for you. After you have completed this simple visual mapping task, take some time to reflect on any new insights or under-standings about your life that have been triggered for you by this activity. Further reflection and discussion could consider how you might inte-grate visual mapping into your work with clients.

Emotions

13

Introduction

When a person wants to talk to a counsellor, at least part of the reason is that they feel bad about something. No matter how much the counselling process focuses on cognitive and rational decision-making and action planning, there is always an emotional dimension to the work. As a result, for the majority of clients who enter into ongoing counselling, there will be a need at some point to look at troubling and painful feelings and emotions, with the goal of resolving them, changing them or making sense of them. This chapter provides an introductory guide to skills for working with emotions in counselling.

Making sense of emotion

On the whole, we live in a world in which rationality is valued and emphasized over emotion. There are a number of reasons for this. Emotion is an immediate, bodily response to a situation, which has direct and clear implications for action. For example, fear triggers flight. Most of us live in complex, crowded urban environments in which we are constantly faced with multiple competing stimuli and rules, where a thoughtful, considered response is usually more effective and appropriate than a spontaneous emotional response. We therefore learn, early on, to suppress our emotions in the interest of getting along with people. In addition, in the past, individuals tended to learn about people and relationships through face-to-face contact, such as listening to another person telling a story, or viewing a drama being enacted on stage. In these situations, the bodily emotion of one person can be directly communicated to others. In contrast, in contemporary societies, we are more likely to learn about people and relationships through watching television, reading books and internet articles, or through social media – all of which are relatively de-emotionalized and disembodied media. For example, when watching a television programme, we are placed in the position of a very distant observer, able to connect with the subjective physical emotion and feeling of any individual actor or character only to a limited extent. We are also in a position of being able to switch off at any moment, and make the character disappear.

Despite the uneasiness and ambivalence about emotion that permeates much of our culture, feelings and emotions remain an essential part of life. One of the most important functions of a counselling relationship is that it provides a space in which there is permission to feel, and to express emotions. In a therapeutic context it is useful to regard emotion and feeling as sources of meaning, or as a signalling system. An inherent aspect of being human is the capacity to perceive, think and reason, to use concepts and ideas to guide action. In parallel to this system of cognitive information-processing and decision-making, there is an emotion-based system, which operates directly on various bodily functions such as heart rate and respiration. While cognitive processing sorts information in terms of possibly thousands of concepts and categories available in language, the emotion system sorts information in terms of a smaller set of categories that have been biologically wired in through evolution: anger, fear, joy, loss, pleasure, disgust. From a counselling perspective, therefore, feeling and emotion always have some *meaning* in relation to what is happening in a person's life space or personal niche. Feeling and emotion are bodily signals that provide information about the basic attitude or action tendency of the person towards an event, other person or situation. For example, certain emotional responses are part of a basic biological 'fight or flight' response, indicating that there is something in the environment that is threatening and which evokes either anger (destroying the threat or making it go away) or fear (escaping from the threat). The emotional reactions that people tend to want to explore in counselling are those where the meaning of the emotion is not clear to the individual, either because the emotion state is fleeting and vague, consisting of a general sense of emotional pain, or is confused/confusing (why do I keep feeling angry and losing my temper?). When a person really knows and accepts what they feel about something, then they usually do not seek counselling. Some of the most profound and intractable issues that people bring to counselling are associated with alienated and discon-nected ways of being where the individual experiences themselves as having lost a capacity to feel, or emotional states that are fragmented, out of control and overwhelming.

The reason why feelings and emotions are often vague and confused is that the individual may have grown up in a family or wider cultural environment in which particular emotions were unacceptable. For instance, many men have learned that it is not 'manly' to feel sadness and loss, or even fear. Many women have been socialized into believing that it is not appropriate for them to feel angry. As a result, men may feel afraid or disgusted about any possibility of personally feeling or expressing sadness. Women may feel fear and self-disgust about any possibility of feeling or expressing anger. Instead of sadness, men may get angry. Instead of anger, women may get anxious or fearful. While these are very broad generalizations, which should never be simplistically applied to individual lives, they do illustrate a basic truth about emotion, which is that *the emotions or feelings that a person exhibits may hide or protect other emotions or feelings that are harder to acknowledge*. It can be useful to take account of the concept of *authenticity* with respect to feeling and emotion. When a person is expressing genuine feelings, what they say has a sense of being authentic, and will have a direct emotional impact on anyone in contact with them. For exam-ple, even listening to a radio interview with a grieving disaster victim, who one has never met, is many thousands of miles away, and speaking in another lan-guage, can be a profoundly moving experience. By contrast, attending a family funeral accompanied by weeping relatives can evoke a sense of detachment. When a person expresses a genuine or authentic feeling or emotion, there is typically a physical sense of relief or release, and a sense of resolution in relation to the issue or problem that is associated with that emotion. These are valuable indicators of whether a feeling or emotion is primary, or may be a secondary emotion that may mask a more basic one. It is rarely helpful to challenge a person seeking help on the grounds that they are expressing false or pretend emotions. The emotions they are expressing are real enough to them, at that moment, and worthy of consideration and respect. The point here, for a counsellor, is to be willing to listen to his or her own gut sense that there *may be more to come.*

It is valuable to make a distinction in counselling between *feeling* and *emotion.* Both are part of the same embodied, internally sensed way of responding to the world. Both are sources of meaning and information. However, feeling can be regarded as an ever-present inner sensing that can be referred to at any moment. Feelings are typically multifaceted – there are many sides to what one feels in a situation, or many threads of feeling of which a person may be aware. Emotion, by contrast, is more specific. It takes over the body, and can usually be identified as one thing, for example anger. In counselling, feelings are always part of the equation. For a counsellor, understanding what a person is talking about is hugely influenced by the feelings they convey, and by what is felt by the counsellor when he or she is listening. In counselling, strong emotion occurs less often. When it does occur, though, it demands attention. Effective counselling skill requires the courage to be willing to be with another person when they are expressing strong emotion, as well as the sensitivity to be able to enter the person's everyday feeling-world.

Types of emotion task in counselling

There are three broad categories of counselling task that require skills in working with feeling and emotion:

1 *Exploring feelings that are elusive, vague or hidden.* The client may have a vague sense of how he or she feels about an issue, but be unable to put this into words, or to stay with the feeling long enough to really know what it is about. Sometimes, a client may claim that they do not feel anything at all. The counselling task here is to bring what is felt sufficiently into awareness for it to become a source of meaning, information and existential groundedness that can be useful to the client.

2 *Giving expression to emotions that are being held back.* If a strong emotion is stimulated by an event, it seems that there is a basic human need to give outward expression to that emotion in some way. If the emotion is not expressed or released, the person may have a sense of incompleteness, or 'unfinished business' which can interfere with normal functioning. The idea that emotions demand expression, and that it can be psychologically and physically damaging to hold back emotion, can be traced to the ancient Greek theory of *catharsis.* The marker for this kind of task may simply be that the client recognizes for themselves that there are emotions near the surface: 'I just need a good cry' or 'I feel so angry inside but I just can't do anything with it'. The counselling task involves creating the conditions for, and facilitating, the safe release of the emotion.

3 *Limiting or managing the expression of emotions that are experienced as being out of control.* The emotion-focused tasks described above share an

aim of learning how to bring buried or suppressed feelings into awareness, and accepting what they may contribute to a client's participation in life. By contrast, another type of emotion-centred task in counselling can comprise the effort to control the experiencing, expression and enactment of emotions that are regarded by the client as unwelcome, or out of proportion to the situations in which they find themselves, such as routinely feeling angry, fearful or sad.

In some cases, either or all of these three forms of emotion work may represent the main focus of counselling. By contrast, in other cases they may be subsidiary to other tasks. For example, helping a person to deal with a relationship problem may often involve feelings of anger or loss with reference to a troublesome family member, alongside meaning-making and acquiring communication and problem-solving skills. The third emotional processing task described above – limiting the expression of emotions that are experienced as being out of control – can be categorized as a type of behaviour change task, and addressed using skills and strategies discussed in Chapter 14. The remainder of the present chapter focuses on counselling skills for situations in which the client needs to make sense of feelings and emotions that are vague and elusive, or are being held back.

Skills for working with emotions in counselling

The following sections discuss a range of skills that can be used to facilitate the awareness and expression of feelings and emotions, and exploration of their meaning.

Developing sensitivity to feeling and emotion

Some counsellors seem to operate as if the emotional life of the people they are trying to help were irrelevant. These are counsellors whose responses predominantly lead the person in the direction of talking about what they *do* and what they *think*, rather than what they *feel*. They pay little attention to emotion cues, or inviting the person to explore feelings. This is a very limited approach to counselling, which misses out on important information about the emotional significance of events in the client's life. Counsellor competence around the awareness of feeling and emotion is based on a willingness to *listen for feelings* at all times during a counselling encounter. Primarily, listening for feelings means being sensitive to the feeling words that a person uses, and weaving these into the conversation. However, it can also involve being on the alert for the *absence* of feeling words. Some people have difficulties in dealing with problems in living because they are unable to refer to their feelings and consciously acknowledge how they feel. The classic example of this is the person who may be very attached to people in their life, but never tells them how much they love them or cares about them, or enjoys their company. A state or condition of lacking feeling words has been labelled 'alexithymia' – some people with psychosomatic complaints may be diagnosed as being alexithymic. A sensitive counsellor may find that a person's body language, tone of voice, or even the events they are describing, hint at a feeling that they seem to be unable to put into words. In these circumstances, it can be helpful for the counsellor very tentatively to offer feeling words for the person to 'try out for size'.

In a counselling situation where it is possible to maintain a relationship with a person over an extended period of time, as a counsellor you may find that the person keeps coming back to the same feeling state again and again. They may consistently get angry, feel tired, get depressed or whatever, no matter what trigger situation they are in. Recurrent feelings that appear to be not quite appropriate to the situation can often be a sign that there are buried feelings in the background. Tears (Knox et al. 2017) and laughter (Gupta et al. 2018; Nelson 2008) can be important markers of underlying emotional states and relationship processes. What seems to happen is that a person can 'specialize' in emotion states that they are familiar with, rather than entering other emotion states that may seem to them to be scary and out of control. As a counsellor, it is valuable at these times to be as sensitive as possible to the presence of possible hidden feeling states – for example by catching the flash of anger that accompanies an expression of repetitive sadness.

A crucial way for any counsellor to heighten their awareness to feelings and emotions in a counselling session is to *listen to your own feelings*. There are at least three ways in which the counsellor's own feelings comprise a vital source of information about what is happening in the counselling relationship. First, a counsellor who listens to their own feelings may become aware that what they are feeling consists of a feeling that they brought into the counselling session, and which has nothing to do with what the person seeking help is talking about. For example, the counsellor may be feeling frustrated and angry because of some work hassles. There is a danger that these feelings may get in the way of tuning into the emotional world of the person seeking help. Part of sound preparation for a counselling session involves setting aside (bracketing) personal emotional processing, in order to be able to concentrate on what the other person is feeling. Second, what a counsellor feels when with a person seeking help can often take the form of a kind of emotional *resonance*: it is as though the counsellor is resonating like a tuning fork to the feelings being emitted by the other person. Therefore, a lot of the time in counselling, how *you* are feeling may be a good clue to how the person is feeling at that moment (although this always needs to be checked out). Third, what the counsellor feels in response to a person may be *how other people also feel in relation to that person*. For example, if you feel angry or annoyed with a person to whom you are offering counselling, it may be that other people (their friends, family, work colleagues) may sometimes feel the same way too. This awareness can be used, carefully, to explore questions such as: What is this person doing to make me feel angry? Do I respond in the same way that others do (which others, and in what circumstances?) and what does this response do in terms of the kinds of relationships this person has with these people?

Emotional sensitivity in counselling is a matter of mastering a kind of dual attention: listening to oneself at the same time as listening to the person seeking help. This is why training in counselling emphasizes the importance of personal development work and the cultivation of therapist self-awareness (see Chapter 9). A huge part of this personal development consists of learning about one's own emotional life, as a means of being better able to tune into the emotional worlds of others.

Making sense of recurring patterns of feeling

People generally do not seek help from a counsellor to deal with transient painful emotions. Instead, the emotional issues that are explored in therapy almost always refer to persistent, recurring patterns of feeling and emotion that the person has recognized as undermining their efforts to maintain satisfying and productive relationships. To be able to make effective use of counselling skills for working with emotions, it is necessary to be able to understand how and why certain emotions become locked into the client's way of living, while other emotions may be almost entirely absent. Some useful theoretical perspectives are summarized below.

Early learning. Transactional analysis (TA) is a good source of ways of thinking about the kinds of psychological and interpersonal processes that trouble people in their lives. In TA theory, it is assumed that people who live productive and healthy lives will have access to, and appropriately express, a wide range of emotions – anger, fear, sadness, happiness – in response to different situations that they encounter. Many of us, however, tend to return to the same feeling state, no matter what the situation. In TA language, such recurrent patterns of feelings are described as *racket feelings*, which can be defined as emotions that are learned and encouraged in childhood, that the individual has a tendency to revert to in stress situations, and are maladaptive in terms of resolving these situations (Stewart and Joines 2012). This phenomenon is explained in terms of a process of *rubber-banding* – the assumption is that when under stress, a person is swiftly and unconsciously catapulted back into what they learned to do as a child, as a way of coping with scary situations. The emotional state that then emerges is the one that was functional, as a child, in gaining parental support and care.

Primary and secondary emotions. A primary emotion is a person's genuine, real, underlying basic response to a situation. However, if a person does not feel safe or comfortable in expressing that primary emotion, they still need to express that emotional energy in some way, so they exhibit a secondary emotion which is safer for them. An example: Donald feels angry (primary emotion) with Andy when he lets him down over a work deadline. Donald has learned to be afraid of his anger because he has been punished in his family for losing his temper. However, in his family everyone was a 'worrier'. There-fore Donald gets anxious when Andy misses the deadline ('Oh dear, I don't know what to do, I'm worried'). The theory of primary and secondary emo-tions is explained in more detail in Greenberg and Pascual-Leone (2006), Elliott and Greenberg (2021) and many other sources. It explains how the persistence of patterns of emotional expression and self-regulation always has a relational dimension. It explains why the emotions that people exhibit in everyday situations – and in therapy – may have a slightly false or inauthentic quality because they do not fully channel the person's underlying bodily response. Finally, it provides a way of understanding why some emotions (primary emotions) are rarely expressed, and why it can be so hard in therapy to access them – they may have been subjected to a lifetime of suppression and avoidance.

The body remembers. The emotions that are felt by a person become biologically locked into their body. This is particularly the case with the intense and extreme emotional responses that occur in trauma, but occurs in other situa-tions as well. It is possible to gain a reasonable appreciation of a person's emotional life by just looking at their facial expressions and how they move their body. Rothschild (2000, 2017) describes these processes as a type of body memory – the body remembers certain emotions, and the events that triggered these emotions, even when the mind is doing its best to forget them. This theory explains the persistence of emotional patterns as being due to the difficulty of being able to talk and reflect on what is happening at a bodily level.

Cultural rules. In addition to the ways that patterns of emotion are shaped by life experience and biological processes, it is also vital to keep in mind that they are also strongly influenced by cultural factors. Within a particular cul-ture, there are unwritten rules around which emotions are permissible and which are not, and the conditions under which certain emotions may be expressed. A cultural perspective explains the persistence of emotions as reflecting cultural factors. Research by Hutchison et al. (2020) suggests that, on the whole, therapists are not particularly sensitive to cultural rules around the communication of emotion. One of the most effective ways to acquire such awareness is participation in a culturally diverse training group (Houdy-shell and Ziegler 2020; Lu et al. 2020).

Creating an environment that is conducive to the expression of emotion

If a person is using counselling to work on an emotion or feeling, it is probable that they are to some extent embarrassed, ashamed or inhibited about acknowledging or expressing that area of emotional life. If the person was *not* embarrassed or ashamed, the chances would be that they would be able to display that emotion openly in everyday circumstances. It is therefore helpful to make sure that the person feels safe enough to express emotion. For instance, the person may be reassured to be told that the counsellor is comfortable with the expression of feelings, or that they can go at their own pace, or have plenty of time for this task. The person may be worried about whether anyone outside the room will hear them, or see them when they leave, or whether there are facilities (tissues, a washbasin, mirror) for putting on a 'face' for the outside world. It is probably easier to express feelings in a soft environment, for example a cushioned armchair that can be hit or stroked, rather than in an office furnished with hard, upright chairs. The counsellor, too, may have concerns in these areas – 'What if my colleagues hear shouting coming from my office?', 'If this person breaks down, I'm sure I will start to cry too, and how will I be able to be ready for my next patient?'

In the process of therapy, a key skill in relation to supporting a client to explore painful emotions is to ensure the availability of sources of emotional safety or self-soothing that the client has identified as being relevant for them. In many situations the relationship with the therapist, or the therapist's use of soft voice or the offer of touch, may be a valuable source of emotional safety. Soothing and self-soothing may take the form of an object such as a blanket, duvet, cushion or soft toy. It may also involve a cognitive dimension, such as imagining and recreating in one's mind a safe place such as being in bed, sitting on a beach or being with one's dog.

Constructing a shared feeling language

Sensitivity to the language with which the person talks about his or her experience can provide a number of possibilities for facilitating feeling and emotion. One of the ways that people avoid getting in touch with their feelings is to talk quickly, or shift topics frequently. People sometimes do these things because they may be aware at some level that talking slowly, or staying with a topic, would mean that the feeling or emotion associated with that topic, or that was being felt at that moment, might become overwhelming. Many standard counselling responses, such as reflecting back what the person has said, allowing silences, and talking in a gentle, measured voice, can have the effect of slowing the person down and helping them to keep in touch with what they are feeling in that moment. There may be specific words, phrases or images that are particularly evocative for the person. Often, these phrases and images will be embedded in the person's speech, produced by the person as he or she is talking about an issue. From the counsellor's perspective, these words can almost jump out of the conversation and very obviously possess a great deal of meaning. The counsellor can reflect these words or images back to the person, or may even invite the person to repeat them, and report on what happens when they try this. Effective development of a shared feeling language requires working together to name feelings. Many counsellors fall back on stock phrases such as 'How does that make you feel?' While there are some situations in which that kind of general invitation to talk about feelings may be helpful, it is better to try to approach feelings in a more intentional manner. This might include tentatively reflecting back feeling words the client has already used, or offering alternative feeling words based on your sense of what might be happening at an implicit level. It might include making a distinction between here-and-now feelings ('and what you're feeling now is…?') and patterns of feeling in everyday life ('what I hear you saying is that there are some social situations where you feel terrified, and others where you feel excited and full of energy…').

Paying attention to what the client's body is saying and doing

Because feeling and emotion are bodily phenomena, there are several ways that careful attention to what is happening at a physical level can be used in emotion work. When a person uses an emotion word, it can be helpful to invite him or her to indicate where that feeling is located in their body, and then to focus their awareness on that part of the body and what they feel right there. Bodily movement is an important means of expressing emotion – when we are happy we dance, and when we are angry we hit things. When a person refers to a feeling or emotion, or seems to be feeling something, it can be valuable to draw their attention to any gestures or movements that seem to accompany the feeling, and either to give words to that movement ('What is your clenched fist saying?', 'If the fingers that are stroking your other arm had a voice, what would they say?') or perhaps repeat and exaggerate the movement ('Clench the fist more, and hold it there for a few moments – what happens when you do that?').

Breathing is closely linked to the expression of feeling and emotion. A highly effective way of controlling or choking off an emotion is to hold one's breath or breathe as shallowly as possible; the release of emotion is typically accompanied by long, deep breaths, sighs and yawning. There may be times when a counsellor can become aware that a person is holding their breath, or is breathing as little as possible. At these moments, it can be useful to point this out to the person, and invite them to breathe deeply and regularly, perhaps also breathing along with them for a few seconds. Another bodily indicator of emotion is tummy rumbling. Some counsellors believe that tummy rumbling, in the absence of overt hunger, is a signal that there is a deeply held, buried feeling struggling to be expressed. If asked, and if they are not too embarrassed, a person will often be able to report on the feeling or desire that lies behind the rumbling. The sensorimotor approach to therapy (Fisher 2019) has developed many skills and strategies around how to observe and work with the bodily expression of emotion.

Two-chair work

When a person wishes to express feelings, but finds it hard to do so, or is struggling to deal with situations and relationships that have an emotional dimension, it may be helpful to use enactment, such as two-chair dialogue, to externalize the underlying emotional process. Usually, a strong emotion is felt *in relation to* another person. For instance, someone may feel angry with a colleague, or feel sad in relation to a partner who has left them. In some instances, the emotion may be felt not in relation to an actual live person, but to an internalized image of a person – for example a father who was absent or critical during the client's childhood years.

When merely talking to a counsellor, there can be a tendency for the person to talk *about* their feelings, for example by describing them, rather than entering directly *into* the feeling. A face-to-face counselling conversation is a situation in which a person will probably be exerting a certain amount of self-control, and will be monitoring what they say rather than allowing themselves to be lost in, or taken over by, feelings. Although this type of conversation may enable the client to develop valuable cognitive understanding of their feelings, it is likely that the feeling itself will still persist. On the basis of both research findings and experience in working with clients, many therapists have discovered that one of the most effective ways of changing a feeling state is to go *into* and *through* the emotion.

Inviting the person to perform their feelings, through dramatically enacting their relationship with the object of their emotions, can be a very effective strategy for facilitating emotional awareness and expression. The person is asked to talk directly to the imagined other person: 'What do you want to say to him or her? Just talk to them as if they were here.' They then move to the other chair, and respond as if they were that other person. The counsellor will typically encourage repetition of key statements ('Say it again – she's not listening to you') in order to heighten the emotional intensity of the interaction. This counselling strategy is often described as 'two-chair work' and is widely used in emotion-focused therapy (EFT) (Elliott and Greenberg 2021; Johnson 2021; Timulak and Keogh 2021) as well as in other approaches to therapy (Kellogg 2004, 2014).

During this kind of enactment, it is usual for the counsellor to sit alongside the client, rather than opposite them. This has two effects. First, it serves to reinforce the intensity of the enactment – the counsellor can coach and support the client to open up to, and give voice to, what they are feeling. Second, it creates a situation where the client is not expressing strong feelings directly at or towards the counsellor: it may be embarrassing or shameful to express anger directly to a counsellor, when the client knows that the true target of their anger is someone else.

What usually happens, when two-chair work is successful, is that there is a softening on both sides of the dialogue, leading to the emergence of different feelings. For example, a client who was locked into a pattern of fearfulness and self-criticism may discover their self-protective anger. Alternatively, a client who was resentful of an absent or controlling father may become aware of sadness around what they have lost in all these years. Two-chair work is effective because it harnesses key emotion-related skills and change processes:

- awareness and expression of emotions, rather than talking 'about' them
- completion of unfinished processing of emotions tied to particular relationships (e.g. 'what I was never able to say to my mother')
- a situation in which the person stays with their feelings long enough for underlying primary emotions to come into awareness and be expressed
- soothing presence of the therapist
- therapist as a supporter and coach who is able to nudge the process along
- opportunity, after the two-chair enactment episode, to make sense of what has been learned and consider its implications for how one lives one's life (see Fosha 2000).

It is also important to recognize that helpful two-chair work seldom occurs in a single episode – typically a client needs to learn how to use this activity, and to feel safe enough with it to fully commit to the process.

Therapists in the EFT tradition have developed a highly differentiated model of how to use two-chair enactment, and offer training courses in the skills required to facilitate this kind of process. Although theory and research in EFT and other emotion-based forms of therapy presents this approach using technical terminology and complex flow diagrams, the reality is quite different. What is happening in two-chair work and other similar interventions is that a person is provided with an opportunity to express powerful feelings and emotions that they may have been holding back for most of their life. While this is helpful in itself, it also has the effect of raising big questions for a person around who they are and how they relate to other people. The key idea here is that it is necessary to view two-chair work as one stage in a longer journey. The symbolic meaning of such a journey is captured very well in the children's story *We're Going on a Bear Hunt* by Michael Rosen and Helen Oxenbury.

As well as two-chair work, there are many other ways that emotion can be externalized and expressed through enactment. One useful variant on the method of enactment involves expressing feelings through a letter written to the other person. This letter may be brought in to a later meeting with the counsellor, may be kept, or may be ritually destroyed to represent the act of moving beyond the feelings that it carries. People may find it useful to write letters on consecutive days, as a way of allowing all of their feelings to emerge, bit by bit. There are also many ways of using art-based and creative methods to facilitate enactment of emotion, such as through sand-play, sculpting, drama, glove puppets, poetry writing, etc.

Experiential focusing

The psychologist, philosopher and psychotherapist Eugene Gendlin developed a method of *experiential focusing*, which is widely applicable in situations where a person is struggling to make sense of, or give expression to, a feeling or emotion (Cornell 1996; Gendlin 2003; Purton 2005). Gendlin argued that the meaning of any situation, relationship or event in which a person is involved is captured in a bodily 'felt sense' to which the person can refer. The felt sense includes a wealth of *implicit* meaning, not all of which is explicitly known or understood by the person at any particular point. If a person can be enabled to stay with (or *focus* on) their felt sense of a situation, then the layers of meaning that are bodily present can begin to be symbolized and consciously known. Usually, symbolization occurs in the form of language – the person finds words and phrases that emerge from the felt sense and seem to capture threads of its meaning. However, symbolization can also take the form of an image, pictorial representation, sound or bodily movement. For Gendlin, the activity of helping a client to focus on an unclear felt sense comprises a basic therapeutic process that occurs in virtually all forms of effective counselling. This is because a central problem that many people have in their lives is that of not allowing themselves to stay close enough to what they are feeling for long enough to allow the broader personal meaning of what is happening in their life to emerge. Gendlin would argue that people avoid focusing on their felt sense of a problem by blocking their internal awareness through incessantly talking, being 'busy' or not paying attention to bodily feelings and sensations. The group of practitioners associated with this approach have developed a set of simple procedures for helping people to access their felt sense and make use of what they find there. They have encouraged the use of these focusing instructions in peer self-help communities worldwide (see Boukydis 1984), and with clients experiencing a variety of health problems. Experiential focusing is a method that is readily incorporated into counselling that takes place embedded in other professional roles. Gendlin's (2003) book, *Focusing*, provides clear guidelines on how to use this method. These guidelines are also available on the International Focusing Institute website: http://www.focusing.org/ This website represents an invaluable starting point for anyone interested in learning more about experiential focusing, including information about local skills training workshops.

Rituals

A ritual is an activity or routine that is invested with special significance by a person or group of people. Human beings have always used rituals as ways of dealing with conflict and marking life transitions. For people seeking to resolve emotional difficulties, ritual may represent a valuable means of expressing troublesome feelings in a controlled setting. For example, a person who is troubled by feelings of depression and hopelessness may counter these emotions by starting each day with a set of yoga exercises which symbolize hope and renewal. Talmon (1990: chapter 3) describes the story of a client, Mary. Mary was angry with her father, for a variety of reasons, and wished to exclude him from her life. Together, she and her husband, along with the counsellor, devised a ritual in which Mary read out, with powerful emotion, a 'decree of divorce' from her father, while the counsellor set on fire a photograph of her father, accompanied by music played by her husband. This ritual, carried out during a counselling session, had an enormous impact on Mary in signalling a transition from a self that had been dominated by her father, to a new self that was free and ready to enter a different phase of her life. In the counselling and psychotherapy literature there are many examples of rituals that have been devised for different therapeutic purposes (Imber-Black and Roberts 1992; McMillan 2006) and which can be adapted for use in counselling situations. Ultimately, in a counselling setting, the rituals that will make most sense for a client are those that are co-constructed – that take shape from the ideas of the counsellor and client together, rather than anything that is entirely preplanned or off the shelf.

CBT techniques

If a person seeks help around the goal of controlling emotions, it may be valuable to consider the use of cognitive-behavioural therapy (CBT) techniques. Cognitive-behavioural therapy encompasses a range of methods that have been designed for, or can be adapted to, the task of emotional self-control. The key idea in CBT is that emotions are controlled by thoughts, and that the most effective way of addressing emotional difficulties is to identify the thought processes through which emotions are regulated, and replace them with different thoughts. For example, a person may respond to a stressful situation with catastrophizing thoughts such as 'I can't cope', 'this is completely awful', etc. These thoughts are likely to trigger feelings of fear, onset of panic and avoidance behaviour that prevents effective coping strategies being developed. The person can be helped to see that these thoughts are exaggerated and irrational by using the CBT skill of Socratic questioning/guided discovery. Alternative thoughts ('I know this is scary but I am confident I can deal with it because…') are then rehearsed and tried out (in CBT behavioural experiments and homework assignments).

Some of the CBT techniques that can be applied in therapeutic work around emotions include:

- Keeping a diary of when and how 'emotion events' occur – with the aim of identifying what triggers them and what seems to prevent them.
- Exploring an emotional event in detail, and working backwards from the event, to the step-by-step sequence of events that preceded it. This can then lead to working together to find ways of interrupting the emotion-inducing sequence (for example, by saying to oneself to 'keep calm', or by thinking about a pleasant image).
- Finding alternatives to the emotion. For example: 'If you did not get angry/burst into tears/freeze with fear, what else could you do?').
- Learning relaxation skills – in many situations, being able to move into a previously learned relaxation or breathing routine can give the person a few

moments to pause and reflect on their choices (e.g. whether to express the troublesome emotion or do something else).

- Identifying the thoughts and processes of 'self-talk' that trigger emotions. For example, someone may make himself or herself angry because they may tell themselves that other people are looking down on them – this is an irrational or dysfunctional thought that can be challenged by the counsellor.

The particular usefulness of CBT techniques lies in its applicability in working with people who do not particularly want to understand their emotion, but are just interested in controlling it, and people who prefer a more structured, rather than exploratory, approach to counselling. People who are scared or embarrassed about expressing their feelings in the presence of the counsellor may also prefer a CBT approach, which on the whole does not require any kind of 'here-and-now' emotional expression. There are many self-help books and websites that provide CBT-based information on how to control emotions such as anger and fear.

Expressive arts

Issues around emotions often centre around the fact that feelings and emotions are processes that take place in a reality that is largely outside of the verbal. Once emotion-oriented counselling gets to the stage where the person can clearly talk about their feelings, either most of the work has been done – or the person has switched into intellectualizing about their feelings, and the opportunity has been lost. The expressive arts comprise a mode of engaging with emotional experience that can powerfully tap into non-verbal ways of knowing and communicating (Rogers 2000). For example, the availability of a lump of plasticine or similar material can give a person an opportunity to allow their hands to express their feelings in the moulding of a shape. The availability of paper and crayons can allow image and colour to be utilized. These are arts tools that are readily accessible, and which will be non-threatening to most people who are seeking counselling. In some situations, more complex forms of expressive activity, such as drama or dance, may also be possibilities. Further information on art-based skills and strategies can be found in McLeod (2019).

Cultural resources

The task of working on feelings and emotions may take place solely in a counselling session, or may include activities that the person decides to pursue elsewhere in their life space. The direct work of the counsellor in relation to feeling and emotion can therefore in some cases be restricted to planning and rehearsing where and how the person might feel safe to express strong emotion. There exists a broad range of cultural resources and settings that can be facilitative for someone struggling to resolve an emotional issue. As mentioned earlier, letter-writing can represent a powerful means of channelling feelings. Other forms of writing, such as poetry, can also be used. Other people may opt to express rage and anger by shouting at a football match, or in the privacy of their car, or allow tears to come by visiting a graveside, spending some time looking at photographs of loved ones or attending a school concert or graduation day. A hugely valuable source of emotional healing for many people is music – listening to, or playing, a piece that evokes a certain emotional state may allow a person to stay with that state long enough for its personal meaning and significance to emerge and be worked through. Movies can allow a person seeking to come to terms with an emotional issue to enter imaginatively into the world of a character who is experiencing a similar issue, and to participate vicariously in the process of resolution as experienced by that figure. Novels can supply a similar sort of learning – the key here is not to suggest to the person seeking help that they should copy the way that a character in a movie or novel has dealt with their emotional difficulties, but that the story can represent one *possible* way of coping. For people who are stuck in an emotional impasse, the idea that there are different possibilities can be liberating. Another important cultural resource is self-help and self-improvement books, for instance around such themes as coping with grief, being more assertive and willing to express anger, or dealing with fears.

Positive emotions

The main focus in this chapter has been on painful emotions such as sadness, loss, fear and anger. However, it can also be helpful to pay attention to what is happening in the client's life around positive emotions such as excitement, interest, enjoyment, beauty and pleasure. The 'broaden and build' theory of working with emotions in therapy provides a useful perspective for making sense of this aspect of practice (Fredrickson 2001). It suggests that negative emotions are associated with intense preoccupation with, and exploration of, a single issue (in order to resolve it). For example, feeling fearful or anxious typically includes persistent or even obsessive rumination about a specific problematic situation. By contrast, even a brief experience of positive feelings allows the person to open up – they have new ideas, generate alternative solutions to problems and try new activities. Positive emotions motivate and encourage the person to go out in the world, while negative emotions require them to find somewhere to stay safe. This idea has important implications for therapy. For example, clients may often mention positive experiences they have had, but only briefly and in passing. Inviting the client to expand on what happened during these positive life events (*broadening*) may encourage them to see the benefits of such activities, and engage in them more often (i.e. *building* a new or more satisfying life). In addition, it can be useful to acknowledge positive feelings that emerge during emotion-oriented interventions within sessions that are primarily aimed at working with negative emotions. For example, when a client uses experiential focusing to attend to what they are feeling inside, they frequently identify not only heavy feelings, but also threads of feeling that they describe as positive energy, excitement or lovingness. Broaden and build theory makes it possible to explain and understand why activating and applying client strengths and cultural resources can be such a useful aspect of therapy. Clearly, a simplistic 'look on the bright side' approach to therapy is disrespectful of clients, in downplaying their suffering and experiences of adversity. On the other hand, ignoring positive experience has the effect of excluding an essential element of human existence. Further discussion of how positive emotions can be integrated into therapy can be found in Fitzpatrick and Stalikas (2008a, 2008b) and Fosha (2004).

Conclusions

Emotions are problematic in contemporary society, and difficulties with emotions lie behind many, or even all, of the main categories of psychological problems for which a person might seek help from a counsellor or psychotherapist. Depression can be understood as a sadness/anger problem. Anxiety is about fear. Low self-esteem can be understood as feeling ashamed to share what you really feel. Being willing and able to move beyond general diagnostic categories such as depression or anxiety, and get closer to what is really bothering a person, in terms of patterns of emotions, represents a significant counselling skill. Working with emotions can be likened to stepping out of 'talking about' problems in living, and stepping into the danger zone where these problems are actually *felt*. This step also takes the person and the counsellor closer to the lived reality of the person's life space or personal niche. This is because emotions are always, ultimately, linked to people, events and objects within that niche. Being sensitive to the person's feelings and emotions allows the counsellor to get beyond general statements such as 'I feel anxious a lot of the time', to more specific statements such as 'I am afraid of my boss, he is a bully.' It is through talking about these specifics that the person and the counsellor can find some leverage in relation to ways of changing what is happening.

There are many skills and strategies that can be employed in counselling situations to help a person who is experiencing difficulty around acknowledging or expressing feelings and emotions. As always, the potential impact of any skill depends on the strength of the relationship between the counsellor and the person seeking help, and on its responsiveness to the needs and preferences of the client – effective emotion-oriented work requires being able to draw from a flexible repertoire of relevant concepts and methods.

Learning activities

The following activities may be explored individually, and/or with a group of learning partners.

1 Your personal emotional profile. How comfortable are you with the expression of emotions? Are there emotions around which you feel relatively comfortable, and other emotions that are hard for you to express or hear? What are the implications of your personal emotional profile for your work as a counsellor?

2 Experiential focusing is probably the single most useful skill in relation to working with emotions. It is impossible to understand this process without direct experience of what it involves. A standard set of guidelines for experiential focusing can be found on the International Focusing Institute website at: https://www.focusing.org/sixsteps These guidelines take you through a procedure that is gentle and safe, and can be stopped at any point without harm. It is not important whether you have been able to experience the whole focusing process, or not. Once you have tried the focusing steps, it is useful to share and discuss your experience with learning partners, to allow you to develop a more complete understanding of how this process can unfold in different ways with different people.

3 How do you control or manage your emotions when they become too strong or intense, and take you out of your comfort zone? What have you learned from your answer to this question that might be helpful in your work as a counsellor?

4 Reflect on a recent occasion when you experienced a strong emotion that was uncomfortable or painful for you. Make notes on the dimensions of that experience that would be considered as potentially significant in the theories and perspectives reviewed in the present chapter: (i) where and how the emotion was expressed in your body; (ii) the internal thoughts, phrases and images that accompanied the emotion; (iii) the relational dimension of what you felt – who triggered it, who was it aimed at, whose voice in your head was telling you to calm down, etc.; (iv) what was in the emotional mix, or different strands of feeling that you were aware of; (v) whether you would retrospectively define it as a primary or secondary emotion. If you intended to use therapy to explore this emotion event, which of these dimensions would you want to focus on, or want to avoid focusing on?

CHAPTER 114

Behaviour change

Introduction

This chapter focuses on practical skills and strategies for facilitating behaviour change in clients. A counselling relationship is based on listening, being receptive, and giving the person a space in which they can begin to develop their own solutions to problems and ways of leaving stuckness behind and moving ahead in their life. Often the primary counselling task that a person is seeking help to fulfil is simply that of *talking*: telling their story, putting feelings, concerns and hopes into words, being heard, reflecting on what has been said, making sense. However, there are other occasions in a counselling relationship when the person may have a very specific idea of what they want to work on, or work out, in terms of a habit or pattern of behaviour that is troubling to them. This chapter focuses on the counselling goal of *behaviour change*. The topic of behaviour change includes a wide range of issues that people may present in counselling, encompassing quite specific, self-contained habits such as 'keeping my paperwork up to date', through more far-reaching behavioural patterns such as weight loss or smoking cessation, changes in interpersonal relating ('How do I stop getting into arguments with my co-workers?') and changes that embrace many aspects of a person's life ('How do I live now that my spouse has died?').

We live in a society in which the pace of change appears to be ever-increasing. Indeed, the rise of psychology as a discipline in the twentieth century can be viewed as a cultural response to the need of ordinary people to get a handle on the challenge of how to change and adapt in the face of new work patterns and social norms. As a result, the counselling and psychotherapy literature contains a proliferation of ideas about how to facilitate change. This chapter introduces some of these ideas. Emphasis is placed on the importance of breaking the change process into achievable step-by-step progress towards an ultimate goal. But first, we consider the key question: why is it so difficult to change behaviour?

Why behaviour change is hard to achieve

One of the major differences between counselling, understood as a skilled and intentional activity, and the type of everyday help-giving that takes place between people who are friends or family members, lies in the way that behaviour change is understood. From a common-sense perspective, if someone has a problem, then the obvious response is to suggest or advise that the person should do something different. This advice is often backed up by personal experience, of the type, 'when that happened to me, what I did was…'. From a counselling perspective, suggestions and advice-giving are unlikely to be helpful in the absence of other strategies. This is because, by the time someone consults a counsellor, they have almost certainly already used all the advice they can find, and it hasn't worked: *if the behaviour was something that was easy to change, they would have done it already.*

There are many reasons why changing behaviour can be difficult:

- *The problem behaviour is being continually reinforced.* A person's behaviour tends to develop in balance with their social environment. In other words, the significant people in an individual's life have come to expect that the person will behave in certain ways, and the subtle 'reward system' that takes place in interactions between people (in the form of approval, affirmation and avoidance of criticism) consistently maintains or reinforces established patterns of behaviour. Self-initiated change ('I wish I could take more exercise') will normally run against the grain of situational forces (e.g. the cost, time and effort of joining a fitness club).

- *Real-life behaviour change takes time, readiness, coaching and practice.* If you reflect on episodes in your life in which you have changed your own behaviour (see Learning activity 1 below) you will typically find that many of these examples involved considerable effort over extended periods of time. For example, learning to swim, ride a bike, drive a car or master a new language – all of these instances of highly valued behaviour change also depend on someone else being willing to devote time to assisting the learner.

- *Ambivalence about change.* A person may well have a personal investment in staying the way they are. No matter how much a person may protest that he or she really, really wants to change, there will be some part of their sense of who they are that identifies with their present pattern of behaviour. Doing something radically different can be scary – it is a step into an unknown. So, no matter how much a student may want to become better organized and get good grades, if he or she has a sense of him/herself as 'someone who just passes and is one of the crowd', then attaining 'A' grades and being noticed by tutors may be quite threatening.

These factors tend to be in play in any situation in which a person seeks help from a counsellor to change their behaviour. Behaviour change is hard in counselling because the problem behaviour is almost certainly firmly embedded in a pre-existing network of relationships, and has turned out to elude resolution through everyday advice-giving. Furthermore, the person seeking help is probably unclear in their own heart about whether they want to change at all.

Skills and strategies for facilitating behaviour change

The following sections discuss various ways of facilitating behaviour change. It is important to keep in mind that behaviour change tasks rarely occur in a vacuum. Even when they comprise the primary focus of counselling, behaviour change is almost always accompanied by complementary tasks around reflection/making sense, emotional clarity and developing more satisfying relationships. Each of the skills and strategies discussed here can be used alone, or combined in a wide variety of ways. In some situations, a single perspective may be sufficient to unlock the door to a different way of being. In other situations, counselling for behaviour change may need to call on multiple approaches. Each skill is supported by extensive theory and research that can be followed up through the suggestions for further reading that are provided.

Clarifying what the client wants to achieve

In relation to behaviour change, it is important to develop a shared understanding of what the client wants to achieve. Issues associated with establishing therapy goals are discussed in Chapter 5. In relation to behaviour change, a specific, future-oriented approach goal (e.g. 'by the time I go on holiday in the summer, I want to be fit enough to walk 10 kilometres each day') is more achievable than a vague avoidance goal ('I don't want to be so fat'). This is because – as outlined in the following sections – a key aspect of effective behaviour change is to construct some kind of step-by-step plan to develop new behaviour, which then replaces the earlier unwanted pattern of behaviour. The accomplishment of each step in the plan or journey helps the person to feel more positive about themselves. By contrast, trying to suppress a pattern of behaviour can have the effect of exacerbating any avoidance and self-criticism tendencies that the person already possesses. Regular reviews of goal attainment, and adjustment or clarification of goal statements, can also be helpful: movement in the direction of a goal usually involves a series of small steps and it is rewarding and motivating to be able to record progress.

Facilitating readiness and commitment to change

Readiness to change represents a key factor in any work around behavioural change. Exploration of the person's views around his or her readiness to do things differently is therefore an important counselling skill. Many practitioners have found that it has been useful to employ the *stages of change* model developed by James Prochaska and Carlo DiClemente. From their experience in working in a health arena, in which many patients were resistant to changing illness-promoting behaviours such as smoking and drinking, these psychologists developed the idea that there are major differences between people in relation to their readiness to change. They formulated a five-stage model of the change process to account for these differences. Their model is known as a 'transtheoretical' theory because it intentionally integrates ideas from various schools of therapy into an overarching framework. The stages of change observed by Prochaska and DiClemente are:

A *Precontemplation*. The person has no immediate intention to make changes in relation to the behaviour that is problematic. For example, someone who is a heavy smoker may be aware that his or her behaviour is a health risk, but is not yet willing to face up to the possibility of quitting.

B *Contemplation*. At this stage, the person has decided to change their behaviour, but at some point in the future, for example at some point in the next six months.

C *Preparation*. Has taken some initial steps in the direction of behaviour change. For example, a person seeking to stop smoking may have collected information about the availability of cessation clinics, nicotine patches, etc.

D *Action*. The person has changed their problematic behaviour for less than six months, and is still in a position of consolidating their new patterns of behaviour, and avoiding temptation.

E *Maintenance*. Avoiding relapse, or coping with episodes of relapse, over a longer period of time.

As further time elapses, and the previously problematic behaviour or habit diminishes, the person can be viewed as entering a final *termination* stage – the problem is no longer relevant to them, and they do not need to give it any attention.

The value of the stages of change model, in relation to working together to do something different, is that it suggests that quite different counselling skills may be required at different stages of the change process. For example, the tasks for helping the person at the precontemplation phase may include consciousness-raising, involving collecting information, and validating and accepting their point of view and state of readiness (rather than establishing a critical or coercive relationship). The tasks at the contemplation stage may include decision-making, and exploring the meaning of the person's ambivalence.

Further information about the stages of change model, and its application in counselling, can be found in Krebs et al. (2019). One of the most useful aspects of the stages of change model that can be applied in counselling for behaviour change, is around understanding the difference between the point at which a person is actively committed to changing their behaviour, and the prior stages where they may be vaguely aware of a need to change, but are not yet ready to commit themselves. The theory and practice of *motivational interviewing* (Miller and Rollnick 2012) offers a set of skills, strategies and methods designed to facilitate/motivate the individual to move beyond precontemplation and contemplation and to engage with the tasks associated with preparation for change and then action. Key skills in motivational interviewing include 'rolling with the resistance' (taking the client's ambivalence seriously, and exploring what it means to them), inviting reflection on disparities between wanting to change and not wanting, and expanding change talk (empathically engaging with, and opening up the meaning and implications of, client positive change statements) (Westra and Aviram 2013). Workbooks for developing motivational interview skills have been published by Matulich (2017) and Wood (2020). There are also many training programmes and online training materials that are available.

Suggestions and advice

As mentioned earlier, the act of offering suggestions and advice is a helping strategy that is widely used in everyday life situations. The central characteristics of advice-giving statements is that they are future-oriented, refer to a set of general norms or rules for dealing with a specific problem ('this is what you *should* do'), and assume or create an implicit unequal relationship between adviser and advisee ('I know better than you', 'I have some special knowledge that you might benefit from'). Although simple, these features help us understand a number of the different ways in which advice can be delivered, as well as some of the reasons why resistance to advice exists. These features of advice-giving are problematic from a counselling perspective that is based on the client being actively involved in finding their own way forward in respect of a problem. However, they are not necessarily problematic for clients, who have lifelong experience of giving and receiving advice in their everyday relationships, as well as familiarity with advice being provided by doctors, nurses, call centres and many other sources.

In many research studies, clients have reported that therapist advice and suggestions, teaching inputs, and what have been described as 'therapist directives' have been helpful for them (see, for example, Swift et al. 2017). In a study of long-term recovery in individuals who had received a diagnosis of psychosis, Bjornes-tad et al. (2018) found that most participants valued advice about how to handle social interactions during the process of re-engaging with society. In a series of studies, Duan et al. (2012, 2015, 2020) observed that therapy clients expected their counsellors to give them advice, and were confident about their capacity for whether or not to follow it. On the other hand, interviews with therapy clients whose weight was in the obese range greatly resented gratuitous advice on weight loss, and regarded it as a form of weight-shaming (Kinavey and Cool 2019).

Taken together, evidence from advice-giving in both everyday life and in therapy indicates that advising is a potentially valuable counselling skill, if used appropriately. Guidelines for advice-giving in therapy include:

- Prefacing any advice by making it clear that what you are going to say may not be helpful for the client, and that they are the only one who knows whether it will be useful or not.
- Using softer word choices, such as 'suggestion', 'possibility' or 'perspective' rather than 'advice'.
- Checking out with the client whether they are interested in hearing your views.
- Later in therapy, once a solid therapy relationship has been established, a client may be in a better position to evaluate advice/suggestions.
- Respecting the client's request for advice.
- From the therapist's perspective, something that would be defined by a client as advice might in fact be the end-point of a process of mutual exploration and decision-making (see, for example, the detailed case examples in Couture and Sutherland 2006).
- Being aware of why you are offering advice – has the client asked for it? Is it for the client, or is it primarily a way to make you feel that you have something to offer?

- At a later session asking the client whether the advice/suggestion has been helpful, and if so, how and why?

Further explanation and discussion of these principles can be found in Duan et al. (2018) and Prass et al. (2020).

The limited value of making helpful suggestions as a means of enabling behaviour change

Transactional analysis (TA) theory includes an elegant analysis of the limitations of naive advice-giving as a strategy for facilitating behaviour change. Berne (1964) suggested that it made sense to regard sequences of apparently self-defeating interactions between people as psychological 'games'. In his model, a 'game' is a series of interactions between two or more people that leads to a well-defined, predictable outcome in the form of an experience of frustration or some other form of negative emotion. Berne regarded games as a substitute for genuine relating between individuals. He believed that although people are often afraid to engage in honest and intimate interaction with others, we all nevertheless have a basic need for social contact – a game provides a structure for such contact without running the risk of too much closeness. In his book *Games People Play*, Berne identifies a large number of psychological games, ranging from all-encompassing long-term life games ('Alcoholic', 'Now I've Got You, You Son of a Bitch') to more benign or briefer interaction sequences such as 'Ain't It Awful'. One of the games that can occur frequently in counselling situations is 'Why Don't You – Yes But' (YDYB). In this game, a person asks for help or advice, and the other players make suggestions. For example:

Person:	My life is so stressful, I feel tired all the time and my social life is suffering. What can I do?
Counsellor:	Why don't you keep a diary and look at how you could cut down on your work commitments?
Person:	I've tried that – there's nothing I can change.
Counsellor:	So what about looking for another job?
Person:	I can't afford to take a drop in salary, so that's not realistic.
Counsellor:	What about trying some relaxation tapes or meditation?
Person:	I've tried them too – finding the time to do them just makes me more stressed...

This kind of interaction is clearly futile, as a piece of counselling. But what makes this kind of suggestion-giving so hopeless? Berne (1964) argues that the apparently rational, Adult-to-Adult request made by the person seeking help in fact conceals a different kind of transaction – between a needy Child and someone (the counsellor) who is unwittingly pushed into the position of all-knowing Parent. The pay-off for the person initiating the game is that the helper will always prove to be inadequate (none of their suggestions will be worth following up), which then leaves the instigator reinforced in a basic sense of being someone who can't be helped, or who is beyond help. In other words, the game allows the person to maintain a superficial contact with another person, without being called upon to explore what is really true for them – in this case a deep feeling of hopelessness and despair about their life.

It can be seen that, in this case, almost any kind of counselling response – empathic reflection, open and curious questioning, encouragement to say more – would be more useful than giving suggestions. Games theory demonstrates that it does not matter how sensible and valid suggestions and advice might be – if they have not arisen out of a shared process of problem-solving based on mutual understanding, they will almost certainly be met with a polite and appreciative response of 'yes… but…'.

Behaviour change as step-by-step progress

Typically, behaviour change is a step-by-step journey that gradually makes progress in the direction of establishing a preferred pattern of behaviour and leaving a dysfunctional one behind. This is a journey that needs to be initiated and sustained by the client, supported by the counsellor and by other people in the client's life. The counselling and psychotherapy literature includes many ideas about how to support and facilitate change. The following sections discuss three contrasting perspectives:

- a collaborative framework for change: goals, tasks and methods
- a cognitive-behavioural approach that uses cognitive change to drive behaviour change
- accomplishing change by building on existing strengths.

There are many ways that these approaches can be combined. However, from the point of view of developing relevant skills, it is useful to consider them as separate.

A collaborative framework for change: goals, tasks and methods

The pluralistic approach to therapy offers a collaborative approach to behaviour change (Cooper and McLeod 2011; McLeod 2018, 2019; McLeod and McLeod 2020). This works by agreeing the goals of therapy, then breaking them down into step-by-step tasks that will contribute to the accomplishment of each goal. This then leads to a discussion around the methods (i.e. activities, interventions) that can be applied to each task. Taken together, these conversations operate as an ongoing process of shared decision-making in which the client and counsellor work together to devise a shared action plan, review progress on a regular basis, and revise the plan as necessary. Any activity, skill, area of personal experience or type of knowledge that is available to the counsellor and client can feed into this process. For example, Sanjit was highly anxious in social situations, and defined his main therapy goal as being able to interact and converse with colleagues in a relaxed manner when they collectively met up for lunch each Friday at a local restaurant. With his counsellor, he was able to identify a set of tasks that needed to be completed in order to achieve his goal: (a) dealing with his physical and cognitive anxiety symptoms; (b) knowing how to participate in an informal conversation; and (c) handling the occasional racist comments that were directed at him in a 'just joking' style. They agreed on a series of breathing, relaxation and CBT techniques (methods) for turning anxiety into positive energy. They practised informal conversational strategies and skills in sessions, and rehearsed stories that Sanjit could tell. Sanjit also recruited to the change project a trusted work colleague who would sit next to him in the restaurant and help him to participate in interactions. Methods for dealing with racist microaggression included both studying the literature on colonialism and white fragility, and learning to accept his own anger and communicate it appropriately. In this way, a collaborative pluralistic approach to behaviour change is able to apply both standard therapy skills and ideas, alongside more idiosyncratic and personal sources.

Using cognitive change to drive behaviour change

The behaviour change methodology that is believed by many specialist counsellors and psychotherapists to be maximally effective in facilitating behaviour change – a position that is backed up by a substantial amount of research – is *cognitive-behavioural therapy* (CBT). Attractive features of this approach, for many practitioners and clients, are that it is businesslike, rational, easy to follow and down-to-earth. The key idea in CBT is to analyse the behavioural patterns of the person (the problem behaviour and the new preferred behaviour) in terms of an A-B-C formula: *antecedents, behaviour* and *consequences*. Anything that a person does on a regular basis is regarded as being elicited or triggered by a stimulus or situation (antecedent) and reinforced or rewarded by its consequences. This formula is the basis for a simple, yet effective behaviour change method. The first step is to collect information, over a period of time, concerning the exact, detailed problem behaviour that is exhibited by the person, the situations in which this behaviour occurs and the consequences that follow from it. The next step is to devise a plan or programme in which the problem behaviour is gradually eliminated or extinguished, while at the same time the desired behaviour is gradually introduced. The third step is to ensure that the new behaviour is maintained, in different situations over a period of time, rather than abandoned when the going gets tough.

The A-B-C formula encourages the person seeking help and their counsellor to devote their attention, initially, to two areas: antecedents and consequences. These are the crucial points of leverage in relation to the problem behaviour.

For example, Trudy was a family counsellor who was called in to work with Andy and his family, on account of Andy's problem with school attendance. Trudy spent a long time listening to the family, asking them to describe exactly what it was that happened on school days, and showing a lively non-judgemental curiosity in everything that they had to say. She also helped them to identify their goals for counselling. At the end of this phase, she brought out a sheet of flip chart paper and some pens, and started to map out what she thought was going on, while inviting the family members to add details or make corrections. She made a list down the centre of the page of all the activities that Andy engaged in on a typical day when he did not go to school – his reason for not wanting to go, the argument with his parents, the parents going to work, Andy having the house to himself, watching TV, and so on. In a different colour, she made a list on the left-hand side of the page of the possible triggers for these events. For example, non-school days were more likely to happen when Andy had not done his homework, or there was a test; unresolved arguments were more likely if both parents needed to be at work earlier than usual. On the right-hand side of the page, in a third colour, Trudy listed some of the consequences of Andy's behaviour – falling behind in his work and feeling panicky, enjoying daytime TV, being on the receiving end of sarcastic comments from teachers, assembling an impressive collection of music downloads, missing out on lunch and games with his friends, and so on. As she was doing this, all of the members of the family started to make connections, and imagine alternatives. For instance, a parent staying at home for two days would have the time to be able to make sure that Andy did his homework in the evening, and to help him with it, as well as making staying at home seem less attractive for Andy, since he would not be able to watch TV and download music from the PC. It also became apparent how stressful, demanding and challenging some aspects of Andy's school life were, and how important it would be to make sure that he received regular rewards in recognition of his efforts. At the end of one meeting, all of the members of the family came away with new behaviours that they agreed to initiate, which were listed in a page pinned to the kitchen noticeboard. Trudy agreed to meet with them two weeks later to check on their progress.

The initial step of how Trudy used a structured approach to helping Andy and his family was primarily oriented towards identifying patterns of behaviour. A further step would usually involve focusing on dysfunctional cognitive processes that function to maintain problem behaviour. For example, Andy might be avoiding doing his homework because of a belief that 'I am stupid'. Trudy might ask Andy to complete worksheets that asked him to list other negative beliefs that might be influencing him, then use the skill of Socratic questioning (see Chapter 12) to gently challenge these negative thought patterns. Later stages in this process would involve working with Andy to identify more constructive forms of self-talk such as 'I know I can work out how to do this if I stick with it and ask for help if I need it', and then applying this new skill in everyday situations.

A key CBT strategy involves designing behavioural experiments that can be implemented between sessions and then reviewed in the next session. For example, the decision by Andy's father to rearrange his work schedule to be more available for his son fits into this category. Some behavioural experiments are particularly emotionally demanding, because they involve exposure to stressful situations. For instance, it turned out that Andy routinely avoided asking his teachers for help, because he was embarrassed about doing this and feared being teased by his friends. Trudy worked closely with Andy to rehearse how he might deal with such situations.

At its heart, CBT is a common-sense approach that relies on the application of some simple, yet powerful ideas in a systematic manner. Like any other method, it works better when there is a good relationship between the person seeking help and the counsellor – notice how respectful and accepting Trudy was, in a counselling situation where it would have been all too easy to be drawn into taking sides and condemning Andy's 'laziness' or inadequacy.

The CBT literature contains a wealth of ideas for behaviour change techniques, and workbooks that can be used by counsellors and clients in relation to specific behaviour change problems. An overview of CBT, with suggestions for further reading, can be found in McLeod (2019). The writings of James Bennett-Levy represent a particularly valuable source. For many years a leading figure in the training of CBT therapists, Bennett-Levy's research into the training process convinced him that self-reflection and self-practice (i.e. the student applying CBT ideas and techniques to their own life problems) was an essential part of learning to be an effective CBT practitioner. With colleagues, he devised an invaluable self-practice manual for self-practice of CBT skills (Bennett-Levy et al. 2015). An alternative CBT skills manual, informed by a deliberate practice perspective, has been published by Boswell and Constantino (2021).

Accomplishing change by building on existing strengths

A quite different method of working with a behaviour change task is to pay attention to occasions when the problem behaviour does *not* occur, rather than the occasions when it *does*. In this approach, the client is invited to identify and reflect on episodes when they were able to deal with a target problem behaviour successfully, as well as on situations in which they failed to deal with it. The underlying idea behind this strategy is to activate the person's existing resources and strengths (i.e. whatever it was that enabled them to have a positive experience) rather than focusing on their weaknesses. This general approach is associated with solution-focused therapy (O'Connell 2012), narrative therapy (Morgan 2001) and combined use of these models (Metcalf 2017). The key idea is that there will almost always be times when the person has in fact been able to behave differently (narrative therapists describe such events as 'unique outcomes' or 'glittering moments'; solution-focused practitioners tend to use the term 'exceptions'), and that the widespread human tendency to become preoccupied with problems (and how awful things are) will have obscured these achievements from view. The job of the counsellor, therefore, is to assist the person to identify the moments of success in relation to the problem behaviour, and then to build on the personal resources that are behind these 'glittering achievements'.

This method can be difficult to implement, if the person seeking help is so over-whelmed by the problem behaviour that he or she just cannot (or will not) allow even the slightest possibility that good moments might occur. On the other hand, it has the potential to be highly energizing and liberating because (a) the solutions that are generated are wholly the product of the person, rather than being sug-gested by the counsellor, and (b) it downplays the failures and deficits of the person and celebrates their achievements. A further positive aspect of this way of supporting behaviour change is that it has the potential to generate learning that transcends the client's initial goals. For example, a person who is trapped in a cycle of disordered eating will be likely to identify therapy goals along the lines of establishing a pattern of healthy eating and appropriate exercise. If a narrative/solution-focused approach turns out to be effective for them, they may end up – in addition to achieving their goals – with an expanded appreciation of their own resourcefulness and strengthened connections with other people in their lives.

A key skill in this approach to behaviour change is to invite the person to stand outside the problem behaviour and view themselves as separate from it. In narrative therapy this is described as *externalizing* the problem. The idea is that the person is not the problem – the problem is the problem. In effect, the client is assumed to be an intelligent, knowledgeable, courageous and resourceful person. For instance, in the case of someone who wishes to control their eating, it might be useful to ask him about when 'the voice of anorexia' (or whatever other phrase the client might choose) visits them, and how it influences their life and relation-ships with others. They might reply that one of the effects of the voice of anorexia is to 'make me different from everyone else'. Further steps in the externalizing process involve using their answers to the question 'How does the problem influence you?' to prepare the ground for the reverse question: 'How do you influ-ence the problem?' Sources of further information on skills for facilitating exter-nalizing conversations can be found in Morgan (2001) and White (2007).

Other skills and strategies for helping a client to appreciate their own strengths and resources, and then apply them to a behaviour change project, include:

- Explaining relevant aspects of a solution-focused or narrative approach to behaviour change, to encourage and enable the client to actively participate in identifying unique outcomes, exceptions, etc.
- Being curious about the client's existing strategies for behaviour change: 'I can see that you have lived with these eating issues for several years – that makes me wonder how you make sense of it yourself in your own mind, and what you have found helpful or unhelpful in managing it', 'I was really struck by how well you seemed able to handle that big life change, or moving to a

new city and starting a new job… is there anything about the way you were able to deal with those situations that could be relevant to the aim of developing a healthier approach to eating?'

- Expanding on innovative moments: the concept of innovative moments refers to the occurrence in client talk of new ways of thinking or acting in relation to a problem (Gonçalves et al. 2009; Nasim et al. 2019). Such moments represent opportunities for the therapist to invite the client to say more, in terms of sharing and elaborating on potential further steps in the direction of sustained behaviour change that are implied in what may often come across as casual remarks made by a client.

- A technique used in solution-focused therapy to maintain a thread of conversation about positive achievements is to ask, towards the start of every session, how much the problem has improved, or how much closer the client has got to accomplishing their goals. This can be given additional focus by using a scale (e.g. 'on a scale of 1 to 10').

- The 'miracle question' is another solution-focused strategy: the client is asked to imagine that a miracle has taken place overnight, and their problem has been completely eradicated. They are then invited to describe what their life is like. This can then lead into conversations about times when the client may have seen pieces of this miracle happening, or steps they can take to begin to make the miracle happen.

Each of these skills and strategies represents different ways of engaging the client's imagination and activating their capabilities. By approaching behaviour change through building on strengths, the assumption is that the client will at some point become able to take charge of the process, because they are essentially assembling and channelling skills and knowledge that they already possess. A lot of the time, this involves drawing on supportive relationships in the everyday life of the client, rather than being dependent on the therapist. Further information about skills and strategies for making use of client strengths and resources in therapy can be found in Fluckiger et al. (2010), Murphy and Sparks (2018), Scheel et al. (2013), Smith (2006) and Sparks and Duncan (2016).

Other aspects of behaviour change

In addition to the broad change pathways outlined above, there are also some recurring themes that arise during counselling for behaviour change that call for the development of specific skills.

Support of others

It is very difficult to make significant behavioural changes on one's own, through individual planning and willpower. Lack of support from other people constitutes an important barrier to change, and ensuring that adequate social support is available represents an important counselling task for many people seeking help around a behaviour change goal. The role of the counsellor in relation to this task can involve checking out with the person the amount of support that is available, and how accessible it is. It may be valuable in some instances to rehearse or run through strategies for enlisting support. Part of this task may involve discussion about the ways in which the counsellor can offer support. In some counselling situations it may be possible to meet with key supporters, to explore their perceptions of how they can help. Support may come from individuals already in the person's social network, such as family, friends and work colleagues, or may encompass new people, such as members of self-help groups. Support may be dispersed over a number of people, or be concentrated on one main 'ally'. Support may be provided face-to-face, by telephone or by email. If the person seeking help has difficulty in identifying potential supporters, it may be useful to invite them to think about 'who would be least surprised to hear about your success in changing this behaviour?' There is no special counselling method that is associated with the task of ensuring support – this is a task that relies on the person and the counsellor being willing to spend some time on it, and pooling their ideas.

Anticipating and preventing relapse

The *stages of change* model, introduced earlier in this chapter, suggests that relapse is an almost inevitable consequence of most attempts to change behaviour – it is very difficult indeed to continue to do something different, without ever slipping back into old ways. An essential counselling task, therefore, when a person is on the point of implementing change, is to consider the issue of relapse. It is usually helpful to explain the concept, and to be candid about the likelihood that some relapse will occur at some point down the line. The questions that may need to be discussed include: How will you know if relapse has happened? What are the factors that might make you vulnerable to relapse? What will you do if you have a relapse? How will you use support at these times? Who will support you? How will you ask for support? How can you learn from a relapse episode about your change strategy? One of the biggest dangers associated with relapse is that the person will catastrophize the situation, jump to an extreme conclusion such as 'I'm no good' or 'it's a waste of time, this isn't going to work', and abandon all the good work that they have done up to that stage. The more that the counsellor has been able to introduce the idea that relapse is normal, routine, predictable and surmountable, the less likely it is that the person will jump to a catastrophic interpretation of what has happened. It is always important to keep in mind that a person engaging in behaviour change that they consider to be significant enough to merit the help of a counsellor, will in all probability be in a state of high emotional vulnerability when they begin to try out new ways of doing things, and will as a result perceive a relapse as a major setback. Planned follow-up sessions, where possible relapse incidents can be explored, can be a valuable source of support for the person, if the counsellor is in a position to offer intermittent contact over a period of time.

Client activity between sessions

Having a really good discussion, in a counselling session, of how and what to do differently, and how to change problematic behaviour, is of little value if the person then does not implement any changes in their everyday life. One of the useful strategies for bridging the gap between the counselling room and real life is the practice of agreeing on *homework* tasks. Homework tasks in counselling can be suggested by the person or by the counsellor, and can range from quite structured and formal tasks, such as writing a journal or completing worksheets, to more informal or flexible tasks such as 'listening to other people more' or 'visiting my grandmother's grave'. Although homework is sometimes considered as a method that is primarily employed by cognitive-behavioural therapists, there is plentiful evidence that counsellors using a wide variety of approaches are all likely to use homework with at least 50 per cent of their cases (Kazantzis and L'Abate 2007; Ronan and Kazantzis 2006).

Based on a review of the research evidence, Scheel et al. (2004) developed some useful guidelines for using homework in counselling. These include: the homework assignment to be based on collaboration between counsellor and client; describing the task in detail; providing a rationale for why the task will benefit the person; matching the task to the person's ability; writing down the task; asking how confident the person is about fulfilling the task, and if necessary modifying the task accordingly; trying out the task during the session; asking about how the person got on with the task, at the next meeting; celebrating or praising the person's achievement of the task. In some counselling situations, it is also possible to use reminders to maximize the chances that the task is carried out. For example, a number of smoking cessation projects phone up patients between sessions to check on their progress. Also, counsellors who use email contact with clients as an adjunct to face-to-face contact can quite easily send a brief email message between meetings.

Conclusions

It is impossible in a chapter of this length to do justice to the huge topic of facilitating behaviour change. The key themes that have been emphasized in the chapter are:

- Behaviour change is difficult to achieve, and there are many barriers to achieving this type of outcome.
- Effective and lasting change requires a step-by-step approach.
- Suggestions and advice can be useful if offered in a collaborative manner.
- There is no one 'right' method to facilitate change – people differ a great deal in terms of the change processes that are meaningful and helpful to them.
- It is seldom effective to try merely to eradicate or extinguish unwanted habits – what works better is to replace these behaviours with alternative activities.
- The single most important thing that a person in a counsellor can do for anyone who is seeking to change their behaviour is to function as a supporter and ally in their journey – the quality of the relationship is crucial in helping the person to persevere with their change objectives.

Learning activities

The following activities may be explored individually, and/or with a group of learning partners.

1   **Your personal experience of change.** Identify one occasion when you attempted to change your own behaviour in some way. What strategies did you use? What worked and what didn't work for you? What have you learned from this experience, that you can use in your work with clients?

2   **Exploring the everyday experience of advice-giving.** Over three consecutive days, make a note of the number of times in your everyday life when you find yourself giving advice to another person, who you gave this advice to, whether that advice was asked for, and how the recipient responded. For the following three days, you should completely refrain from giving advice at all, and instead make notes each day on occasions when you wanted to give advice (and to whom), the reactions of recipients to not receiving advice, what you and they did next, and any impact that not giving advice had on your relationship. On completion of

this sequence, reflect (on your own and/or with learning partners) on the implications for your work as a counsellor from what you have learned from this activity. (The source of this exercise is a study by Blakemore et al. 2019.)

3   **Your capacity to support behaviour change**. Divide a piece of paper into three columns:

A   Skills and strategies I am confident that I can already use to support behaviour change

B   Skills and strategies that I would like to learn more about and become more competent with

C   Approaches to behaviour change that I have heard about but do not fit with my values or style as a counsellor

Your answers should reflect your wider reading and experiences, in addition to material covered in the present chapter. Once you have filled in each column, reflect on your lists (on your own and/or with learning partners) in terms of what you can do to shift items in column B into column A, and the implications for your practice of the items in column C, in terms of how you might respond to clients who favour or need such ways of working.

Difficult situations

Introduction

Central themes in this book have been the idea that counselling skills are used to create a collaborative, blame-free, safe space for reflection on problems in living, and the development of solutions and new ways of understanding. The aim of the present chapter is to consider some of the issues involved in maintaining the counselling space during *difficult situations* – moments in counselling where it may become impossible to continue with a counselling or therapeutic conversation.

It is important for a skilled counsellor to be able routinely to monitor what is happening in the counselling relationship, as a means of staying alert to the possibility that a threat to the therapeutic space may be building up. In order to be able to respond to the person in a caring and responsible manner, anyone in a counselling role needs to have a clear idea of their strategies for dealing with difficult situations. For this reason, preparation and training for offering a counselling relationship should always involve a process of working through worst-case scenarios, so that the counsellor is as ready as he or she can be to cope with any difficult situations that may arise. In these situations, the person seeking help may be at their most vulnerable, so it is especially important for their counsellor to have a clear idea of how they will handle whatever comes up.

In this chapter, a range of difficult situations are discussed, along with skills for responding effectively to them. Within the limits of the chapter, it is not possible to provide exhaustive coverage of all the critical situations that might arise, or all the strategies that might be employed in dealing with these scenarios. In many cases, organizations will have their own protocols for handling difficult issues, which will draw on resources that may be available, for example the immediate involvement of a more experienced colleague or supervisor.

The topic of skills and strategies for repairing a breakdown or rupture in the client–therapist relationship (alliance) are discussed in Chapter 8.

Ethical dilemmas

In the course of exploring the issues that have brought them to counselling, clients may sometimes refer to experiences and situations that are ethically problematic. For example, a client may describe unlawful activity by themselves or another person. They may report intention to engage in violence, self-harm or suicide to an extent that the counsellor believes that they have a moral responsibility to revoke the client's right to confidentiality and autonomy, and initiate the involvement of external agencies such as the client's GP. The client themselves may regard some aspect of their counsellor's behaviour as harmful or unethical, and wish to make a complaint. If any such issues arise, the counsellor needs to pause the ongoing therapeutic process and address the ethical issue that has arisen.

Responding to such ethical dilemmas is seldom straightforward. The client may be in a state of vulnerability and as a consequence may be open to exploitation or manipulation. Implicit in the way that the client describes his or her problem, or the counsellor formulates a potential solution to that problem, are multiple (and often contradictory) assumptions around values. Events and lines of action that are explored in counselling sessions may have implications for other people, such as family members, who have their own rights. The counsellor may fear that acting on an ethical dilemma may jeopardize the therapeutic relationship and lead to the client dropping out of therapy. In professions such as nursing, medicine and social work, ethical dilemmas can almost always be discussed within a team, over a period of time, leading to a collective decision. By contrast, ethical issues in counselling can often arise in the moment, in situations where other colleagues cannot have access to the same amount of information about the client.

All counselling and psychotherapy professional associations publish ethical codes that specify rules of conduct for their members, and all training programmes include extensive inputs on ethics and professional standards. It is assumed that anyone who reads this book will be broadly familiar with such codes. The aim of the present chapter, therefore, is not to revisit what is already known, or can be readily accessed through relevant websites, but to concentrate instead on practical skills and strategies for responding to ethical dilemmas that arise in the course of counselling.

Skills and strategies for responding to ethical dilemmas in counselling can be divided into two broad categories: *awareness and sensitivity to potential ethical issues*, and *facilitating ethical problem-solving*.

Awareness and sensitivity around potential ethical issues

One of the central aspects of learning and using counselling skills is the development of awareness: being able to differentiate between helpful and unhelpful ways of implementing a skill, and sensitivity to situations that call for the use of specific skills. A key focus in any skills training is learning to recognize what is happening and make sense of it in terms of categories and concepts. Similarly, ethical competence requires a capacity to be sensitive to markers of potential ethical dilemmas. Being able to identify potential ethical problems early – and engage in preventative action – is a valuable skill in itself.

At one level, the ethics of counselling is grounded in a *common-sense* appreciation of what is the 'right' thing to do, based on shared core *values* such as respect for the person, and belief in a person's capacity to develop and learn. These values are reflected in an array of personal *virtues* such as honesty and integrity. The existence of this kind of everyday, common-sense moral sensibility means that, in many situations, counsellors are intuitively aware that something may be ethically not quite 'right'.

The everyday moral basis of practice is also reinforced by *ethical principles*, which seek to provide a more formal framework for being aware of ethical issues. An important statement of the core ethical principles that inform counselling practice was made by Karen Kitchener (1984), who proposed that ethical decision-making in any counselling situation should be based on five fundamental moral constructs:

- *autonomy*: people are understood as individuals who have the right to freedom of action and freedom of choice, in so far as the pursuit of these freedoms does not interfere with the freedoms of others
- *non-maleficence*: the injunction to all helpers or healers that they must 'above all do no harm'
- *beneficence*: the intention to promote human welfare
- *justice*: the fair distribution of resources and services
- *fidelity*: being loyal and reliable, and acting in good faith.

In recent years, there has been a growing appreciation that it is necessary for counsellors to be able to interpret ethical principles within a relational context, leading to frameworks for understanding *relational ethics* (Gabriel and

Casemore 2009). The key characteristics of relational ethics is exemplified in a study by Jennings et al. (2005) in which experienced psychotherapists were interviewed about the values that informed their work with clients. The themes that emerged from analysis of these interviews illustrate the extent to which a relational ethos permeated the ethical thinking of these practitioners. They reported that their responsibility to their clients could only be fulfilled if they continued to maintain and build their knowledge, skills and competence in two areas. *Relational connection* referred to a commitment to relationships with clients, colleagues, family and friends, and members of the community. *Humility* referred to an appreciation of their limitations as practitioners and as human beings. Further ethical frameworks have been developed to reflect ethical values associated with different cultural and faith traditions, and feminist values (see McLeod 2019 for further information).

There are a number of aspects of counselling that may trigger ethical dilemmas. These include:

- working within the law
- negotiating informed consent;
- maintaining confidentiality
- safeguarding and child protection
- competence (being aware of your limits as a counsellor)
- taking care around dual relationships
- dealing with risk and self-harm
- using touch.

Across these domains, it is possible to identify three broad categories of ethical issue. The category that emerges most often in practice refers to ethical dilemmas arising from some aspect of the client's life, such as the client wishing to end their life, disclosing information about sexual abuse, or not wanting the counsellor to take notes or discuss their case in supervision. A second category, which occurs less often but is more likely to lead to ethical complaints to professional bodies, is the unethical behaviour of the counsellor themselves. For example, a counsellor may want to develop a friendship or sexual relationship with a client, operate outside the limits of their competence, have impaired competence on health grounds, or prolong counselling for financial gain. A third category refers to ethically problematic policies at an organizational level, such as limits on the number of sessions, discrimination against certain groups of clients, bullying of staff, etc. Beyond these categories, there are also occasions when the client may act unlawfully towards the therapist, for instance by being violent or stalking them.

Ethical issues associated with the topics listed above are discussed in more detail in McLeod (2019) and Reeves and Bond (2021).

The development of awareness and sensitivity around ethical issues needs to be multifaceted and ongoing. Tools for awareness, in the form of concepts, examples and stories, can be found in professional organizations, the counselling clinic or agency where one works, supervisors and colleagues. New ethical challenges, and new perspectives on well-known challenges, continue to emerge, for example in recent years in respect of online therapy and therapist presence on social media. Learning about ethical dimensions of practice is therefore a career-long process.

Skills for facilitating ethical problem-solving

The main skills and strategies for dealing with ethical dilemmas centre on *preparation and anticipation*, and *implementing a decision-making framework*.

Preparation and anticipation refers to providing ethical information to clients, and allowing them to ask questions and discuss any difficulties, at the start of therapy. The general ethical principle of informed consent means that this kind of procedure routinely needs to take place in any case. It also creates a shared understanding or ethical anchor-point for exploring ethical dilemmas that emerge in the course of therapy.

When a client arrives for an intake or assessment session, or for their first counselling session, they will have many concerns on their mind over and above informed consent. A client may be too emotionally troubled to take in ethical information. It is therefore necessary to regard ethical preparation as a process that may include information being available on a website, some kind of standard statement made by the intake interviewer or counsellor, space for questions and discussions, and then one or more follow-up probes at subsequent sessions to check whether the client has further questions or worries. The counselling agency may specify what should be said to clients, and may offer training around this task. Training programmes also provide similar inputs. It is important for counsellors to use deliberate practice to personalize and rehearse what they are going to say, and how they will invite questions, so that they come across to the client as comfortable and knowledgeable in respect of these issues.

Because significant types of ethical dilemma are associated with the actions of therapists themselves, and their employers, it is essential that preparatory information should include complaints procedures. This should incorporate not only internal procedures, but also external sources, such as information on service user group websites about how to respond to malpractice, and on professional body websites.

In respect of both ethical questions raised by clients at the start of therapy, and dilemmas that arise later on, it is helpful for a counsellor to have internalized a step-by-step decision-making framework that they can follow. Sometimes, ethical dilemmas are shocking and frightening (e.g. disclosure of sexual abuse, or expressed intention to commit suicide), or highly complex, leading to an immediate counsellor reaction of fearfulness, being 'thrown', panic, not knowing what to do, confusion, etc. The client is likely to be aware of such reactions, no matter how much the therapist strives to maintain their professional composure.

At one level, the counsellor's authentic response may be helpful if it conveys a sense of the seriousness of the issue and how deeply they have been touched by the client's predicament. On the other hand, the client may well be feeling shame about the situation they are describing, and may be very sensitive to any signs (as they see it) of counsellor judgement. And, ultimately, they are looking to the counsellor to find a way through the dilemma.

In abstract or general terms, a decision-making framework might include the following steps:

1 Explicitly acknowledging that there is an ethical issue that needs to be addressed, and naming it.

2 Collecting all relevant information, starting by helping the client to tell their story. It is useful to collect information about the preferences and resources of the person seeking help ('What do you think would be a good way to deal with this?'), yourself as the counsellor, and the possible views of other people who might be affected.

3 Opening out the issue by looking at who benefits from different courses of action. Identify the benefits of what could be done, from the points of view of the person, the counsellor and others.

4 Considering consequences. Identify the consequences of any action, from the points of view of the person, the counsellor and others.

5 Identifying duties. To whom does a duty exist, in the case being examined? For example, does the counsellor have a primary duty or responsibility to the person, or to a wider group, such as the person's family, or society as a whole? To whom does the organization in which the counsellor is employed have a duty or responsibility? What is the counsellor's duty to themself?

6 Consulting. Use consultation and discussion with others, for example a counselling supervisor or members of the client's cultural community, and published sources to develop a more complete understanding of duties, benefits and consequences, and to check out your own assumptions in these areas. Invite the client to engage in consultation that might be available appropriate to them.

7 Deciding. Bring together these various factors into a preliminary plan of action.

8 Testing the plan. Consult again, to check how the plan appears to other people and to the client.

9 Reviewing. Once a course of action has been set in motion, check out how it is working, and whether the client might want further support or to engage in further conversation.

In practice, there are occasions when a counsellor may feel that a decision needs to be made immediately, and there is not enough time to work through the steps outlined above. However, even when this happens, it can be valuable afterwards to sit down and work out the intricacies of duty, benefit and consequence that were at stake. It is always important to consult – ethical dilemmas are an important topic for supervision.

One of the key skills in implementing an ethical decision-making process is that the counsellor needs to actively take the initiative in broaching the topic. This can be hard to do, because it may cut across the ongoing flow of whatever personal issue the client is exploring at that moment, and because it leads the conversation into an area of uncertainty. In addition, the counsellor may be aware of a burden of responsibility, and may fear that their relationship with the client may be compromised. Because such incidents occur rarely, the counsellor may lack confidence in their capacity to handle it. The counsellor may also be unsure of how external stakeholders (e.g. the manager of the counselling agency, the child protection social worker or GP they phone up) may respond. What can happen, in the light of these factors, is that the counsellor avoids broaching the topic, in the hope that it will resolve itself. Avoidance is rarely a good option because the client has chosen to talk about particular areas of their life that they have probably already worked out are ethically problematic, and may wonder what is happening when their therapist appears to ignore the implications of what they are hearing. It is also a poor option because, as in many areas of life, early intervention is more effective than crisis firefighting.

From a collaborative perspective, an important aspect of skilful ethical decision-making is the capacity to explain and discuss ethics using everyday language that makes sense to the client. Concepts such as 'boundaries', and even 'ethics' may be mystifying for clients, and have the effect of positioning the counsellor in an expert, controlling stance.

When developing and then applying skills for responding to ethical dilemmas that emerge during therapy, it is essential for the counsellor to be aware that their capacity to deal with what is happening does not just require rehearsal and practice of key phrases and questions and an internalized model of ethical decision-making. It also involves awareness of the personal meaning of experiences such as the wish to end one's life, the intention to harm someone else, being a vulnerable child, or being betrayed. Being invited into engaging with these issues in the context of the life of a client may be highly challenging for a counsellor, in the sense of being overwhelmed in the moment by unresolved emotions and memories triggered by the client's story.

Finally, when developing skills for handling ethical dilemmas, it is essential to acknowledge that responding to such situations always involves collective responsibility. No one (including the client) would want or expect a counsellor to take an important ethical decision on their own.

When a client is hard to reach

Sometimes a client will withdraw from contact or be consistently hard to reach or connect with. This kind of process can occur when a person is exploring a life problem that has a strong emotional content, and reaches a stage at which they become overwhelmed by fear to the point that they are unable to continue to engage in rational dialogue. It is as though the person's psychological processes close down to keep them safe, and they become out of touch and detached from what other people might consider to be 'reality'. Examples of this process include:

- panic attacks
- dissociation
- hearing voices
- withdrawal
- being angry with the counsellor.

Each of these phenomena make it hard, or even impossible, to continue to pursue routine counselling tasks that call for a capacity to respond to another person and engage in some kind of collaborative conversation or dialogue. The person has withdrawn from dialogue with external others, and is largely focusing on some aspect of their own inner experiencing.

Panic attacks are associated with a set of reactions that take place when a person experiences high levels of anxiety in a specific situation. Typically, a person will have a panic attack when he or she feels trapped and enclosed, with no possibility of escape. This may happen in a lift, aeroplane or any other enclosed space. A counselling session, where a person might have a sense of being 'on the spot' or under pressure, can quite easily be experienced in this kind of way. What seems to happen in a panic sequence is that the person begins to have thoughts of being trapped and powerless, which then in turn trigger a physical 'flight' response, characterized by fast, shallow breathing. This physiological activity quickly produces a whole set of other physical symptoms, such as a feeling of pins and needles in hands and arms, pressure across the chest and a sense of faintness. The person then pays attention more and more to these symptoms, which are experienced as highly alarming, and this generates an even higher level of thoughts of being out of control, or even of dying. In turn, these thoughts and images of being out of control and dying lead to even faster, shallower breathing, and more physical symptoms. A panic attack is a spiral which can lead to loss of consciousness or actual flight (the person runs away, or tries to).

Dissociation can be regarded as a cognitive process for dealing with overwhelming threatening thoughts (e.g. memories of highly distressing and traumatic events) and emotions by not allowing these thoughts and emotions into awareness. The person achieves this by focusing their attention on something that is neutral or safe, as an alternative to what is threatening and painful. There are usually two processes that enable a person to do this. First, the person may attempt to stop breathing. This cuts off their awareness of what they are feeling, and almost makes time 'stand still'. Second, the person may find an image in their mind to attend to, or may focus their attention on an apparently meaningless object in the room, such as the corner of a radiator, or a light bulb. From the perspective of the counsellor, the person will be experienced as having 'gone away' – they will act as though they do not hear what the counsellor is saying, and are almost unaware of the counsellor's presence. A less extreme variant of this pattern can occur when a person deals with threatening thoughts and emotions by changing the topic of conversation – from the perspective of the counsellor this activity is experienced as a lack of continuity or coherence in the conversation.

Sometimes a client may withdraw inside themselves as a form of self-protection. This kind of reaction is less extreme than dissociation. For example, the person may be able to explain that this is what they need to do, and may be quite calm. Withdrawal from here-and-now interpersonal contact may be a long-established strategy for coping with too much stimulation, as in individuals on the autism spectrum. Alternatively, it may be a response to physical pain, or an intentional choice to engage in silent contemplation.

Hearing voices (sometimes described as hallucinations or delusions) can be viewed as ways that a person has developed over a period of time for dealing with persistent impossibly difficult and stressful thoughts, emotions and life situations. What seems to happen is that these thoughts and emotions become organized into voices that the person hears, and/or imaginary people or objects that are present for them.

A further situation in which a client may withdraw from active participation in a session may be when the counsellor has made an error, or has responded in a way that is disrespectful or hurtful to the client, or is viewed by the client as being generally lacking in competence, sensitivity and insight. This kind of scenario can be described as a 'rupture' in the therapy relationship or alliance. It has been widely studied, and is discussed in Chapter 8.

Skills for working with people who are hard to reach

It is important to respond to moments of client withdrawal respectfully, and not jump to conclusions that what is happening might be a sign of underlying pathology. Any of the scenarios described in the previous section can be understood as a normal and understandable way of dealing with a stressful situation. In the majority of cases, a gentle open question along the lines of 'I am wondering what is happening – you seem to have gone into your own space... Is that OK for you? ... Is there anything you would like me to do?' will prompt the client to explain what they need. Further discussion may take place at a later point when the client has re-established contact.

However, it can also be valuable to be able to utilize additional skills and strategies if necessary. The American person-centred therapist Garry Prouty has developed some useful methods for making basic emotional and interpersonal contact with people who are hard to reach. He recommends that a counsellor faced by a person who is withdrawn or unable to communicate effectively should concentrate on solely making concrete and literal empathic reflections. Prouty et al. (2002) describes five types of basic contact-making reflections:

- *Situational reflections*: statements of the counsellor's awareness of the person's situation or environment. For example: 'You are sitting on the sofa'.
- *Facial reflections*: statements that seek to capture the pre-expressive feelings of the person, as embodied in their face. For example: 'You are smiling', 'You are frowning'.
- *Word-for-word reflections*: restatements of single words, sentences and other sounds made by the person.
- *Body reflections*: the counsellor moves his or her own body to match the postures or movements made by the person.
- *Reiterative reflections*: if any of the previous types of statements appear to be effective in establishing contact, they are repeated.

The assumption behind these literal empathic reflective methods is that the person has for the moment lost contact with the external world, and that if recontact is to occur, it needs to begin with simple moves that are unthreatening, under the control of the person, and uncomplex. Of course, it is essential to offer these statements in a gentle and respectful manner. Prouty et al. (2002) offers an example of his work with an older woman, Dorothy, who was an institutionalized resident of a psychiatric facility. She mumbled for about ten minutes, while Prouty reflected back whatever words he could make out. Then she made a clear statement, 'come with me', which Prouty again reflected back. She then led him to the corner of the day room, and they stood there silently for some time. She put her hand against the wall and said 'cold'. He put his hand also on the wall, and repeated 'cold'. Prouty noted that Dorothy was holding his hand and would tighten her grip when he made a reflection, conveying that she had received and appreciated what he had said or done. Gradually Dorothy's words began to make more sense and she was able to talk about how unhappy she was. Further information about this set of skills can be found in Erskine (2015), Prouty et al. (2002) and Peters (1999). What it offers is a disciplined and caring means of patiently staying as close as possible to the experience of someone who is withdrawn, until the point where they feel able to enter into a reciprocal relationship.

More broadly, beyond Prouty's contact reflection approach, a counsellor confronted with a client who seems to be withdrawing from contact needs to be able to engage constructively at the *cognitive, bodily* and *social-interpersonal* levels. At a cognitive level, the person may be generating a steady stream of 'self-talk' (things they are saying to themselves in their head, or are being said by voices or internalized critical others) that is quite destructive and negative – for example 'I can't cope', 'I am going to die', 'I am worthless' and so on. It can be helpful for a counsellor to keep talking, in a calm and reassuring manner, and introduce more positive self-statements into the person's awareness, such as 'you will be all right', 'my sense is that you are afraid now, but we can see this through together'.

It may be that the counsellor can introduce hopeful images or statements that the person has shared on a previous occasion. It may also be helpful for the counsellor to offer an explanation of what is happening and what can be done, such as 'I think that what you were beginning to talk about was something that is very frightening for you, and now you need to cut yourself off from it by … I think what might be helpful now could be if you listen to me and…'.

An important area for a counsellor to attend to is the physical or bodily response of the person, particularly their breathing. People who are in a process of 'losing it' are often breathing fast and shallow, or slow (holding breath). It can be useful for a counsellor to draw the person's attention to their breathing ('I'm aware that you seem to be…') and instruct them in breathing regularly and deeply. For example, it may be effective to invite the person to 'breathe with me – in as far as you can – one, two, three, four, five, six, seven – and out again – one, two…'). In panic situations, it can be useful for a person to breathe into and out of a bag, or their cupped hands, as a means of reducing their oxygen intake. In some situations, the person's posture may be frozen, or hunched over (which inhibits breathing), and it can be useful to encourage them to begin to move, perhaps to walk.

Finally, a common feature of these ways of coping is a withdrawal of contact from the other, and a retreat into a private world. It can be helpful to encourage the person to look at the counsellor, to engage in eye contact and (if appropriate in the context of the relationship) to touch. Accompanied by calm, confident talking on the part of the counsellor, the re-establishment of interpersonal contact can both enable the person to pay less attention to their own inner processes, and to gain a sense of safety and security ('there is someone here I can trust, and rely on') that can make whatever it was that was scary seem a bit more bearable. These are not methods, in themselves, that are necessarily going to eliminate panic, dissociation or voice-hearing from a person's life forever – they are strategies for helping someone who is seeking counselling to manage their thoughts and feelings in the moment, so that they may, if they choose, continue to engage in a counselling conversation.

In Western society, experiences of panic, dissociation and hallucination are often addressed through psychiatric interventions such as administration of drug treatment, or by specialist psychotherapeutic interventions such as cognitive-behaviour therapy (CBT). However, in many other cultures the same phenomena are accepted and valued as part of being human. Although the methods being described here are consistent with a psychiatric or CBT approach, they are better viewed as routine skills and strategies that are intended to enable the person to make use of a counselling relationship. In some cases, it can be helpful to explore with the person the potential value of receiving more specialist help for their panic, voice-hearing or dissociation. In other cases, there may be indigenous forms of help that are more relevant. Anyone offering a counselling relationship needs to be informed about the possibilities for specialist help and consultation that are available in their community.

When a client is going through a crisis

There can be occasions when a counselling client is going through a crisis, and unable to engage with the process of counselling. Crises can take the form of disruptions to practical living arrangements, health problems that make everyday functioning impossible or mental health breakdown (Gullslett et al. 2016). Sometimes a crisis will lead the client to take time out of counselling, or quit completely. Alternatively, a client may view counselling as a source of support, and continue attending.

There exists a substantial practical, theoretical and research literature around principles of responding to crisis (James and Gilliland 2016). There are also many brief (and longer) training programmes that have been developed for members of the public as well as professionals, that provide crisis response skills. These include mental health first aid (Jorm and Ross 2018) and the Applied Suicide Intervention Skills Training (ASIST) package. Information about how to access these programmes locally is readily available through an internet search. Many counsellors have found such programmes to be a valuable supplement to their main skills training. The kind of skills that are covered include being aware of warning signs, how to initiate conversations about the crisis, listening in a non-judgemental and caring manner, providing information and helping the person to make contact with practical sources of support (e.g. family members).

When a client is at risk of harming themselves

One of the most challenging situations for a counsellor is when a person seeking help talks or acts in a way that suggests that he or she may be at risk of harming themselves or harming another person. There are several different forms that risk may take in counselling. The person may:

- plan to take their own life
- be engaged in self-harming behaviour such as cutting, purging, starving, alcohol or drug abuse, unsafe sex, etc.
- be engaged in, or planning, inflicting harm on another person (which may include the counsellor), through physical, verbal or sexual violence, harassment or stalking, criminal activity or unprotected sex (for instance in cases of HIV/AIDS infection).

A person may believe it is acceptable to kill themselves, if they have arrived at a position where life is unliveable, or possibly even to threaten other people who they perceive to have wronged them. However, when a person refers to risky behaviour in the context of a conversation with a counsellor or other practitioner, they are almost certainly asking for help to avoid doing anything harmful. It is therefore essential for anyone acting in a counselling role to be prepared to respond constructively and actively to such situations. Times when a person seeking counselling talks about risk to self or others can be very difficult for a counsellor to deal with. There is a sense of a great pressure of responsibility, and typically there may be little or no opportunity to consult colleagues – the counsellor needs to respond, one way or another, in the moment. For reasons of space, the following discussion focuses specifically on skills that are relevant for responding to risk of suicide. Reeves (2015) is an invaluable source of information on all aspects of risk in counselling.

Skills for responding to risk of suicide need to be built on an understanding of the meaning and nature of suicide, based on reading, training and talking to colleagues. Serious suicidal behaviour is relatively rare, and it is likely that a practitioner involved in offering counselling would personally come across only a relatively small number of cases over the course of their career, unless they were working in a specific area such as psychiatry or a suicide helpline. As a result, expertise and confidence arising from cumulative first-hand experience is generally not a realistic option. Particularly valuable study resources are articles that bring together the learning and insights of therapists who have worked with many suicidal clients (Aherne et al. 2018; Meichenbaum 2005), case studies that allow the reader to look 'over the shoulder' of a therapist working with a suicidal client (Pratt et al. 2016), and psychological autopsy studies that retrospectively reconstruct the suicide victim's story (Draper et al. 2008; Rasmussen et al. 2014a, 2014b). It is also valuable to develop a theoretical understanding of suicide, and examine one's own assumptions, feelings and experiences around this topic.

Key counselling skills include: (a) listening for indications from the person that some kind of harm may take place; (b) exploring: engage the person in conversation around their intentions, and the meaning that the harm event holds for them; (c) estimating the level of risk; (d) implementing strategies for avoiding harm; (e) maintaining counsellor effectiveness through consistent self-care and peer/supervisor support.

On many occasions where harm is an issue, the person seeking help may be quite open and explicit about what is in their mind. At other times, however, the person may convey their intentions in a disguised, vague or metaphorical way of talking. There is some evidence that counsellors are not good at picking up subtle clues about harmful behaviour. High levels of sensitivity and awareness are particularly important in this area of work because many clients are unwilling to admit to suicidal thoughts, or downplay them, because they are ashamed to talk about them or fear that their therapist will initiate a psychiatric intervention if they do say anything (Blanchard and Farber 2020). In a study carried out by Reeves et al. (2004), a group of highly trained specialist counsellors were recorded in sessions with 'standardized clients', who had been instructed by the researcher to talk vaguely about suicidal intentions. Very few of the counsellors followed up the implicit cues the clients were expressing around suicidality in the sessions. One explanation for this finding could be that these counsellors were more tuned into the positive aspects of what their clients were saying, and less focused on negatives. Another explanation was that they lacked skill and confidence in initiating conversations around risk. A further explanation might be an underlying (and false) belief that talking about suicide might encourage the client to act.

Assessing the severity of suicide risk usually involves collecting information that has been found to be associated with suicide attempts and completion:

- evidence of previous attempts
- current suicidal thoughts and plans
- access to means and opportunity
- attitude towards help
- current or past mental health problems
- current circumstances and quality of support available from professional and informal supporters
- current alcohol and drug use
- recent life events or anniversaries
- hopelessness and negative attitude towards the future
- reasons for living
- male aged 16–30.

In general, ongoing counselling or psychotherapy tends to be regarded in the profession as relevant for a person when their expression of suicidal is vague, when the person and their circumstances are known to the counsellor, and when the person is actively engaged in help-seeking. Otherwise, many practitioners and therapy organizations would deem it as essential to give serious consideration, in collaboration with the person if at all possible, to organizing some form of continuing support in which the person's safety and well-being can be ensured while they find a way through their current life difficulties. Usually, this would require the involvement of the client's GP and referral to a crisis team or centre. There are many examples of effective combination of ongoing counselling with attendance at a crisis centre (see, for example, Andreoli et al. 2016).

The integration of an in-depth risk assessment into a therapy session can be problematic. If a counsellor abruptly switches from an exploratory, collaborative mode of being with the client to a more interviewing/assessment mode, the client may feel that they have been turned into a 'case' rather than a person. In response to this dilemma, some groups of therapists have developed ways of assessing risk alongside exploring strategies for making sense of suicidal thoughts and developing a shared plan for mitigating risk. The most widely used examples of this kind of collaborative approach are dialectical behaviour therapy (DBT) (Harned et al. 2017; Linehan et al. 2012) and the Collaborative Assessment and Management of Suicidality (CAMS) model (Ellis 2004; Jobes 2016; Monahan et al. 2020). These approaches are supported by extensive training materials and courses that enable therapists to develop relevant skills.

In addition, there are many specific suicide prevention techniques, such as contracts, outreach and safety plans that draw on basic skills that most therapists already possess, and as a result are readily assimilated into practice (Rudd et al. 2006).

Being a therapist for a client who is suicidal can have a profound effect on the practitioner (Webb 2011). A further aspect of responding to a client with suicidal intentions is that the difficulties do not cease if the client does eventually end their life. Therapists, and other people involved with the client, are likely to be deeply affected by the outcome (Jordan and McIntosh 2011), and may need to draw on skills and knowledge from the field of suicide postvention.

Conclusions

A central theme that has run through this chapter is the idea of *crisis* – difficult situations in counselling tend to be those in which there is a crisis to be resolved, either a crisis in the life of the person seeking help, a crisis in the relationship between the person and the counsellor, or a crisis around knowing what is an ethically sound course of action. In responding to crisis, it is important not to assume that the acute difficulty being experienced is necessarily characteristic of the person (or the relationship) as a whole. James and Gilliland (2016) suggest that a crisis is an event or situation that is intolerable and urgently needs to be addressed, because it exceeds the immediately available resources and coping mechanisms of an individual or group. The task of the counsellor is to provide a secure base within which client and therapist can work together to begin to access resources that are not immediately available, but can be brought to bear on the situation.

The difficult situations discussed in this chapter are not smooth or easy. They are hard work and even scary. However, they provide opportunities for taking the relationship between a person and a counsellor, their mutual understanding, and the bond of trust between them, much further. An important aspect of longer-term counselling is that it makes it possible for counsellor and client to weather successive storms.

Learning activities

It can be helpful to carry out these activities with colleagues or learning partners, as a means of sharing experience and discussing implications for practice.

1   An important skill for any counsellor is to be able to access the support, knowledge and experience of other people in relation to therapy situations that test the limits of their competence or capacity to cope. Make a list of the sources of consultation, referral and specialist knowledge that are currently available to you. Identify any gaps in your support network, and reflect on how they might be filled.

2   What do you say to prospective clients about what is involved in counselling? When do you say it? Is this information backed up by written materials? If you have been a client yourself, what kind of consent procedure was conducted? As a result of the information you were given did you have a sense of actively giving consent for counselling to take place, and what counselling would be like? Consent conversations are not merely an ethical requirement, but also set the scene for what happens in therapy. In relation to both what you might say to a client, or your experience of being a client, how might different ways of talking about (or not talking about) consent have an effect on how the process of therapy unfolds?

3   Information for clients about ethical standards and how to complain. Carry out an internet search of the information provided for clients by counselling and psychotherapy agencies and professional bodies around how to make complaints about treatment, services or the conduct of their therapist, and how complaints are handled. Imagine you are an aggrieved client. How might you feel at the point of wanting to make a complaint? What might you be thinking? Who might you turn to for information and support? In respect of these questions, how satisfactory and helpful were the internet sources you have found? How might they be improved, particularly in relation to empowering clients and therapists to address difficulties that may arise in their relationship with each other?

4   Hard to reach role-play. Meet up with learning partners to take turns in being client, counsellor and observer(s) around sessions in which the client plays the role of a person who is hard to reach, based on the material in the relevant section of this chapter. The counsellor should use this as an opportunity either to try out different skills, or to focus on one key skill. At the end of the session, the client should provide honest feedback on what the counsellor did that was helpful or otherwise. Sufficient time should be allowed to enable the client to share their experience of being a person who was looking for help but was hard to reach.

References

Aherne, C., Coughlan, B. and Surgenor, P. (2018) Therapists' perspectives on suicide: A conceptual model of connectedness, *Psychotherapy Research*, 28(5): 803–19.

Alexander, A. and Hulse-Killacky, D. (2005) Childhood memories and receptivity to corrective feedback in group supervision, *Journal for Specialists in Group Work*, 30(1): 23–45.

Anderson, H. (1996) Reflection on client–professional collaboration, *Families, Systems, & Health*, 14(2): 193–206.

Anderson, H. (2007) The heart and spirit of collaborative therapy: A way of being, in H. Anderson and D. Gehart (eds) *Collaborative Therapy: Relationships and Conversations that make a Difference*. Taylor & Francis, pp. 43–59.

Anderson, S. and Brownlie, J. (2011) Build it and they will come? Understanding public views of 'emotions talk' and the talking therapies, *British Journal of Guidance & Counselling*, 39(1): 53–66.

Anderson, T., Crowley, M.J., Himawan, L., Holmberg, J. and Uhlin, B. (2016a) Therapist facilitative interpersonal skills and training status: A randomized clinical trial on alliance and outcome, *Psychotherapy Research*, 26(5): 511–29.

Anderson, T., Finkelstein, J.D. and Horvath, S.A. (2020) The facilitative interpersonal skills method: Difficult psychotherapy moments and appropriate therapist responsiveness, *Counselling & Psychotherapy Research*, 20(3): 463–9.

Anderson, T. and Hill, C.E. (2017) The role of therapist skills in therapist effectiveness, in L.G. Castonguay and C.E. Hill (eds) *How and Why are Some Therapists Better than Others?: Understanding Therapist Effects*. Washington, DC: American Psychological Association, pp. 139–57.

Anderson, T., McClintock, A.S., Himawan, L., Song, X. and Patterson, C.L. (2016b) A prospective study of therapist facilitative interpersonal skills as a predictor of treatment outcome, *Journal of Consulting and Clinical Psychology*, 84(1): 57–66.

Anderson, T., Ogles, B.M., Patterson, C.L., Lambert, M.J. and Vermeersch, D.A. (2009) Therapist effects: Facilitative interpersonal skills as a predictor of therapist success, *Journal of Clinical Psychology*, 65(7): 755–68.

Anderson, T., Perlman, M.R., McCarrick, S.M. and McClintock, A.S. (2019) Modeling therapist responses with structured practice enhances facilitative interpersonal skills, *Journal of Clinical Psychology*, 76(4): 659–75.

Andreoli, A., Burnand, Y., Cochennec, M.F. et al. (2016) Disappointed love and suicide: A randomized controlled trial of 'abandonment psychotherapy' among borderline patients, *Journal of Personality Disorders*, 30(2): 271–87.

Angus, L. (2012) Toward an integrative understanding of narrative and emotion processes in emotion-focused therapy of depression: Implications for theory, research and practice, *Psychotherapy Research*, 22(4): 367–80.

Angus, L. and Greenberg, L. (2011) *Working with Narrative in Emotion-focused Therapy: Changing Stories, Healing Lives*. Washington, DC: American Psychological Association.

Angus, L.E. and Rennie, D.L. (1988) Therapist participation in metaphor generation: Collaborative and noncollaborative styles, *Psychotherapy*, 25(4): 552–60.

Angus, L.E. and Rennie, D.L. (1989) Envisioning the representational world: The client's experience of metaphoric expressiveness in psychotherapy, *Psychotherapy*, 26(3): 373–9.

Aponte, H.J. and Kissil, K. (2014) 'If I can grapple with this I can truly be of use in the therapy room': Using the therapist's own emotional struggles to facilitate effective therapy, *Journal of Marital and Family Therapy*, 40(2): 152–64.

Aponte, H.J. and Kissil, K. (eds) (2016) *The Person of the Therapist Training Model: Mastering the Use of Self*. New York and Abingdon: Routledge.

Arnd-Caddigan, M. (2012) Imagining the other: The influence of imagined conversations on the treatment process, *American Journal of Psychotherapy*, 66(4): 331–48.

Arnd-Caddigan, M. (2013) Imagined conversations and negative countertransference, *Journal of Psychotherapy Integration*, 23(2): 146–57.

Arnett, R.C., Arneson, P. and Holba, A. (2008) Bridges not walls: The communicative enactment of dialogic storytelling, *Review of Communication*, 8(3): 217–34.

Arnold, K. (2014) Behind the mirror: Reflective listening and its Tain in the work of Carl Rogers, *The Humanistic Psychologist*, 42(4): 354–69.

Aronov, N.E. and Brodsky, S.L. (2009) The river model: A metaphor and tool for training new psychotherapists, *Journal of Contemporary Psychotherapy*, 39(3): 187–95.

Arthern, J. and Madill, A. (1999) How do transitional objects work?: The therapist's view, *British Journal of Medical Psychology*, 72(1): 1–21.

Arthern, J. and Madill, A. (2002) How do transitional objects work? The client's view, *Psychotherapy Research*, 12(3): 369–88.

Audet, C.T. and Everall, R.D. (2010) Therapist self-disclosure and the therapeutic relationship: A phenomenological study from the client perspective, *British Journal of Guidance & Counselling*, 38(3): 327–42.

Austin, J.T. and Austin, J.A. (2018) Initial exploration of therapeutic presence pedagogy in counselor education, *International Journal for the Advancement of Counselling*, 40(4): 481–500.

Bailenson, J.N. (2021) Nonverbal overload: A theoretical argument for the causes of Zoom fatigue, *Technology, Mind and Behaviour*, 2(1): 1–6.

Baker, S.B., Daniels, T.G. and Greeley, A.T. (1990) Systematic training of graduate-level therapists: Narrative and meta-analytic reviews of three major programs, *The Counseling Psychologist*, 18(3): 355–421.

Baldwin, M. (ed.) (2013) *The Use of Self in Therapy*, 3rd edn. New York and Hove: Routledge.

Balmforth, J. and Elliott, R. (2012) 'I never talked about, ever': A comprehensive process analysis of a significant client disclosure event in therapy, *Counselling & Psychotherapy Research*, 12(1): 2–12.

Bamford, J. and Akhurst, J. (2014) 'She's not going to leave me' – counsellors' feelings on ending therapy with children, *British Journal of Guidance and Counselling*, 42(5): 459–71.

Banham, J.A. and Schweitzer, R.D. (2017) Therapeutic conversations: Therapists' use of observational language contributes to optimal therapeutic outcomes, *Psychology and Psychotherapy: Theory, Research & Practice*, 90(3): 264–78.

Barrett-Lennard, G.T. (1981) The empathy cycle: Refinement of a nuclear concept, *Journal of Counseling Psychology*, 28(2): 91–100.

Barrett-Lennard, G. (1993) The phases and focus of empathy, *British Journal of Medical Psychology*, 66(1): 3–14.

Barrett-Lennard, G.T. (1998) *Carl Rogers' Helping System: Journey and Substance*. London: Sage.

Barrett-Lennard, G. (2014) *The Relationship Inventory: A Complete Resource and Guide*. Chichester: Wiley-Blackwell.

Bateman, A.W. and Fonagy, P. (eds) (2019) *Handbook of Mentalizing in Mental Health Practice*, 2nd edn. Washington, DC: American Psychiatric Association.

Battles, M.B. and Berman, J.S. (2012) The impact of conversational acknowledgers on perceptions of psychotherapists, *Psychotherapy Research*, 22(6): 648–55.

Bayne, H.B. and Jangha, A. (2016) Utilizing improvisation to teach empathy skills in counselor education, *Counselor Education and Supervision*, 55(4): 250–62.

Bedi, R.P., Davis, M.D. and Williams, M. (2005) Critical incidents in the formation of the therapeutic alliance from the client's perspective, *Psychotherapy: Theory, Research, Practice, Training*, 42(3): 311–23.

Bedi, R.P. and Duff, C.T. (2014) Client as expert: A Delphi poll of clients' subjective experience of therapeutic alliance formation variables, *Counselling Psychology Quarterly*, 27(1): 1–18.

Benecke, C., Peham, D. and Bänninger–Huber, E. (2005) Nonverbal relationship regulation in psychotherapy, *Psychotherapy Research*, 15(1–2): 81–90.

Bennett-Levy, J. (2019) Why therapists should walk the talk: The theoretical and empirical case for personal practice in therapist training and professional development, *Journal of Behavior Therapy and Experimental Psychiatry*, 62: 133–45.

Bennett-Levy, J. and Finlay-Jones, A. (2018) The role of personal practice in therapist skill development: A model to guide therapists, educators, supervisors and researchers, *Cognitive Behaviour Therapy*, 47(3): 185–205.

Bennett-Levy, J., Waites, R., Haarho, B. and Perry, H. (2015) *Experiencing CBT from the Inside Out: A Self-Practice/Self-Reflection Workbook for Therapists*. New York: Guilford Press.

Berdondini, L., Grieve, S. and Kaveh, A. (2014) The INSPIRE project: Using the 'unknown' to co-construct a training course on humanistic counselling in Afghanistan, *International Journal for the Advancement of Counselling*, 36(3): 305–16.

Berdondini, L., Kaveh, A. and Grieve, S. (2019) Counselling training in Afghanistan: The long term development of the INSPIRE project, *International Journal for the Advancement of Counselling*, 41(2): 230–39.

Berg, H., Antonsen, P. and Binder, P.E. (2016) Sediments and vistas in the relational matrix of the unfolding 'I': A qualitative study of therapists' experiences with self-disclosure in psychotherapy, *Journal of Psychotherapy Integration*, 26(3): 248–58.

Berg, H., Bjornestad, J. Våpenstad, E.V., Davidson, L. and Binder, P.E. (2020) Therapist self-disclosure and the problem of shared-decision making, *Journal of Evaluation in Clinical Practice*, 26(2): 397–402.

Berne, E. (1964) *Games People Play: The Psychology of Human Relationships*. London: Penguin.

Berthoud, L. and Noyer, T. (2021) Therapist anger: From being a therapeutic barrier to becoming a resource in the development of congruence, *Person-Centered & Experiential Psychotherapies*, 20(1): 34–47.

Bike, D.H., Norcross, J.C. and Schatz, D.M. (2009) Processes and outcomes of psychotherapists' personal therapy: Replication and extension 20 years later, *Psychotherapy*, 46(1): 19–31.

Bimont, D. and Werbart, A. (2018) 'I've got you under my skin': Relational therapists' experiences of patients who occupy their inner world, *Counselling Psychology Quarterly*, 31(2): 243–68.

Binder, J.L. and Strupp, H.H. (1997) 'Negative process': A recurrently discovered and underestimated facet of therapeutic process and outcome in the individual psychotherapy of adults, *Clinical Psychology: Science and Practice*, 4(2): 121–39.

Bjornestad, J., Veseth, M., Davidson, L. et al. (2018) Psychotherapy in psychosis: Experiences of fully recovered service users, *Frontiers in Psychology*, 9: article 1675, https://doi.org/10.3389/fpsyg.2018.01675

Blakemore, T., Agllias, K. and Pallas, P. (2019) 'What you need to do is...': Social work students' reflections on an advice-giving audit exercise, *Journal of Social Work Practice*, 33(1): 67–80.

Blanchard, M. and Farber, B.A. (2016) Lying in psychotherapy: Why and what clients don't tell their therapist about therapy and their relationship, *Counselling Psychology Quarterly*, 29(1): 90–112.

Blanchard, M. and Farber, B.A. (2020) 'It is never okay to talk about suicide': Patients' reasons for concealing suicidal ideation in psychotherapy, *Psychotherapy Research*, 30(1): 124–36.

Blenkiron, P. (2010) *Stories and Analogies in Cognitive Behaviour Therapy*. Chichester: Wiley-Blackwell.

Blue, A.W., Darou, W.G. and Ruano, C. (2015) Through silence we speak: Approaches to counselling and psychotherapy with Canadian First Nation clients, *Online Readings in Psychology and Culture*, 10(3): article 6, http://dx.doi.org/10.9707/2307-0919.1095

Bodie, G.D., Worthington, D.L. and Gearhart, C.C. (2013) The Listening Styles Profile (LSP-R): A scale revision and evidence for validity, *Communication Quarterly*, 61(1): 72–90.

Bohart, A.C. (1993) Emphasizing the future in empathy responses, *Journal of Humanistic Psychology*, 33(2): 12–29.

Bohart, A.C. (2000) The client is the most important common factor: Clients' self-healing capacities and psychotherapy, *Journal of Psychotherapy Integration*, 10(2): 127–48.

Bohart, A.C. (2021) *The Art of Bohart: Person-Centred Therapy and the Enhancement of Human Possibility*. Monmouth: PCCS Books.

Bohart, A.C. and Tallman, K. (1996) The active client: Therapy as self-help, *Journal of Humanistic Psychology*, 36(3): 7–30.

Bohart, A.C. and Tallman, K. (1999) *How Clients Make Therapy Work: The Process of Active Self-Healing*. Washington, DC: American Psychological Association.

Bordin, E.S. (1979) The generalizability of the psychoanalytic concept of the working alliance, *Psychotherapy: Theory, Research & Practice*, 16(3): 252–60.

Börjesson, S. and Boström, P.K. (2020) 'I want to know what it is used for': Clients' perspectives on completing a routine outcome measure (ROM) while undergoing psychotherapy, *Psychotherapy Research*, 30(3): 337–47.

Boswell, J.F. and Constantino, M.J. (2021) *Deliberate Practice in Cognitive Behavioral Therapy*. Washington, DC: American Psychological Association.

Boukydis, K.M. (1984) Changes: Peer counselling supportive communities as a model for community mental health, in D. Larson (ed.) *Teaching Psychological Skills: Models for Giving Psychology Away*. Belmont, CA: Brooks/Cole, pp. 306–17.

Bozarth, J.D. (1984) Beyond reflection: Emergent modes of empathy, in R.F. Levant and J.M. Shlien (eds) *Client-Centered Therapy and the Person-Centered Approach: New Directions in Theory, Research, and Practice*. Westport, CT: Praeger Publishers/Greenwood Publishing Group, pp. 59–75.

Brar-Josan, N. and Yohani, S.C. (2019) Cultural brokers' role in facilitating informal and formal mental health supports for refugee youth in school and community context: A Canadian case study, *British Journal of Guidance & Counselling*, 47(4): 512–23.

Brattland, H., Høiseth, J.R., Burkeland, O., Inderhaug, T.S., Binder, P.E. and Iversen, V.C. (2018) Learning from clients: A qualitative investigation of psychotherapists' reactions to negative verbal feedback, *Psychotherapy Research*, 28(4): 545–59.

Brazelton, N. (2019) Listening from places of survival: The role of story listening in the empowerment of female victims of violence, *International Journal of Listening*, 33(3): 154–7.

Brock, R.L., O'Hara, M.W. and Segre, L.S. (2017) Depression treatment by non-mental-health providers: Incremental evidence for the effectiveness of Listening Visits, *American Journal of Community Psychology*, 59(1–2): 172–83.

Brown, G., Kainth, K., Matheson, C., Osborne, J., Trenkle, A. and Adlam, J. (2011) An hospitable engagement? Open-door psychotherapy with the socially excluded, *Psychodynamic Practice*, 17(3): 307–24.

Brownlie, J. (2011) Not 'going there': Limits to the professionalisation of our emotional lives, *Sociology of Health & Illness*, 33(1): 130–44.

Brownlie, J. (2014) *Ordinary Relationships: A Sociological Study of Emotions, Reflexivity and Culture*. Basingstoke: Palgrave Macmillan.

Brownlie, J. and Anderson, S. (2017) Thinking sociologically about kindness: Puncturing the blasé in the ordinary city, *Sociology*, 51(6): 1222–38.

Brownlie, J. and Shaw, F. (2019) Empathy rituals: Small conversations about emotional distress on Twitter, *Sociology*, 53(1): 104–22.

Burkholder, D., Toth, M., Feisthamel, K. and Britton, P. (2010) Faculty and student curricular experiences of nonerotic touch in counseling, *Journal of Mental Health Counseling*, 32(2): 168–85.

Burks, D.J. and Robbins, R. (2011) Are you analyzing me? A qualitative exploration of psychologists' individual and interpersonal experiences with authenticity, *The Humanistic Psychologist*, 39(4): 348–64.

Bury, S.M., Jellett, R., Spoor, J.R. and Hedley, D. (2020) 'It defines who I am' or 'It's something I have': What language do [autistic] Australian adults [on the autism spectrum] prefer?, *Journal of Autism and Developmental Disorders*, doi: 10.1007/s10803-020-04425-3.

Campbell, P. and Wilson, J. (2017) Palagi counsellors and effective counselling practice with Pasifika youth, *New Zealand Journal of Counselling*, 37(2): 90–102.

Carey, T.A., Tai, S.J. and Stiles, W.B. (2013) Effective and efficient: Using patient-led appointment scheduling in routine mental health practice in remote Australia, *Professional Psychology: Research and Practice*, 44(6): 405–14.

Carkhuff, R.R. (1969a) *Helping and Human Relations, Vol. 1: Selection and Training*. New York: Holt, Rinehart and Winston.

Carkhuff, R.R. (1969b) *Helping and Human Relations, Vol. 2: Practice and Research*. New York: Holt, Rinehart and Winston.

Cash, R.W. (1984) The Human Resources Development model, in D. Larson (ed.) *Teaching Psychological Skills: Models for Giving Psychology Away*. Belmont, CA: Brooks/Cole, pp. 245–70.

Chang, D.F., Dunn, J.J. and Omidi, M. (2021) A critical-cultural-relational approach to rupture resolution: A case illustration with a cross-racial dyad, *Journal of Clinical Psychology*, 77(2): 369–83.

Chow, D. (2018) *The First Kiss: Undoing the Intake Model and Igniting First Sessions in Psychotherapy*. n.p.: Correlate Press.

Chow, D.L., Miller, S.D., Seidel, J.A., Kane, R.T., Thornton, J.A. and Andrews, W.P. (2015) The role of deliberate practice in the development of highly effective psychotherapists, *Psychotherapy*, 52(3): 337–45.

Chui, H., Hill, C.E., Ain, S. et al. (2014) Training undergraduate students to use challenges, *The Counseling Psychologist*, 42(6): 758–77.

Churchman, A., Mansell, W. and Tai, S. (2020) A process-focused case series of a school-based intervention aimed at giving young people choice and control over their attendance and their goals in therapy, *British Journal of Guidance & Counselling*, 49(4): 565–86.

Claxton, G. (2012) Turning thinking on its head: How bodies make up their minds, *Thinking Skills and Creativity*, 7(2): 78–84.

Claxton, G. (2015) *Intelligence in the Flesh: Why your Mind Needs your Body Much More than it Thinks*. New Haven, CT: Yale University Press.

Colosimo, K.A. and Pos, A.E. (2015) A rational model of expressed therapeutic presence, *Journal of Psychotherapy Integration*, 25(2): 100–14.

Cooper, M. (2012) *The Existential Counselling Primer*. Monmouth: PCCS Books.

Cooper, M. (2021) Directionality: Unifying psychological and social understandings of well-being and distress through an existential ontology, *Journal of Humanistic Counseling*, 60(1): 6–25.

Cooper, M. and Knox, R. (2018) Therapists' self-reported chronic strategies of disconnection in everyday life and in counselling and psychotherapy: An exploratory study, *British Journal of Guidance & Counselling*, 46(2): 185–200.

Cooper, M. and Law, D. (eds) (2018) *Working with Goals in Psychotherapy and Counselling*. Oxford: Oxford University Press.

Cooper, M. and Norcross, J. C. (2016) A brief, multidimensional measure of clients' therapy preferences: The Cooper-Norcross Inventory of Preferences (C-NIP), *International Journal of Clinical and Health Psychology*, 16(1): 87–98.

Cooper, M. and McLeod, J. (2011) *Pluralistic Counselling and Psychotherapy*. London: Sage.

Cornell, A.W. (1996) *The Power of Focusing: A Practical Guide to Emotional Self–Healing*. Oakland, CA: New Harbinger.

Cornell, W.F. (2018) *Self-Examination in Psychoanalysis and Psychotherapy: Countertransference and Subjectivity in Clinical Practice*. Abingdon: Routledge.

Costa, B. (2020) *Other Tongues: Psychological Therapies in a Multilingual World*. Monmouth: PCCS Books.

Costa, B. and Dewaele, J.M. (2018) The talking cure – building the core skills and the confidence of counsellors and psychotherapists to work effectively with multilingual patients through training and supervision, *Counselling & Psychotherapy Research*, 19(3): 231–40.

Couture, S.J. and Sutherland, O. (2006) Giving advice on advice-giving: A conversation analysis of Karl Tomm's practice, *Journal of Marital and Family Therapy*, 32(3): 329–44.

Cowen, E.L. (1982) Help is where you find it: Four informal helping groups, *American Psychologist*, 37: 385–95.

Crews, J., Smith, M.R., Smaby, M.H. et al. (2005) Self-monitoring and counseling skills: Skills-based versus interpersonal process recall training, *Journal of Counseling & Development*, 83(1): 78–85.

Cuttler, E., Hill, C.E., King, S. and Kivlighan, D.M., Jr (2019) Productive silence is golden: Predicting changes in client collaboration from process during silence and client attachment style in psychodynamic psychotherapy, *Psychotherapy*, 56(4): 568–76.

Dalenberg, C.J. (2004) Maintaining the safe and effective therapeutic relationship in the context of distrust and anger: Countertransference and complex trauma, *Psychotherapy: Theory, Research, Practice, Training*, 41(4): 438–47.

Daniel, T. and McLeod, J. (2006) Weighing up the evidence: A qualitative analysis of how person-centred counsellors evaluate the effectiveness of their practice, *Counselling & Psychotherapy Research*, 6(4): 244–9.

Day-Vines, N.L., Ammah, B.B., Steen, S. and Arnold, K.M. (2018) Getting comfortable with discomfort: Preparing counselor trainees to broach racial, ethnic, and cultural factors with clients during counseling, *International Journal for the Advancement of Counselling*, 40(2): 89–104.

Day-Vines, N.L., Cluxton-Keller, F., Agorsor, C. and Gubara, S. (2021) Strategies for broaching the subjects of race, ethnicity, and culture, *Journal of Counseling & Development*, 99(3): 348–57.

Day-Vines, N.L., Cluxton-Keller, F., Agorsor, C., Gubara, S. and Otabil, N.A.A. (2020) The multidimensional model of broaching behavior. *Journal of Counseling & Development*, 98(1), 107–118.

De Jager, A., Tewson, A., Ludlow, B. and Boydell, K. (2016) Embodied ways of storying the self: A systematic review of body-mapping, *Forum Qualitative Sozialforschung/Forum: Qualitative Social Research*, 17(2): article 22, doi: https://doi.org/10.17169/fqs-17.2.2526.

De Roten, Y., Gilliéron, E., Despland, J.N. and Stigler, M. (2002) Functions of mutual smiling and alliance building in early therapeutic interaction, *Psychotherapy Research*, 12(2): 193–212.

Denborough, D. (2008) *Collective Narrative Practice: Responding to Individuals, Groups, and Communities who have Experienced Trauma*. Adelaide: Dulwich Centre Publications.

Denborough, D. (2018) *Do you Want to Hear a Story? Adventures in Collective Narrative Practice*. Adelaide: Dulwich Centre Publications.

Diamond, G.M. (2014) Attachment-based family therapy interventions, *Psychotherapy*, 51(1): 15–19.

Dogan, T. (2018) The effects of the psychodrama in instilling empathy and self-awareness: A pilot study, *PsyCh Journal*, 7(4): 227–38.

Dollarhide, C.T., Shavers, M.C., Baker, C.A., Dagg, D.R. and Taylor, D. T. (2012) Conditions that create therapeutic connection: A phenomenological study, *Counseling and Values*, 57(2): 147–61.

Dos Santos, O. and Dallos, R. (2012) The process of cross-cultural therapy between white therapists and clients of African-Caribbean descent, *Qualitative Research in Psychology*, 9(1): 62–74.

Draper, B., Snowdon, J. and Wyder, M. (2008) A pilot study of the suicide victim's last contact with a health professional, *Crisis*, 29(2): 96–101.

Duan, C., Hill, C., Jiang, G. et al. (2012) Therapist directives: Use and outcomes in China, *Psychotherapy Research*, 22(4): 442–57.

Duan, C., Hill, C.E., Jiang, G. et al. (2015) The counselor perspective on the use of directives in counseling in China: Are directives different in China as in the United States?, *Counselling Psychology Quarterly*, 28(1): 57–77.

Duan, C., Hill, C., Jiang, G. et al. (2020) Client views of counselor directives (指导): A qualitative study in China, *Counselling Psychology Quarterly*, https://doi.org/10.1080/09515070.2020.1768049

Duan, C., Knox, S. and Hill, C.E. (2018) Advice giving in psychotherapy, in E.L. MacGeorge and L.M. Van Swol (eds) *The Oxford Handbook of Advice*. New York: Oxford University Press, pp.175–98.

Duffey, T. and Haberstroh, S. (2013) Deepening empathy in men using a musical chronology and the emerging life song, *Journal of Counseling & Development*, 91(4): 442–50.

Dunn, D.S. and Andrews, E.E. (2015) Person-first and identity-first language: Developing psychologists' cultural competence using disability language, *American Psychologist*, 70(3): 255–84.

Edwards-Stewart, A. and Norcross, J.C. (2019) Integrating self-help and psychotherapy, in J.C. Norcross and M.R. Goldfried (eds) *Handbook of Psychotherapy Integration*, 3rd edn. New York: Oxford University Press, pp. 357–74.

Egan, G. (1984) Skilled helping: A problem-management framework for helping and helper training, in D. Larson (ed.) *Teaching Psychological Skills: Models for Giving Psychology Away*. Belmont, CA: Brooks/Cole, pp. 133–50.

Egan, G. and Reese, R. (2021) *The Skilled Helper*, 12th edn. Boston, MA: Cengage.

Ekman, P. and Friesen, W.V. (2003) *Unmasking the Face: A Guide to Recognizing Emotions from Facial Clues*. Los Altos, CA: Malor Books.

Elliott, R., Bohart, A.C., Watson, J.C. and Murphy, D. (2018) Therapist empathy and client outcome: An updated meta-analysis, *Psychotherapy*, 55(4): 399–410.

Elliott, R. and Greenberg, L. (2021) *Emotion-Focused Counselling in Action*. London: Sage.

Ellis, R.J.B., Carmon, A.F. and Pike, C. (2016) A review of immediacy and implications for provider–patient relationships to support medication management, *Patient Preference and Adherence*, 10: 9–18, doi: 10.2147/PPA.S95163.

Ellis, T.E. (2004) Collaboration and a self-help orientation in therapy with suicidal clients, *Journal of Contemporary Psychotherapy*, 34(1): 41–57.

Ericsson, K.A. and Pool, R. (2016) *Peak: Secrets from the New Science of Expertise*. Boston, MA: Houghton Mifflin Harcourt.

Erskine, R. (2015) Meeting Vincent: Reconnections from behind the wall – pre-therapy in a psychiatric unit context, *Person-Centered & Experiential Psychotherapies*, 14(4): 300–9.

Eubanks, C.F., Sergi, J., Samstag, L.W. and Muran, J.C. (2021) Commentary: Rupture repair as a transtheoretical corrective experience, *Journal of Clinical Psychology*, 77(2): 457–66.

Farber, B.A. (2006) *Self-Disclosure in Therapy*. New York: Guilford Press.

Farber, B.A., Blanchard, M. and Love, M. (2019) *Secrets and Lies in Psychotherapy*. Washington, DC: American Psychological Association.

Finlay, L. (2015) Sensing and making sense: Embodying metaphor in relational-centered psychotherapy, *The Humanistic Psychologist*, 43(4): 338–53.

Fisher, J. (2019) Sensorimotor psychotherapy in the treatment of trauma, *Practice Innovations*, 4(3): 156–65.

Fiske, A. (2019) *Kama Muta: Discovering the Connecting Emotion*. Abingdon and New York: Routledge.

Fiske, A.P., Seibt, B. and Schubert, T. (2019) The sudden devotion emotion: Kama muta and the cultural practices whose function is to evoke it, *Emotion Review*, 11(1): 74–86.

Fitzpatrick, M.R. and Stalikas, A. (2008a) Positive emotions as generators of therapeutic change, *Journal of Psychotherapy Integration*, 18(2): 137–54.

Fitzpatrick, M.R. and Stalikas, A. (2008b) Integrating positive emotions into theory, research, and practice: A new challenge for psychotherapy, *Journal of Psychotherapy Integration*, 18(2): 248–58.

Fluckiger, C., Wüsten, G., Zinbarg, R. and Wampold, B. (2010) *Resource Activation: Using Clients' Own Strengths in Psychotherapy and Counseling*. Oxford: Hogrefe and Huber.

Flyvbjerg, B. (2001) *Making Social Science Matter: Why Social Inquiry Fails and How it can Succeed Again*. Cambridge: Cambridge University Press.

Fosha, D. (2000) Meta-therapeutic processes and the affects of transformation: Affirmation and the healing affects, *Journal of Psychotherapy Integration*, 10(1): 71–97.

Fosha, D. (2004) 'Nothing that feels bad is ever the last step': The role of positive emotions in experiential work with difficult emotional experiences, *Clinical Psychology and Psychotherapy*, 11(1): 30–43.

Fowler, J.C., Hilsenroth, M.J. and Handler, L. (2000) Martin Mayman's early memories technique: Bridging the gap between personality assessment and psychotherapy, *Journal of Personality Assessment*, 75(1): 18–32.

Fredrickson, B.L. (2001) The role of positive emotions in positive psychology: The broaden-and-build theory of positive emotions, *American Psychologist*, 56(3): 218–26.

Friedberg, R.D. and Wilt, L.H. (2010) Metaphors and stories in cognitive behavioral therapy with children, *Journal of Rational-Emotive & Cognitive-Behavior Therapy*, 28(2): 100–13.

Gabriel, L. and Casemore, R. (2009) *Relational Ethics in Practice: Narratives from Counselling and Psychotherapy*. Hove and New York: Routledge.

Gait, S. and Halewood, A. (2019) Developing countertransference awareness as a therapist in training: The role of containing contexts, *Psychodynamic Practice*, 25(3): 256–72.

Geller, S.M. (2017) *A Practical Guide to Cultivating Therapeutic Presence*. Washington, DC: American Psychological Association.

Geller, S. (2020) Cultivating online therapeutic presence: Strengthening therapeutic relationships in teletherapy sessions, *Counselling Psychology Quarterly*, doi: 10.1080/09515070.2020.1787348.

Gelso, C.J. and Perez-Rojas, A.E. (2017) Inner experience and the good therapist, in L.G. Castonguay and C.E. Hill (eds) *How and Why are Some Therapists Better than Others?: Understanding Therapist Effects*. Washington, DC: American Psychological Association, pp. 101–15.

Gelso, C.J., Pérez Rojas, A.E. and Marmarosh, C. (2014) Love and sexuality in the therapeutic relationship, *Journal of Clinical Psychology*, 70(2): 123–34.

Gendlin, E.T. (1984) The politics of giving therapy away: Listening and focusing, in D. Larson (ed.) *Teaching Psychological Skills: Models for Giving Psychology Away*. Belmont, CA: Brooks/Cole, pp. 287–305.

Gendlin, E.T. (2003) *Focusing: How to Open up your Deeper Feelings and Intuition*. New York: Rider.

Genuchi, M.C., Hopper, B. and Morrison, C.R. (2017) Using metaphors to facilitate exploration of emotional content in counseling with college men, *Journal of Men's Studies*, 25(2): 133–49.

Gerwing, J. and Li, S. (2019) Body-oriented gestures as a practitioner's window into interpreted communication, *Social Science & Medicine*, 233: 171–80.

Gibbs, M., Griffiths, M. and Dilks, S. (2020) A grounded theory of how service users experience and make use of formulation in therapy for psychosis, *Psychosis*, 12(3): 245–56.

Gibson, A., Cooper, M., Rae, J. and Hayes, J. (2020) Clients' experiences of shared decision making in an integrative psychotherapy for depression, *Journal of Evaluation in Clinical Practice*, 26(2): 559–68.

Gilbert, J. (2002) Cross-cultural issues in counselling skills training: Lessons from Lesotho, *Journal of Social Development in Africa*, 17(1): 123–35.

Gilligan, C. (2015) The Listening Guide method of psychological inquiry, *Qualitative Psychology*, 2(1): 69–77.

Gilligan, C. and Eddy, J. (2017) Listening as a path to psychological discovery: An introduction to the Listening Guide, *Perspectives on Medical Education*, 6(2): 76–81.

Gladding, S.T. and Drake Wallace, M.J. (2016) Promoting beneficial humor in counseling: A way of helping counselors help clients, *Journal of Creativity in Mental Health*, 11(1): 2–11.

Gladwell, M. (2006) *Blink: The Power of Thinking Without Thinking*. London: Penguin.

Goedert, M. (2020) Racism in the countertransference, *Psychoanalytic Quarterly*, 89(4): 715–40.

Goldberg, S.B. and Sachter, L.D. (2018) The zentensive: A psychodynamically oriented meditation retreat for psychotherapists, *Practice Innovations*, 3(1): 18–31.

Goldman, R.N., Vaz, A. and Rousmaniere, T. (2021) *Deliberate Practice in Emotion-Focused Therapy*. Washington, DC: American Psychological Association.

Goldstein, G. and Suzuki, J.Y. (2015) The analyst's authenticity: 'If you see something, say something', *Journal of Clinical Psychology*, 71(5): 451–6.

Gonçalves, M.M., Matos, M. and Santos, A. (2009) Narrative therapy and the nature of 'innovative moments' in the construction of change, *Journal of Constructivist Psychology*, 22(1): 1–23.

Goode, J., Park, J., Parkin, S., Tompkins, K.A. and Swift, J. K. (2017) A collaborative approach to psychotherapy termination, *Psychotherapy*, 54(1): 10–14.

Goodman, G. (1984) SAHSAtapes: Expanding options for help-intended communication, in D. Larson (ed.) *Teaching Psychological Skills: Models for Giving Psychology Away*. Belmont, CA: Brooks/Cole, pp. 271–86.

Gordon, K.M. and Toukmanian, S.G. (2002) Is *how* it is said important? The association between quality of therapist response and client processing, *Counselling & Psychotherapy Research*, 2(2): 88–98.

Gordon, T. (1984) Three decades of democratising relationships through training, in D. Larson (ed.) *Teaching Psychological Skills: Models for Giving Psychology Away*. Belmont, CA: Brooks/Cole, pp. 151–70.

Granello, D.H. and Gibbs, T.A. (2016) The power of language and labels: 'The mentally ill' versus 'people with mental illnesses', *Journal of Counseling & Development*, 94(1): 31–40.

Greenberg, L.S. and Geller, S. (2001) Congruence and therapeutic presence, in G. Wyatt (ed.) *Rogers' Therapeutic Conditions: Evolution, Theory and Practice*, Vol. 1. Monmouth: PCCS Books, pp. 131–49.

Greenberg, L.S. and Pascual-Leone, A. (2006) Emotion in psychotherapy: A practice-friendly research review, *Journal of Clinical Psychology*, 62(5): 611–30.

Greenberg, L.S., Rice, L.N. and Elliott, R. (1993) *Facilitating Emotional Change: The Moment-by-Moment Process*. New York: Guilford Press.

Gross, B. and Elliott, R. (2017) Therapist momentary experiences of disconnection with clients, *Person-Centered & Experiential Psychotherapies*, 16(4): 351–66.

Guerney, B.G., Jr (1984) Relationship enhancement therapy and training, in D. Larson (ed.) *Teaching Psychological Skills: Models for Giving Psychology Away*. Belmont, CA: Brooks/Cole, pp. 171–205.

Gulbrandsen, P., Clayman, M.L., Beach, M.C. et al. (2016) Shared decision-making as an existential journey: Aiming for restored autonomous capacity, *Patient Education and Counseling*, 99(9): 1505–10.

Gullslett, M.K., Kim, H.S., Andersen, A.J. and Borg, M. (2016) 'Emotional darkness without solutions': Subjective experiences of mental health crisis, *International Journal of Mental Health*, 45(3): 161–70.

Gupta, S., Hill, C.E., and Kivlighan, D.M., Jr (2018) Client laughter in psychodynamic psychotherapy: Not a laughing matter, *Journal of Counseling Psychology*, 65(4): 463–73.

Hansen, J.T. (2009) Self-awareness revisited: Reconsidering a core value of the counseling profession, *Journal of Counseling & Development*, 87(2): 186–93.

Hanson, J. (2005) Should your lips be sealed? How therapist self-disclosure and non-disclosure affects clients, *Counselling & Psychotherapy Research*, 5(2): 96–104.

Harned, M.S., Lungu, A., Wilks, C.R. and Linehan, M.M. (2017) Evaluating a multimedia tool for suicide risk assessment and management: The Linehan suicide safety net, *Journal of Clinical Psychology*, 73(3): 308–18.

Haroutunian-Gordon, S. and Laverty, M.J. (2011) Listening: An exploration of philosophical traditions, *Educational Theory*, 61(2): 117–24.

Hart, C. (2020) Even though our bodies cannot be in the same place, focussing on body process is helpful in video mediated psychotherapy, *Journal of Child Psychotherapy*, 46(3): 367–72.

Hauke, G. and Kritikos, A. (eds) (2018) *Embodiment in Psychotherapy: A Practitioner's Guide*. Cham, Switzerland: Springer.

Hawley, L.D. (2006) Reflecting teams and microcounseling in beginning counsellor training: Practice in collaboration, *Journal of Humanistic Counseling, Education and Development*, 45(2): 198–207.

Hayes, J.A. and Vinca, M. (2017) Therapist presence, absence, and extraordinary presence, in L.G. Castonguay and C.E. Hill (eds) *How and Why are Some Therapists Better than Others?: Understanding Therapist Effects*. Washington, DC: American Psychological Association, pp. 85–99.

Heide, F.J. (2010) The agonistic metaphor in psychotherapy: Should clients battle their blues?, *Psychotherapy: Theory, Research, Practice, Training*, 47(1): 68–82.

Henretty, J.R. and Levitt, H.M. (2010) The role of therapist self-disclosure in psychotherapy: A qualitative review, *Clinical Psychology Review*, 30(1): 63–77.

Heritage, J., Robinson, J.D., Elliott, M.N., Beckett, M. and Wilkes, M. (2007) Reducing patients' unmet concerns in primary care: The difference one word can make, *Journal of General Internal Medicine*, 22(10): 1429–33.

Hernández, W. and Grafanaki, S. (2014) Social development with focusing through the pause, *FOLIO*, 25(1): 172–85.

Heron, J. (1976) A six-category intervention analysis, *British Journal of Guidance & Counselling*, 4(2): 143–55.

Hill, C.E. (2003) *Dream Work in Therapy: Facilitating Exploration, Insight, and Action*. Washington, DC: American Psychological Association.

Hill, C.E. (2018) *Meaning in Life: A Therapist's Guide*. Washington, DC: American Psychological Association.

Hill, C.E. (2019) *Helping Skills: Facilitating Exploration, Insight, and Action*, 5th edn. Washington, DC: American Psychological Association.

Hill, C.E., Anderson, T., Gerstenblith, J.A., Kline, K.V., Gooch, C.V. and Melnick, A. (2020) A follow-up of undergraduate students five years after helping skills training, *Journal of Counseling Psychology*, 67(6): 697–705.

Hill, C.E., Kline, K.V., O'Connor, S. et al. (2019a) Silence is golden: A mixed methods investigation of silence in one case of psychodynamic psychotherapy, *Psychotherapy*, 56(4): 577–87.

Hill, C.E., Knox, S. and Pinto-Coelho, K.G. (2018) Therapist self-disclosure and immediacy: A qualitative meta-analysis, *Psychotherapy*, 55(4): 445–60.

Hill, C.E. and Lent, R.W. (2006) A narrative and meta-analytic review of helping skills training: Time to revive a dormant area of inquiry, *Psychotherapy: Theory, Research, Practice, Training*, 43(2): 154–72.

Hill, C.E., Lu, Y., Gerstenblith, J.A., Kline, K.V., Wang, R.J. and Zhu, X. (2019b) Facilitating client collaboration and insight through interpretations and probes for insight in psychodynamic psychotherapy: A case study of one client with three successive therapists, *Psychotherapy*, 57(2): 263–72.

Hill, C.E., Spangler, P.T., Jackson, J.L. and Chui, H. (2014) Training undergraduate students to use insight skills: Integrating the results of three studies, *The Counseling Psychologist*, 42(6): 800–20.

Hill, C.E., Stahl, J. and Roffman, M. (2007) Training novice psychotherapists: Helping skills and beyond, *Psychotherapy: Theory, Research, Practice, Training*, 44(4): 364–73.

Hill, C.E., Thompson, B.J. and Ladany, N. (2003) Therapist use of silence in therapy: A survey, *Journal of Clinical Psychology*, 59(4): 513–24.

Hinchliffe, G. (2002) Situating skills, *Journal of Philosophy of Education*, 36(2): 187–205.

Hollingworth, A. (2017) So, you think your counselling practices are collaborative?, *Psychotherapy and Counselling Journal of Australia*, 5(1), https://pacja.org.au/fifth-issue-volume-5-no-1-july-2017/

Holmes, J. (2017) Reverie-informed research interviewing, *International Journal of Psychoanalysis*, 98(3): 709–28.

Honos-Webb, L. and Stiles, W.B. (1998) Reformulation of assimilation analysis in terms of voices, *Psychotherapy*, 35(1): 23–33.

Houdyshell, M. and Ziegler, N. (2020) Graduate students share their experiences of building helping skills: A case study, *Journal of Curriculum Studies Research*, https://doi.org/10.46303/jcsr.2020.4

Hulse-Killacky, D., Orr, J.J. and Paradise, L.V. (2006) The Corrective Feedback Instrument – Revised, *The Journal for Specialists in Group Work*, 31(3): 263–81.

Hutchison, A.N., Gerstein, L.H., Millner, A., Reding, E.M. and Plumer, L. (2020) Counseling psychology trainees' knowledge of cultural display rules, *The Counseling Psychologist*, 48(5): 685–715.

Imber-Black, E. and Roberts, J. (1992) *Rituals for our Times: Celebrating Healing and Changing our Lives and Relationships*. New York: HarperCollins.

Irving, K. (2019) The role of humor in priming intersubjectivity, *Psychoanalytic Psychology*, 36(3): 207–15.

Ivers, N.N., Rogers, J.L., Borders, L.D. and Turner, A. (2017) Using interpersonal process recall in clinical supervision to enhance supervisees' multicultural awareness, *The Clinical Supervisor*, 36(2): 282–303.

Ivey, A.E. and Galvin, M. (1984) Microcounseling: A metamodel for counselling, therapy, business, and medical interviews, in D. Larson (ed.) *Teaching Psychological Skills: Models for Giving Psychology Away*. Belmont, CA: Brooks/Cole, pp. 207–28.

Ivey, A.E., Ivey M. and Zalaquett, C. (2018) *Intentional Interviewing and Counseling: Facilitating Client Development in a Multicultural Society*, 9th edn. Boston, MA: Cengage Learning.

Jack, D.C. and Ali, A. (2010) *Silencing the Self Across Cultures: Depression and Gender in the Social World*. New York: Oxford University Press.

Jackson, D. (2018) Aesthetics and the psychotherapist's office, *Journal of Clinical Psychology*, 74(2): 233–8.

Jager, M., Huiskes, M., Metselaar, J., Knorth, E.J., De Winter, A.F. and Reijneveld, S.A. (2016) Therapists' continuations following I don't know – responses of adolescents in psychotherapy, *Patient Education and Counseling*, 99(11): 1778–84.

James, R.K. and Gilliland, B.E. (2016) *Crisis Intervention Strategies*, 7th edn. Boston, MA: Cengage Learning.

Jennings, L. and Skovholt, T.M. (1999) The cognitive, emotional and relational characteristics of master therapists, *Journal of Counseling Psychology*, 46(1): 3–11.

Jennings, L. and Skovholt, T. (eds) (2016) *Expertise in Counseling and Psychotherapy: Master Therapist Studies from Around the World*. New York: Oxford University Press.

Jennings, L., Sovereign, A., Bottoroff, N., Mussell, M.P. and Vye, C. (2005) Nine ethical values of master therapists, *Journal of Mental Health Counseling*, 27(1): 32–47.

Jobes, D.A. (2016) *Managing Suicidal Risk: A Collaborative Approach*, 2nd edn. New York: Guilford.

Johnsen, C. and Ding, H.T. (2021) Therapist self-disclosure: Let's tackle the elephant in the room, *Clinical Child Psychology and Psychiatry*, 26(2): 443–50.

Johnson, S.M. (2021) *A Primer for Emotionally Focused Individual Therapy (EFIT): Cultivating Fitness and Growth in Every Client*. New York and Abingdon: Routledge.

Johnson, W.B., Barnett, J.E., Elman, N.S., Forrest, L., Schwartz-Mette, R. and Kaslow, N.J. (2014) Preparing trainees for lifelong competence: Creating a communitarian training culture, *Training and Education in Professional Psychology*, 8(4): 211–25.

Johnstone, L. and Dallos, R. (eds) (2014) *Formulation in Psychology and Psychotherapy: Making Sense of People's Problems*, 2nd edn. Hove: Routledge.

Jones, C.T. and Welfare, L.E. (2017) Broaching behaviors of licensed professional counselors: A qualitative inquiry, *Journal of Addictions & Offender Counseling*, 38(1): 48–64.

Jones, J.K. (2018) A phenomenological study of the office environments of clinical social workers, *HERD: Health Environments Research & Design Journal*, 11(3): 38–48.

Jones, J.K. (2020) A place for therapy: Clients reflect on their experiences in psychotherapists' offices, *Qualitative Social Work*, 19(3): 406–23.

Jones, S.M. (2011) Supportive listening, *International Journal of Listening*, 25(1–2): 85–103.

Joo, E., Hill, C.E. and Kim, Y.H. (2019) Using helping skills with Korean clients: The perspectives of Korean counselors, *Psychotherapy Research*, 29(6): 812–23.

Jordan J.R. and McIntosh, J.L. (eds) (2011) *Grief after Suicide*. New York and Hove: Routledge.

Jordan, J.V. (2000) The role of mutual empathy in relational/cultural therapy, *Journal of Clinical Psychology*, 56(8): 1005–16.

Jordan, J.V. (2017) Relational–cultural theory: The power of connection to transform our lives, *Journal of Humanistic Counseling*, 56(3): 228–43.

Jordan, J.V., Hartling, L.M. and Walker, M. (eds) (2004) *The Complexity of Connection: Writings from the Stone Center's Jean Baker Miller Training Institute*. New York: Guilford Press.

Jorm, A.F. and Ross, A.M. (2018) Guidelines for the public on how to provide mental health first aid: Narrative review, *BJPsych Open*, 4(6): 427–40.

Josselson, R. (2004) The hermeneutics of faith and the hermeneutics of suspicion, *Narrative Inquiry*, 14(1): 1–28.

Kagan, N. (1980) Influencing human interaction – eighteen years with IPR, in A.K. Hess (ed.), *Psychotherapy Supervision: Theory, Research and Practice*. New York: Wiley, pp. 262–86.

Kagan, N. (1984) Interpersonal process recall: Basic methods and recent research, in D. Larson (ed.) *Teaching Psychological Skills: Models for Giving Psychology Away*. Belmont, CA: Brooks/Cole, pp. 229–44.

Kagan, N.I. and Kagan, H. (1990) IPR – a validated model for the 1990s and beyond, *The Counseling Psychologist*, 18(3): 436–40.

Kagan, N., Schauble, P., Resnikoff, A., Danish, S.J. and Krathwohl, D.R. (1969) Interpersonal process recall, *Journal of Nervous and Mental Disease*, 148(4): 365–74.

Kahlon, S., Neal, A. and Patterson, T.G. (2014) Experiences of cognitive behavioural therapy formulation in clients with depression, *The Cognitive Behaviour Therapist*, 7: article e8, https://doi.org/10.1017/S1754470X14000075

Kahn, M. (2001) *Between Therapist and Client*. New York: St Martin's Press.

Kazantzis, N. and L'Abate, L. (eds) (2007) *Handbook of Homework Assignments in Psychotherapy: Research, Practice, and Prevention*. New York: Springer.

Kazantzis, N. and Stuckey, M.E. (2018) Inception of a discovery: Re-defining the use of Socratic dialogue in cognitive behavioral therapy, *International Journal of Cognitive Therapy*, 11(2): 117–23.

Kehoe, L.E., Hassen, S.C. and Sandage, S.J. (2016) Relational ecologies of psychotherapy: The influence of administrative attachment on therapeutic alliance, *Psychodynamic Practice*, 22(1): 6–21.

Keij, S.M., van Duijn-Bakker, N., Stiggelbout, A.M. and Pieterse, A.H. (2021) What makes a patient ready for shared decision making? A qualitative study, *Patient Education and Counseling*, 104(3): 571–7.

Kellogg, S. (2004) Dialogical encounters: Contemporary perspectives on 'chairwork' in psychotherapy, *Psychotherapy: Research, Theory, Practice, Training*, 41(3): 310–20.

Kellogg, S. (2014) *Transformational Chairwork: Using Psychotherapeutic Dialogues in Clinical Practice*. Washington, DC: Rowman & Littlefield.

Kelly, M., Nixon, L., Broadfoot, K., Hofmeister, M. and Dornan, T. (2019) Drama to promote nonverbal communication skills, *The Clinical Teacher*, 16(2): 108–13.

Kelly, M.A., Nixon, L., McClurg, C., Scherpbier, A., King, N. and Dornan, T. (2018) Experience of touch in health care: A meta-ethnography across the health care professions, *Qualitative Health Research*, 28(2): 200–12.

Kelly, M., Svrcek, C., King, N., Scherpbier, A. and Dornan, T. (2020) Embodying empathy: A phenomenological study of physician touch, *Medical Education*, 54(5): 400–7.

Killick, S., Curry, V. and Myles, P. (2016) The mighty metaphor: A collection of therapists' favourite metaphors and analogies, *The Cognitive Behaviour Therapist*, 9: article e37, doi: 10.1017/S1754470X16000210

Kinavey, H. and Cool, C. (2019) The broken lens: How anti-fat bias in psychotherapy is harming our clients and what to do about it, *Women & Therapy*, 42(1–2): 116–30.

King, B.R. and Boswell, J.F. (2019) Therapeutic strategies and techniques in early cognitive-behavioral therapy, *Psychotherapy*, 56(1): 35–40.

King, K.M. (2021) 'I want to, but how?' Defining counselor broaching in core tenets and debated components, *Journal of Multicultural Counseling and Development*, 49(2): 87–100.

King, K.M. and Borders, L.D. (2019) An experimental investigation of white counselors broaching race and racism, *Journal of Counseling & Development*, 97(4): 341–51.

Kitchener, K.S. (1984) Intuition, critical evaluation and ethical principles: The foundation for ethical decisions in counseling psychology, *Counseling Psychologist*, 12(3–4): 43–55.

Kivlighan, D.M., Jr (2014) Three important clinical processes in individual and group interpersonal psychotherapy sessions, *Psychotherapy*, 51(1): 20–4.

Kleinman, A. (1988) *The Illness Narratives: Suffering, Healing and the Human Condition*. New York: Basic Books.

Kleinman, A. (2012) Caregiving as moral experience, *The Lancet*, 380(9853): 1550–1.

Kline, K.V., Hill, C.E., Morris, T. et al. (2019) Ruptures in psychotherapy: Experiences of therapist trainees, *Psychotherapy Research*, 29(8): 1086–98.

Knapp, S., Gottlieb, M.C. and Handelsman, M.M. (2017) Self-awareness questions for effective psychotherapists: Helping good psychotherapists become even better, *Practice Innovations*, 2(4): 163–72.

Knox, R., Murphy, D., Wiggins, S. and Cooper, M. (eds) (2013) *Relational Depth: New Perspectives and Developments*. Basingstoke: Palgrave Macmillan.

Knox, S., Cook, J., Knowlton, G. and Hill, C.E. (2018) Therapists' experiences with internal representations of clients, *Counselling Psychology Quarterly*, 31(3): 353–74.

Knox, S., Goldberg, J.L., Woodhouse, S.S. and Hill, C.E. (1999) Clients' internal representations of their therapists, *Journal of Counseling Psychology*, 46(2): 244–56.

Knox, S., Hill, C.E., Knowlton, G., Chui, H., Pruitt, N. and Tate, K. (2017) Crying in psychotherapy: The perspective of therapists and clients, *Psychotherapy*, 54(3): 292–306.

Kolden, G.G., Wang, C.-C., Austin, S.B., Chang, Y. and Klein, M.H. (2018) Congruence/genuineness: A meta-analysis, *Psychotherapy*, 55(4): 424–33.

Kolmes, K. and Taube, D.O. (2019) Yelped: Psychotherapy in the time of online consumer reviews, *Practice Innovations*, 4(4): 205–13.

Kopp, R.R. and Craw, M.J. (1998) Metaphoric language, metaphoric cognition, and cognitive therapy, *Psychotherapy: Theory, Research, Practice, Training*, 35(3): 306–11.

Kopp, R. and Eckstein, D. (2004) Using early memory metaphors and client-generated metaphors in Adlerian therapy, *Journal of Individual Psychology*, 60(2): 163–74.

Krebs, P., Norcross, J.C., Nicholson, J.M. and Prochaska, J.O. (2019) Stages of change, in J.C. Norcross and B.E. Wampold (eds) *Psychotherapy Relationships that Work, Vol. 2: Evidence-Based Therapist Responsiveness*, 3rd edn. New York: Oxford University Press, pp. 296–328.

Kumari, N. (2011) Personal therapy as a mandatory requirement for counselling psychologists in training: A qualitative study of the impact of therapy on trainees' personal and professional development, *Counselling Psychology Quarterly*, 24(3): 211–32.

Kuyken, W., Padesky, C.A. and Dudley, R. (2008) The science and practice of case conceptualization, *Behavioural and Cognitive Psychotherapy*, 36(6): 757–68.

Kykyri, V.L., Karvonen, A., Wahlström, J., Kaartinen, J., Penttonen, M. and Seikkula, J. (2017) Soft prosody and embodied attunement in therapeutic interaction: A multimethod case study of a moment of change, *Journal of Constructivist Psychology*, 30(3): 211–34.

Ladany, N., Hill, C.E., Thompson, B.J. and O'Brien, K.M. (2004) Therapist perspectives on using silence in therapy: A qualitative study, *Counselling & Psychotherapy Research*, 4(1): 80–9.

Lakoff, G. and Johnson, M. (1980) *Metaphors we Live By*. Chicago: University of Chicago Press.

Lakoff, G. and Johnson, M. (1999) *Philosophy in the Flesh: The Embodied Mind and its Challenge to Western Thought*. New York: Basic Books.

Lambert, M.J., Whipple, J.L. and Kleinstäuber, M. (2018) Collecting and delivering progress feedback: A meta-analysis of routine outcome monitoring, *Psychotherapy*, 55(4): 520–37.

Larson, D. (ed.) (1984) *Teaching Psychological Skills: Models for Giving Psychology Away*. Belmont, CA: Brooks/Cole.

Lavik, K.O., Frøysa, H., Brattebø, K.F., McLeod, J. and Moltu, C. (2018) The first sessions of psychotherapy: A qualitative meta-analysis of alliance formation processes, *Journal of Psychotherapy Integration*, 28(3): 348–66.

Lawson, G. (2005) The hero's journey as a developmental metaphor in counseling, *Journal of Humanistic Counseling, Education and Development*, 44(2): 134–44.

Lee, B. (2017) Language matters in counselling diversity, *British Journal of Guidance & Counselling*, 45(5): 500–7.

Lee, B. and Prior, S. (2013) Developing therapeutic listening, *British Journal of Guidance & Counselling*, 41(2): 91–104.

Lee, B. and Prior, S. (2016) 'I have to hear them before I hear myself': Developing therapeutic conversations in British counselling students, *European Journal of Psychotherapy & Counselling*, 18(3): 271–89.

Lee, S.A. (1997) Communication styles of Wind River Native American clients and the therapeutic approaches of their clinicians, *Smith College Studies in Social Work*, 68(1): 57–81.

Leibovich, L., Wachtel, P.L., Nof, A. and Zilcha-Mano, S. (2020) 'Take a sad song and make it better': What makes an interpretation growth facilitating for the patient?, *Psychotherapy*, 57(3): 400–13.

Lent, R.W., Hill, C.E. and Hoffman, M.A. (2003) Development and validation of the Counselor Activity Self-Efficacy Scales, *Journal of Counseling Psychology*, 50(1): 97–108.

Levitt, H., Korman, Y. and Angus, L. (2000) A metaphor analysis in treatments of depression: Metaphor as a marker of change, *Counselling Psychology Quarterly*, 13(1): 23–35.

Lindwall, O. and Ekström, A. (2012) Instruction-in-interaction: The teaching and learning of a manual skill, *Human Studies*, 35(1): 27–49.

Linehan, M.M., Comtois, K.A. and Ward-Ciesielski, E.F. (2012) Assessing and managing risk with suicidal individuals, *Cognitive and Behavioral Practice*, 19(2): 218–32.

Links, M.J., Watterson, L., Martin, P., O'Regan, S. and Molloy, E. (2020) Finding common ground: Meta-synthesis of communication frameworks found in patient communication, supervision and simulation literature, *BMC Medical Education*, 20(1): 1–16.

Lohr, C., Pietrzak, T. and Hauke, G. (2018) Therapeutic alliance: Grounding interaction in space, in G. Hauke and A, Kritikos (eds) *Embodiment in Psychotherapy: A Practitioner's Guide*. Cham, Switzerland: Springer, pp. 231–308.

Lu, Y., Hill, C.E., Hancock, G.R. and Keum, B.T. (2020) The effectiveness of helping skills training for undergraduate students: Changes in ethnocultural empathy, *Journal of Counseling Psychology*, 67(1): 14–24.

Macaskie, J., Lees, J. and Freshwater, D. (2015) Talking about talking: Interpersonal process recall as an intersubjective approach to research, *Psychodynamic Practice*, 21(3): 226–40.

MacIntosh, H.B. (2017) A bridge across silent trauma: Enactment, art, and emergence in the treatment of a traumatized adolescent, *Psychoanalytic Dialogues*, 27(4): 433–53.

Mackrill, T., Ebsen, F., Birkholm Antczak, H. and Leth Svendsen, I. (2018) Care planning using SMART criteria in statutory youth social work in Denmark: Reflections, challenges and solutions, *Nordic Social Work Research*, 8(1): 64–74.

Mackrill, T. and Sørensen, K.M. (2020) Implementing routine outcome measurement in psychosocial interventions – a systematic review, *European Journal of Social Work*, 23(5): 790–808.

Markus, H. and Nurius, P. (1986) Possible selves, *American Psychologist*, 41(9): 954–69.

Maroda, K.J. (2009) *Psychodynamic Techniques: Working with Emotion in the Therapeutic Relationship*. New York: Guilford Press.

Maroda, K. (2019) Working with enactment: The analyst's willingness to be both confrontive and vulnerable, *Psychoanalytic Inquiry*, 39(3–4): 234–40.

Matson, J.L. and Burns, C.O. (2017) History of social skills, in J.L. Matson (ed.) *Handbook of Social Behavior and Skills in Children*. Cham, Switzerland: Springer, pp. 1–8.

Matsumoto, K. (2020) Ma – The Japanese concept of space and time. Available at: https://medium.com/@kiyoshimatsumoto/ma-the-japanese-concept-of-space-and-time-3330c83ded4c (accessed 20 August 2021).

Matulich, B. (2017) *How to Do Motivational Interviewing: A Guidebook*. Amazon Kindle edition.

McAdams, D.P. (1993) *Stories We Live By: Personal Myths and the Making of the Self*. New York: William Murrow.

McCarthy, C. and French, K. (2017) Student perceptions of online video cases to promote helping skills training, *The Journal of Counselor Preparation and Supervision*, 9(2): article 4. https://doi.org/10.1080/15401383.2020.1800543

McCarthy, J., Shannon, E. and Bruno, M. (2020) Creative question-framing: 12 ideas for counselors-in-training, *Journal of Creativity in Mental Health*, 1–12, https://doi.org/10.1080/15401383.2020.1800543

McCarthy, K.S. and Barber, J.P. (2009) The Multitheoretical List of Therapeutic Interventions (MULTI): Initial report, *Psychotherapy Research*, 19(1): 96–113.

McCluskey, U. and O'Toole, M. (2019) *Transference and Countertransference from an Attachment Perspective: A Guide for Professional Caregivers*. Abingdon and New York: Routledge.

McCormack, B. (2011) The work of John Heron, *International Practice Development Journal*, 1(2): article 10.

McGrath, R. (2013) Commenting on process, *Journal of Psychotherapy Integration*, 23(2): 193–203.

McHenry, B. and McHenry, J. (2020) *What Therapists Say and Why They Say It: Effective Therapeutic Responses and Techniques*, 3rd edn. New York and Abingdon: Routledge.

McLellan, J. (1991) Formal and informal counselling help: Students' experiences, *British Journal of Guidance & Counselling*, 19(2): 149–58.

McLeod, John (1997) *Narrative and Psychotherapy*. London: Sage.

McLeod, John (1999) A narrative social constructionist approach to therapeutic empathy, *Counselling Psychology Quarterly*, 12(4): 377–94.

McLeod, John (2004) The significance of narrative and storytelling in postpsychological counseling and psychotherapy, in A. Lieblich, D. McAdams and R. Josselson (eds) *Healing Plots: The Narrative Basis of Psychotherapy*. Washington, DC: American Psychological Association, pp. 11–27.

McLeod, John (2018) *Pluralistic Therapy: Distinctive Features*. Abingdon and New York: Routledge.

McLeod, John (2019) *An Introduction to Counselling and Psychotherapy: Theory, Research and Practice*, 6th edn. Maidenhead: Open University Press.

McLeod, John and McLeod, Julia (2013) *Personal and Professional Development: A Practical Guide for Counsellors, Psychotherapists and Mental Health Practitioners*. Maidenhead: Open University Press.

McLeod, John and McLeod, Julia (2016) Assessment and formulation in pluralistic counselling and psychotherapy, in M. Cooper and W. Dryden (eds) *Handbook of Pluralistic Counselling and Psychotherapy*. London: Sage, pp. 15–27.

McLeod, John and McLeod, Julia (2020) The pluralistic approach, in N. Moller, A. Vossler, D.W. Jones and D. Kaposi (eds) *Understanding Mental Health and Counselling*. London: Sage, pp. 341–68.

McLeod, Julia (2021) How students use deliberate practice during the first stage of counsellor training, *Counselling & Psychotherapy Research*, online early view, https://doi.org/10.1002/capr.12397

McMillan, D.W. (2006) *Emotion Rituals: A Resource for Therapists and Clients*. New York: Routledge.

McMullen, L.M. (1989) Use of figurative language in successful and unsuccessful cases of psychotherapy: Three comparisons, *Metaphor and Symbol*, 4(4): 203–25.

McMullen, L.M. (1999) Metaphors in the talk of 'depressed' women in psychotherapy, *Canadian Psychology*, 40(2): 102–11.

Mearns, D. and Thorne, B. (2013) *Person-Centred Counselling in Action*, 4th edn. London: Sage.

Meekums, B., Macaskie, J. and Kapur, T. (2016) Developing skills in counselling and psychotherapy: A scoping review of interpersonal process recall and reflecting team methods in initial therapist training, *British Journal of Guidance & Counselling*, 44(5): 504–15.

Meichenbaum, D. (2005) 35 years of working with suicidal patients: Lessons learned, *Canadian Psychology*, 46(2): 64–72.

Metcalf, L. (2017) *Solution Focused Narrative Therapy*. New York: Springer.

Miklavcic, A. and LeBlanc, M.N. (2014) Culture brokers, clinically applied ethnography, and cultural mediation, in L.J. Kirmayer, J. Guzder and C. Rousseau (eds) *Cultural Consultation: Encountering the Other in Mental Health Care*. New York: Springer, pp. 115–37.

Miller, E. and McNaught, A. (2018) Exploring decision making around therapist self-disclosure in cognitive behavioural therapy, *Australian Psychologist*, 53(1): 33–9.

Miller, J.B. (1992) *Toward a New Psychology of Women*. Boston, MA: Beacon Press.

Miller, W.R. and Rollnick, S. (2012) *Motivational Interviewing: Preparing People for Change*, 3rd edn. New York: Guilford Press.

Minulescu, M. (2015) Symbols of healing and transformation in psychotherapy: The Bridge, *Procedia-Social and Behavioral Sciences*, 165: 103–7.

Mjelve, L.H., Ulleberg, I. and Vonheim, K. (2020) 'What do I share?' Personal and private experiences in educational psychological counselling, *Scandinavian Journal of Educational Research*, 64(2): 181–94.

Monahan, M.F., Crowley, K.J., Arnkoff, D.B., Glass, C.R. and Jobes, D.A. (2020) Understanding therapists' work with suicidal patients: An examination of qualitative data, *OMEGA–Journal of Death and Dying*, 81(2): 330–46.

Morgan, A. (2001) *What is Narrative Therapy? An Easy-to-Read Introduction*. Adelaide: Dulwich Centre Publications.

Morgan, E. and Nutt Williams, E. (2021) A qualitative study of psychotherapists' in-session tears, *Psychotherapy*, 58(1): 150–9.

Mosher, C.M. (2017) Historical perspectives of sex positivity: Contributing to a new paradigm within counseling psychology, *The Counseling Psychologist*, 45(4): 487–503.

Mousavi, S.B., Lecic-Tosevski, D., Khalili, H. and Mousavi, S.Z. (2020) To be able, or disable, that is the question: A critical discussion on how language affects the stigma and self-determination in people with parability, *International Journal of Social Psychiatry*, 66(5): 424–30.

Moyers, T.B. and Miller, W.R. (2013) Is low therapist empathy toxic?, *Psychology of Addictive Behaviors*, 27(3): 878–84.

Muran, J.C. and Eubanks, C.F. (2020) *Therapist Performance under Pressure: Negotiating Emotion, Difference, and Rupture*. Washington, DC: American Psychological Association.

Muran, J.C., Eubanks, C.F. and Samstag, L.W. (2021) One more time with less jargon: An introduction to 'Rupture Repair in Practice', *Journal of Clinical Psychology*, 77(2): 361–8.

Murphy, D., Liao, F., Slovak, P. et al. (2020) An evaluation of the effectiveness and acceptability of a new technology system to support psychotherapy helping skills training, *Counselling & Psychotherapy Research*, 20(2): 324–35.

Murphy, D., Slovak, P., Thieme, A., Jackson, D., Olivier, P. and Fitzpatrick, G. (2019) Developing technology to enhance learning interpersonal skills in counsellor education, *British Journal of Guidance & Counselling*, 47(3): 328–41.

Murphy, J.J. and Sparks, J.A. (2018) *Strengths-Based Therapy: Distinctive Features*. Abingdon: Routledge.

Myers, S.A. and White, C.M. (2010) The abiding nature of empathic connections: A 10-year follow-up study, *Journal of Humanistic Psychology*, 50(1): 77–95.

Najavits, L. (1993) How do psychotherapists describe their work? A study of metaphors for the therapy process, *Psychotherapy Research*, 3(4): 294–9.

Nasim, R., Shimshi, S., Ziv-Beiman, S. et al. (2019) Exploring innovative moments in a brief integrative psychotherapy case study, *Journal of Psychotherapy Integration*, 29(4): 359–73.

Ncube, N. (2006) The tree of life project: Using narrative ideas in work with vulnerable children in Southern Africa, *International Journal of Narrative Therapy and Community Work*, 1: 3–16.

Nelson, J. (2008) Laugh and the world laughs with you: An attachment perspective on the meaning of laughter in psychotherapy, *Clinical Social Work Journal*, 36(1): 41–9.

Nemec, P.B., Spagnolo, A.C. and Soydan, A.S. (2017) Can you hear me now? Teaching listening skills, *Psychiatric Rehabilitation Journal*, 40(4): 415–17.

Nerdrum, P. and Rønnestad, M.H. (2002) The trainees' perspective: A qualitative study of learning empathic communication in Norway, *The Counseling Psychologist*, 30(4): 609–29.

Nerdrum, P. and Rønnestad, M.H. (2004) Changes in therapists' conceptualization and practice of therapy following empathy training, *The Clinical Supervisor*, 22(2): 37–61.

Neukrug, E., Bayne, H., Dean-Nganga, L. and Pusateri, C. (2013) Creative and novel approaches to empathy: A neo-Rogerian perspective, *Journal of Mental Health Counseling*, 35(1): 29–42.

Newberger, J. (2015) The (K)Not of self-disclosure: One therapist's experience, *Psychoanalytic Social Work*, 22(1): 39–51.

Newman, C.F. (2000) Hypotheticals in cognitive psychotherapy: Creative questions, novel answers, and therapeutic change, *Journal of Cognitive Psychotherapy*, 14(2): 135–47.

Ng, C.T.C. and James, S. (2013) Counselor empathy or 'Having a heart to help'? An ethnographic investigation of Chinese clients' experience of counseling, *The Humanistic Psychologist*, 41(4): 333–47.

Nissen, B. (2018) The debate on frequency: Can low-frequency psychoanalysis be free-floating?, *International Journal of Psychoanalysis*, 99(5): 1212–20.

Norcross, J.C. (2006) Integrating self-help into psychotherapy: 16 practical suggestions, *Professional Psychology: Research and Practice*, 37(6): 683–93.

Norcross, J. C. and Cooper, M. (2021) *Personalizing Psychotherapy: Assessing and Accommodating Patient Preferences*. Washington, DC: American Psychological Association.

Norcross, J.C., Zimmerman, B.E., Greenberg, R.P. and Swift, J.K. (2017) Do all therapists do that when saying goodbye? A study of commonalities in termination behaviors, *Psychotherapy*, 54(1): 66–75.

Notess, S.E. (2019) Listening to people: Using social psychology to spotlight an overlooked virtue, *Philosophy*, 94(4): 621–43.

Nummenmaa, L., Glerean, E., Hari, R. and Hietanen, J.K. (2014) Bodily maps of emotions, *Proceedings of the National Academy of Sciences of the United States of America*, 111(2): 646–51.

O'Connell, B. (2012) *Solution-Focused Therapy*, 3rd edn. London: Sage.

Oddli, H.W., McLeod, J., Nissen-Lie, H.A., Rønnestad, M.H. and Halvorsen, M.S. (2021) Future orientation in successful therapies: Expanding the concept of goal in the working alliance, *Journal of Clinical Psychology*, 77(6): 1307–29.

Oddli, H.W. and Rønnestad, M.H. (2012) How experienced therapists introduce the technical aspects in the initial alliance formation: Powerful decision makers supporting clients' agency, *Psychotherapy Research*, 22(2): 176–93.

Omer, H. (1997) Narrative empathy, *Psychotherapy*, 25: 171–84.

Ong, A.D., Burrow, A.L., Fuller-Rowell, T.E., Ja, N.M. and Sue, D.W. (2013) Racial microaggressions and daily well-being among Asian Americans, *Journal of Counseling Psychology*, 60(2): 188–99.

Oster, G.D. and Crone, P.G. (2004) *Using Drawings in Assessment and Therapy: A Guide for Mental Health Professionals*. Abingdon: Brunner-Routledge.

Østlie, K., Stänicke, E. and Haavind, H. (2018) A listening perspective in psychotherapy with suicidal patients: Establishing convergence in therapists' and patients' private theories on suicidality and cure, *Psychotherapy Research*, 28(1): 150–63.

Overholser, J.C. (2018) Guided discovery: A clinical strategy derived from the Socratic Method, *International Journal of Cognitive Therapy*, 11(2): 124–39.

Owen, J., Drinane, J.M., Tao, K.W., DasGupta, D.R., Zhang, Y.S.D. and Adelson, J. (2018) An experimental test of microaggression detection in psychotherapy: Therapist multicultural orientation, *Professional Psychology: Research and Practice*, 49(1): 9–21.

Owen, J., Reese, R.J., Quirk, K. and Rodolfa, E. (2013) Alliance in action: A new measure of clients' perceptions of therapists' alliance activity, *Psychotherapy Research*, 23(1): 67–77.

Owen, J., Tao, K.W., Imel, Z.E., Wampold, B.E. and Rodolfa, E. (2014) Addressing racial and ethnic microaggressions in therapy, *Professional Psychology: Research and Practice*, 45(4): 283–90.

Oyserman, D., Terry, K. and Bybee, D. (2002) A possible selves intervention to enhance school involvement, *Journal of Adolescence*, 25(3): 313–26.

Papayianni, F. and Cooper, M. (2018) Metatherapeutic communication: An exploratory analysis of therapist-reported moments of dialogue regarding the nature of the therapeutic work, *British Journal of Guidance & Counselling*, 46(2): 173–84.

Paré, D.A. (1999) Using reflecting teams in clinical training, *Canadian Journal of Counselling and Psychotherapy*, 33(4): 293–306.

Paulick, J., Deisenhofer, A.K., Ramseyer, F. et al. (2018) Nonverbal synchrony: A new approach to better understand psychotherapeutic processes and drop-out, *Journal of Psychotherapy Integration*, 28(3): 367–89.

Pedersen, P. (1994) Simulating the client's internal dialogue as a counselor training technique, *Simulation & Gaming*, 25(1): 40–50.

Pérez-Rojas, A.E., Palma, B., Bhatia, A. et al. (2017) The development and initial validation of the Countertransference Management Scale, *Psychotherapy*, 54(3): 307–19.

Peters, H. (1999) Pre-therapy: A client-centered/experiential approach to mentally handicapped people, *Journal of Humanistic Psychology*, 39(4): 8–29.

Phelan, J.E. (2009) Exploring the use of touch in the psychotherapeutic setting: A phenomenological review, *Psychotherapy: Theory, Research, Practice, Training*, 46(1): 97–111.

Pinto-Coelho, K.G., Kearney, M.S., Sarno, E.L. et al. (2018) When in doubt, sit quietly: A qualitative investigation of experienced therapists' perceptions of self-disclosure, *Journal of Counseling Psychology*, 65(4): 440–52.

Pistole, M.C. (2003) Dance as a metaphor: Complexities and extensions in psychotherapy, *Psychotherapy: Theory, Research, Practice, Training*, 40(3): 232–43.

Postle, D. (2021) Psycommons website. Available at: https://wildernessweb.org (accessed 4 September 2021).

Potter, S. (2020) *Therapy with a Map: A Cognitive Analytic Approach to Helping Relationships*. West Sussex: Pavilion.

Prass, M., Ewell, A., Hill, C.E. and Kivlighan, D.M., Jr (2020) Solicited and unsolicited therapist advice in psychodynamic psychotherapy: Is it advised?, *Counselling Psychology Quarterly*, 34(2): 253–74.

Pratt, D., Gooding, P., Awenat, Y., Eccles, S. and Tarrier, N. (2016) Cognitive behavioral suicide prevention for male prisoners: Case examples, *Cognitive and Behavioral Practice*, 23(4): 485–501.

Prescott, D., Maeschalck, C. and Miller, S.D. (eds) (2017). *Reaching for Excellence: Feedback–Informed Treatment in Practice*. Washington, DC: American Psychological Association.

Probst, B. (2015) The other chair: Portability and translation from personal therapy to clinical practice, *Clinical Social Work Journal*, 43(1): 50–61.

Prouty, G., Van Werde, D. and Portner, M. (2002) *Pre-Therapy: Reaching Contact-Impaired Clients*. Monmouth: PCCS Books.

Prytz, M., Harkestad, K.N., Veseth, M. and Bjornestad, J. (2019) 'It's not a life of war and conflict': Experienced therapists' views on negotiating a therapeutic alliance in involuntary treatment, *Annals of General Psychiatry*, 18(1): 1–10.

Puhl, R.M. (2020) What words should we use to talk about weight? A systematic review of quantitative and qualitative studies examining preferences for weight-related terminology, *Obesity Reviews*, 21(6): e13008.

Punzi, E. and Singer, C. (2018) 'Any room won't do.' Clinical psychologists' understanding of the consulting room. An interview study, *Psychodynamic Practice*, 24(4): 319–33.

Purton, C. (2005) *Person-Centred Therapy: The Focusing-Oriented Approach*. Basingstoke: Palgrave Macmillan.

Råbu, M. and Haavind, H. (2018) Coming to terms: Client subjective experience of ending psychotherapy, *Counselling Psychology Quarterly*, 31(2): 223–42.

Råbu, M., Halvorsen, M.S. and Haavind, H. (2011) Early relationship struggles: A case study of alliance formation and reparation, *Counselling & Psychotherapy Research*, 11(1): 23–33.

Rantanen, A. and Soini, H. (2013) Development of the counselor response observation system, *Measurement and Evaluation in Counseling and Development*, 46(4): 247–60.

Rantanen, A.P. and Soini, H.S. (2018) Changes in counsellor trainee responses to client's message after peer group consultation (PGC) training, *British Journal of Guidance & Counselling*, 46(5): 531–42.

Rasmussen, B. (2000) Poetic truths and clinical reality: Client experiences of the use of metaphor by therapists, *Smith College Studies in Social Work*, 70(2): 355–73.

Rasmussen, B. and Angus, L. (1996) Metaphor in psychodynamic psychotherapy with borderline and non-borderline clients: A qualitative analysis, *Psychotherapy*, 33(4): 521–30.

Rasmussen, M.L., Dieserud, G., Dyregrov, K. and Haavind, H. (2014a) Warning signs of suicide among young men, *Nordic Psychology*, 66(3): 153–67.

Rasmussen, M.L., Haavind, H., Dieserud, G. and Dyregrov, K. (2014b) Exploring vulnerability to suicide in the developmental history of young men: A psychological autopsy study, *Death Studies*, 38(9): 549–56.

Rasting, M. and Beutel, M.E. (2005) Dyadic affective interactive patterns in the intake interview as a predictor of outcome, *Psychotherapy Research*, 15(3): 188–98.

Redhead, S., Johnstone, L. and Nightingale, J. (2015) Clients' experiences of formulation in cognitive behaviour therapy, *Psychology and Psychotherapy: Theory, Research and Practice*, 88(4): 453–67.

Rees, A., Hardy, G.E., Barkham, M., Elliott, R., Smith, J.A. and Reynolds, S. (2001) 'It's like catching a desire before it flies away': A comprehensive process analysis of a problem clarification event in cognitive-behavioral therapy for depression, *Psychotherapy Research*, 11(3): 331–51.

Reeves, A. (2015) *Working with Risk in Counselling and Psychotherapy*. London: Sage.

Reeves, A. and Bond, T. (2021) *Standards and Ethics for Counselling in Action*, 5th edn. London: Sage.

Reeves, A., Bowl, R., Wheeler, S. and Guthrie, E. (2004) The hardest words: Exploring the dialogue of suicide in the counselling process – a discourse analysis, *Counselling & Psychotherapy Research*, 4(1): 62–71.

Regev, D., Chasday, H. and Snir, S. (2016a) Silence during art therapy – The client's perspective, *The Arts in Psychotherapy*, 48: 69–75.

Regev, D., Kurt, H. and Snir, S. (2016b) Silence during art therapy: The art therapist's perspective, *International Journal of Art Therapy*, 21(3): 86–94.

Renger, S. (2021) Therapists' views on the use of questions in person-centred therapy, *British Journal of Guidance & Counselling*, doi: 10.1080/03069885.2021.1900536.

Rennie, D.L. (1998) *Person-Centred Counselling: An Experiential Approach*. London: Sage.

Rice, L. and Wagstaff, A. (1967) Client voice quality and expressive style as indexes of productive psychotherapy, *Journal of Consulting Psychology*, 31(6): 557–63.

Ridley, C.R., Kelly, S.M. and Mollen, D. (2011) Microskills training: Evolution, reexamination, and call for reform, *The Counseling Psychologist*, 39(6): 800–24.

Rober, P. (2002) Constructive hypothesizing, dialogic understanding and the therapist's inner conversation: Some ideas about knowing and not knowing in the family therapy session, *Journal of Marital and Family Therapy*, 28(4): 467–78.

Rogers, C.R. (1958) A process conception of psychotherapy, *American Psychologist*, 13(4): 142–59.

Rogers, C.R. (1961) *On Becoming a Person*. Boston, MA: Houghton Mifflin.

Rogers, C.R. (1975) Empathic: An unappreciated way of being, *The Counseling Psychologist*, 5(2): 2–10.

Rogers, C.R. and Stevens, B. (eds) (1968) *Person to Person: The Problem of Being Human*. Lafayette, CA: Real People Press.

Rogers, J. (2016) *Coaching skills*, 4th edn. Maidenhead: Open University Press.

Rogers, N. (2000) *The Creative Connection: Expressive Arts as Healing*. Monmouth: PCCS Books.

Romanelli, A. and Tishby, O. (2019) 'Just what is there now, that is what there is' – the effects of theater improvisation training on clinical social workers' perceptions and interventions, *Social Work Education*, 38(6): 797–814.

Ronan, K.R. and Kazantzis, N. (2006) The use of between-session (homework) activities in psychotherapy, *Journal of Psychotherapy Integration*, 16(2): 254–9.

Roth, A.D. and Pilling, S. (2008) Using an evidence-based methodology to identify the competences required to deliver effective cognitive and behavioural therapy for depression and anxiety disorders, *Behavioural and Cognitive Psychotherapy*, 36(2): 129–47.

Rothschild, B. (2000) *The Body Remembers: The Psychophysiology of Trauma and Trauma Treatment*. New York: W.W. Norton.

Rothschild, B. (2017) *The Body Remembers, Volume 2: Revolutionizing Trauma Treatment*. New York: W.W. Norton.

Rousmaniere, T.G. (2016) *Deliberate Practice for Psychotherapists*. New York: Routledge.

Rousmaniere, T.G. (2018) *Mastering the Inner Skills of Psychotherapy: A Deliberate Practice Handbook*. Seattle, WA: Gold Lantern Press.

Rousmaniere, T.G., Goodyear, R.K., Miller, S.D. and Wampold, B.E. (eds) (2017) *The Cycle of Excellence: Deliberate Practice to Improve Supervision and Training*. Hoboken, NJ: Wiley.

Rudd, M.D., Mandrusiak, M. and Joiner, T.E., Jr (2006) The case against no-suicide contracts: The commitment to treatment statement as a practice alternative, *Journal of Clinical Psychology*, 62(2): 243–51.

Sachse, R. and Elliott, R. (2002) Process-outcome research on humanistic outcome variables, in D.J. Cain and J. Seeman (eds) *Humanistic Psychotherapies: Handbook of Research and Practice*. Washington, DC: American Psychological Association, pp. 83–115.

Safran, J.D. (1993) Breaches in the therapeutic alliance: An arena for negotiating authentic relatedness, *Psychotherapy*, 30(1): 11–24.

Safran, J.D. and Muran, J.C. (2000) Resolving therapeutic alliance ruptures: Diversity and integration, *Journal of Clinical Psychology – In Session: Psychotherapy in Practice*, 56(2): 233–43.

Sahu, A., Console, K., Tran, V. et al. (2021) A case using the process model of multicultural counseling competence, *The Counseling Psychologist*, 49(4): 568–85.

Salazar Kämpf, M., Nestler, S., Hansmeier, J., Glombiewski, J. and Exner, C. (2020) Mimicry in psychotherapy – an actor partner model of therapists' and patients' non-verbal behavior and its effects on the working alliance, *Psychotherapy Research*, 31(6): 752–64.

Sandage, S.J., Moon, S.H., Rupert, D. et al. (2017) Relational dynamics between psychotherapy clients and clinic administrative staff: A pilot study, *Psychodynamic Practice*, 23(3): 249–68.

Sandberg, J., Gustafsson, S. and Holmqvist, R. (2017) Interpersonally traumatised patients' view of significant and corrective experiences in the psychotherapeutic relationship, *European Journal of Psychotherapy & Counselling*, 19(2): 175–99.

Sarpavaara, H. and Koski-Jännes, A. (2013) Change as a journey—clients' metaphoric change talk, *Qualitative Research in Psychology*, 10(1): 86–101.

Scheel, M.J., Davis, C.K. and Henderson, J.D. (2013) Therapist use of client strengths: A qualitative study of positive processes, *The Counseling Psychologist*, 41(3): 392–427.

Scheel, M.J., Hanson, W.E. and Razzhavaikina, T.I. (2004) The process of recommending homework in psychotherapy: A review of therapist delivery methods, client acceptability, and factors that affect compliance, *Psychotherapy: Theory, Research, Practice, Training*, 41(1): 38–55.

Schnellbacher, J. and Leijssen, M. (2009) The significance of therapist genuineness from the client's perspective, *Journal of Humanistic Psychology*, 49(2): 207–28.

School of Life (2021) *Drawing as Therapy: Know Yourself Through Art*. London: School of Life Press.

Schröder, T., Wiseman, H. and Orlinsky, D. (2009) 'You were always on my mind': Therapists' intersession experiences in relation to their therapeutic practice, professional characteristics, and quality of life, *Psychotherapy Research*, 19(1): 42–53.

Seedall, R.B. and Butler, M.H. (2006) The effect of proxy-voice intervention on couple softening in the context of enactments, *Journal of Marital and Family Therapy*, 32(4): 421–37.

Segre, L.S., Stasik, S.M., O'Hara, M.W. and Arndt, S. (2010) Listening visits: An evaluation of the effectiveness and acceptability of a home-based depression treatment, *Psychotherapy Research*, 20(6): 712–21.

Shafran, N., Kline, K., Marks, E. et al. (2020) The final session of psychodynamic psychotherapy for satisfied and unsatisfied clients who initiate the end of treatment, *Counselling Psychology Quarterly*, 33(4): 583–97.

Shakespeare, J., Blake, F. and Garcia, J. (2006) How do women with postnatal depression experience listening visits in primary care? A qualitative interview study, *Journal of Reproductive and Infant Psychology*, 24(2): 149–62.

Sharpley, C.F., Halat, J., Rabinowicz, T., Weiland, B. and Stafford, J. (2001) Standard posture, postural mirroring and client-perceived rapport, *Counselling Psychology Quarterly*, 14(4): 267–80.

Sharpley, C.F. and Sagris, A. (1995a) Does eye contact increase counsellor–client rapport?, *Counselling Psychology Quarterly*, 8(2): 145–55.

Sharpley, C.F. and Sagris, A. (1995b) When does counsellor forward lean influence client-perceived rapport?, *British Journal of Guidance & Counselling*, 23(3): 387–94.

Shedler, J. (2006) That was then, this is now: Psychoanalytic psychotherapy for the rest of us. Available at: http://jonathanshedler.com/writings/ (accessed 20 August 2021).

Shedler, J. (2010) The efficacy of psychodynamic psychotherapy, *American Psychologist*, 65(2): 98–109.

Shelton, K. and Delgado-Romero, E.A. (2011) Sexual orientation microaggressions: The experience of lesbian, gay, bisexual, and queer clients in psychotherapy, *Journal of Counseling Psychology*, 58(2): 210–21.

Shirota, N. (2021) *Nagara* listening: Japanese listeners' behavior in multi-activity settings, *International Journal of Listening*, doi:10.1080/10904018.2021.1883434.

Shoaib, K. and Peel, J. (2003) Kashmiri women's perceptions of their emotional and psychological needs, and access to counselling, *Counselling & Psychotherapy Research*, 3(2): 87–94.

Sinclair, S.L. and Monk, G. (2004) Moving beyond the blame game: Toward a discursive approach to negotiating conflict within couple relationships, *Journal of Marital and Family Therapy*, 30(3): 335–47.

Singer, J.A., Blagov, P., Berry, M. and Oost, K.M. (2013) Self-defining memories, scripts, and the life story: Narrative identity in personality and psychotherapy, *Journal of Personality*, 81(6): 569–82.

Skatvedt, A. (2017) The importance of 'empty gestures' in recovery: Being human together, *Symbolic Interaction*, 40(3): 396–413.

Smith, E.B. (2019) Holding the tension of opposites: Counselors' experiences of the therapeutic internalization process, *Journal of Humanistic Counseling*, 58(3): 204–22.

Smith, E.J. (2006) The strength-based counseling model, *The Counseling Psychologist*, 34(1): 13–79.

Solomonov, N., McCarthy, K.S., Gorman, B.S. and Barber, J.P. (2019) The multitheoretical list of therapeutic interventions – 30 items (MULTI-30), *Psychotherapy Research*, 29(5): 565–80.

Solstad, S.M., Castonguay, L.G. and Moltu, C. (2019) Patients' experiences with routine outcome monitoring and clinical feedback systems: A systematic review and synthesis of qualitative empirical literature, *Psychotherapy Research*, 29(2): 157–70.

Solstad, S.M., Kleiven, G.S. and Moltu, C. (2021) Complexity and potentials of clinical feedback in mental health: an in-depth study of patient processes, *Quality of Life Research*, 30(11), 3117–25.

Solstad, S.M., Kleiven, G.S., Castonguay, L.G. and Moltu, C. (2020) Clinical dilemmas of routine outcome monitoring and clinical feedback: A qualitative study of patient experiences, *Psychotherapy Research*, 31(2): 200–10.

Sommers-Flanagan, J. and Bequette, T. (2013) The initial psychotherapy interview with adolescent clients, *Journal of Contemporary Psychotherapy*, 43(1): 13–22.

Sonne, J.L. and Jochai, D. (2014) The 'vicissitudes of love' between therapist and patient: A review of the research on romantic and sexual feelings, thoughts, and behaviors in psychotherapy, *Journal of Clinical Psychology*, 70(2): 182–95.

Spangler, P.T., Hill, C.E., Dunn, M.G. et al. (2014) Training undergraduate students to use immediacy, *The Counseling Psychologist*, 42(6): 729–57.

Sparks, J.A. and Duncan, B.L. (2016) Client strengths and resources: Helping clients draw on what they already do best, in M. Cooper and W. Dryden (eds) *The Handbook of Pluralistic Counselling and Psychotherapy*. London: Sage, pp. 68–79.

Spence, D.P. (1984) Perils and pitfalls of free floating attention, *Contemporary Psychoanalysis*, 20(1): 37–59.

Spencer, J., Goode, J., Penix, E.A., Trusty, W. and Swift, J.K. (2019) Developing a collaborative relationship with clients during the initial sessions of psychotherapy, *Psychotherapy*, 56(1): 7–10.

Stewart, I. and Joines, V. (2012) *TA Today: A New Introduction to Transactional Analysis*, 2nd rev. edn. Nottingham: Lifespace Publishing.

Stewart, J. (ed.) (2011) *Bridges Not Walls: A Book About Interpersonal Communication*, 11th edn. Maidenhead: McGraw-Hill.

Stewart, S. and Schröder, T. (2015) Emotional homework: A systematic literature review of patients' intersession experiences, *Journal of Psychotherapy Integration*, 25(3): 236–52.

Stickley, T. (2011) From SOLER to SURETY for effective non-verbal communication, *Nurse Education in Practice*, 11(6): 395–8.

Stiggelbout, A.M., Pieterse, A.H. and De Haes, J.C. (2015) Shared decision making: Concepts, evidence, and practice, *Patient Education and Counseling*, 98(10): 1172–9.

Stiles, W.B. (2001) Assimilation of problematic experiences, *Psychotherapy*, 38(4): 462–5.

Stiles, W.B. (2011) Coming to terms, *Psychotherapy Research*, 21(4): 367–84.

Stiver, I.P., Rosen, W., Surrey, J. and Miller, J.B. (2008) Creative moments in relational-cultural therapy, *Women & Therapy*, 31(2–4): 7–29.

Stoddard, J. and Afari, N. (2014) *The Big Book of ACT Metaphors: A Practitioner's Guide to Experiential Exercises and Metaphors in Acceptance and Commitment Therapy*. Oakland, CA: New Harbinger.

Stott, R., Mansell, W., Salkovskis, P., Lavender, A. and Cartwright-Hatton, S. (eds) (2010) *Oxford Guide to Metaphors in CBT: Building Cognitive Bridges*. Oxford: Oxford University Press.

Strong, T. (2000) Six orienting ideas for collaborative counsellors, *European Journal of Psychotherapy, Counselling and Health*, 3(1): 25–42.

Stroud, D., Olguin, D. and Marley, S. (2016) Relationship between counseling students' childhood memories and current negative self-evaluations when receiving corrective feedback, *International Journal for the Advancement of Counselling*, 38(3): 237–48.

Sudnow, D. and Dreyfus, H.L. (2001) *Ways of the Hand: A Rewritten Account*. Cambridge, MA: MIT Press.

Sue, D.W. (2010) *Microaggressions in Everyday Life: Race, Gender, and Sexual Orientation*. Hoboken, NJ: Wiley.

Sue, D.W., Capodilupo, C.M., Torino, G.C. et al. (2007) Racial microaggressions in everyday life: Implications for clinical practice, *American Psychologist*, 62(4): 271–86.

Sunderani, S. and Moodley, R. (2020) Therapists' perceptions of their use of self-disclosure (and non-disclosure) during cross-cultural exchanges, *British Journal of Guidance & Counselling*, 48(6): 741–56.

Sundet, R., Kim, H.S., Karlsson, B.E., Borg, M., Sælør, K.T. and Ness, O. (2020) A heuristic model for collaborative practice – Part 1: a meta-synthesis of empirical findings on collaborative strategies in community mental health and substance abuse practice, *International Journal of Mental Health Systems*, 14: article 42, doi: 10.1186/s13033-020-00376-5.

Swank, J.M. and McCarthy, S. (2013) The Counselor Feedback Training Model: A developmental approach to teach feedback skills, *Adultspan*, 12(2): 100–12.

Swank, J.M. and McCarthy, S. (2015) Effectiveness of the Counselor Feedback Training Model, *Journal of Counselor Preparation and Supervision*, 7(1): article 4, http://dx.doi.org/10.7729/71.1078

Swift, J.K., Tompkins, K.A. and Parkin, S.R. (2017) Understanding the client's perspective of helpful and hindering events in psychotherapy sessions: A micro-process approach, *Journal of Clinical Psychology*, 73(11): 1543–55.

Talmon, S. (1990) *Single Session Therapy: Maximising the Effect of the First (and often only) Therapeutic Encounter*. Hoboken, NJ: Jossey-Bass.

Tay, D. (2014) An analysis of metaphor hedging in psychotherapeutic talk, in M. Yamaguchi (ed.) *Approaches to Language, Culture, and Cognition*. Basingstoke: Palgrave Macmillan, pp. 251–67.

Thompson, L., Howes, C. and McCabe, R. (2016) Effect of questions used by psychiatrists on therapeutic alliance and adherence, *British Journal of Psychiatry*, 209(1): 40–7.

Timulak, L. and Keogh, D. (2021) *Transdiagnostic Emotion-Focused Therapy: A Clinical Guide for Transforming Emotional Pain*. Washington, DC: American Psychological Association.

Tomasello, M. (2015) *Becoming Human: A Theory of Ontogeny*. Cambridge, MA: Belknap Press.

Tomasello, M., Carpenter, M., Call, J., Behne, T. and Moll, H. (2005) Understanding and sharing intentions: The origins of cultural cognition, *Behavioral and Brain Sciences*, 28(5): 675–91.

Tomicic, A., Martinez, C. and Krause, M. (2015) The sound of change: A study of the psychotherapeutic process embodied in vocal expression. Laura Rice's ideas revisited, *Psychotherapy Research*, 25(2): 263–76.

Topor, A., Bøe, T.D. and Larsen, I.B. (2018) Small things, micro-affirmations and helpful professionals everyday recovery-orientated practices according to persons with mental health problems, *Community Mental Health Journal*, 54(8): 1212–20.

Topor, A., von Greiff, N. and Skogens, L. (2021) Micro-affirmations and recovery for persons with mental health and alcohol and drug problems: User and professional experience-based practice and knowledge, *International Journal of Mental Health and Addiction*, 19(5): 374–85.

Trower, P., Bryant, B. and Argyle, M. (1978) *Social Skills and Mental Health*. London: Methuen.

Tsai, M., Gustafsson, T., Kanter, J., Plummer Loudon, M. and Kohlenberg, R.J. (2017) Saying good goodbyes to your clients: A functional analytic psychotherapy (FAP) perspective, *Psychotherapy*, 54(1): 22–8.

Tsai, M., Plummer, M.D., Kanter, J.W., Newring, R.W. and Kohlenberg, R.J. (2010) Therapist grief and functional analytic psychotherapy: Strategic self-disclosure of personal loss, *Journal of Contemporary Psychotherapy*, 40(1): 1–10.

Tsai, M., Yoo, D., Hardebeck, E.J., Loudon, M.P. and Kohlenberg, R.J. (2019) Creating safe, evocative, attuned, and mutually vulnerable therapeutic beginnings: Strategies from functional analytic psychotherapy, *Psychotherapy*, 56(1): 55–61.

Tschacher, W. (2018) Embodiment of social interaction: Our place in the world around us, in G. Hauke, and A, Kritikos (eds) *Embodiment in Psychotherapy. A Practitioner's Guide*. Cham, Switzerland: Springer, pp. 57–68.

Tschacher, W. and Meier, D. (2020) Physiological synchrony in psychotherapy sessions, *Psychotherapy Research*, 30(5): 558–73.

Tummala-Narra, P. (2015) Cultural competence as a core emphasis of psychoanalytic psychotherapy, *Psychoanalytic Psychology*, 32(2): 275–90.

Vanaerschot, G. (1993) Empathy as releasing several micro-processes in the client, in D. Brazier (ed.) *Beyond Carl Rogers*. London: Constable.

Vandenberghe, L., Coppede, A.M. and Bittencourt, M.V. (2018) Building and handling therapeutic closeness in the therapist–client relationship in behavioral and cognitive psychotherapy, *Journal of Contemporary Psychotherapy*, 48(4): 215–23.

Versammy, K.-J. and Cooper, M. (2021) Helpful aspects of counselling for young people who have experienced bullying: A thematic analysis, *British Journal of Guidance & Counselling*, 49(3): 468–79.

Wahlström, J. (2018) Discourse in psychotherapy: Using words to create therapeutic practice, in O. Smoliak and T. Strong (eds) *Therapy as Discourse*, The Language of Mental Health. New York: Springer, pp. 19–44.

Warren, J.A. and Nash, A. (2019) Using expressive arts in online education to identify feelings, *Journal of Creativity in Mental Health*, 14(1): 94–104.

Wasil, A., Venturo-Conerly, K., Shingleton, R. and Weisz, J. (2019) The motivating role of recovery self-disclosures from therapists and peers in eating disorder recovery: Perspectives of recovered women, *Psychotherapy*, 56(2): 170–80.

Wearn, A., Clouder, L., Barradell, S. and Neve, H. (2019) A qualitative research synthesis exploring professional touch in healthcare practice using the threshold concept framework, *Advances in Health Sciences Education*, 25(3): 731–54.

Webb, K.B. (2011) Care of others and self: A suicidal patient's impact on the psychologist, *Professional Psychology: Research and Practice*, 42(3): 215–21.

Webb, K., Schroder, T.A. and Gresswell, D.M. (2019) Service users' first accounts of experiencing endings from a psychological service or therapy: A systematic review and meta-ethnographic synthesis, *Psychology and Psychotherapy: Theory, Research & Practice*, 92(4): 584–604.

Werbart, A., Gråke, E. and Klingborg, F. (2020) Deadlock in psychotherapy: A phenomenological study of eight psychodynamic therapists' experiences, *Counselling Psychology Quarterly*, advance online publication, https://doi.org/10.1080/09515070.2020.1863186

Westra, H.A. and Aviram, A. (2013) Core skills in motivational interviewing, *Psychotherapy*, 50(3): 273–8.

White, M. (2007) *Maps of Narrative Practice*. New York: W.W. Norton.

Winslade, J.M. (2005) Utilising discursive positioning in counselling, *British Journal of Guidance & Counselling*, 33(3): 351–64.

Withers, R. (2006) Interactive drawing therapy: Working with therapeutic imagery, *New Zealand Journal of Counselling*, 26(4): 1–14.

Wood, A. (2020) *The Motivational Interviewing Workbook: Exercises to Decide What You Want and How to Get There*. Emeryville, CA: Rockridge Press.

Worthington, D.L. and Bodie, G.D. (eds) (2020) *The Handbook of Listening*. Hoboken, NJ: Wiley.

Wosket, V. (2008) *Egan's Skilled Helper Model: Developments and Implications in Counselling*. Hove and New York: Routledge.

Yalom, I.D. (2002) *The Gift of Therapy: Reflections on Being a Therapist*. London: Piatkus.

Yoshida, T. (2020) The Triad Training Model in counseling, cultural diversity, and intercultural training, in D. Landis and D.P.S. Bhawuk (eds) *The Cambridge Handbook of Intercultural Training*, 4th edn. Cambridge: Cambridge University Press, pp. 377–406.

Zemel, A. (2016) Embedded instruction: Proxy voicing in couples therapy, *Journal of Pragmatics*, 97: 21–36.

Ziv-Beiman, S., Keinan, G., Livneh, E., Malone, P.S. and Shahar, G. (2017) Immediate therapist self-disclosure bolsters the effect of brief integrative psychotherapy on psychiatric symptoms and the perceptions of therapists: A randomized clinical trial, *Psychotherapy Research*, 27(5): 558–70.

Zur, O. and Nordmarken, N. (2011) *To Touch or Not to Touch: Exploring the Myth of Prohibition on Touch in Psychotherapy and Counselling. Clinical, Ethical and Legal Considerations*. Available at: https://drzur.com/touch-in-therapy/ (accessed 20 August 2021).

Index

Page numbers with 't' are tables.

"PSIA information can be obtained
www.ICGtesting.com
ited in the USA
'W020031100723
)61LV00004B/480

9 780335 250158